D0160625

MORE PRAISE FOR ROBERT L. BERNSTEIN

"No matter how serious our agenda, Bob Bernstein always leaves me smiling or laughing. . . . Hidden behind the humor in those anecdotes is a serious attitude: the optimistic courage to volunteer for hard tasks and to find a way on, despite the odds against. I think of this as the Bernstein style. What must be done can be done. Somehow."

—Robert Fulghum, author of *All I Really Need to Know I Learned in Kindergarten*

"When he was at the height of his corporate influence and visibility, Bernstein never flagged in seizing the moment to speak out and act . . . he showed how success in commerce and the corporate world could be reconciled with the principled exercises of citizenship."

—Leon Botstein, president of Bard College

"Bob Bernstein's lifetime accomplishments for promoting international human rights, for founding crucial nongovernmental organizations, and for personally helping so many prominent dissidents in their time of need . . . have been stunning, historic, and transformative."

—Harold Koh, former assistant secretary of state for democracy, human rights, and labor

"Bob Bernstein's leadership in the struggle for human rights is truly peerless in depth and scope."

—Trevor Morrison, dean, NYU School of Law

SPEAKING FREELY

MY LIFE IN PUBLISHING
AND HUMAN RIGHTS

Robert L. Bernstein

with

Doug Merlino

THE NEW PRESS

NEW YORK
LONDON

Every effort has been made to trace copyright holders and to obtain their permission for the use of copyrighted material in this book. Should anyone be aware of any errors or omissions, kindly provide any corrections to the publisher. These corrections will then be incorporated in future reprints or editions of this book.

Requests for permission to reproduce selections from this book should be mailed to:
Permissions Department, The New Press, 120 Wall Street, 31st floor, New York, NY 10005.

Published in the United States by The New Press, New York, 2016
Distributed by Perseus Distribution

LIBRARY OF CONGRESS CATALOGING-IN-PUBLICATION DATA

Names: Bernstein, Robert L., 1923– author. | Merlino, Doug, author.
Title: Speaking freely : my life in publishing and human rights / Robert L.
    Bernstein with Doug Merlino.
Description: New York : The New Press, 2016. | Includes index.
Identifiers: LCCN 2016001938 (print) | LCCN 2016003084 (ebook) | ISBN
    9781620971710 (hardcover : alk. paper) | ISBN 9781620971727 (e-book)
Subjects: LCSH: Bernstein, Robert L., 1923– | Publishers and
    publishing—United States—Biography. | Random House (Firm)—History. |
    Human rights workers—United States—Biography. | Human Rights Watch
    (Organization)—History.
Classification: LCC Z473.B43 A3 2016 (print) | LCC Z473.B43 (ebook) | DDC
    070.5092—dc23
LC record available at http://lccn.loc.gov/2016001938

The New Press publishes books that promote and enrich public discussion and understanding of the issues vital to our democracy and to a more equitable world. These books are made possible by the enthusiasm of our readers; the support of a committed group of donors, large and small; the collaboration of our many partners in the independent media and the not-for-profit sector; booksellers, who often hand-sell New Press books; librarians; and above all our authors.
www.thenewpress.com

Book design and composition by Bookbright Media
This book was set in Sabon and Berkeley Oldstyle

Printed in the United States of America

10 9 8 7 6 5 4 3 2 1

To my dear Helen, who has broadened my life in more ways than I can count, nurturing our family and creating a world full of joy and purpose

CONTENTS

Foreword by Toni Morrison ⸱ ix

Preface ⸱ xiii

1 Youth ⸱ 1

2 Office Boy in Waiting ⸱ 19

3 At Random ⸱ 47

4 On Top, Suddenly ⸱ 72

5 Politics and Publishing ⸱ 95

6 The Russians ⸱ 118

7 The Birth of Helsinki Watch ⸱ 140

8 From RCA to Newhouse ⸱ 159

9 Finding Our Footing: Human Rights, 1980–85 ⸱ 174

10 The Soviet Union Implodes: Human Rights, 1985–90 ⸱ 201

11 Random House in the 1980s: The Newhouse Years ⸱ 226

12 China ⸱ 250

13 A New Organization, a New Approach ⸱ 276

14 Some Thoughts on the Future of Human Rights in the Middle East ⸱ 292

Epilogue ⸱ 321

Acknowledgments ⸱ 327

Index ⸱ 333

FOREWORD

I KNEW OF BOB BERNSTEIN IN 1965 (WHEN I JOINED THE L.W. Singer Company, based at that time in Syracuse, New York, but recently purchased by Random House and already scheduled within the year to move to New York City). I met him in 1967 when he visited that subsidiary. I remember a cigar (Fidelistic), height (much too tall), and restless, impatient eyes. The cigar was gone the next time I saw him, but the height remained as did the impatience. But the restlessness seemed to have been replaced with what I understood now to be an intense curiosity: things interested him; people interested him; ideas interested him. I had had only one employer like that before—someone who cherished knowledge for its own sake, got passionate about it, and who was willing to act on that knowledge and passion in ways not immediately (or even ultimately) beneficial to himself.

Since that meeting, fifty years ago, there have been many more, and I came to know him both as employer and friend. It ought to be a contradiction in terms: "boss" and "friend." It ought to be a contradiction because one of the deepest pleasures of working at a certain level in a company, or a factory, or a university, or a laboratory, or a shop, is the real joy one can take knowing not only that your boss is not your friend, but that you can do his work better, and that you are secretly or obviously better equipped to run the

place than those who do. That if only they would do what you advised, all would be well.

Robert Bernstein deprived me of that joy by becoming a friend
I could rely on, instituting or examining and dismissing all the
improvements I could think of. And Random House prospered,
thrived, flourished in spite of the fact that he refused to take di-
rections from me. A great deal of that prosperity I connect with
that impatience and curiosity that I noticed in 1967. Impatient with
obstacles to first-rate work, he was curious about what might be
a better way and what other people thought. What is wrong, he
seemed always to be saying, and how can I fix it? Or, as he said to
me once, when I was trying to make an important decision about
my work life: "If you had it like you wanted it, what would it be?"
No one had ever asked me that before (or since) and it humiliated
me to think I had never asked it of myself. It also overpowered me
to hear it from my employer (who need not have concerned himself)
and from a friend (who clearly was concerned). What it said to me
was: Difficult things are possible, problems can be solved if you are
clear in your own mind about your purpose. It may sound obvious
now, but then, at that moment, it was the opening of a small gate
in my personal China Wall. It was a moment that crystallized the
clarity of purpose that had been evolving in him during those years
since 1967.

Robert Bernstein presided over a company in the business of
turning ideas artfully expressed into profit. Somewhere along the
line, he got interested in turning profit into ideas—in being insistent on the rights of authors to say what they wished and to let the
worth of the saying rest on its own merit, which might not coincide
with the desires of the marketplace. The resources of the company
at his insistence were well used in defending the rights of Marchetti
and Marks (*The CIA and the Cult of Intelligence*) against the restrictions of the CIA; the resources of the company were well and
significantly employed in the publishing of public servants and dissident writers who could be and were perceived as commercially
unpromising. His disdain for the "hot" but corrupt title on the ho-
rizon was legend among us. And always this tremendous curiosity:

What if . . . followed by the determination to do something about it. Is a new employee badly placed? Where should he or she be? Are there other Black people who might want to work in publishing if they knew about it? Recruit them, gather them, and give them real jobs rather than hopeless summer vacations in the stockroom. Is the entering salary too low? What is competitive and let's change it. Is there an imprisoned, shackled, tortured, defenseless writer? Where? And how can he or she be helped?

Protective of talent in the workplace, he used his time, his own talent and resources to protect writers in the world. When I recall his work as Chairman and President of Random House, and refresh my memory about the organizations he has founded, co-founded, or led, when I think of his testimony before august government bodies, the consequences in real terms of the alleviation of personal distress, or a dialogue begun, a mind freed, information exchanged—the consequences of his trip to Russia, China, Nicaragua, Norway—it occurs to me that his life is not only an interesting one, a coherent one, but one that turns on a moral axis. That is no small thing in a world where indifference is not only easy, it's chic. From my vantage point, he functions almost like the Praetorian guard for those of us whose work is language.

Who are these people who forbid us to speak the language: The language we dream in, the language we fall in love in, the language that lets our fellows know we are dying or living or fighting or winning—the language we know the world by and by which the world knows us. Language that can change a mind or console it. Language that negotiates power and is itself power. Language that topples regimes and spawns them and holds them to account. The right to have language, to use it, to dissect it, to share it, to take it with you into other states and nations, to roar it—these things Bob Bernstein has made his business. He publishes language, penetrates borders with language to let other languages escape; he also takes care of those who husband it, produce it, accomplish it, distribute it. With grace, I might add. And humor. And perseverance. He has extricated ideas as text and as discourse from the paws of those terrified by them.

This battle for the free expression and exchange of ideas seems forever, but because of Robert Bernstein and those like him, it is not forever elusive. He has engaged life; evil does not awe or paralyze him; civic life is enhanced by his presence in it.

—Toni Morrison

PREFACE

IN THE FALL OF 1976, MY WIFE HELEN AND I WENT TO MOSCOW AT the invitation of the Soviet government. The Soviets wished to introduce us to Russian authors because I had been on the team of publishers that convinced the Soviets to join the Universal Copyright Convention in 1973. While the Soviets tried to schedule every hour of our trip, we, of course, had different plans. On our first night in Moscow, the *New York Times* bureau, headed by Christopher Wren with his talented colleague David Shipler, arranged a dinner party for us.

When Helen and I arrived, we saw the Russian nuclear physicist turned dissident activist Andrei Sakharov sitting on the couch with his wife, Elena Bonner. At Random House, where I was in my tenth year as president, we had published a few books of Sakharov's translated writings and speeches, but I had never met him in person. A year earlier, he had won the Nobel Peace Prize, but the Soviet regime had stopped him from attending the ceremony. At the invitation of Bonner, Helen and I had gone to Oslo to watch her accept the award on her husband's behalf. After the moving experience Helen and I had at the ceremony, we felt like we really knew him. We immediately went over and met them.

I was astounded by his accomplishments, but, in person, he was very modest. He was in his mid-fifties and balding, wore big glasses, and spoke in a soft voice. He always wore sweaters, and that night, as I recall, he had on a gray sweater with red plaid on the front and gray slacks—he was obviously not very interested in clothes.

Sakharov had become a hero in the Soviet Union for his breakthroughs in developing the hydrogen bomb after World War II. He had gone on to make major scientific advances that helped the Soviets build their nuclear power capability. In return, he was given all the perks the regime could offer: fame, a nice house, a car and driver, and honors such as being named a "Hero of Socialist Labor."

But Sakharov's role in building nuclear weapons troubled him so much that he had to speak out. In the late 1960s, he published an essay denouncing the nuclear arms race. Though he began to lose his privileges, he continued to call for openness, democracy, and peace. He also helped a small group of brave Russian dissidents speak out for human rights, who often did so at great personal cost.

Bonner's eyesight was failing because of a degenerative condition for which she was having a hard time getting medical care, so she wore thick glasses. She chain-smoked and stepped in to translate for us when needed.

I became completely engrossed in what Sakharov had to say. For over an hour, he spoke about what was happening in Russia, what he thought was necessary for his country to come out of it, and the precarious situation in which he, his wife, and other activists found themselves.

As he spoke, I kept thinking what an amazing story his life was. Impulsively, I said, "I've got to publish your autobiography."

"I'd like you to do that," he said.

I was thrilled. "I don't want to lose a moment," I said. "How do I get you a contract?"

He held out his right hand, and I shook it. "There," he said. "Now we have a contract. You work out the details."

It was a moment when the two great passions of my life—publishing and human rights—came together in a very special and significant way. I was fifty-three years old, and I had been working in book publishing for thirty years, since first landing a job by chance at Simon & Schuster—at the time still headed by Dick Simon and Max Schuster—after coming home from World War II.

Subsequently, I'd moved on to Random House, where I was hired by its founders, Bennett Cerf and Donald Klopfer.

Growing up on the sales side, I had first looked at publishing as a business, but after a decade as president of Random House, I had certainly realized the tremendous importance of books in carrying the great ideas of mankind to every corner of the world in so many different ways. Imagine a job where in your work you talk to E.L. Doctorow, James Michener, Eudora Welty, Dr. Seuss, John Hersey, Maya Angelou, Richard Kluger, Nora Ephron, Robert Caro, Truman Capote, Robert Penn Warren, Toni Morrison, and many, many others.

In the late 1960s and early 1970s, I'd had to guide Random House through a series of acquisitions and mergers while working to keep its independence and integrity. At the same time, we'd gone to court against the U.S. government and the CIA to protect what we saw as our freedom to publish. Instinctively I felt that one of the jobs of a publisher is to protect the ability of authors to bring forth their ideas, and this naturally led to a commitment to work for authors who were denied this privilege. Publishers, of course, had been doing this work in the United States, on their own initiative and later through the efforts of the Association of American Publishers' International Freedom to Publish Committee and other industry and independent groups. These efforts included fighting book banning in libraries, government interference in publishing, and other attempts to stop the free flow of ideas in our country.

But the harsh treatment of the Soviets in silencing authors such as Sakharov went far beyond—writers were imprisoned, banned, and exiled simply for the act of expressing thoughts the regime found threatening.

Meeting Sakharov that evening was a personal turning point. He was, for me and many others, both an inspiration and a moral beacon. In the days that followed, I met several other dissident Soviet writers and returned to the United States feeling that I had to use my position to try to help ease their plight. In 1977, I worked with a small band of people with a deep interest in Eastern Europe and Russia to found Helsinki Watch, which was dedicated to helping Soviet dissidents fight for human rights behind the Iron

Curtain. Over the next two decades, Helsinki Watch grew into Human Rights Watch, one of the world's largest international human rights organizations. My interests in human rights expanded to Latin America, China, and the Middle East.

This book tells the story of how that came about, as well as the experiences of a lifetime involved in books and the spread of ideas. After a seven-decade career, I believe more strongly than ever in one core principle: that one book, one voice, has the power to change the world.

SPEAKING FREELY

1

YOUTH

LIKE A LOT OF NEW YORK STORIES, MINE HAS ROOTS SOMEWHERE in the Pale of Settlement, the strip of land in Eastern Europe that ran from Lithuania down to the Black Sea, making up the western border of Imperial Russia. In 1791, Catherine the Great declared that Russian Jews had to live within the Pale, forcing the relocation of Jews from Moscow and other cities.

If you've seen *Fiddler on the Roof*, you've got an idea of what village life was like in the shtetls of the Pale—very poor. After revolutionaries assassinated Tsar Alexander II in 1881, the Russian government made the Jews the scapegoat and unleashed a wave of pogroms in the Pale. Mobs destroyed homes, pillaged, and murdered. Next came laws that, among other things, blocked Jews from going to school. The idea was either to kill them off or force them to leave.

Around 1883, my paternal great-grandfather—like a couple million other Jews over the coming decades—got the message. The story, as it has come down in my family, is that he began walking toward Germany from his village, located in what is now Lithuania. Eventually, he found his way into the hold of a ship and sailed across the Atlantic, and that's how he arrived in New York.

He ended up in Poughkeepsie, and, like a lot of other newly landed Jews, he got a horse and cart and went from farmhouse to farmhouse peddling "notions"—household items like thread, fabrics, scissors, and pots and pans. His son, my grandfather, came to Manhattan and started a business making "wash suits," which were shorts and tops for little boys who were not yet ready for long pants, each one with a little whistle attached. After my father, Alfred Bernstein, graduated from Columbia University in 1913, he stayed in the clothing business.

My maternal grandfather had emigrated from Germany when he was sixteen years old. My mother, Sylvia, had a budding career when she met my father. She modeled hats but was also quite an opera singer. She was scheduled to appear at the opening of Radio City Music Hall with two male singers, Robert Weede and Jan Peerce, who went on to become stars at the Metropolitan Opera. My father, I think, convinced her to give up singing and become a mother.

To round out the family, I had a wonderful younger sister, Barbara.

I grew up in an apartment on West Seventy-Fifth Street in the Upper West Side of Manhattan, and my formative years were what I call "middle-class humdrum." Every Friday night, we'd meet either at my family's apartment or that of one of my father's brothers, Ben and Harry, who were married to Pearl and Toddy, respectively. Uncle Ben was observant, so we'd recite Friday night prayers, light candles, and then have dinner.

My father used to work a half-day on Saturdays and then take me to the City Athletic Club, down on West Fifty-Fourth Street. It was all male and all Jewish because many other clubs in the city—notably the New York Athletic Club—did not accept Jews. While my father played handball, I shot baskets. When he was done, we'd go down to the steam room, and afterward we'd take a swim in the club's huge pool.

We always had to be home by five thirty because my parents had their card night. They had the same five couples over every weekend of their married lives—they called themselves the "Saturday Nighters." The men and women split up and went to separate rooms. The men always played bridge. The women started with mah-jongg, but after several years they switched to canasta when it became popular. At exactly eleven o'clock, they always stopped their games to eat cold cuts. Even when I was in high school and went out with friends on Saturday nights, I always tried to be home by eleven because the food was so good.

On Sunday, my mother, father, younger sister, and I always ate lunch together and it was always the same: roast beef, creamed spinach, and roasted potatoes. My parents were not at all religious—we went to synagogue only on Yom Kippur and Rosh Hashanah. Our rabbi was Mordecai Kaplan, who was famous for his interpretations of the Bible and the Talmud, but nevertheless, as a young person, I found that I was just not very interested in religion.

I was always aware I was Jewish, however, particularly at Christmas. We celebrated the holiday by getting a Christmas tree at the last moment, when they were on sale, and I always liked getting and giving presents. I especially liked singing Christmas carols but could never say "Christ, our Lord."

My father, who wasn't one for a lot of words, certainly didn't have any noticeable religious or political passions. His favorite piece of advice in life for me was "Don't get involved!"

He was not a joiner, unlike his brother Ben, who was mixed up with everything. Uncle Ben was the head of his synagogue and was always on this and that committee. When my father learned about one of Ben's new projects, he would look up from his copy of the *New York Sun*, shake his head, and tell me, "Don't be like Ben. Stick to your business!"

The Upper West Side was, at that time, the main Jewish neighborhood in Manhattan along with the Lower East Side. This didn't make much of an impression on me at the time. I was a tall, skinny, good-natured but somewhat shy kid with red hair and freckles. One day, when I was around ten years old, a man stopped my father and me on the street and told us he was casting a movie and needed some Irish kids, and that he would pay $200 a week. My father thought for a moment and said, "For $200 a week, he can be Irish!"

As kids, we had the run of the neighborhood. We played on the block of Amsterdam Avenue between Seventy-Third and Seventy-Fourth Streets. There was a savings bank on the street but not many other stores, and there was hardly ever much traffic on the block. We played stoopball, where you threw a small ball against a two-foot-high ledge on a building and tried to send it flying off at a weird angle—the guy playing the field behind you had to catch it in the air or you'd get a run—and we played hockey on roller skates with metal wheels that made a terrible noise as they scraped against the pavement.

It was the early days of broadcast radio, and I got addicted to shows like *Little Orphan Annie*, *Dick Tracy*, and *Jack Armstrong*, which always finished with a cliff-hanger that pulled you back for the next episode. The movies were the other big thing—we'd go on Saturday afternoons, when the theater would have a double feature, cartoons, and a few games of bingo. You'd walk in at one p.m. and get out four hours later. The other option on Saturday afternoons was free movies at the American Museum of Natural History, which were always packed with kids. The museum showed films like *Nanook of the North*, a documentary about the Inuit, which totally fascinated me.

My father had gone into business with his two brothers and had an office on Thomas Street in what is now Tribeca. He was a textile converter, a profession that doesn't exist anymore. Essentially, he bought plain, unbleached cotton cloth and had several artists who designed patterns for it. My father then sent the plain cloth to a cloth printer, who printed the artists' designs on it and sent it back, and my father's firm sold it to other companies that made inexpensive cotton dresses. Later, after I had started my career in book publishing, my father would remark to me that "we're both essentially in the same business"—the only difference was he printed on cloth and I printed on paper.

His office building had a lunch club on the top floor, which seemed like a great luxury to me. When I would visit my father, and he had time, we'd eat there. When he didn't, I would go out with one of the guys from the stockroom, who were always cutting pieces to send out as samples to various manufacturers. My lunch was two hot dogs and an orange drink from Nedick's, which was a chain of hot dog stands. It always came to 15¢ in total.

Fortunately, the family business did all right after the Great Depression started, but it was obvious just from walking around the Upper West Side that a lot of people were really hurting. It seemed like there were men on every corner selling apples for 5¢ or offering to shine your shoes. There were shantytowns in Central Park and Riverside Park, where people lived in shacks made of cardboard and corrugated tin. They looked like the areas you would see outside Cape Town in South Africa today.

My sister Barbara and I had a governess—today, it would be a "nanny"—a student at New York University, who took us to school in the mornings, picked us up after school, and watched over us on the weekends. On the weekends, she would take me through the encampments to talk with people—I think she probably had leftist political leanings. We would enter Central Park on the west side at Eighty-First Street and then walk to the middle of the park, to the Great Lawn, just north of Belvedere Castle.

Even though I was only ten years old, it was humbling. Men and women wearing ragged clothes stooped over little cooking fires. The people were always very nice, and when my governess stopped to speak with them, they would offer me something like a cup of hot cocoa. There was no electricity or plumbing, and I always wondered where they went to the bathroom. It made you wonder what you would do if everything was taken away. I also began to realize that a lot of people had it very rough in the world.

My father was always a bit of a stoic, a friendly man but shy. Looking back, my grandfather on my mother's side, Jacob Bloch, was really a big influence on me. He had little formal education but a lot of street smarts. After emigrating from Germany, he started a wholesale butcher business that sold meat to hotel restaurants around town. He was a very good-looking man and very much into looking good—he always wore a coat with a velvet collar and a gray felt hat, and he carried a cane with a silver handle. He didn't really need the cane; it was just the fashion of the day to have one. To top it off, he always placed a white carnation in his lapel.

The Depression had crushed my grandfather, financially. He had gotten out of the meat business in 1924 and gone into real estate. By the 1930s, he owned several brownstones up in Harlem, which was really Harlem then—you didn't see a white person north of 110th Street in those days. My grandfather always went up to collect the rent on the places he owned in person, but after the Depression started, many of his tenants couldn't pay. A lot of other landlords started mass evictions, but my grandfather didn't want to do that—I remember when he came back, my grandmother would ask if he had gotten the rent, and he always had an excuse about why he hadn't. In the end, he couldn't make his payments, and he lost everything. After that, my grandparents were supported by my parents and my mother's siblings, though from just seeing my grandfather you would never guess that he was broke. My grandparents had a great apartment with a large terrace, which was where my grandmother, who had diabetes and had lost a leg, spent her days in her wheelchair.

My grandfather loved to make these somewhat grandiose gestures. For example, once a year, he took my cousin Charles and me out to dinner and the theater. One year, when I was about fifteen years old, he decided that we should all go in tuxedos. We had a terrific dinner at the Astor Hotel, where my grandfather still knew the headwaiter from his days in the meat business. Then we went to see a show called *Hellzapoppin'*, which was a burlesque comedy that was very popular at the time. I remember one moment from the show: a baby in one of the boxes started crying and yowling so loud that you couldn't hear anyone, and everybody started to look at the box. The baby was just screaming its head off. One of the guys on the stage yelled out, "Usher, quiet that baby!" And then you heard "Bang!" That was what passed for humor.

Shortly after Hitler came to power in 1933, my grandfather figured out that things weren't going to be very good for Jews in Germany. He decided that it was his responsibility to get the people in his hometown, Randegg, near the border with Switzerland, out of the country. In 1934, my grandfather wrote to the Jews in the town to let them know that he wanted to help. Then, over the course of several years, he sent an affidavit to the American consul for each one who wanted to leave, swearing that he would support them and offering his property as a guarantee. According to an old newspaper article I have on him, my grandfather got at least sixty-eight people out of Germany in this way.

When they arrived and thanked him, my grandfather would break the news: "Well, I can't support you, but I had to get you out. You've got to get a job somehow, but I want to be sure you and your family have one good meal a day. I don't know how bad things are going to be or how good. So if you call us by three in the afternoon, you're always welcome for dinner at our house."

So my whole childhood I remember going to dinner at my grandparents' apartment with the "refugees," which is what we called them. They would arrive around five o'clock, and my grandfather would take out a bottle of gin, a bottle of Scotch, and a bottle of schnapps, and he'd put out some crackers and cheese. On the better days, my grandfather would pick up some smoked salmon from Barney Greengrass, the "Sturgeon King," a delicatessen right around the corner.

The refugees would come in and tell stories about looking for jobs and their lives in New York City and the lives they had left behind, and then they'd stay for dinner—on any evening, there would usually be between three and eight of them at the apartment. My grandmother's standard meal was pot roast, salad, red cabbage and potatoes, and, for dessert, lemon pound cake with sugar icing.

I remember one man telling me he'd been a prominent doctor in Berlin, with a weekend country house and a car and driver, until Hitler took away the licenses of Jewish doctors. When I asked him what he was doing now that he was in New York, he told me that the only job he could find was changing the marquee on a movie theater. He said, "I climb up this big ladder after eleven at night, when the theater is closed and they're changing the film, and I put in the letters for the new film."

One of the refugees, an ear doctor, invented a machine that could measure deafness. He had it patented, started to sell it, and was making pretty good money. My grandfather went to him and said, "Look, I consider all the people I brought over as sort of a socialist state. You're doing much better than the others. Would you give some of your income to support the others?"

My grandfather was shocked when the man said no.

The group of refugees, as a whole, made a huge and lasting impression on me. Watching them, I began to develop a philosophy that if you are going to help people, don't judge them too closely. From afar, it's easy to think in romantic terms about people who are suffering in other parts of the world; when you meet them, you find that they are just people, with all the good and bad aspects of people everywhere. You can't expect them to meet some artificial standard of behavior that you have in your head.

It also struck me that the refugees were people who had been prominent and wealthy professionals back in Germany. Their lives had been turned completely upside down by the rise of Hitler. Many years later, after I got married, I would sometimes wonder what my wife and I would do if we were forced to become refugees in a foreign country, such as China, and what we would do if—like many adult immigrants—we weren't able to learn the language. I finally decided that Helen would make cheesecakes, brownies, and coffee cakes, and I would be the delivery boy for them. Fortunately, it hasn't come to that yet.

In 1934, when I was starting the seventh grade, my parents somehow got me into the Lincoln School, an experimental school that was run by Columbia University's Teachers College and designed to implement the progressive educational philosophies of John Dewey, who believed that students should learn through experience.

I don't know why exactly my parents enrolled me there—my father was a pretty conservative man—but it was a great place to go to school, located in a building up on 123rd Street between Amsterdam and Morningside Avenues, right across from Morningside Park. A big part of the education was to go and see things for ourselves, so we took field trips to places like a farm in Massachusetts, to see how our food was produced, and a coal mine in West Virginia.

There are two excursions I remember vividly. One was to the slums in Harlem near our school, where we saw rats running up and down the stairways and kids and their parents hanging out, sort of hollow eyed and beaten, completely despairing, living in tenements that smelled of urine. This was only a few blocks from our school, where we had a gorgeously kept gym and swimming pool.

The other trip was to one of the jails in downtown Manhattan, where the guards brought us to a cell and had us talk with a prisoner who was a heroin addict. He held up his arm and showed how it was completely scabbed over from where he had been searching for a vein. The man spoke to us quite calmly, and you almost immediately realized how powerful his addiction must have been to make him damage himself as he had done.

Though I would later go to court against the U.S. government over First Amendment issues, I think my first free speech fight came against Mr. Stolper, my tenth-grade English teacher. Mr. Stolper was in his sixties, always wore a suit and tie, and was really a wonderful teacher. He was also something of an authoritarian who tended to expound at length on his opinions.

Mr. Stolper started a newspaper that he called the *Public Press*—it was two pages that weren't distributed, but tacked up on the classroom wall. As the advisor, he had the final say in what could and could not go in the paper, and I guess I didn't agree with his editorial direction. So, without telling anyone, a friend and I made our own newspaper in secret, called the *Private Press*, which we said included everything not allowed in Mr. Stolper's paper. We had it printed and hung it on the wall next to the *Public Press*. In it, we included a cartoon of the police interrogating a man in a chair, whom we labeled "Stolper." One of the policemen was explaining to the other, "We can't get him to stop talking!"

I learned that in freedom of the press battles, there are some fights you win and some that you lose. It was the first and last issue of the *Private Press*.

Overall, I was interested in politics as a kid but not especially political. For example, I remember writing a letter in support of the Scottsboro Boys, nine African American teenagers from Alabama who had been railroaded after being falsely accused of raping two white women. But when I was at Lincoln School, Joe Lash, a student at City University who later became a biographer of Franklin and Eleanor Roosevelt, started the American Student Union, which was for socialist revolution. Several of my classmates joined, but

I wasn't interested. My lack of interest wasn't really based on the political merits; I think I just wanted to spend my time playing basketball instead of organizing rallies.

Most weekends I played bridge with a group of three close friends, and our games sometimes lasted straight through from Friday to Sunday evening, with pauses only to sleep. I didn't have a lot of dates, and I remember, when I was fifteen years old, being very excited to finally go out with Delia Heming, who was very attractive and always had boyfriends. We went to the New Yorker Hotel to hear the Tommy Dorsey big band, but I don't think she was very impressed when I only had enough money to buy her a drink, and I settled for a glass of water.

Back then, the Ivy League schools had a deal with certain private schools—if you were in the upper seventh of your class, you didn't have to take the entrance exams. I did well enough academically at Lincoln to get into Cornell and Harvard, even though Harvard at the time had quotas on how many Jews it would let in.

Coming from Lincoln, which after all was "progressive," I thought Harvard was kind of snobby. I didn't like the privileged and had decided I wanted to be in the middle of the world, not an elitist. So I wanted to go to Cornell, where my father had actually gone for his first three years, until he couldn't afford it and had to come back to New York City to work while he finished at Columbia. I was admitted and everything was set, except that I forgot to apply for a room. Cornell wrote me and told me that the dorms were full and that I'd have to rent a room off campus. That seemed a little too adventurous to me, so I went to Harvard.

I began my freshman year in the fall of 1940, a year after Germany invaded Poland to start World War II. That year, I did the normal two semesters and another in the summer. On December 7, 1941, when I was in my sophomore year, the Japanese bombed Pearl Harbor. The draft was reinstated, and Harvard—like many universities across the country—went to a twelve-month calendar, meaning that there were three semesters a year instead of two. You were also allowed to take five or even six classes a semester, so you could graduate in three years or less.

I didn't particularly like Harvard. The first year I was lonely, and I wasn't very good at making friends. Most of the classes were huge lectures of a few hundred people where some famous professor, sometimes looking totally bored, would read a lecture he'd been giving each year for decades. I didn't think it was the best way to get an education. With six courses a semester and a considerable amount of reading for each, there was a tremendous volume of work just to keep up, so I took part in only a few extracurricular activities.

One was the Harvard band. At the start of my freshman year, the manager of the band came to speak to our class and said, "We want all of you to come out, whether you can play an instrument or not." I always wanted to be in a marching band, but I couldn't play anything, so I thought this was my golden opportunity.

I stood in line the next day and soon noticed that everybody had an instrument except me. When I got to the head of the line, the manager asked what I played, and I told him I didn't play anything. He asked what I was doing there then. I said, "Look, last night you said you wanted every freshman to come out for the band whether they played an instrument or not. I want to be in a band very badly. I'll be happy to pull the bass drum."

Harvard had a really huge bass drum that had a big maroon "H" painted on it, about eight feet across. It was kept on a little cart that was wheeled onto the field, and a guy walked next to it and hit it with a big drumstick every once in a while. The manager said that job had already been filled but asked if I thought I could play the cymbals. I told him I thought I would be great.

It wasn't quite that simple. In rehearsal, it was easy to hear the band and know when to hit them. But when I got out on the street—we marched from Eliot House, which was on the river, across the bridge and into the stadium—I was in the back, and it was really hard to hear the music, so I never knew when exactly to crash the cymbals. The other thing was that a girl had to really like you to want to sit next to the cymbal player in the stadium.

Harvard also had a newly launched radio station, which was closed-circuit and distributed only to the campus. It was on every day from four in the afternoon until ten at night. I became the program director, which meant that I had to come up with ideas for shows. One was, as I think about it now, pretty sexist. But it taught me one thing, which is that it's usually best to be up front about things.

The show was called *Test Your Line*. We would play a song, and the first guy to call us up at the station and name the song got a chance to come up and "test his line."

We had the pictures and phone numbers of ten girls from Radcliffe, Harvard's sister college. The guy could call whomever he wanted, and we would broadcast the conversation (the girl didn't know it was on air). The deal was that if the contestant could get the girl to agree to go out on a date, we would pay for it.

It was very interesting. The guys ended up being very erratic and the girls very consistent. Some guys called up and said, "I saw you walking across the campus and I had to find out who you were. I was swept away just by the look of you," and usually the girl would hang up.

The better approach was to say, "Look, you don't know me. I'm calling because the Harvard radio station has this program called *Test Your Line* and I'm here on it, so our conversation is being broadcast and I want you to know that. And here's the way it works: if we decide that we want to go out and take a chance and have dinner together, they'll pay for the whole thing. And I'd like to try it. Would you?" The girl would usually say, "Sure."

After a few years at Harvard, I knew I was going to be drafted soon. I decided that I might as well find an army specialty I was interested in and enlist, so the military wouldn't choose a specialty for me. I looked into several and, though I was majoring in American history, decided that I might like meteorology. So I entered the military on January 1, 1943, as a trainee meteorologist. I left Harvard one semester short of graduation, and I never went back.

I had signed up for what was called Meteorology B, which was meteorology for people who didn't have science backgrounds. I was assigned to Brown University for classes with about two hundred other aspiring weathermen. It was like college but with a martial twist. We got up at six in the morning and did calisthenics for half an hour. Then we ran around the campus for a few miles. After each class, we gathered into a formation and marched to our next class or to the meal hall.

After six months, I graduated from Meteorology B and was assigned to MIT for Meteorology A, which was where you learned to do weather maps, synoptic meteorology, and dynamic meteorology. I really struggled, as the sciences were hard for me. In December 1943, I was elated that I'd passed every course. Then the army announced it had overestimated the number of meteorologists it needed and told MIT to cut 50 percent of the class from the program. That included me.

Now the army had to do something with us, a bunch of would-be meteorologists. We were all college students, but we nevertheless ended up at a base in Goldsboro, North Carolina, which happened to be where anybody who was cut from any course anywhere in the army was sent. So it was the bottom half of everything— the cooks who couldn't cook, the bakers who couldn't bake, the truck drivers who crashed their trucks, and a bunch of mediocre meteorologists.

With the way my life had been to that point—going to a progressive New York City high school and then Harvard—Goldsboro was a shock to me. A lot of guys in the barracks had southern drawls so thick I could hardly understand them. It seemed like every sentence had at least one "fuck" or "shit" in it.

I was really surprised when I realized that a lot of the men were pretty much illiterate. We had a lot of time to kill, and the army printed these wonderful books that were long and narrow so that you could fit them in your back pocket. Once, on a long bus ride, I asked the guy next to me why he didn't have a book, and he said, "I can't read."

Goldsboro was also totally segregated. On weekends, you could go into town to catch a movie or grab something to eat. The army had shuttle buses that ran back and forth. There were two lines for the buses: one for whites and one for blacks. When the bus came, the whites would board first, and if there were any seats left, the the blacks got on. Fifteen minutes later, when the next bus came, it was the same thing, so that the whites always got on and the black line kept backing up. It would take a white person ten to fifteen minutes to get on a bus, while a black person would wait much longer.

I thought this was really wrong. I talked to another guy and asked, "Shouldn't I report this? This isn't the way the army should treat citizens."

He told me, "Buddy, if I were you I would keep my mouth shut, because if you report it you'll be reporting it, probably, to a southern officer. The southern officer won't say anything, but all of a sudden you'll be shifted over to the Battle of the Bulge or something else in the most dangerous part of Europe, and believe me, nothing will change."

So I didn't say anything. Later on, when I began to work with human rights activists from repressive countries, one of the reasons I was so blown away by them is that they went ahead and spoke their consciences despite the sometimes terrible consequences to themselves. I also learned that speaking up isn't enough. You have to have actual ideas for how to bring about change. It's not easy.

In February 1944, I got my orders to ship out. I loaded into a boat with seven thousand other soldiers to cross the Atlantic. We were part of a convoy of about twelve ships, protected by cruisers and battleships. I stayed in one cavernous room in the hold with four hundred other men. The bunk beds were stacked about seven high. Most of our time was taken up with getting something to eat—you were fed twice a day and given a time to get in line. You waited an hour or two to get your food. Not long after you finished, it was time to line up again.

We landed in Casablanca. As part of my job as company clerk, I knew that each serviceman was supposed to get a carton of cigarettes and some chocolate when we landed. It ended up that our captain took all of it and sold it on the black market—he had some soldiers deliver the cigarettes and chocolate to an address he gave them. A couple of days later, the boat sailed back to America with the captain on it to pick up another load of troops. I always wondered how much money he made through that scam.

We stayed in a camp outside Casablanca until the army loaded us on a train and sent us to Oran, Algeria—the city on the Mediterranean coast where Albert Camus set *The Plague*—where we set up in another camp just outside town. The rumor was that we were going to be sent to Italy as replacement troops for soldiers who had been killed, but just as we got to Oran, there was a big breakthrough in the Italian campaign and we weren't needed.

So there we all were. The army decided, instead, to send troops to India. We were all loaded onto a former cruise ship that sailed under the British flag. Under the British army rules, the officers had tremendous privileges over the enlisted men, which wasn't as true of the U.S. Army. It was June, and we were going through the Suez Canal. The temperature on deck was around 105 degrees, and belowdecks, at night, it would go up to 120. You just couldn't stay there, so you had to sleep on deck.

Meanwhile, when you were on deck, you looked into air-conditioned lounges in which the officers were sitting and being served mint juleps by barefoot Indians in white jackets and white pants. At night, the officers all went to their quarters and these air-conditioned living rooms sat empty. So one night an enlisted sergeant said, "This is ridiculous. We're out here in the heat and those air-conditioned rooms aren't even in use. Let's just let in as many men as can sleep on the floor."

The British officers immediately tried to eject them, but they were enormously outnumbered. The British and Egyptian officers said this was a mutiny and we'd all be tried when we landed, but the American officers interfered and said, "The troops are right. Why aren't we using these air-conditioned rooms at night, at least relieving some of the people?" So after a big fight, it was resolved, mainly because the Americans had numerical superiority.

We arrived in Bombay (now Mumbai), a beautiful city, but one rife with poverty. At some of the best hotels in Bombay, where we'd sit and have a drink and maybe a meal, there'd be big signs outside saying: "For Europeans Only." I was appalled. On Grant Road, there was one whorehouse after another. It was explained to me that most of the women there were the wives of Indian men who had run up debt, and in order to pay it off they were allowed to put their wives into these brothels. When the debt was paid off—and who knows how long they were kept there—they could come back to their homes.

A little while later, I went to Calcutta (now.Kolkata), which was in the midst of a famine. People would stand in food lines for hours, hoping to get something to eat. Often, they'd die in line because there was nothing. I watched as their bodies were loaded into trucks, wondering whether they were really dead or had just passed out.

Finally, we were put on a riverboat and sent to the state of Assam, in northeast India, near the town of Chabua. We ended up at a camp near an airstrip. I was a staff sergeant by then and in an intelligence unit of the Air Service Command. I reported to a major who had worked for the New York Telephone Company and was an expert on radiotelephone. He would sit there with this big machine talking to Burma (now Myanmar) to find out where exactly the Japanese were. Then we'd tell our planes where to fly so that they wouldn't get shot at. It sounds like an important job, but the Japanese line moved very slowly through the Burmese jungle, and our planes always flew far north of them.

Because we were in the middle of thousands of acres of tea fields, I learned something about the British-owned East India Company, which managed the tea plantations. All the hard labor was done by Indians, who were called "wogs," and every mile or two there'd be quite a nice house, the home of the man the East India Company sent out to administer the fields.

He lived in this house, which was staffed with servants, and also had a mistress supplied to him, usually an Anglo-Indian woman and usually very attractive. The administrator would be there for two years, and then he'd be brought back to company headquarters in England. Then another overseer would arrive from England. He would have the same mistress. Under the circumstances, it's not hard to understand that most of the Anglo-Indian women whom I met were all trying to get an American officer to fall in love with them, marry them, and take them to America.

I'd been in Assam for almost a year and a half when the atomic bombs were dropped on Hiroshima and Nagasaki in August 1945. I was relieved—we had heard terrible stories about what happened to soldiers taken prisoner by the Japanese. The dropping of the A-bombs changed everything; now, the war would end. Later, especially after I read John Hersey's *Hiroshima* and learned about the terrible destruction the bombs caused, I wondered whether it was the right thing to do. I don't think there are any easy answers.

Even though the war was over, the army told us we would have to stay in India for a while longer because it didn't have enough ships to get us home quickly. There was really nothing to do except sit in the heat and drink the case of beer you were allotted every month. The University of Maryland had courses it offered to soldiers, so, to combat the boredom, I arranged for the school to send us the list of its classes. Once you signed up for a class, it would send the textbooks. After you read the textbooks, you filled in some study materials and got college credit for it. In the months after the end of the war, I had several thousand soldiers sign up throughout the valley. We called it "Assam University," and I got nicknamed "Dean Bernstein."

I first learned about the Holocaust during that period, when the army sent Fred Friendly, who was a master sergeant, to our camp. When the American troops entered Germany, the army newspaper in India—it was called the *CBI Roundup*, for the China, Burma, and India theater of war—had sent Fred and a photographer to go through the concentration camps as they were liberated. Fred produced a slide show about it, and when he returned to India, the army sent him to its bases to give a presentation. Because I had been assigned to Education and Information, my job was to drive Fred around in a Jeep to the camps in the Assam region.

Fred was a wonderful speaker and obviously had been deeply touched by what he had seen. As he showed the photos, men in the audience were equally moved. One day, after Fred gave a speech at one of the camps, the colonel who was in charge invited him to eat with the officers. Fred was about twenty-seven at the time, and typical of him, as I saw in later years, he told the colonel he was honored, but he was an enlisted man and felt that he should eat with the other enlisted men. The colonel looked shocked, but he didn't make it an order. When I asked Fred about it, he said, "I think it's important that the enlisted men have a chance to ask me questions and talk to me about what happened, rather than just a few officers."

Fred, of course, subsequently became well known for his journalistic work as Edward R. Murrow's producer on *See It Now* and later became president of CBS News. From those initial encounters in India, we became lifelong friends.

Overall, everybody was just anxious to get home, and at the beginning of 1946, we finally heard that the army was ready to ship us out. So we went to Calcutta and then were flown to Karachi, in what is now Pakistan. We stayed in a windblown, dusty camp on the outskirts of town. After another month, the army put us on a ship and sent us back to Calcutta, and from there we sailed to Manila and finally to Seattle.

My experiences in India left a lasting impression on me. I never forget that despite all the problems the United States has with its own poor and struggling, these just don't compare to other places in the world. Once you've seen the slums in a place like Calcutta, you see how deeply rooted some global problems are. Seventy years later, India still has 500 million people who can't read or write and 300 million without easy access to fresh water. It's staggering when you think about it.

The only dangers I faced in the army were a bad stomach—at six-foot-three, I weighed 165 pounds when I left the States and 146 pounds when I returned—and a close call in Assam with a poisonous snake. In Seattle, we loaded on a train and headed east. It was February and very cold, and the train broke down somewhere in the middle of Montana in a terrible snowstorm. It took many hours for help to come, and as the temperature dropped in the train, men began to panic. I thought at the time it would be a fitting ending that I'd been in a world war and come all the way around the globe only to freeze to death in Montana. But help eventually arrived, the train was repaired, and I got my discharge in February 1946. I was back in New York City without a clue about what I was going to do next.

2

OFFICE BOY IN WAITING

BY EARLY 1946, DISCHARGED SOLDIERS WERE FLOODING BACK INTO New York City. Although the economy was entering a decades-long postwar expansion, no one knew that at the time and memories of the Great Depression were still fresh. I was worried I wasn't going to be able to get a job.

While I was in Assam, I received a letter from Harvard letting me know that it had granted me credit for the courses I had taken at Brown and MIT while I was in the army's meteorology program and had given me a degree in absentia (I was only a credit and a half shy when I left). Since I didn't know what I wanted to do, I applied to Harvard's business school. I got in but I decided not to go. My reasoning was that when I graduated in two years, all the good jobs might already be taken. With people coming out of the army in droves, I thought I'd better try to land something fast.

Writing for radio or television seemed appealing. I didn't know exactly where to start, so I wrote letters to twenty-seven advertising agencies. I got several interviews, and I remember thinking that if I was really charming with the receptionist, she'd put in a good word when she went in to talk with her boss. Either my theory was flawed or my charm was lacking, because I didn't get a single job offer. I finally got my foot in the door at WNEW, a radio station, where I worked for $25 a week as a receptionist from two in the afternoon until ten at night. The station was run by Bernice Judis, the general manager, and Ted Cott, the programming director. It was one of the biggest moneymakers in New York, and its big show was *Make Believe Ballroom* with Martin Block, in which Block would play records and then describe a scene to the audience as if he were watching people dance in a ballroom. I could never understand it, but people would come to watch Block do the show, and part of my job was to let them into the studio.

My first job in book publishing, which set the course for my entire professional life, was a total fluke. My father happened to have a salesman in his textile business named Clarence Dorman, who was a lovely guy, but he never got things quite right. When Clarence heard that I was looking for a writing job, he thought that I wanted to write books. He went and made an appointment for me with his friend Albert Leventhal, who was vice president of Simon & Schuster. I had never even considered publishing, but I thought that since Clarence had been nice enough to make the appointment, I might as well keep it.

So I went in to see Leventhal, but I told him, "Mr. Leventhal, our mutual friend, Clarence, made this appointment. But I want to tell you right off, I never thought of publishing in my life. I know nothing about it, and I really want to work in radio or television."

I don't know what Albert Leventhal saw in me, but he said, "You really don't want to work in radio or television. It's a terrible business. You won't like the people. The stuff you turn out, for the most part, is junk. You should really go into book publishing. It's a great business."

The only problem, Leventhal told me, was that he didn't have any jobs available right then. "I'll tell you what," he said. "We're going to promote our office boy to manuscript reader soon. Come in and help him out until we do, and we'll go from there. Just get in here and we'll see what happens. If you don't like it, you can always do something else. But I think you'll like it." He told me he would start me at $30 a week, a raise of $5 over what I was making at the radio station.

I caught on to Leventhal's enthusiasm and thought I might as well give it a try. I began at Simon & Schuster in the summer of 1946, working with the office boy. So I always say that I started in the business at a new low. Everybody in publishing has a title. I decided mine was "office-boy-in-waiting."

Simon & Schuster occupied two floors of an office building at Sixth Avenue and Forty-Eighth Street. As I quickly learned, it was a small business dominated by the quirks of the men who ran it.

Dick Simon and Max Schuster, the firm's namesakes, were very different personalities. Simon was tall, outgoing, handsome, and something of a Renaissance man—he was an excellent pianist, bridge player, and photographer. The son of a successful women's hat maker, Simon had grown up wealthy on the Upper East Side.

Schuster was born in Austria and came to the United States with his family when he was a baby. His father opened a stationery and cigar store in Harlem, and Schuster went to public school in Washington Heights. While Simon was a great salesman, Schuster was the editor of the pair. He was short and intense, usually off in his own world, thinking about whatever book he happened to be working on. Where Simon was polished, suave, and charming, Schuster was awkward, nervous, and shy.

Though both went to Columbia University, they met in 1921, after they had graduated. Simon, who had taken a job selling pianos, went to see Schuster, who was editing the trade magazine of the Motor & Equipment Manufacturers Association. Simon had gotten a tip that Schuster might want to buy a piano. He didn't, but the two began to talk and struck up a friendship.

Simon soon took a new job as a salesman for the larger-than-life publisher Horace Liveright. By 1923, when he was twenty-five years old, Simon had decided he wanted to start his own publishing house. He spoke with his friend Schuster, and they came up with $4,000 in capital.

They opened for business in January 1924 in a one-room office on West Fifty-Seventh Street without a thing to publish. They put their names on the door—"Simon & Schuster, Publishers"—and the story goes that when they came back to the office from lunch on the first day, someone had pinned a note next to "Publishers" asking, "Of what?"

After a slow first day, Simon had dinner with his aunt, who told him her daughter was crazy about a new game that had started to run in the *New York World* on Sundays. Simon talked to Schuster about it, and in a few months the pair published the first book of crossword puzzles.

It was an incredible break for them. Crossword puzzles became a national craze, and the book was an instant success. The pair hurried out two follow-ups, and by the end of the year they had sold a total of 375,000 copies of all three books. The first books included a pencil, and the story I heard was that one of the early business decisions was that the books would sell just as well without it, so they dropped the pencil.

Just as Simon & Schuster (S&S) celebrated its first early success, the publishing world happened to be beginning a generational and cultural shift.

Until the early 1900s, American publishing had been dominated by staid, old families who ran their houses more like private clubs than businesses. These houses—such as G.P. Putnam; Doubleday; Harcourt, Brace; Harper and Brothers; Macmillan; and Scribner's in New York City, and Little, Brown; Atlantic Monthly Press; and Houghton Mifflin in Boston—were WASP enclaves, conservative in what they published and high-handed toward their authors. They didn't seem to hire Jews—or any other ethnic or racial minority, for that matter—for jobs anywhere above the mailroom.

In the 1920s, a new group of publishers emerged in New York City and shook up the industry. Dick Simon and Max Schuster joined this young and predominantly Jewish bunch, which included Horace Liveright of Boni & Liveright; Ben Huebsch and Harold Guinzburg of Viking Press; Alfred A. Knopf and his wife, Blanche; and Bennett Cerf and Donald Klopfer of Random House.

The "Jewish houses" revolutionized the business. They actively sought out authors, published books that included more controversial and racy material, and promoted their titles with snappy, eye-catching ads and artwork.

As one of this vanguard, S&S had great success. After the crossword puzzles, the firm's next big book came quickly, when Schuster noticed in a bookstore a collection of 5¢ pamphlets on philosophy written by a Columbia University professor named Will Durant. Schuster convinced Durant to combine and expand them into a book, *The Story of Philosophy*, which summarized the ideas of the great philosophers. It was a huge bestseller.

By the 1930s, S&S was an established name, thanks to a string of hits, many of which came from the publishers' personal passions. Simon, for example, convinced his friend George Gershwin—the two had been students together at Columbia—to publish a book of his songs. Until that point, songs had been published only as sheet music, which was sold in music stores. After the Gershwin book took off, Simon convinced two other Columbia grads—composer Richard Rodgers and lyricist Lorenz Hart—to do the same thing with their music (many others followed, including Noël Coward, Cole Porter, and Gilbert and Sullivan). Simon later followed his passion for photography and published the first books featuring the work of great photographers such as Henri Cartier-Bresson and Philippe Halsman. Schuster loved art and published the first big book that reproduced great works of art, *A Treasury of Art Masterpieces*. (The story around S&S was that Schuster owned one painting by Georges Braque. When he saw that the *Treasury* was going to include a work by Braque, he arranged to have his appear in the book, over the words "From the collection of M. Lincoln Schuster.")

The biggest bestseller was brought in by the firm's business manager, Leon Shimkin, who really had about as much responsibility in running the house as the two founders. Shimkin, who was born in Brooklyn, joined S&S in 1924 just after the firm had its first success with the crossword puzzle books. Only seventeen at the time, Shimkin worked at S&S while going to night school at New York University's School of Commerce, Accounts, and Finance. As it turned out, the business-oriented Shimkin was a useful counter to the outgoing and fun-loving Simon and the somewhat reclusive and bookish Schuster.

Shimkin was a very shy man. In 1934, he took a fourteen-week course that was supposed to teach you how to relate better with people. Shimkin was so impressed with it that he signed the teacher to turn the course into a book. When it came out in 1937, *How to Win Friends and Influence People* was a massive bestseller; its author, Dale Carnegie, became a household name. By 1939, the book had sold more than a million copies. It subsequently spent ten years on the *New York Times* bestseller list and has now sold more than 16 million copies.

Schuster and Simon were very appreciative of their business manager's editorial acumen and, I was told, offered him a $25,000 bonus. Shimkin, reportedly, turned it down and asked for one-third ownership in the firm, which he got. From then on, the cognoscenti always referred to him as the third "S" in S&S.

Shimkin also seized on the next opportunity that appeared at the door.

Robert Fair de Graff had started as a salesman for Doubleday and later ran a firm that did hardcover reprints, which were reissues of previously published books. Hardback reprints sold for a buck or two, but de Graff was convinced that they could be even cheaper and he came up with what was then a novel idea: paperback books. He approached Simon, Schuster, and Shimkin about investing in his idea. The partners signed on, but Shimkin took a special interest, taking charge of the business side of the new imprint.

In the spring of 1939, Pocket Books put out its first ten titles, which included Shakespeare's *Five Great Tragedies*, *Wuthering Heights*, and *The Murder of Roger Ackroyd*, an Agatha Christie book. The books proved to be more popular than the partners had expected—on the day of the launch, the bookstore in Grand Central Station called and ordered a restock.

A big part of the success of Pocket Books was the distribution model. Because traditional bookstores were not warm to the idea— they were doing just fine with hardbacks—Pocket Books hooked up with the national network of independent magazine wholesalers. You could get the books at newsstands, cigar shops, grocery stores, hotels, and anywhere else you could buy a magazine or items like toothpaste and razor blades. In effect, Pocket Books were everywhere. In 1940, the firm sold 5 million paperbacks. Sales ratcheted up even further during World War II as the military bought books by the boatload for servicemen.

The success of Pocket Books attracted the attention of Marshall Field III, the owner of the Chicago department store of the same name. Field wanted to diversify his holdings, and when he found out that the owners of Simon & Schuster owned Pocket Books, he made an offer for both firms in 1944. Simon was staunchly opposed, but the interests of Schuster, Shimkin, and de Graff prevailed. The two houses were sold to Field for about $3 million. The deal included the stipulation that the companies would have autonomy and the former owners would receive long-term contracts with performance bonuses.

A few years later, in 1946, I arrived on the scene.

When I started at S&S, I was twenty-three and had absolutely no idea about business. At that age, I just knew I didn't want to be broke—I wanted to earn enough to buy an apartment and live reasonably well. Of course, I also knew that I wasn't going to get there as assistant to the office boy.

Albert Leventhal had hired me, and when I started, his big thing was managing Little Golden Books, a series that was conceived by Georges Duplaix, an elegant Frenchman who ran the editorial operations of Western Printing & Lithographing, a company based in Racine, Wisconsin. His idea was to establish a line of inexpensive children's titles, so he came up with these small four-color books that each had a little story in them, like *Scuffy the Tugboat*, *Tootle* (about a locomotive), and *The Poky Little Puppy*. Duplaix brought the concept to Shimkin, who agreed that S&S would distribute them.

Little Golden Books launched in 1942, and, like Pocket Books, they were sold in magazine racks and grocery stores around the country. They cost 25¢ and were instantly successful. During the first fifteen years of the series, 400 million Little Golden Books were sold. S&S brought out about three or four new books a month, and it was normal for each book to sell more than a million copies. There weren't even any royalties to pay because the authors sold the rights, for as little as $300 a book, as I remember.

Later on, Big Golden Books, which were larger in size and more expensive, came out and also did very well. Golden Coloring Books and Golden Pop-Up Books followed. These made Simon & Schuster, with Western Printing, one the largest publishers of children's books in the country.

Duplaix, who had a deal that he would get 2 percent of sales, made out tremendously. He started spending more and more time in France and less and less time doing any work. The story is that Shimkin called him in and said, "You know, Georges, we're paying you several hundred thousand dollars a year, and you're not working very hard." Shimkin practically had a heart attack when Duplaix said, "Well, you know, Mr. Shimkin, we have this arrangement where I get 2 percent of sales. It doesn't say anything about work. If you want me to work, you'll have to pay me extra."

When you start as office-boy-in-waiting, it's quite obvious that you have to figure out how to get promoted quickly. Seeing that the lines of Golden Books were exploding, I thought about how to help that part of S&S. One of the saving graces of my life is that I've always been able to come up with ideas. They just pop into my head. A lot of them might be garbage—at least, in other people's opinions—but sometimes there's something good in there. I soon came up with a proposal.

Libraries at the time had storytelling hours every Saturday morning when people would come in and tell stories to the kids—I had gone to them when I was a child. My idea was that S&S should announce a national storytelling contest and have people submit the best original stories from these Saturday morning sessions. The stories would be broadcast every week on a radio program, and they would be printed in little pamphlets and put into cereal boxes. At the end of the year, Simon & Schuster would pick from all the ones submitted and publish a book—the best original children's stories coming out of the library system of the United States.

Leventhal was very enthusiastic about the idea. We went to see Dancer-Fitzgerald-Sample, the ad agency for Kellogg's Corn Flakes, and it said it was interested. For a while, there was a lot of excitement in the office, and here I was, an office boy walking around with the vice president, planning this new series. It seemed too good to be true, and it was—in the end, the radio broadcast fell through and Kellogg's backed off the idea, so it never happened.

But it served me very well. I was promoted from office boy right away. The managers didn't know what to do with me, so they tried me out in different departments. I went to advertising, where I worked very briefly for Nina Bourne, who over the coming decades became legendary for her great copy and layouts. She gave me a book called *How to Clean Everything*, and I wrote the ad headline "Grape Juice on the Rug?" My second book was an economy travel guide to Florida, and my headline for that one really worked: "Florida on a Shoestring."

They moved me to the sales department next, and that's where I settled in.

At the time, Little Golden Books were being sold through independent distributors, which were in every city and town in America. They were monopolies and controlled the distribution of magazines and newspapers as well as paperback books to drugstores and stationery stores. If you tried to go around them, they would threaten to cut off the stores you were dealing with. There was reportedly Mafia involvement in the business in a few cities.

Nevertheless, Shimkin wanted to see what would happen if we took some of that work in-house, so he set up a trial project in Bridgeport, Connecticut. My job was to go from account to account to make sure each had a steady supply of Little Golden Books and to fill orders from the trunk of my car.

I hated being a salesman. I drove up to Bridgeport on Monday and stayed the week in the Stratford Hotel. During the day, I went from store to store, checking on accounts. At night, I ate dinner by myself. It was lonely and boring. I came home Fridays, anxious to get back to the city.

My most memorable account was a small magazine store. It had five big racks of Little Golden Books up front, but every time I went in, it never seemed to have sold any. After a few weeks, I started to nose around. I went to the back, looking for the owner, and found about eight bookies taking bets on the horses. The whole thing was a front.

Before long, the wholesaler S&S was using, Fairfield County News, told Shimkin that if we kept trying to go our own way with Little Golden Books, it would tell our customers that it was going to stop supplying them with books and magazines. That ended that, and I was released from my duties in Connecticut. My next assignment was to work with Shimkin's nephew, Arthur Shimkin, who was starting something called Little Golden Records, an audio spin-off of the books.

The idea was to produce six-inch records of children's songs that could be sold alongside the books. At the time, the maximum you could squeeze onto one side of a six-inch record was one and a half minutes, so that was basically one very short song on each side.

We hired Mitch Miller, an unknown but extremely talented oboe player, to put together an orchestra and oversee the recordings (a few years later Miller became famous for leading his own orchestra and hosting his television program, *Sing Along with Mitch*). Arthur's job was to get the songs written and get the manufacturing done, and my responsibility was to take the finished records and sell them. A lot of the songs we did were tie-ins with stories in the Little Golden Books series, but we also had a contract with Disney and recorded songs from Disney films. Occasionally, we did independent songs. One of the most popular was "How Much Is That Doggie in the Window?"

It developed into a very profitable business, though we had one brush with disaster at the beginning. We made a deal with a man named Al Massler—he later made a fortune in plastics—who told us he had a new way to make records very inexpensively by injection molding instead of pressing. The problem was that children's phonographs were made very cheaply, and they had heavy arms compared with those of regular record players. For our first printing, we used the new plastic and shipped records all over the country before we realized that the heavy arm of a children's record player would dig into the groove and start to peel it off. You could play the record about five times before it was destroyed.

We had invested a lot of money in these records, which were beautifully made and packaged, and had sold about six hundred thousand copies. We didn't know what to do and were expecting a huge amount of returns. Going back to the lesson I learned at Harvard with the girls and the *Test Your Line* radio show, we wrote a straightforward letter to all our retailers telling them about the problem. We asked them to refund any customers who brought the records in and let us know how many had been returned, and said we would reimburse them. In the end, few came back, and our customers were pleased that they had been warned about the problem and that it could be so easily handled.

Once we had the issues with the plastic worked out, I began to travel to sell the line. At the time, every city usually had one or two really big department stores. For example, there was Shillito's in Cincinnati, L.S. Ayres in Indianapolis, and Marshall Field's in Chicago.

On the road, which can be very lonely, dinner invitations are treasured. There was a wonderful buyer at the Maison Blanche department store in New Orleans who always wore great big hats. She invited me to dinner and told me she had an old New Orleans house and I should come and see it. When I arrived, I saw it had a huge front porch, and as I climbed the steps to it I didn't notice her mean-faced bulldog dozing there. The evening got off to a bad start when he bit me.

In Cleveland, the big department store was Higbee's. Anne Udin, its book buyer, was one of the best known and most popular in the business. If she got behind a book, all of Cleveland would know about it.

However, it was questionable whether department store book sections would buy records, so I was very eager to sell Anne and tell all the other stores that she was carrying Little Golden Records. When I went into her small office, I was greeted with a great smile, so I thought things would go well, but I was certainly surprised when I learned why they would.

"Look," she said, "I'm going out with this guy tonight to a baseball game, and I want to impress him, but I don't know beans about baseball. If you'll spend the half-hour that you'd be selling me and tell me about baseball instead, you can write any order you want for your records, I'll sign it, and I'll promote them."

Little Golden Records did well, and in 1949, Albert Leventhal called me into his office and told me I was getting a bonus of $8,000. Since my salary was only $10,000, I was ecstatic. I didn't realize that this particular bonus would have such a tremendous influence on my later life.

A day or two later, I was surprised when Leventhal came back and asked me, "Would you mind if we cut your bonus to $5,000?"

I asked him why.

He said, "Well, Leon Shimkin believes that we're bringing you along at the wrong rate and that an $8,000 bonus is too big a percentage of your salary. He thinks $5,000 is the correct rate of growth."

"Well, Mr. Leventhal," I said, "frankly, if you'd offered me $5,000, I would have thought it was great. But after offering me $8,000, I really wouldn't like to have it cut. If it puts you in any kind of bad position, though, of course I'll accept the five. So if you want me to do it, tell me, and it's done."

He said, "No, I don't want you to do it. I don't think Leon is right. But he has asked me to ask you if you would volunteer to take $5,000."

I thought about it for a moment and said, "Well, I don't agree with the reasoning. I think people go along at all different rates. Some go along at a fantastic rate and some never make any progress. So I won't agree to voluntarily cut it."

Leventhal said, "I'll tell him that. That's what I wanted to ask you. And it's fine with me."

The next thing I knew, I got called into Dick Simon's office. He said, "Bob, I hear you're having a discussion about your bonus with Leon Shimkin. I want to tell you, I think you're right. I've heard the story. But Leon Shimkin is in charge of this. We've given him the responsibility. And if you don't give in to him he will never forget it. He will hold it against you for your whole life. I'm telling you as a friend, it's not worth having Leon Shimkin as an enemy for $3,000. So you ought to consider volunteering to do this."

I said, "Mr. Simon, I can tell you right off I'm sure you're right. I just don't think he's right to be asking it. I think the company should have done their thinking before offering me the $8,000. Albert Leventhal has told me it would be no problem for him. If it was, I would gladly give it back."

"Well, you do as you see fit, it's up to you," he said. "I just thought I would give you the benefit of my knowledge of Leon Shimkin."

So then I was called into Shimkin's office. I couldn't believe there was all this fuss over $3,000. It was mind-boggling to me. And I was getting more and more intrigued and sort of enjoying the whole process—here were the owners of the company, engaging themselves over the size of a twenty-seven-year-old's bonus.

Shimkin explained to me that you make logical progress in business. I said, "Mr. Shimkin, there is no such thing as logical progress in business. Look at Frank Sinatra. He emerged as a star and made a fortune at a very young age."

I continued: "To tell you the truth, Mr. Shimkin, I love this business, and if you made me president right now I think I could run the company."

That was not the right thing to say, because Shimkin wanted to run the company himself. Even though he was a partner, he was not considered quite on the level of the two founders. His face turned red, and he said, "Well, I understand that you won't do this voluntarily, and we'll have to make a decision."

A few days later Leventhal told me, "Mr. Shimkin cut your bonus to $5,000."

That was that.

About a month later I got a raise from $10,000 to $15,000, and the following year I got a bonus of $12,000, and there was no discussion of any kind.

I thought that the incident was over and forgot about Dick Simon's warning.

In my early years at S&S, I was painfully self-conscious and a bit shy. Part of publishing is the social life—meeting and chatting with people at cocktail parties—and that was very difficult for me (it still is to this day). I never really knew what to talk about, or if the person was at all interested in what I was saying. When people invited me to parties and dinners, I always wondered if they really wanted me there, or if they just invited me because they felt they had to. At about age thirty-five, I simplified my life a lot by just deciding that if I was invited someplace, all I had to do was to make up my mind whether I wanted to go, and not worry about the rest of it.

At S&S, Albert Leventhal and editor in chief Jack Goodman were both exactly the opposite of me as far as comfort in social situations, and they both took a liking to me. They soon started to make efforts to get me involved in both the business and their social lives.

Leventhal, while technically vice president, was really running S&S by the time I arrived. Since the sale in 1944 to Marshall Field, Dick Simon had faded into the background, Max Schuster's focus was really just on the books he was editing, and Leon Shimkin looked after the financial aspects but was most involved with Pocket Books. So Leventhal oversaw all the business operations, particularly the huge operation of Golden Books.

In 1933, Simon had hired Goodman, who was then twenty-four, to write advertising copy. Right after he started, Goodman recommended to Simon that he hire his close friend and bridge partner, Leventhal, who was then a reporter at a newspaper in Brooklyn. Leventhal came on as an assistant in the sales department, and from that point on, his and Goodman's careers at the house rose in tandem.

They were personable, funny, and outgoing men who liked the same things, including bridge, poker, golf, tennis, and pretty secretaries. They were so close that, in their early days at S&S, they did something I've never heard of anyone else doing.

They were worried that if one of them got promoted faster than the other and got a bigger salary, it might get in the way of their friendship. So they decided to form a corporation, and the deal was that whatever money they made went to the partnership, not to either of them as individuals. Whatever the money was, they each took half, so that Goodman never went ahead of Leventhal, and Leventhal never went ahead of Goodman. It worked out particularly well for Goodman, because Leventhal had an arrangement where he got a percentage of the sales of Golden Books, which soared.

After I started, Leventhal and Goodman really took me under their wings. Leventhal would invite me over to these big dinner parties he had at his apartment, which were always very jolly.

Goodman took me out to parties around town. I remember one for White Russians—the monarchist Russians who had fought and lost to the Bolsheviks in the Russian Civil War of 1918–20. I couldn't get a conversation started with anybody. Half of the guests were speaking in Russian, and with the other half, I didn't know what they were talking about.

When we left I said to Goodman, "That was the dullest party I ever went to. Why did we go to that?"

"Yeah, it was," Goodman said, "but you didn't help it much."

When I asked him what he meant, he said, "Well, you just decided everybody else was dull. You could have started questioning them; you could have done something to liven it up."

Then he gave me some advice I've remembered ever since. He said, "I suggest to you, Bob, whenever you find yourself in a dull situation, don't just assume that you're not part of it. See if you can improve it. You'll get much more out of life."

That same night, we went to Sherman Billingsley's famous Stork Club on East Fifty-Third Street, where the gossip columnist Walter Winchell held court nearly every night at table 50. Goodman had a date with a beautiful young woman named Leila, and I was trying to figure out why he had brought me along. When Goodman went to the men's room and I was sitting alone with Leila, I asked her if she would like to dance. I'll always remember her response: "I really can't, because for me dancing is a sexual experience."

I moved on to another subject.

One night, Goodman took me to dinner with Margaret Bourke-White, who was one of the most famous photographers of the day. We met at the Lafayette Hotel, on University Place, then a hangout for artists and writers. After the main course, Bourke-White got up and said, "I can't stay for dessert. I'm flying to India. I'm going on a tiger hunt with some maharajah, and I'll call you when I get back."

I was pretty impressed with that. We saw her again when she returned, and she said the tiger hunt was a big disappointment. She told us they all sat in a blind with their rifles, and when a tiger finally came up, he could hardly move—it was like he was half asleep. When Bourke-White asked what was wrong with the animal, they told her that a few days before the hunt, they put out a dead goat full of dope and hung it from a tree. The tiger, of course, had eaten it. Bourke-White was really disgusted with the whole thing, and she said it certainly didn't make for exciting photographs.

Goodman also took me to the Century Country Club, which at that time was all Jewish. In its early days, in fact, I was told that the club took only German Jews and excluded Russian Jews—I guess everybody has to be better than somebody.

On the way there, Goodman said, "Bob, I want you to know I always make a social error of some kind at this club. I'm only here to play golf, but I always screw it up, so expect something to go wrong."

When we pulled up to the entrance and took out our golf clubs, all the parking attendants were standing there. Goodman turned to one of them and said, "Here, would you mind taking my clubs down to the first tee? We'll be down in a minute."

The guy looked at him and said, "I beg your pardon. I'm a member."

Goodman turned to me and said, "See what I mean?"

I don't know how much Jack Goodman's efforts to build my social skills helped, but he sure tried, introducing me to girls and even selling me his pea-green convertible at a discount price. In 1950, though, I was still single.

At the time, one of my best friends from the Lincoln School, Bob Ginsberg, got engaged to a woman named Helen Rosenau, who had also graduated from Lincoln School. I wasn't having much luck romantically, so I asked Helen to give me a list of her three best friends who were single.

One of them I never managed to get on the phone. Another I went out with and had her back in two hours—we had nothing to say to each other, and the two hours seemed like two weeks. The other girl on the list was Helen Walter.

So I called her up and made a date. She had a great apartment on Fifty-Fourth Street between Fifth and Sixth Avenues, right across from the Museum of Modern Art. When I rang the bell, Helen answered the door with only a bath towel wrapped around her. She said, "As you can see, I'm not quite ready. Could you come back in fifteen minutes?"

When I returned, she told me she was running late because she had gone to get tickets for the Sadler's Wells ballet company—a troupe from England that came to New York once a year—which had gone on sale that day. The line ended up being much longer than Helen expected. She told me she had planned on buying two tickets, which would have cost around $15, but when she saw how in demand the seats were, she had bought $100 worth of tickets. She thought her friends would want to go, so she planned on selling the extra tickets to them.

This was April 1950, and the ballet wasn't until September. Impulsively, I said, "I'll tell you what. I'll buy two tickets for September, and I'll take you."

Helen looked at me like I was crazy. "These tickets were very hard to get," she said, "and I don't even know if I'll know you in September."

I told her, "Okay, I guess we'll see."

So we went out on our first date. We had dinner at Charles à la Pomme Soufflée, a restaurant that was famous because it had these little potatoes that it puffed up with air, kind of like a dinner roll. We ate in the garden dining area, and afterward we went to hear the piano player at Delmonico's. It was a weeknight and there was maybe one other couple in the place. Helen told me later that she thought I had chosen it because I didn't want to be seen with her. She was wrong!

Helen had just graduated from Bard College and taken a job working at *The Reporter*, a current affairs magazine. She was petite and had brown hair, blue eyes, and an irreverent sense of humor. She had grown up in Woodmere, Long Island. Her father was a German Jew from Munich who had immigrated and started a business manufacturing lace and embroidery.

I was very smitten with Helen (and still am). When the summer came, she went away for the month of August to Nantucket with her friends. My parents had rented a large colonial summerhouse in Connecticut, and Helen came to visit from Nantucket for the Labor Day weekend. We were going to dinner with my parents at the Silvermine Tavern, which still exists, and were standing in the upstairs laundry room of the house, folding clothes my mother had given us to put away. Helen asked me what she could talk about with my parents at dinner. I said I had an idea and asked her to marry me. She was completely taken aback—which she rarely is—but she said yes.

One of the joys of my life with Helen was getting to know her father, Tony Walter, an outgoing man who never lost his thick German accent—he sounded a lot like Henry Kissinger. My father-in-law was a very emotional man, and he always had an interesting and original way of looking at things. When Helen and I got married, Tony impulsively took off his very costly Jaeger-LeCoultre watch and gave it to me. He said, "I want you to have this at this moment."

Later that day, we were talking and he said to me, "Bob, getting married is very expensive. There's Helen's clothes, there's furniture for your apartment, there's your own car. I don't want you and Helen to have any financial worries."

I listened carefully to see what was coming, and then Tony, with a big smile on his face, said, "So if you ever need any money, don't hesitate . . ." He waited a beat and then added, "To go to your father."

There are a few things I always remember about him. One is that he always left big tips for restroom attendants. When I asked him about it, he said, "Well, like me, they're usually immigrants, so I think, 'There but for the grace of God go I.'" Then he smiled and added: "Besides, do you know anyone who's ever gotten rich by under-tipping in men's rooms?"

Tony loved to drink Scotch. He always kept a bottle in his office and put it on his desk at noon. I think he drank about half of it in a day, but I never saw him drunk and drove home with him many times. He told me once he was having a hard time finding a doctor. "Bob," he said, "I talked to seven before I found one who said Scotch is good for you."

Tony lived in Hewlett, Long Island, with a case of Johnnie Walker Black Label stored in his basement closet with a big padlock on the door. Nevertheless, he noticed that bottles of Scotch were disappearing from the closet. He guessed that James, half of the wonderful couple—Rebecca and James—who worked for the Walters for many years, must have found his way in. Tony reasoned that if he confronted James, they might leave, and he certainly didn't want to lose them over a few bottles of Scotch. Rebecca took James to church every Sunday, and that gave Tony an idea. He got a big piece of cardboard, wrote on it, "God is watching you," and put it on top of the case of Scotch in the closet. From then on, not a single bottle went missing.

Helen and I spent our honeymoon in Ocho Rios, Jamaica. The first night, we received a bottle of champagne with a note: "Have a wonderful honeymoon, Dick Simon." I thought it was very nice, considering that he hardly even knew me. The next night, we got another bottle, and this note read: "Congratulations! One-half from Max Schuster, one-half from Leon Shimkin." Again, I found it very nice. I told Helen we should write a thank-you note right away, but she said it could wait until we got back.

When we checked out, we noticed there was a letter with our bill. Helen noticed it was in her father's handwriting and asked to see it. The staff said it wasn't for her, but Helen insisted. We saw that Tony had sent the champagne and had instructed the staff what to write on the cards.

On the flight back to New York, I became more and more upset as I thought about how embarrassing it would have been if we had sent a thank-you note to my bosses for gifts they hadn't sent. By the time we landed, I had worked up a full head of steam.

Tony adored his only daughter, and even though we returned on a weekday afternoon, he was there to pick us up. I marched right up to him and said: "Tony, what were you thinking? Make any jokes you want, but please stay out of my business life! What if Helen had written Dick and Max and Leon thank-you notes?"

He looked a little hurt. He was quite proud of his prank. "Bob," he said, "you've known Helen for six months. I've known her for twenty-three years. There wasn't a chance she was going to write thank-you notes on her honeymoon."

I realized he was right. When I cooled down and thought about it, I said, "I should have known. Who would send a gift and sign it 'One-half from Max Schuster, one-half from Leon Shimkin'?"

Tony looked at me and said, "Well, Bob, from the way you talk about them, particularly Leon, they don't sound like the types to send a whole bottle!"

* * *

Almost all of our friends who had gotten married were having trouble having kids, so Helen and I decided to try it right away. In 1951, eleven months after our wedding, we had Peter, and then Tom was born thirteen months later (Helen's father called them "Pete and Re-Pete"). After that, we thought we should take a break. Bill, our only planned child, was born in 1956.

After Tom's birth, we decided that we should move out of New York City to a place where the kids could have a yard and room to play. We found a house in Scarsdale, a short forty-minute commute from Grand Central, that I thought was perfect. It was a white colonial with a big magnolia tree in front. It had a steep driveway and a brook that ran behind the house. Next door, there was a big vacant lot where the kids could play. The only problem was the price. At $42,000, I thought it would be a stretch to make the payments.

I really agonized over it. My father told me that I would be crazy to spend more than $25,000. But then Tony gave me some advice that I've always thought was some of the best I ever got in my life.

He told me that it's really important where you live, that it affects your whole way of thinking about yourself. He said, "If you go home to some hovel at night, it's going to be depressing. A decent home is the one thing you should overspend on in your life. Because you live there. You go there. It influences so much more of your head than you realize."

So he said, "Overspend for a house."

We did, and I never regretted it.

In 1952, I was promoted to be Simon & Schuster's sales manager. My job was to oversee the national sales force of about twenty-five people, meet with the buyers for big bookstores and chains, and generally keep on top of all the trends in the business.

The 1950s was really when mass-market publishing took off in America. World War II had nearly destroyed the economies of Europe and Japan, which left the United States far and away as the economic powerhouse in the noncommunist world. Manufacturing boomed in this country, and suddenly people could afford consumer products they had never dreamed of buying before—things like refrigerators, vacuum cleaners, and, of course, new cars.

Broadcast television, then in its birth stages, offered a way for corporations to advertise to huge national audiences. And the postwar baby boom fueled a demand for all types of products, not the least of which were children's books and records.

No one took advantage of this new market better than Walt Disney, who figured out how to market his art in this new age. Disney had a deal with Western Printing to put out his books and records, and Western Printing partnered with Simon & Schuster. As I've noted, a lot of Disney books came out through the Little Golden Books and Little Golden Records lines—for example, we did the songs from *Snow White*.

When Disneyland opened in July 1955, Walt Disney invited us to the opening. Helen and I, along with several people from Western Printing, took the train out. As I remember, it took three days to get from Chicago to Los Angeles, and there was nothing to do but read and drink. It turned out that the people from Western Printing were very good at the latter.

Helen and I had been married for almost five years by this time, but, with two young sons, we'd had little time to get away on our own. We decided we wanted to have an experience when we got to L.A., so we booked ourselves into the famous Beverly Hills Hotel.

The hotel had a grand entrance—cars drove up its big circular driveway and then out. We checked in and found ourselves in a room facing the driveway. Helen noticed it immediately and said that we'd have car lights coming at us all night. I called the front desk and asked for another room, which they gave us.

There was a bowl of fruit in the room and Helen picked it up. I said, "Helen, there will be a bowl in our new room, believe me." She said, "You never can tell," and marched down the hall with the bowl of fruit in hand. We got to the new room and couldn't quite believe it. It was the identical room, just on the other side of the entrance.

I called down again. They apologized and said they would find another room. Helen, ever on the alert, spotted another bowl of fruit and picked it up. I begged her to leave it but she wouldn't. I pretended not to know her as we went to our third room, which overlooked a garden and was great, and settled in with our three bowls of fruit.

The Beverly Hills Hotel had a restaurant called the Polo Lounge, which was the place to be seen in Los Angeles. All the agents would go there to meet with their stars. Helen and I decided to have breakfast there, but I was ready a little before her, so she suggested that I go down and get our table.

At the time, the hotel had a bellhop named Johnny, who was a dwarf. He wore a red jacket with gold braids, black pants, and a round cap. When people got phone calls, he would yell out their names, such as: "Call for Mr. Smith! Call for Mr. Smith!" It was a big deal to be paged by Johnny at the Polo Lounge.

I went and took a seat. A few minutes later, Johnny announced, "Call for Robert Bernstein! Call for Robert Bernstein!" I put up my hand, and he walked over with a white phone on a tray and plugged it in at the table. When I picked it up, it was Helen.

"Helen, what are you doing?" I asked. "I just left you two minutes ago."

"I know, I know," she said, "but I didn't want you to be the only one not to get a call."

Later that day, we went out to play on the hotel's tennis courts, which were separated by a fence covered with canvas so that you couldn't see the people playing in the adjacent court. All we heard was a steady stream of "Oh, shit! Oh, shit! Oh, shit!"

The voice sounded really familiar, and finally we couldn't resist. When we peeked over the partition, we saw Katharine Hepburn taking a lesson and looking magnificent in her tennis whites.

The opening of Disneyland was really exciting—a theme park on that scale was a completely new thing, and no one knew if it was actually going to work.

The night before the opening, Walt Disney hosted a dinner for some of his business partners. He was very gracious and gave all of us signed prints. That night we were also given the opportunity to invest $5,000 in the Disneyland Hotel, if we wanted. The hotel was going to be in Anaheim, and I turned it down because I thought nobody would want to stay there—I figured they'd all want to go back to Los Angeles. Of course, since the hotel opened, it has pretty much operated at full occupancy. So much for my feel for real estate.

The next day, we were very happy to be among the first people to walk into Disneyland. And then the crowds hit. I had never seen anything like it. I was told there were 37,000 of Disney's closest friends in the park. The place was absolutely wall-to-wall bodies. You'd hear that something was going on in Fantasyland, but there was no way to get there through the crowds. The temperature climbed to more than 100 degrees, and, because of a plumbers' strike, hardly any of the drinking fountains worked. Some of the cement was so fresh that women's high heels sank in.

My cousin Charles, whom I had grown up with in New York, had become a public relations man out in Los Angeles. We met him and he took us to a tent, where we watched the whole thing on television.

After a while, I began to get bored with managing the sales force, so I started to look for other things to do, which is how I got involved with Kay Thompson and Eloise.

By 1957, Kay was famous. She was born in St. Louis in 1909, the daughter of a jewelry shop owner. She made her first splash as a piano prodigy, playing Franz Liszt with the St. Louis Symphony at age sixteen. In 1929, she moved out to Los Angeles and worked as a singer and choir director on the radio. She became a sought-after Hollywood voice coach, and her clients included Judy Garland (Kay told me that Garland was often so nervous before a show that Kay had to push her onto the stage). That led to work with MGM as a musical arranger and composer.

Kay stepped out on her own in 1947, when she started a cabaret act in which she sang and danced and was backed by the four Williams brothers (Andy Williams later became a star in his own right). Kay's show toured the country and eventually settled in for a long run in New York City. In 1956, Kay starred in the movie *Funny Face* along with Fred Astaire and Audrey Hepburn. Kay played the editor of a fashion magazine, and her big song was "Think Pink."

She was an incredibly talented woman—a great actress, singer, dancer, composer, and choreographer.

Kay lived in the Plaza Hotel on Fifth Avenue and Central Park South, and in the early 1950s she got an idea to write a book about a precocious six-year-old girl who lived there with very little adult supervision. She teamed up with the illustrator Hilary Knight, and Simon & Schuster published the first Eloise book in 1955. It was an immediate success. There was something really fun and appealing about this little girl running around in this fancy hotel getting into trouble.

When the book took off, Kay decided she wanted to release a line of Eloise merchandise. She needed someone to manage it and asked her friend Dick Grossman, S&S's head of advertising, for a recommendation. He suggested that she try me since I had experience with Little Golden Books and Little Golden Records.

Kay and I hit it off right away—she was completely irrepressible, constantly telling jokes. But she was also very chic; she always dressed very elegantly—she had a taste for furs—and had very short, perfectly coiffed blond hair. Kay was wonderful and impossible at the same time, very charming, but with an iron will.

We got permission from S&S to work together—I was basically moonlighting—and formed Eloise Ltd., of which she owned 60 percent and I owned 40 percent. We had a five-year contract.

We made Eloise dolls, which were a nightmare because there were all kinds of problems with the production process—first the doll manufacturer didn't make the doll right, and then the dress manufacturer didn't make the dresses right. It took a lot of coordination to make sure one part went with another.

Then we developed the Eloise Emergency Hotel Kit for little girls. It was a tiny hatbox with a very elegant handle. Inside, there was toothpaste and a toothbrush, a little shoeshine rag, a little block to put your gum on, and a million other little things. I figured that since it was a form of advertising, we could get all these items for free. So I wrote to Colgate and, sure enough, it asked me how many tiny tubes of toothpaste I wanted. I decided to start with ten thousand, which I stored in our garage in Scarsdale.

Unfortunately, we sold only 7,500 Eloise kits. That left me with

2,500 tubes of toothpaste. At Halloween, I said to Helen, "Let's be very original. Instead of candy, we'll give the trick-or-treaters a tube or two of toothpaste." I thought that since the kids were going to be overloading on candy, some toothpaste would be useful for them.

The next day when our kids came home from school, they told Helen and me, "Everybody hates us!" One kid actually took the toothpaste and squirted it all over our lawn.

The one really good deal I lined up for Eloise was with Kraft Foods. Kleenex had already had a big success by using a comic character named Little Lulu in its advertising, so Kraft decided that maybe it could duplicate that by having Eloise in its ads for Kraft Caramels. It offered a quarter of a million dollars against a percentage of the advertising that it ran every year. I was ecstatic. That was going to mean $100,000 a year to me and $150,000 for Kay, a huge amount of money in the 1950s.

But when I told Kay, she thought a minute and said, "We can't do it."

I was aghast. "What do you mean?" I asked.

"Eloise hates Kraft Caramels," she said. "She would never eat them. It's just not in her character to eat Kraft Caramels."

At the time, there was a boutique candy store in New York called Rosemarie de Paris. It had only one store in New York, where it sold very elegant chocolates. It also had a classy horse and carriage that it used to deliver candy all around the city. Kay said, "Bob, Eloise really prefers Rosemarie chocolates."

"But, Kay," I explained, "Rosemarie is not going to do a national advertising campaign!"

Kay looked at me and shook her head. "I talked to Eloise and she says she wouldn't be caught dead with Kraft Caramels." We passed on the deal.

I loved working with Kay, even with all her quirks. She frequently called in the dead of night when I was home in Scarsdale. My youngest son, Bill, was just one year old, and by the time we got to bed, we were thoroughly exhausted, so it was not totally welcome when the phone rang at two in the morning. I'd pick it up and hear Kay say, "Bob, I have a great idea."

"Kay, it's the middle of the night," I'd tell her.

She would apologize sincerely and profusely and say, "Oh, Bob, I forgot that you're a day person."

The kids, of course, always wanted to meet Eloise. Kay had this wonderful Eloise voice, so when she called up she'd say, "Hello, Peter, it's me, Eloise! I'm at the Plaza. Why don't you come down for cocoa?"

Peter and Tom would get all excited, and we'd all get in the car and drive to New York City. When we got to the Plaza, Kay would come out and say, "Oh, I'm so sorry. You just missed her." The kids didn't mind that much, though, because they loved going and having cocoa with Kay.

Over the years I worked at S&S, Leon Shimkin took on more and more responsibility for running the business. Max Schuster, always the less outgoing member of the original partnership, retreated into his own world of books—his wife, Ray, was by far the more dominating personality of the couple. Dick Simon, who was still relatively young—he'd been born in 1899—had a rapid decline in his health, suffering from heart attacks and a series of strokes in the 1950s.

By 1956, Shimkin was practically in charge all alone. He had hired Emil Staral, who had come from the oil business in Texas, as his right-hand man and company treasurer. Since Shimkin was busily employed at Pocket Books, he let Staral take on some responsibility for the rest of the firm. Staral noticed that editors came in at all different times of day, but certainly most of them later, around ten in the morning or even eleven. So he decreed that they had to be in at nine like everybody else.

Within a few weeks, there were large boxes of manuscripts piled up outside each editor's office that hadn't been there before. When Staral asked what they were, the lead editor said, "We're really quite behind." Staral asked how this had happened. The lead editor said, "Well, we used to read at home at night, frequently late into the night, but with this nine-to-five rule of yours, we all decided that it was no longer our responsibility to do that."

The decree was quickly rescinded.

One day in October 1956, Shimkin sent Staral down to see me.

He was brief and to the point. He said, "Bob, I want you to know I'm very fond of you, but Leon has asked me to deliver this message. He would like you to leave the company by the end of the year."

"Why?" I asked.

"He didn't give me a reason," Staral said. "But he said that's the way he wants it."

"Well, when can I see Mr. Shimkin?" I asked.

"He said to tell you that he didn't want to speak with you."

So that was it. I was completely shocked. I knew I was well thought of at S&S and in the industry, and I really loved the firm. It was full of young, bright, interesting people like the editor Bob Gottlieb; Tony Schulte, who was working for me in sales; Lee Wright, who had founded the Inner Sanctum Mysteries series; Tom Bevans, who ran production; Dick Krinsley, who was also in sales; Joe Barnes, who had come from a distinguished career at the *Herald Tribune*; and many others.

I was never given a reason for why I was fired. I have always assumed that Dick Simon's advice to me, seven years before, was right on the mark, and that Shimkin was getting his revenge because I wouldn't voluntarily give up $3,000 of my bonus. Shimkin just waited until he was in a position of complete authority. Of course, neither Shimkin nor I immediately realized what a fantastic break it was for me to get fired.

As it turned out, S&S as I knew it was just about finished. Marshall Field III, the hands-off owner who had bought the house in 1944, died in November 1956. His family had no interest in the publishing business and sold the firm back to Simon, Schuster, and Shimkin. Shimkin finally got his wish and became president.

Albert Leventhal had been taking care of the day-to-day running of the business. When he saw Shimkin ascendant, he decided to get out, taking a job with Western Printing. Leventhal's close friend, Jack Goodman, the editor in chief who had tried to expand my social horizons, died of a heart attack in the summer of 1957.

As for me, I decided to leave right away instead of waiting until the end of the year. I was thirty-three years old and didn't really know what I was going to do. I thought that I would work on merchandising Eloise for Kay Thompson and see what else came up.

I went over to the Plaza Hotel and spoke with the manager. I said if he gave me an office space, the Plaza could really advertise itself as the "Home of Eloise." He loved it. In fact, he said, there was a big room on the second floor that the hotel only rented when it was totally full, because it had a balcony that attracted a lot of pigeons, which guests didn't like. He gave me that as my office.

So I moved into my free office on Central Park South and began to think about what type of Eloise products little girls might pester their parents into buying.

3

AT RANDOM

I'D BEEN IN MY NEW OFFICE AT THE PLAZA FOR ONLY TWO OR three weeks when I got an unexpected telephone call from Bennett Cerf, the president of Random House. Bennett and I didn't know each other, but he said that Lou Langfeld, the owner of Books Inc., a big chain in San Francisco, had told him that he should keep his eye on me, that he thought I was a bright fellow. Bennett asked me to come over for a meeting.

Bennett is probably the only publisher in American history who was a household name. At the time, he was juggling several careers at once. In addition to being the chairman and one of the principal owners of Random House, he wrote Trade Winds, a column on the book publishing business, for the *Saturday Review of Literature*. He had published several books of his stories and jokes that sold very well—*Try and Stop Me* was the best known—and he had a newspaper joke column. He was also a big draw on the lecture circuit. And, since 1950, he'd appeared every Sunday as a panelist on the popular television show *What's My Line?* As you could see if you watched the show, Bennett was the embodiment of the urbane New Yorker. He always seemed to have a perfectly witty response for any situation.

I went over to meet Bennett at the Random House offices, which were in the Villard Mansion on Madison Avenue between Fiftieth and Fifty-First Streets, right across from the back of St. Patrick's Cathedral. We hit it off immediately, and Bennett offered me a job. I was reluctant, though, to go back to work at another company after my experience with Leon Shimkin. I thought maybe I wasn't made for the corporate life and it might be nice to start something of my own. I told that to Bennett, and he said, "Well, think it over." Bennett, thank God, called again two weeks later and said, "Come on back here, I really want to talk to you."

In the meantime, I'd felt like a fool. I hadn't even let him give me an offer, and I had a new house in Scarsdale and three young sons to support. I began to think it was pretty stupid to turn down a job at Random House, especially since I hadn't even asked what the job was. When I walked back in, Bennett said, "Look, we want you to come here. Write down on a piece of paper what you want to come."

It was really one of the great breaks of my life, and I've come to realize you really need only one.

I hastily wrote a figure as high as I thought practical, because by then I really wanted the job. I don't think he even looked at the piece of paper. He said, "Okay, you've got a deal."

Bennett said he'd like me to begin right away. I told him that I'd like to, but I couldn't start for eight weeks.

"What do you mean? You're unemployed," he said.

I told Bennett that when I left S&S, Leon Shimkin said I would get severance pay for twelve weeks, but I had to come in each week to get it. He wouldn't give it to me in a lump sum. If I took a job before the twelve weeks was over then I wouldn't need the money, so I wouldn't get my severance pay. I was pretty angry at being fired, and I didn't want to let him out of the severance pay.

Bennett thought a moment and said, "Here's what we'll do. I'd like you to come here for eight weeks on trial, at no salary and with no commitment from us. At the end of eight weeks, if we like your work, we'll hire you, and we'll pay you double for the first eight weeks that you're employed." And then he winked and asked, "Will that fit your requirements?"

"That will fit my requirements very well," I said.

"That should teach you a lesson, Bob," Bennett said. "There's always a way to screw a son of a bitch."

I laughed, and Bennett looked pleased. "Then we have a deal," he said.

A little hesitantly, I said, "There's really one more thing."

"What?" Bennett asked.

"Well, I have this letter from Helen. She feels wives should make a deal also."

I handed him an envelope that had "Demands of Helen Bernstein" written on the outside.

Bennett was obviously a little taken aback, but when he opened the envelope and began to read the letter inside, he let out into one of his roaring laughs, the same laugh he often broke into after telling you a joke. It often carried you with him whether you liked the joke or not. Helen's letter said, "The only thing I want is parking in the Random House courtyard."

Bennett said, "She's smarter than you are. That's the only tangible asset we have. Tell her she's got it, and I'll tell you why."

He explained that the courtyard had ten spaces and that the archdiocese owned the other two buildings in the Villard Mansion. Bennett said that when he bought the Random House building, the monsignor came over and they got to talking about the parking spaces. The monsignor said, "Well, Mr. Cerf, since the church has two buildings and Random House has one, I guess we get seven spaces and you get three."

Bennett said, "No, we get three and one-third."

The monsignor pointed out that no one could park in one-third of a parking space.

"Yes, that's true," Bennett said, "but you can't park in two-thirds of a space, either."

When the monsignor asked Bennett what he wanted to do, Bennett suggested they flip a coin for the space. The monsignor said that he was a man of the cloth and couldn't gamble, but Bennett said he wouldn't tell anyone. Bennett won the toss.

Bennett told me that he had a space, Donald Klopfer had a space, and Tony Wimpfheimer, Donald's stepson, had a space. But since Bennett won the toss with the monsignor, the fourth space was available for Helen. (Let's not discuss Bennett's promise to keep the coin toss a secret.)

* * *

So I started at Random House right away. I told Kay Thompson I was going to continue with Eloise, but I'd be doing it from Random House. The company gave me a tiny office, about the size of a walk-in closet. I had my desk and a chair, a chair on the other side of the desk, and one little bookshelf on the side. It was actually in a space right outside the office of Lew Miller, the executive vice president of Random House and sales director, and my new boss. The offices were separated by a big bookcase.

When I came back from lunch my first day, I found six pigeons roosting in my little area. There was a big sign on my desk that read: "Welcome to Random House from Eloise."

At the Plaza Hotel, there were always pigeons outside on the balconies, and when you look at the pictures in the Eloise books, there are always loads of the creatures.

"Come on, Kay," I said. "Wherever you're hiding, come out."

Kay popped out of the closet.

"Kay, it's my first day here!" I said. "What are we going to do about the pigeons?"

She said, "Now don't get excited, Bob. You don't think I'd just have ordinary pigeons here? These are theatrical pigeons. The trainer's here, and in no time they'll be back in their cage."

So I relaxed and started laughing.

Four hours later, Kay was still walking around behind the trainer, who had a big net. The ceilings in the Villard Mansion were very high and the pigeons were on the light fixtures. Kay was screaming at the guy, "Dammit, you told me they were trained!"

One flew into Lew Miller's office and pooped all over his desk. Everybody in the place came out, from all the floors, to find out what was going on. So, from my very first day on the job, people knew who I was. Depending on how you look at it, it was either an auspicious or an inauspicious start.

When I started at Random House in late 1956, I was one of about eighty people working there. Though it was one of the leading American publishing houses, the firm had yearly sales of only around $4 million. It was still, in every sense, a small family business.

Random House's founders, Bennett and his partner, Donald

Klopfer, met in 1919 while they were students at Columbia University, where Bennett edited the *Daily Spectator*, the school newspaper, and *The Jester*, the campus humor magazine. After graduation, Bennett, who was a few years older than Donald, took a job on Wall Street. In 1923, the year I was born, Bennett's friend Dick Simon called and told him he was leaving a job with the firm of Boni & Liveright and would recommend Bennett as his replacement. Bennett had inherited some money from his grandfather, a jeweler. When he met Horace Liveright, the publisher, he was offered the position of vice president in exchange for a loan of $25,000, which says about all you need to know about Liveright's financial management skills.

As Bennett relates in his memoir, *At Random*, Liveright not only had movie-star looks, he tried to live like one, too. In the 1920s, during Prohibition, bootleggers delivered alcohol to the office, and every afternoon there would be a cocktail party. In warm weather it moved outside to the office's roof garden, which was lined with plants and rattan couches and chairs. On a given afternoon, the guests might include any of the firm's authors, writers such as Eugene O'Neill, William Faulkner, Theodore Dreiser, and Dorothy Parker. Liveright paid for all of it, which probably was why he was always short of cash.

Bennett's break came in 1925, when Liveright, who had started to bankroll Broadway productions, again ran into financial trouble and needed money fast.

While Liveright published many prestigious authors—as well as many not-so-prestigious bestsellers—his most valuable property was the Modern Library, a series of reprints of mostly classic books bound in leather. They sold for 95¢ each. This was before the advent of paperback books, so the Modern Library had the most affordable versions of books such as *Moby-Dick* and *The Scarlet Letter*. The line was immensely popular. Bennett thought he could do better with it, though. One day over lunch, as Liveright was lamenting his money problems, Bennett offered to buy it. By the time they returned to the office, Liveright had agreed to sell the Modern Library to him for $200,000. Bennett called Donald, who had gone into his father's diamond-cutting business, and offered him an equal partnership if he could come up with half the purchase price, and Donald did.

The Modern Library was for decades the financial bedrock of Random House. There were 108 titles in the series when Bennett and Donald bought it. They began to trim out the ones that weren't selling, revamped the whole line by redesigning the typeface and binding, came up with a flashy new catalog, and started to make sales calls up and down the East Coast. Sales took off. By 1927, it was doing so well that the partners decided they wanted to publish new authors they liked—"at random," so to speak—and that's how Random House got its name.

It was the height of the Roaring Twenties, and with the stock market going up and up, there was a huge demand for limited edition, luxury versions of classic books. Random House's first book was a deluxe edition of Voltaire's *Candide*, illustrated by the artist Rockwell Kent, who also designed the Random House colophon.

The house really started to come into its own in 1932, when Bennett and Donald decided to challenge the American ban on James Joyce's *Ulysses*, which was thought to be obscene because of passages such as Molly Bloom's monologue about masturbation. Bennett had met Joyce in Paris and cut a deal with him that if Random House could get the obscenity ruling overturned, it would get the right to publish the book in America.

To test the book in a U.S. court, you would have to have copies in the United States. Bennett, always a smart businessman, decided that instead of doing a whole print run, he would bring one copy over, get it confiscated, and sue the government to get it made legal.

Reportedly, when he arrived back in New York, Bennett had it at the top of his suitcase and was going through customs on a hot July day. The customs inspector said, "Go on through, you're okay."

"You're supposed to open my suitcase to see if I'm bringing anything illegal into the U.S.," Bennett said.

So the inspector, grudgingly, had Bennett open the suitcase. The copy of *Ulysses* was right there. Bennett said, "That book is illegal in the United States."

"Oh, one copy won't hurt," the inspector said. Bennett, though, insisted he confiscate it, which cleared the way for the court case.

Bennett got Morris Ernst, a high-powered attorney, to represent the case in exchange for a small cut of future royalties if they won. That turned out to be a great deal for Ernst and his heirs. In the landmark freedom of speech case that followed, Judge John Woolsey ruled that the book was not obscene, but "a sincere and serious attempt to devise a new literary method for the observation and description of mankind."

Ulysses really launched Random House. *Ulysses* was the house's first important contemporary book, and the publicity from the case was great promotion. At little cost, Donald and Bennett won a victory for free speech, gained a reputation as publishers who were on the side of literary freedom, and published a book that also happened to make them a lot of money—they sold sixty thousand copies of *Ulysses* before putting it in the Modern Library, where it sold over one hundred thousand more. I think Judge Woolsey's decision is still printed in every copy of the book.

Random House grew into a formidable publisher over the next two decades. In 1936, it absorbed the firm of Smith & Haas— Robert Haas became the third partner until retiring and selling his share back to Bennett and Donald in 1956—which added authors including Faulkner, Isak Dinesen, André Malraux, Robert Graves, and Jean de Brunhoff, who wrote the Babar children's books. Random House also hired legendary editors Harry Maule, Robert Linscott, and Saxe Commins, and they brought authors such as Sinclair Lewis and Robert Penn Warren with them.

When I joined in late 1956, Random House had a bit of a mystique. Part of that came from its location in the Villard Mansion, which was designed by the architect Stanford White and built in the 1880s for the publisher and railroad magnate Henry Villard. It was a Renaissance-style mansion built around a courtyard. When you walked inside the black-and-white marble lobby, a grand staircase to the left led up to the second floor. Some of the high-ceilinged rooms that were used as offices had balconies that overlooked the courtyard.

It was normal for Random House authors to just wander in and hang out, so that you might run into Ralph Ellison on the staircase. Truman Capote swept through trailing his personality behind him—he called Bennett "Great White Father." I remember Faulkner walking in when he finished a book. He would show up unexpected, with his manuscript in one hand and a bottle of bourbon hidden inside a brown paper bag in the other. He would proceed into the small office of Albert Erskine, his editor, which was right next to Bennett's, and for the next few days Albert would cancel all his appointments as they went through the draft pages, I assume sipping the whisky as they went (Saxe Commins, Faulkner's longtime editor, retired shortly before I started at Random House).

Bennett was also in large part responsible for Random House's prominence. He loved the spotlight. Going over to Bennett's house for dinner parties was one of the joys of working at Random House, because he always had celebrities, intellectuals, and authors over, people ranging from Norman Podhoretz to Frank Sinatra. Some people took Bennett for a showbiz person because he appeared on TV and was always joking around, but they certainly misjudged him—that was only one side of him. He was also a very good businessman, which you can see not only by all the authors he signed and managed to keep over many years, but also by his skill in putting together a publishing house that consisted, in my view, of the best talent in the business. People stayed not only for money or a job, but because they felt Random House was a special place to be in the literary world. I was completely awed by Bennett's ability to keep several careers going and, at the same time, to always appear relaxed and interested in who the guy was.

At times, Bennett's huge number of acquaintances got the better of him. He lived out in Mount Kisco, about an hour from the city, and one day he came into the office and told us that a man had approached him on the commuter train platform and started a conversation. The man obviously knew Bennett, but Bennett drew a total blank. As one does in these situations, Bennett started to ask questions that might give him a hint of who the guy was. Bennett thought the man must have published a book with Random House, but beyond that, he had no clue. After the train arrived, the man came and sat next to Bennett and continued the conversation. When it finally became apparent that Bennett had no idea who he was, the man, looking exasperated, said, "Bennett, I'm your dentist!"

* * *

Bennett and Donald treated people extremely well. One story that always went around about them was that one day they were planning to fire an editor who wasn't working out. Donald and Robert Haas waited outside Bennett's office while Bennett called in the editor to tell him the bad news. A little while later, the editor came out with a big smile on his face. When Haas and Donald rushed in to ask how it went, Bennett had on his very sheepish grin that everyone knew meant trouble. It turned out that as soon as the guy came in, he started to talk about how his wife really wanted to move into a new place, but they couldn't afford it. "Well, did you fire him?" Haas asked. "Not exactly," said Bennett. "I seem to have lent him $10,000 to buy a house."

With all the projects he had going, Bennett was really stretched thin, which left Donald to run the day-to-day business. In temperament, the two were almost opposite. Donald avoided the spotlight as much as Bennett sought it. While Bennett could get carried away with his ideas, Donald was a stabilizing influence, vetting Bennett's whims before they could be put into action. In *At Random*, Bennett's memoir, he says of Donald: "I would blow my top, and Donald always knew how to handle me. He would sit there, chewing the earpiece of his glasses, and listen very calmly. Then after seven or eight minutes, when he saw that I had had my say, he would get up and say, 'Oh, shut up,' and walk out of the office."

Donald was the office father figure—everybody came to him with their problems. He was completely closemouthed, so you felt that you could tell him anything. I went to Donald's home much less, socially, than to Bennett's, but I saw Donald in the office and had lunch with him a lot. We almost always ate in, at his desk. Donald really taught me how to run a company—how to give raises, how to tackle problems, and, above all, how to manage people.

In a publishing house with editors of many different temperaments, the latter is vital. I believe my own success was due principally to keeping on very talented editorial staff—for many years we added people, but very few ever left or were let go. There were times when an editor seemed to be losing his or her ability to bring in books. I would always sweat it out, even if it lasted for a few years.

It was like a baseball player being in a batting slump. It almost always worked out in the end.

Lew Miller was the other person who had a significant say in the business when I started as sales manager. Lew, as executive vice president, was my direct supervisor. He was a private man, smart, staid, and knew his opinion on everything. He was also very dominant. He had what Bennett called a strong sense of amour propre. Because of that, I always made sure to defer to him, but he was cordial and friendly—a very fine man.

Lew had, I think, made one big mistake. Bennett and Donald had offered Lew a partnership in the firm. They even offered to lend him the money and let him work it out over his share of the profits, but he turned it down. I think he regretted it. But Bennett and Donald treated him like a partner—they regarded him as a third voice on all their big decisions.

Lew gave me one very good piece of advice. It was my job, under him, to hire the salesmen, and I was interviewing and interviewing for one territory out west, I think Nebraska and Iowa. Lew had told me, "Now don't hire a real hotshot for this territory, because if you do, he's not going to be very happy in these little stores. So get a smart, capable guy who's going to be content roaming around the Midwest selling books."

After I had a candidate in mind, I went in and said to Lew, "I just can't decide about this guy. Here are his good points and here are his bad points. How does it sound to you?"

Lew said, "Look, you're making the decision, not me. But I'll give you only one piece of advice: No matter who you hire, you have to buy the whole person."

I've always remembered that expression. Everybody's got strengths and faults. You just have to evaluate them. Whenever I've had to fire somebody, I think I made half the mistake. They may have made an error in taking a job they couldn't do, but I made a mistake also in judgment; I also knew more about the job than they did. This was one of the reasons I was always very liberal with severance pay.

Shortly after I started at Random House, Bennett was scheduled to speak at a luncheon put on by the *New York Herald Tribune*, which back then was the main competitor of the *New York Times*. The *Herald Tribune* luncheons were given at the Waldorf Astoria and hosted by Irita Van Doren, the famous editor of the newspaper's book review and a member of the prominent Van Doren family. All the ladies would come and fill the tables and have lunch, and three or four authors would speak.

When Bennett was announced as a speaker, my mother decided she was going to go. Being the aggressive woman she was, at the end of the luncheon she pushed her way through the crowd to Bennett.

"I'm Sylvia Bernstein. My son, Bob, works for you. Do you know him?" my mother asked.

Bennett said, "Of course I know Bob. We hired Bob Bernstein and Jason Epstein the same day, and we call them 'mass' and 'class.'"

Now, Jason had come to Random House from Doubleday, where he had started Anchor Books, the first really distinguished line of higher-priced, larger-formatted paperback books. His idea was to take quality literature and publish it in paperback—until then it was all in hardcover. They were very classy.

I had just come from Simon & Schuster and knew a lot about juvenile publishing.

The details of my various ventures and Jason's were not known to my mother, so when Bennett said we were "mass" and "class," she asked, "Which one is Bob?"

Children's books really fueled my career.

Bennett had thrown an incentive into my contract that all the editors had. He gave me 2 percent of sales on any book I brought in, even though, as sales manager, that was technically not my job. But Bennett figured that the more hooks out, the higher chance the house had of landing good books.

Kay Thompson immediately came over with me from Simon & Schuster, which prompted Leon Shimkin to call Bennett to explain that he thought what I was doing—stealing an author—was immoral. Bennett took the position that authors decided where they wished to be published and suggested that Leon call Kay and discuss it with her.

In the few weeks in my office at the Plaza Hotel—after I left S&S

and before I took the job at Random House—I had become the literary agent for a new client. My good friend Mike Dann had left his post as vice president at NBC to work for a TV packager founded by the producer Henry Jaffe. The company had signed Shirley Temple to be the hostess of a children's TV series, which was going to do dramatizations of all the great children's stories. Mike called me and said I should agent it and sell a book version to a publisher.

Shirley, of course, had been a huge child movie star in the 1930s (think of her singing songs like "On the Good Ship Lollipop"). As she got older—she was born in 1928—her box office appeal dimmed a bit, and she had retired from the industry in 1949. So her television show was a bit of a comeback for her.

I flew out to California and met Shirley and was pretty sure I was onto a good thing, but before I sold the project, I took the job at Random House. So I asked Mike and Shirley if they minded if I sold the book to myself at Random House. They were delighted. We ended up putting out one big book of stories, which was also split up and published as three less expensive books. And here's an example of how lucrative children's books can be: while Random House was doing about $4 or $5 million in sales at the time, the Shirley Temple books alone had sales of over a million dollars.

Not exactly class, but definitely mass, which was fine with me. In general, I kept my eyes open for things that I thought would have broad appeal. Many of these weren't world-stopping events in publishing, but they sold well.

For example, I decided that when you went on vacation, you shouldn't have to carry around a big, fat travel guide everywhere you went. I got the idea that we could do city instead of country guides. I wanted them to be thin enough to fit into the pocket of a man's coat, so you didn't lose them all the time by leaving them someplace. There was a popular travel magazine at the time called *Holiday*, so I teamed up with the publisher and we called them *Holiday* Travel Guides. They were quite successful for several years.

Another very popular series was a line of books on the continents, each one quite lavish and beautifully illustrated, which was brought to me by a book packager named Paul Steiner. A book packager was really a publisher that did everything but sell the book. The packager would get the idea, make all the arrangements with the authors, even coordinate the printing and sell the finished copies of the book to the publisher. Steiner's company was called Chanticleer Press and he was one of the best in the business. His biggest success, which Knopf published, was the Audubon nature guides, which still sell very well today.

People also loved the books on the continents. It's always good to bring in a project with the potential for a series, because if people like the first one, you have a built-in market for more to follow. You don't have to reinvent the wheel every time.

Of course, I was not always successful in landing the projects I wanted. In 1961, Knopf had a great hit when it published Julia Child's *Mastering the Art of French Cooking*. I thought I might be able to duplicate it if I could sign Henri Soulé, the famous chef of Le Pavillon, New York's leading French restaurant. Though many publishers had tried, no one had been able to get him to do a cookbook.

I called Soulé and was invited to lunch. After we had some small talk, Soulé soon explained to me, in his heavily accented English, why I was not going to be able to persuade him to become an author. "Let me explain how busy I am," he said. "I have three mistresses, and I haven't seen any of them in two years."

One of the longest-lasting relationships I formed in my first years at Random House was with Ted Geisel, otherwise known as Dr. Seuss. At the time we met, Ted had published several books, but he had not really broken out yet.

Ted was born in 1904 in Springfield, Massachusetts, the son of German immigrants (his father was actually a brewmaster). He went to Dartmouth College, where he wrote stories for the campus humor magazine and signed them "Seuss," which was his mother's maiden name and his middle name. Toward the end of Ted's time in college, his father asked him what he planned on doing after graduation, and Ted told him he'd received a scholarship to study at Oxford. After Ted's father reported the news to the local newspaper in Springfield, Ted confessed that he'd made it up. In order to save face, Ted's father decided to pay for him to go to England to study. Ted thought he would get a PhD and become a professor. While he was in England, though, another American student named Helen Palmer complimented him on the doodling he had done in a class. She told him he should become an artist. He not only took her advice, but he also married her (the "Dr." in Dr. Seuss, as Ted would always say, was for the PhD he never earned).

When Ted and Helen returned to the United States, Ted found work as an advertising copywriter with Standard Oil and as a freelance cartoonist for publications such as *Life* and *Vanity Fair*. As a result, Ted's first really well-known work was for an insecticide called Flit. The tagline: "Quick, Henry, the Flit!" The story I heard was that the ad was so successful that Standard Oil, which manufactured Flit, paid Ted for his full time so he wouldn't do ads for other companies. The ads took very little of Ted's energy, so he decided to write children's books in his spare time.

In 1937, Ted published his first book, *And to Think That I Saw It on Mulberry Street*, the story of a boy who watches as a passing parade becomes increasingly bizarre. Though Ted would go on to become one of the best-selling authors of all time—there are more than 220 million copies of his books now in print—he wasn't an instant success. *Mulberry Street* was rejected by twenty-seven houses before an old Dartmouth friend who worked at Vanguard Press got it published there. The next year, Ted published *The 500 Hats of Bartholomew Cubbins*. Though neither book was a tremendous seller, they were well reviewed and caught the eye of Bennett, who signed Ted to Random House.

Vanguard, of course, made a huge mistake in letting Ted go. Later in life, I bought the entire company just to get *Mulberry Street* and *Bartholomew Cubbins*. I wanted Random House to have the rights to all the Dr. Seuss books.

Ted published two books with Random House in 1939, *The King's Stilts* and *The Seven Lady Godivas*, which was one of the few books he ever did for an adult audience. The thesis was that no *one* nude woman riding through Coventry could have caused such a fuss, so there must have been seven. Ted used the idea to create wonderfully amusing drawings, such as one that showed a nude woman on a horse disappearing around a corner as another was coming onto the scene.

Years later, when I was with Ted—I think in Madison, Wisconsin —and he was receiving an award for being the great Dr. Seuss, a little old lady came up with a copy of *The Seven Lady Godivas* for him to autograph. Ted laughingly told her he would sign it, but she should hide it, as it could ruin his career as a children's book author. He was always very proud of the book and flummoxed that it hadn't done better. Decades later, he convinced us to republish it, and it still failed to sell well.

Ted had his first moderate success with *Horton Hatches the Egg*, which came out in 1940. He didn't publish another book until 1947.

After the start of World War II, he began to draw several political cartoons a week for *PM*, a New York newspaper. In 1943, Ted joined the army and worked in Frank Capra's Signal Corps. He ran a propaganda unit and made films for American soldiers with titles such as *Your Job in Germany* and *Our Job in Japan*.

The major turning point in Ted's career came in 1957, right after I joined Random House. *Life* magazine had published "Why Do Students Bog Down on First R," an article reporting that illiteracy was rising among American children. According to the author, John Hersey, the reason was that schoolbooks were too boring. At the time, the standard texts for young kids were from the Dick and Jane series. Hersey called for more imaginative use of drawings and language, and he even mentioned Dr. Seuss as an example of what children's books could be like if done well.

After the article came out, Houghton Mifflin, which published textbooks, asked Ted if he would do a school textbook reader that could be jointly published with Random House. Houghton Mifflin sent Ted a list of beginning reader words, the same vocabulary in the Dick and Jane books. Ted struggled with the task, but eventually used 236 words. The result was *The Cat in the Hat*. It had all the visual quirks and verbal twists of Ted's other books, but with a basic vocabulary. Young kids loved it, and suddenly Ted's books were accessible to a much broader market. It totally revolutionized what people thought about children's books and what they could be.

I hadn't read Ted's books when I joined Random House, but the minute I did, I fell in love with them. I thought he was a genius.

He was also, in person, charming, modest, and funny. I told him that we could really increase his sales if children got to know Dr. Seuss. Back then, author tours weren't really a commonplace thing, but I thought the publicity we could generate through word of mouth would be more valuable than any advertising we could do. I said if he would do it, I would personally go on the trip with him, just the two of us, and he agreed.

So I arranged book signings in Chicago, Minneapolis, Detroit, and Rochester. In Detroit, we rented a helicopter, and Ted flew from one branch of the J.L. Hudson department store chain to another, landing in the parking lot like Santa Claus. The press ate it up, putting it on the front page, and huge lines of kids and parents waited for him at every store. Ted was shocked when the last store we went to that day had to stay open two hours after closing to accommodate all the kids who were waiting.

In Chicago, at Marshall Field's, Ted was signing books when he noticed in one copy that just at the spot where he wanted to write his name, the book was already signed "Chief White Cloud." Ted looked around and noticed a man in full Native American costume, with a wonderful feathered headdress, walking along the line of kids, signing their Dr. Seuss books and handing out a card informing them that "Chief White Cloud dances at the Orpheum on Sunday at 3 p.m." Ted called me over and very gently, with a bit of hurt in his voice, asked if I didn't think I could arrange for the chief to have his own autographing party. I spoke with the book buyer for Marshall Field's, who was horrified, and the store's security people quickly convinced the chief to leave.

In Minneapolis, as I stood around while Ted signed hundreds of books, I got a little bored and took two books from children in the line and inscribed them "Chief White Cloud." The first passed Ted without a reaction. When the second appeared, Ted looked up and called out to me in pain, "Bob, the damned Indian has followed us all the way to Minneapolis!"

Over the coming decades, I would go out about once a year to see Ted at his home in La Jolla, California, where he and his wife, Helen, had bought an old observation tower on top of a hill overlooking the Pacific Ocean. They had built their house around the tower, and Ted's circular office was at the top. He had corkboards all around the circle, where he mounted all the pages of a book as he wrote it. He would walk around and around, correcting and changing the text and improving the artwork little by little. Just as there are a few songwriters who compose both the music and lyrics, Ted was one of the few authors who created both the text and the drawings.

I loved to arrive when he was finishing a new book. He would rush me to his studio and show me the pages, still mounted on the cork wall. He would read them to me and then anxiously ask what I thought. This can be an uncomfortable moment with some authors, but I looked forward to it with Ted—his work always thrilled me.

Mostly, Ted kept in touch through the stream of stuff he sent in the mail, drawings and little bits of verse. He constantly churned out material.

Once I told him a story about something my son Peter had said. I was putting some fertilizer on the lawn, taking it out of the bag and spreading it, and Peter asked, "What's that?" I said, "It's cow manure." Peter asked what cow manure was, and I explained where it came from. So Peter, who was around eight years old, asked, "How do they get them to do it in the bag?" Not long after I told Ted the story, I got a drawing from him in the mail, of a cow looking at a farmer and saying, "In a bag?"

Though my job title was sales manager, I became involved in many other parts of the company. I ran the sales department, of course, but also ended up deciding on printings, tinkering with ads, and doing the hiring and firing on the business side. I began to work closely with Bennett, Donald, and Lew. In 1962, they promoted me to first vice president.

Bennett frequently included me on business decisions. Sometimes he wanted my opinion, and at other times I think he just wanted me to be there as a witness.

For example, one day Bennett urgently called me down to his office to sit in on a negotiation. John Budlong, from New American Library, had come over to see Bennett about buying the paperback rights to a yet-to-be-published book called *Wanderers Eastward,*

Wanderers West, by Kathleen Winsor. Her previous book, *Forever Amber*—which was not published by Random House—had been loaded with sex and was a massive hit. We had paid a large advance to get *Wanderers Eastward, Wanderers West*. Unfortunately, when the manuscript arrived, we all agreed it wasn't really that good, she was a one-book author, and this book, in our opinion, was not going to make it.

Budlong thought otherwise. So, after I came in, Budlong said, "Look, I'm going to make you an offer for the paperback rights. But the offer is only good while I'm in your office. You have to accept it, because I don't want you to shop it and maybe get a better offer. I'm going to make a large offer, because we really want to take a chance on this book."

Bennett told him that was fine, and Budlong named his price—a half million dollars.

Bennett turned to me and said, "Bob, I don't need your opinion."

He looked at Budlong and said, "John, we accept."

We both knew we were getting off the hook for a book we thought would not earn back its advance, and we were delighted.

So Bennett, very pleasantly, said, "John, I hope the book does well, and I hope you're making a good buy, and we're delighted that you bought it. It couldn't be in better hands."

I thought Bennett made it sound a little insincere when he couldn't resist adding, because he loved his own humor, "John, do you mind if I walk you back to your office? I want to be sure nothing happens to you."

In the 1950s, the actor, singer, and comedian Danny Kaye became a roving ambassador for UNICEF, a position he stayed dedicated to for more than three decades. After I started at Random House, I got the idea that we could do a Danny Kaye storybook that would be a collection of children's stories from around the world.

I knew that Bennett knew Kaye and his wife, Sylvia Fine, and I asked for an introduction. When Kaye was in town, Bennett took me to the Pierre hotel to meet him.

When we got there, Kaye told us he had just read a book called *Folk Medicine*, by some doctor in Vermont, and that he had learned about a drink made out of apple juice and vinegar that would stop you from getting colds all winter. He had just made a batch and he insisted on sharing some with Bennett and me.

He handed us each a glass. Bennett, looking a little quizzical, took the first sip. I don't remember whether he just spit it out or swallowed it and grimaced, but he looked at Kaye and said, "Danny, I have to tell you, I don't want the book bad enough to have to drink your concoction!"

Instead of taking a conflict head-on, Bennett usually found a humorous way around it.

One Monday, he came into the office and said he'd been at a party with Zsa Zsa Gabor over the weekend. Gabor, a Hollywood actor and socialite, had asked him for a whole set of the Modern Library, which by then included around four hundred books.

"Can you imagine the gall?" Bennett asked.

A few weeks later, Bennett came in and said he'd run into Gabor again, and she had repeated her request. This time he had an idea.

We still had thousands of copies of a book we had published called *The Wandering Jew*, which had not sold well at all. Bennett called the warehouse and asked the staffers to take four hundred or so copies of *The Wandering Jew*, put the dust jackets from the Modern Library around them, and send them to Zsa Zsa Gabor. They did, and for several weeks, we waited for Gabor to phone. After a while with no word, we forgot about it.

About a year later, Gabor called Bennett. She was incensed.

"You son of a bitch!" she said. "I had a guest who reads!"

I gradually turned a lot of the sales manager job over to my assistant, Anne Marcovecchio. When I arrived at Random House, Anne had been working for Dick Lieberman, the sales manager before me. Lew Miller asked me if I was bringing anybody in to be my secretary. When I said no, he said, "You can try Anne out, and if she suits you, keep her on, it's up to you."

Foolishly, at some point I told Anne this story, and over the course of the thirty-seven years we worked together, I can tell you it was thrown in my face every now and then. She would stop me in my tracks many times, saying, "Well, you know what Lew Miller told you . . . you don't have to keep me on!"

The first six years with Anne, when I would ask people to leave a message with her, they would always ask, "Who?" So I would say, "'Marco,' like in Marco Polo, and 'Vecchio,' like in Ponte Vecchio, the bridge in Florence." After six years working together, a wonderful thing happened—she married a man named Hugh Johnson, so for the next thirty-one years, life was much simpler.

One thing you learn as sales manager is that book buyers from around the country love to call up and talk with New York, sometimes with a problem, but also a lot of times just to gossip. I was terrible at small talk and always very busy, and I really didn't want to talk to the buyers about all their problems. But Anne was great with them—every time they called, she'd chat with them for a few minutes about what was happening in Denver or Indianapolis or wherever.

Finally, I said to Anne, "Look, just between you and me, you be sales manager." Most of the time, the buyers were calling because they needed an emergency order, or they didn't get an order, or an order was lost. And when they said, "I'd like to talk about this with Bob," Anne would say, "Oh, he's on the phone. Let me take a crack at it." And every time she'd do it. Of course, if they really wanted to talk to me, she would pass them on, but since she was so charming with them—much more than me—that hardly ever happened.

Anne's abilities went well beyond sales. Ted Geisel was very fond of her, and he relied on her for everything. She made all the arrangements and appointments for him when he came to New York City. When he had a new Dr. Seuss book in tow, he insisted that Anne and I sit in my office and listen to him read it. Then he would point out that under his contract there was a clause on "acceptance of manuscript," and he sought both of our official approval for Random House. Ted was very serious about it. He would look up quizzically after he finished reading the book and always say, first to Anne, "What do you think?" and then he'd ask me. Needless to say, for both of us, it was never a very difficult decision, and I always used to wonder about this genius of a man wanting or needing reassurance.

By the early 1960s, the group of publishers that had shaken up the business in the first half of the century—men such as Bennett, Donald, and Alfred Knopf—had become respected figures of the establishment. Nearing retirement, they had to think about their estates and tax issues. This happened at the same time that corporations were getting interested in the publishing business, so the conditions were ripe for the wave of mergers and acquisitions that would sweep over publishing in the following decades.

A major turning point—I don't think we clearly saw how important it would be at the time—came in October 1959, when Bennett and Donald took Random House public on the stock market. Random House stock, which was offered at $11.25, rose to $14. In the fall of 1961, the stock was up around $40.

As Michael Korda, a longtime Simon & Schuster editor, noted in his memoir, *Another Life*, the sale of stock in Random House had a profound effect across the industry. Even though Bennett and Donald kept enough shares to retain control of the firm, they now had to, as a public company, issue financial disclosures. In publishing, traditionally a business that paid relatively small salaries, this meant people knew how much the house was making in revenues and what the top officers earned. Not only did the people who worked in the business begin to think they should make more money, but authors (and their agents) saw the figures and got the same idea as well. Until the 1960s, handshake deals were still commonplace—with Faulkner, for example, we usually didn't even bother to sign a contract until after one of his books was published; he just expected us to pay him a fair amount. Now, with money in the air, we found ourselves dealing more and more with agents who bargained hard for their clients.

The other change was apparent right away. With the sale of the stock, Bennett and Donald suddenly had an excess of cash. Naturally, they started to look around for something to do with it.

As it happened, they'd had their eyes on Alfred Knopf's house for years. Knopf had probably the most prestigious list of literary authors in publishing—his backlist included Thomas Mann, Willa Cather, Albert Camus, and H.L. Mencken, and he had contemporary authors such as John Hersey, John Updike, and Roald Dahl.

Knopf, who ran the house with his wife, Blanche, was getting old (he was born in 1892). It had seemed as if his son, Alfred A. "Pat"

Knopf Jr., would take over the firm, but in 1959 Pat left to start his own house, Atheneum. In the spring of 1960, Bennett and Donald approached Alfred with a proposition for a merger. Under the deal, Random House would acquire Knopf, but Alfred and Blanche would remain in complete control of the imprint.

Alfred asked Bennett if the deal was fair.

"If I didn't think it was fair, I wouldn't be offering it," Bennett said.

That was enough for Alfred. They shook hands, and that was that.

At the time, Random House was doing around $8 million in volume, and Knopf was doing around $5 million. The *New York Times* ran a story—by Gay Talese, then the paper's publishing beat reporter—about the merger on the front page. Alfred explained: "Merging with Random House seemed the logical thing to do. What prompted us to do it was, I think, Mr. Cerf's great desire to have it come about. Since we've been friends for thirty-odd years, and since their list is a very fine list, we have no editorial compunction about being associated with Random House."

Before long, the Federal Trade Commission (FTC) came in, to see if Random House was so big that the merger would restrain trade. Bennett told me, "You see them. I hate seeing people like that."

So I met with the men from the FTC, who asked about the size of our business.

"Thirteen million dollars," I said.

"Is that your profit?" they asked.

"No, it's our sales."

"It's your sales? Thirteen million dollars?"

"Yes."

They asked why the *Times* had made such a big deal out of the merger.

"You'll have to ask them," I said, "but my guess is that it's for the quality of our authors rather than the size of our business."

"Well," they said, "it's ridiculous, our being here to look into a $13 million business."

They left, but Knopf was only the first of the acquisitions Random House would make over the next three decades. We made two other major deals right away.

Later the same year, in 1960, we bought L.W. Singer, a major textbook publisher that was located in Syracuse, New York (the deal would later, indirectly, bring us one of our most revered authors).

Then in 1961, Random House acquired Pantheon, which had been founded in 1942 by Kurt Wolff and his wife, Helen. Wolff had been a prominent German publisher in the 1920s and 1930s before coming to New York to escape the Holocaust. The Wolffs were soon joined by Jacques Schiffrin, a French Jew who left Europe for the same reason. The house specialized in European intellectuals, some well known, such as André Gide, and others obscure and unprofitable. It had the occasional bestseller with books such as *Dr. Zhivago* and *The Tin Drum*, but overall it tended to break even or return a modest profit.

Bennett and Donald paid less than a million dollars for Pantheon, which they saw as an acquisition for prestige rather than profit. Donald later explained, "These are the sort of books that have to be published. Not all of them will necessarily make money, but someone has to do them. All we ask is that Pantheon break even. We can afford that sort of publishing."

I would later have to battle to defend that line of thought. Bennett and Donald took it for granted that a house should publish some books simply because they were important.

One day in October 1965, Bennett walked into my office and said, "Look, I think I want to step down as president of Random House. I'll stay as chairman of the board for another couple of years after that. But I want to do some writing, and I want to take it easier. And I'd like you to be president."

"Bennett," I said, "I think you ought to tell me closer to the time. You're not going to do that for years. You know that. Now that you've told me, I'm going to keep wondering when it will happen."

He said, "It's October. Suppose we do it January first?"

"Well, that's certainly quick enough," I said.

I was completely shocked. I'd had no idea it was going to happen, and it hadn't been discussed by either Bennett or Donald before this. They were such fixtures that it almost seemed inconceivable.

After the succession was announced, the *New York Times* came to do a story. A photographer took a picture of Bennett and me.

When the article appeared the next day, I was surprised to see that Bennett looked about twice as big as me—even though we'd been standing side by side, he appeared to be huge.

I pointed it out to Bennett, and he laughed. "I'll let you in on a little secret," he said. "Whenever you're getting your picture taken, and you want to stand out, what you do is you just lean forward right as the photographer is about to snap it."

Though Bennett and Donald were staying on as chairman and vice chair, respectively, I suddenly had to step up to a whole new level of responsibilities.

It might seem hard to believe, but I had never really thought about running the company or had any conscious plan to position myself to take it over. Thinking back, it was probably better that it happened the way it did, because if I'd had time to think about it for very long, it might have completely overwhelmed me.

Of course, I knew the nuts and bolts of publishing—sales, marketing, distribution, and things like that. More important, I had internalized the way Bennett and Donald ran the house. They kept an eye on everything but they also knew that they had smart and dedicated people in every department of the business. They treated them more like associates than employees, and it was totally genuine. I know I inherited this from them and I like to think that I followed their example and that Random House remained a special place after I took it over.

I had just turned forty-three when I became president of Random House at the beginning of 1966. Suddenly I was the head of America's premier publishing house, which by then had a sales force of 150 and annual sales of almost $35 million.

The country was about to go through one of the most socially turbulent periods in its history. I felt that it was very important to carry on the tradition of the house, which was to both make money and to publish books that mattered. But nothing I had learned from

Bennett and Donald quite prepared me for what was ahead. There was no way to foresee some of the challenges that were coming—from the government, the industry, and from within Random House itself.

4

ON TOP, SUDDENLY

ON A WEEKEND MORNING IN JANUARY 1966, RIGHT AFTER MY FIRST week as president of Random House, my kids ran up to me in a state of excitement. They said something strange was happening outside and that I had to come look. I went to the door and saw that a limousine had parked outside our little house in Scarsdale. Two footmen in full livery, complete with white gloves, got out, walked up to our door, and, in a very dignified manner, each handed me a brown paper bag.

I opened one and found a note from Mike Dann, the same friend who had introduced me to Shirley Temple a decade earlier and was now chief programming executive for CBS, one of the most powerful jobs in television. He'd written: "This is how the president of Random House should get his Sunday morning bagel and lox."

It was, in hindsight, the most genteel moment I had in publishing. At the time I became president, in fact, the industry was quickly moving away from its small-time roots.

By the mid-1960s, Bennett and Donald were both nearly seventy years old, and they realized that it would be smart to sell the house for tax reasons—if one of them was to die suddenly, it would have been a nightmare for their estates. Random House stock was doing well, and the timing seemed right to make a move.

The publishing business was actually, for a short period of time, in vogue. Bennett and Donald's decision to list Random House on the New York Stock Exchange in 1959 helped to bring what had been a low-key business to the attention of analysts and business journalists. Book sales had been climbing since the 1950s, fueled in large part by the baby boom and an increasing demand for children's books. In addition, the Russian launch of Sputnik into space in 1957 set off a panic that the U.S. educational system was falling behind, which increased government spending for new and revised textbooks. These two factors together made it seem logical that the market for juveniles and textbooks was only going to keep expanding exponentially, giving publishing the one thing all Wall Street analysts look for: growth prospects.

The other part of the equation was that corporations such as IBM and RCA were developing computers to sell commercially. One of the hot products of the future was going to be the "teaching machine," which, looking back at it, was basically a rudimentary personal computer. The idea was that all types of material, such as children's books, textbooks, and encyclopedias, would be available through the machines. The teaching machines would go into classrooms around the nation, so that kids could sit at them and learn at their own speed. The market was potentially huge, and publishing houses were seen as prospective suppliers of the raw material the machines would need to operate.

This line of thinking led the Radio Corporation of America (RCA) to buy Random House in January 1966 for $40 million, the same month that I became president. Despite Random House's illustrious history and its list of major authors, RCA was mainly attracted by our recent acquisition of L.W. Singer, which, in all honesty, was really a small, undistinguished textbook publisher at the time.

Bennett and Donald had insisted as part of the deal that Random House maintain editorial independence and control of hiring and firing. At the time, that was all right with RCA, which was expecting to deal only with the relatively small educational part of our business.

Though I didn't totally realize it at the time, Bennett and Donald's sale of the firm marked the beginning of a permanent change in publishing. Houses that had been run by their founders were acquired one by one to become divisions within larger companies, subject to the whims of their corporate parents. Much of my job in the coming decades would be to try to balance the tradition established by Bennett and Donald against increasing pressure for higher profits.

To understand RCA—and what it meant for Random House to be acquired by it—you need to know the story of David "the General" Sarnoff, who dominated his company as much as Bennett did ours. Just as Bennett's career encompassed the development of publishing from 1920 to 1970, Sarnoff's story matches that of the birth of modern mass communications during the same time period.

Born dirt-poor near Minsk in 1891, Sarnoff immigrated to New York City with his Russian Jewish parents when he was nine years old. When his father died in 1906, Sarnoff dropped out of school and took a full-time job as a messenger boy for a cable company. Within a few years, he became a telegraph operator for American Marconi, and in 1912 he began to work in the company's station on the top floor of the Wanamaker's department store at Broadway and Ninth Street (the store thought that having a telegraph operator on-site helped to draw customers, who could send messages or just watch him at work).

At the time, radiotelegraphy—sending telegrams without the use of wires—was state-of-the-art communications. Several times already, people on board sinking ships had been saved after telegraphing for help. Sarnoff happened to be on duty for the biggest shipwreck of all, when the *Titanic* hit an iceberg on April 14, 1912.

Working at Wanamaker's, Sarnoff picked up a signal from a boat in range of the *Titanic*'s telegraph. For seventy-two hours, Sarnoff stayed at his post, becoming the link between the rescue operation and the United States as he gathered the names of survivors, which were relayed to relatives gathered outside on Broadway.

The next year, Sarnoff moved to the business side of the company, knowing he could make more money as a manager than as an engineer. At the time, the technology for radio broadcasting was in its infancy, and in 1916, Sarnoff wrote a memo to his bosses encouraging the company to develop a "radio music box" that people would buy and then use at home to listen to broadcasts of music and lectures. He figured that at $75 each, the company could sell at least one million.

Sarnoff's bosses rejected his idea. But in 1919, GE took over American Marconi, renamed it Radio Corporation of America, and put it in the business of selling radios. Sarnoff, by then the firm's general manager, began to think of ways to make broadcast radio commercial. His insight was to give consumers a reason to buy radios. In July 1921, he arranged the broadcast of a prizefight between Jack Dempsey and Georges Carpentier to the New York City area, drawing tens of thousands of listeners. Radio sales exploded. RCA stock became the hot stock of its day, its share price heading straight up until it was leveled by the 1929 crash.

Sarnoff, in the meantime, realized there was a lot of money to be made selling advertising during radio programs, and he began to stitch together local radio stations to make a national network. He launched the National Broadcasting Company in 1926, effectively setting the template for mass communications for the rest of the century.

By the early 1930s, Sarnoff, who had become president of RCA, directed his engineers to work on developing television technology. Sarnoff, who was given to grand pronouncements about technology and the future, believed he was building a democratic medium that would not only be used for entertainment, but would encourage people to become involved and informed citizens. When NBC aired its first television broadcast in 1939, Sarnoff said: "It is with a feeling of humbleness that I come to this moment of announcing the birth in this country of a new art so important in its implications that it is bound to affect all society."

Sarnoff, with his drive, brains, and vision, completely overshadowed RCA—his name became synonymous with the company, much as Steve Jobs was with Apple and Mark Zuckerberg is with Facebook. During World War II, Sarnoff served as a communications consultant to General Eisenhower and was later named brigadier general, earning him his beloved nickname. At the same time, RCA moved heavily into defense contracting, selling the military everything from radar to walkie-talkies to satellites. By 1965, RCA—with divisions in broadcasting, manufacturing TVs and radios, computers, and military contracting—had revenues of more than $2 billion. It employed one hundred thousand people.

Random House and its imprints, at the time, brought in around $35 million and had a few hundred employees. While a lot of the authors we published were familiar names—William Faulkner, James Michener, E.L. Doctorow, Dr. Seuss, John Updike, and Julia Child—we barely constituted a speck on RCA's organizational chart.

That we had moved into a bigger league financially became apparent right away, when General Sarnoff hosted a dinner to celebrate the deal at his apartment on East Seventy-Second Street, which had not only a swimming pool but also a barber chair, so that Sarnoff did not have to go out for a haircut. Helen and I and other top executives from Random House and RCA took our places at the very long table in the huge dining room, about ten people on each side.

It was all very entertaining. The General was a stern, rather authoritarian man. He sat on one end of the table, and his wife, Lizette, who was French and Jewish, sat on the other. Lizette, who had a thick French accent, was very funny. At one point, she announced, "I always like to have a party this size. It makes the help get down all the dishes and wash them." Later, she called out to the General, "David, could you be quiet while I'm interrupting you?"

Bennett, of course, was not one to be outdone. At around ten o'clock, he announced that his special guest had arrived, and Frank Sinatra walked in and joined us. A bit later, Lizette told Sinatra, "Frankie, I could really go for you, except that David is such a great provider."

I did not get to work too deeply with David Sarnoff. As it happened, David Sarnoff, like Bennett, gave up the presidency of RCA in January 1966. He became chairman, and his son Robert "Bobby" Sarnoff took over the presidency of the company. He continued his father's policy of non-interference for Random House.

At one point during my time as president of Random House, a writer for *Fortune* magazine came to interview me. It was a rare visit, because, at the time, publishing wasn't seen as much of a business —profits jumped up and down from year to year, and a release by a big author such as James Michener could really affect your numbers. The writer, who wanted to know about our recent acquisitions, asked, "Tell us the secret of how Random House is growing so fast." I told him that as far as I was concerned, the reason for the company's success could be summed up in one phrase: "Hire and delegate."

In publishing, the key job, which is acquiring books, has to be done by editors simply because, as head of the company, I couldn't do all the reading that would be required. I couldn't control everything from the center because publishing, done right, is an individual job. I couldn't scale it. Every book is the product of an individual author and an individual editor, and every book poses different challenges. There is no way to get around the fact that producing a good book is time-consuming, labor-intensive work.

So from a practical point of view, as head of the house, I got involved only if there was to be a large advance, and even in that case, I would usually exert my authority in a rather subtle way. The fact that the editor would have to talk to me to give a large advance, I believed, would make the editor think a little bit harder about what he or she was about to spend.

I had loved how Bennett and Donald managed Random House, but when I became president, I also realized that I was going to have to do some things differently. I wanted to keep the warm, personal atmosphere that they had built, but now I had to do that in a growing company.

As Random House grew larger, it became harder to do what Bennett and Donald had done so brilliantly, which was to make authors a part of their social life. I was aware of this from the very beginning. Helen and I entertained as much as we could, but what really worked for Random House was that many of the authors not only liked their editors, but also appreciated the quality of the advice they were getting from them. In many cases, close friendships developed.

I wanted each imprint to have what basically amounted to autonomy as far as the books it published and its internal operations. When necessary, I would deal with the agents of our best-selling authors and have a say over big-money acquisitions. For the most part, though, I tried to monitor things by staying in frequent contact with the managers on both the editorial and business sides. I engaged in what I would call troubleshooting, which would be to zero in on a part of the business that for some reason or another did not seem to be functioning well and work to turn it around. Delegating the maximum authority possible did two things: one, the people running each imprint realized that faith was being put in them and, I think, therefore derived tremendous satisfaction from their successes; and two, when they succeeded, they knew it was through their own efforts.

I think this arrangement helped to attract and keep talented people, because they were given leeway and didn't have me breathing down their necks all the time. So while individual editors and imprints retained control over their lists, they also had the financial protection and distribution that came from being part of a larger firm.

My other business philosophy, which is really the corollary of "hire and delegate," has always been: "Beware of articulate incompetents." I've always found, particularly in creative businesses, that there are people who sound great in an interview but then can't do anything once you hire them. I relied a lot on intuition to defend against the articulate incompetent, and, for the most part, if I ignored my gut feeling, I regretted it later.

One of the most useful pieces of management advice I got came from an unusual source: Dr. Seuss.

Not long after Bennett made the announcement that I was going to be president, Ted came into my office and asked me when I was going to move to a bigger one. I told him I hadn't thought about it at all and said I might just stay where I was.

"That would be a mistake," he said. "When you have a big office, no one questions if you have authority. They can see it. People want to see that the boss has a big office. It makes them feel like you're in charge. The setup does the work for you. If you have a small office, people question if you really have any power, especially because you are succeeding such a successful and well-known man, Bennett, and he has a huge office."

Since Ted had not worked very much in big companies, I wondered how he had come to this thought, and then I realized that, particularly during World War II, he had done a lot of work in the studios of Hollywood. I took the advice and moved into an office in the Villard Mansion one floor above Bennett's, but exactly the same size. And when we had to give up the Villard Mansion and move to a Third Avenue skyscraper, Bennett and I had identical offices at separate corners of the same floor.

But it took me a while to grow into my new role. Of course, as president, my social profile rose, and I quickly became aware that people like to know the president of an organization they are associated with.

In late 1966, the first year of my presidency, Truman Capote sent out invitations to his famous Black and White Ball, a party he was giving in honor of Katharine Graham, the publisher of the *Washington Post*. The party was to be at the Plaza Hotel, and, for some people, it became crucial to be on the star-studded guest list of five hundred, which was to include everyone whom Capote deemed "important" in society. I was delighted that Helen and I were invited, though I knew I had my recent promotion to thank for the inclusion.

When I heard that Joe Fox, Truman's editor, and his wife, Jill, were also going, we arranged to go together and hired a limousine so that we would arrive in proper style at the Fifth Avenue entrance of the Plaza, which had a red carpet stretched from the curb and up the broad steps leading into the hotel. There were wooden barriers on each side of the carpet, behind which stood crowds of people with cameras who were taking pictures of the arriving celebrities, who included Andy Warhol, Jackie Kennedy, Leonard Bernstein, Tennessee Williams, Richard Burton, Greta Garbo, and many others.

Joe, Jill, Helen, and I got out of the car and were approaching the steps, looking at the camera-laden crowd, when we heard the shrill voice of a young boy with his own camera. He looked at us and then turned around and yelled at the crowd: "They're nobody!"

Being around famous authors for most of my life, I quickly got used to this role.

* * *

Bennett always liked to compare Random House to the New York Yankees. In order to maintain their greatness, the Yankees were always looking ahead and thinking about when their current managers and players were going to retire. Instead of resting on their laurels, they kept developing a pipeline of new talent, so that there was no drop in quality when a coach or player left.

Coming into the presidency, I had the advantage of that pipeline. Our authors included James Michener, Robert Penn Warren, John Hersey, Eudora Welty, William Styron, John Updike, and Philip Roth. We also had great editors: Jim Silberman was editor in chief of Random House, backed up by great editors such as Joe Fox, Bob Loomis, Jason Epstein, Lee Wright, and Charlotte Mayerson. André Schiffrin, Jacques Schiffrin's son, headed Pantheon.

We also had Beginner Books, a tremendously profitable children's imprint founded by Ted Geisel; his wife, Helen; and Phyllis Cerf, Bennett's wife. The idea, which they came up with after the runaway success of *The Cat in the Hat*, was to have an imprint dedicated to releasing books for younger kids. From the time that Beginner Books was founded, Ted wrote some of his books for it—usually under the name "Theo. LeSieg," with drawings by another illustrator—and Random House continued to publish his more complex work aimed at older readers.

One area of concern was Knopf. Alfred, without a doubt, was one of the greatest publishers of the twentieth century, but he was getting older (he would turn seventy-eight in 1970). His wife, Blanche, had died in 1966. I wanted to make sure there was a team in place to succeed Alfred.

There was no question who would be ideal. I had worked with Bob Gottlieb, Nina Bourne, and Tony Schulte when I was at Simon & Schuster. The three were so close that they were something of their own club.

Gottlieb was a brilliant editor, combining several talents that are usually not found in a single person: he had an eye for the overall structure of a book and the ability to line edit with amazing skill and speed, and he could read the market for a book. He was also a great leader, inspiring the people around him and creating a place that combined loyalty, hard work, and fun. Gottlieb had many successes at S&S, one of the biggest being Joseph Heller's antiwar book, *Catch-22*.

Bourne was S&S's advertising head—I had actually worked for her briefly when I started at S&S—and she was, in my opinion, the best ad person in the business. She had a genius for ad layout and design and highlighting the perfect quotes. The ads she had designed for S&S just jumped off the page.

Schulte, who was always upbeat, served as a liaison between the editorial and business sides at S&S, coordinating things like sales strategies, advertising, release dates, and distribution. He had a somewhat rare trait in publishing in that he understood business but could also just as easily sit for hours and talk books with Gottlieb. I think it's safe to say that he was one of the most well-liked people in the book business.

For several years, I had let Gottlieb, Bourne, and Schulte know that if they ever wanted to leave S&S, Random House would be happy to hire all of them, either individually or as a threesome. While Gottlieb was perhaps the star among the three, I didn't want Bourne and Schulte to feel that I wanted them only if Gottlieb came. In the 1960s, good editors almost never left their publishing houses, particularly because after having signed all of their authors to a house, leaving could be complicated. It was almost unheard of for a star editor like Gottlieb to make a move. But, over time, there were a few things working in Random House's favor.

At S&S, Gottlieb still had to contend with Leon Shimkin, who had kept a tight rein on the company. While Shimkin had promised Gottlieb much, he kept to his old ways, doling out pay increases incrementally and grudgingly. By 1967, Schulte, Bourne, and Gottlieb had started to look elsewhere and had even considered the possibility of buying another house to run.

I wanted them to come to Knopf and began a series of clandestine meetings with the trio—if anyone saw us together, the news would have been all over the industry before we got back from lunch.

I had the perfect place. When I had become president of Random House, Bennett told me that I needed to have a place in the city in addition to our home in Scarsdale. I was resistant—I had three kids at home—but he insisted there were times when it would come in useful. He set up a meeting for me with his friend Claudette Colbert.

Claudette, who was born in France but grew up in New York, had been a huge film star in the 1930s and 1940s and had won the Best Actress Oscar for the 1934 Frank Capra film *It Happened One Night*. By the mid-1960s, she was splitting her time among New York City; Barbados, where she had a house; and Beverly Hills, where her husband, Joel "Jack" Pressman, a surgeon, lived, with occasional jaunts to Paris to brush up her French and buy shoes.

Since she was in New York so little, Bennett had suggested that she rent her small apartment to me. So I found the address on the Upper East Side and rang the bell. The door was opened by the beautiful Claudette Colbert, in a housedress and holding a mop in her hand. She said, "Oh, I thought you were coming at six thirty and it's only six."

Then she looked at the mop. "I guess I should explain this," she said. "We have a very good maid but she just won't reach up and clean those moldings at the top of this high ceiling, so I have to do it myself."

I then started what I thought was a negotiation with Claudette about the rent and other arrangements for the apartment. I asked what the rent would be. She said, "Well, I'm paying this amount, that's what it will be."

"Claudette," I said, "the apartment is beautifully furnished and has absolutely everything in it. Don't you think you should get something for that?"

"No, no," she said. "That's all here anyway."

She then looked at her watch and said, "It's getting late, when are you going to have dinner?"

When I told her I was going to eat when I got back to Scarsdale, she insisted on making me a hamburger.

So I ate a hamburger. She told me about her place in Barbados and how great it was. I asked her what she was going to do now that she wouldn't have an apartment. She said she was in New York City for only three weeks out of the year, so she would just get a hotel room.

I told her that Bennett had pushed me into renting the apartment. "I can easily go without it whenever you're in town," I said. "Consider it your apartment whenever you're here, just as though you had never sublet it to me." She agreed that it was a great idea.

Before I left that evening, she said, "Oh, you have to come to Barbados in the winter. Bennett and Phyllis come all the time; you'll have to come too." I told her it would be great and left it at that. Little did I know that it would lead to one of the great friendships in Helen's and my life.

Bennett's foresight about my needing a place was clear as I started the meetings with Gottlieb, Bourne, and Schulte. We met during the day at Claudette's apartment. Each time a different person was responsible for bringing lunch.

My line of argument was that if they bought a publishing house, they would have to deal with the financial side. If they took a job somewhere else, that's what it would be—a job. I could offer them their own imprint, and not just any imprint, but Alfred A. Knopf, one of the most storied in publishing.

They were obviously interested but didn't immediately accept. One day, when it was Bourne's turn to supply lunch, she brought sandwiches with thick slices of smoked salmon and raw onions on dark brown bread. The raw onion was horrible. I told them, "Look, I can't take any more of this. You've got to make a decision."

So, at the beginning of 1968, they finally agreed. It was a great coup within the industry. S&S was shocked, and I admit it gave me a great deal of pleasure to get back at Leon Shimkin.

In a short time, Gottlieb, Bourne, and Schulte managed to both charm and please Alfred, who certainly could be difficult at times. The one time things nearly went bad happened early on, in 1968, when Knopf published Joseph Heller's second book, *We Bombed in New Haven*. Until then, every Knopf book ever published had included the imprint's borzoi logo on the cover (it is still on the spine of every book Knopf publishes). For some reason, they left it off the Heller book (the cover was actually quite striking—it was simply the text of the title and Heller's name in the shape of a bomb against a white background).

As soon as the ads for the book hit the paper, Alfred called me.

He was at LaGuardia Airport, just about to go on vacation, and he was livid. He demanded that I immediately fire Bourne, Schulte, and Gottlieb.

Trying to calm him down, I suggested that he meet with the three of them to discuss it. Alfred set up a lunch date with the trio in the Pool Room of the Four Seasons Restaurant. As it was told to me later, things were tense, until Alfred and Gottlieb began to talk about obscure English novelists they both loved. Apologies were made, and two hours later everyone left very happy.

As it turned out, Bob Gottlieb, aided by Tony Schulte and Nina Bourne, ran the imprint very successfully for the next two decades. Years later, I received a note from Alfred, who wrote that despite his initial reservations, things had worked out at Knopf better than he had ever expected.

After Blanche Knopf died in 1966, a woman named Helen Hedrick, who'd published a novel with Knopf many years earlier, sent Alfred roses. They married a year later. She was wonderful for him. She had come from a small town in Oregon and loved the outdoors, which worked very well with Alfred's love for the national parks. He seemed to become mellower and to be really enjoying life with her. She was also a great hostess and I'm sure was a fantastic help behind the scenes in making Alfred appreciate how well the transition was working for Knopf and how the imprint would retain all the luster it had when he ran it. Alfred gradually phased out of the house, and he died in 1984 at the age of ninety-one.

Shortly after I became president, I went up to Syracuse to visit L.W. Singer, the textbook publisher we had bought a few years earlier. It was really a small place with not all that much going for it, but Bennett thought we needed to be in textbooks. It was difficult, because none of us knew anything about publishing elementary school textbooks, which was very different from trade publishing. On top of that, none of us was really very interested in the business, and L.W. Singer had a small niche in a highly competitive field.

As I walked around talking with people, I ended up in the office of one of the editors, a young African American woman. I asked her what she was up to, and she told me about an anthology of African stories she was editing. She was charming and funny and described the book she was editing in a way that really made it come alive. It was not hard to tell that she was an unusual person. When I asked how she had ended up at L.W. Singer, she told me she had moved up to Syracuse because she was divorced and thought it would be a good place to raise her two young sons. I asked her, now that Random House had bought L.W. Singer, what job she would really want. In an instant, she said she'd like to be an editor at Random House.

"Well, I've just become president, I'll see what I can do," I said. I went back to New York City and spoke with Jim Silberman. At the time, I thought that we needed to add diversity to our editorial staff—African Americans were not just underrepresented in the business; they were practically nonexistent. So we offered Toni Morrison a job as a Random House editor.

A few years after Toni started working at Random House, I spotted her first novel, *The Bluest Eye*, on display in a bookstore. I was surprised to see it had been published by Henry Holt. I went back to the office and asked Toni why she hadn't brought it to us. She told me she didn't want to be published by the same house where she was an editor.

I told her a story about George Brett, who had been the president of Macmillan in 1946 when a young editor came to him with a manuscript he had written. Brett said, "Look, you're a good editor, but you really should forget about the writing."

The editor went uptown to the offices of Random House, then at Fifty-Seventh Street, and met with Bennett, who signed him. The man was James Michener and the book was *Tales from the South Pacific*.

"Toni," I said, "I don't want to be George Brett."

Looking back, I feel very smart, of course, but it was just a hunch.

I told her that she could continue to be an editor at Random House, and I'd introduce her to Bob Gottlieb at Knopf. If Knopf published her, she would not be at the same imprint where she worked. She's been there ever since, and Gottlieb is still her editor.

When I became president of Random House at age forty-three, I was a generation below Bennett and Donald's and one above that of our younger editors. At the time, I gave money here and there to political causes, but I was not deeply involved with anything except running Random House, which was thinly staffed, and coping with three teenage kids in Scarsdale.

I leaned to the left, I think, for a few reasons. Growing up around the "refugees" who gathered at my grandparents' house had made me aware that a lot of people needed help at times for reasons beyond their control. And then at Lincoln School, I was made very conscious about the problems of poverty in America. Finally, during my three years in the army, I had seen enormous poverty and suffering in India.

By 1966, the political situation in the country was rapidly heating up. America had already seen the main breakthroughs of the civil rights movement—the 1955–56 Montgomery bus boycott, the 1963 March on Washington, and the passage of the 1964 Civil Rights Acts—but the mass demonstrations against the Vietnam War, the assassinations of Martin Luther King Jr. and Bobby Kennedy, black power, hippies, the feminist movement, and Nixon were still to come. Of course, all of these things had an impact on the book business—if nothing else, they produced a lot of new books.

You can see the changing political and cultural trends in the best-sellers we published in the years directly after I became president. They included *My Lai 4*, Seymour Hersh's exposé of the massacre of Vietnamese villagers by American troops; *The Greening of America*, Charles A. Reich's love letter to the counterculture, which argued that hippies were changing the world's consciousness; *The Strawberry Statement*, a student's account of the Columbia University campus riots of 1968; *I Know Why the Caged Bird Sings*, Maya Angelou's first book, an autobiographical novel that deals with issues such as rape and racism; *Division Street*, Studs Terkel's first bestseller, an oral history of Chicago; and *Portnoy's Complaint*, Philip Roth's comic masterpiece about sex, psychoanalysis, and being Jewish.

Dr. Seuss became more political as well. In 1970, Ted began work on *The Lorax*. The title character is a creature who "speaks for the trees" and tries to stop the greedy Once-ler from cutting down a forest of wooly Truffula trees to produce a Thneed, which is a strange-looking knitted garment. The Once-ler doesn't listen and cuts down the forest, only to find that he has made a polluted wasteland. At the end of the book, he gives a tree seed to a boy and asks him to replant the forest. The environmental movement loved the book, and Ted later said that it was his favorite.

I thought I had my finger on the political pulse. But then an art catalog, authored by the Metropolitan Museum of Art and distributed by Random House, turned into an exceedingly controversial event.

As in the rest of the United States, race relations in New York City at the end of the 1960s were strained. In 1964, the first major race riot of many across the country that decade had broken out in Harlem after a white police officer shot a fifteen-year-old African American boy.

Four years later, in May 1968, one month after the assassination of Martin Luther King Jr., a black school board in Brooklyn fired eighteen white teachers on the grounds that the teachers were opposed to "local control" of the schools. The fallout was horrible. The teachers' union went on strike to support the fired teachers, and more than one million kids in New York City were shut out of school. Many prominent white liberals—such as Mayor John Lindsay and the Ford Foundation's McGeorge Bundy—supported the black activists in their demands for more power in the school system. Many Jewish groups, traditionally allies with black civil rights causes, sided with the teachers' union (which was also heavily Jewish). By the time the strike ended and the teachers were reinstated, the city had been polarized, and there was a nasty rift in the relationship between Jews and blacks.

It was against this backdrop that Thomas Hoving, the ambitious new director of the Metropolitan Museum of Art, announced that the Met—which until then had been anything but in the vanguard of cultural change—was going to present a major exhibition dedicated to the history of Harlem. Hoving had the admirable goal of drawing more African Americans to the institution, which until then wasn't perceived as inclusive. He also wanted to shake things up, and he ended up getting his wish.

Allon Schoener, the show's curator, had previously done an

exhibition about the experiences of Eastern European Jews in New York for the Jewish Museum. *Harlem on My Mind* was to take the same approach, using photographs, newspaper clippings, and sound recordings to put together a multimedia composite history of African Americans in Harlem.

Schoener's agent approached the editor in chief of Random House, Jim Silberman, and told him there was going to be a catalog for the exhibition. The Met wanted forty thousand paperback copies to sell in its gift shop, and there would also be a hardbound book that Random House would distribute to bookstores. We didn't see any problem with publishing it. Schoener and the Met were already doing all the editorial work, so we had little overhead in the project.

From its inception, though, the exhibition was troubled. One of the first issues to come up was that Schoener was a Jew with no particular expertise in black culture or history, which opened him up to charges of exploitation. Though Schoener hired black researchers, he had a testy relationship with members of a Harlem advisory board, which complained to the press that Schoener had ignored its input. In addition, Schoener announced that the show was going to be only documentary, with no artwork. That drew protests from black artists who asked how an art museum could put on an exhibition with no art.

Despite all that, the preparations continued, and when the show opened on January 18, 1969, it drew a huge and varied crowd—it was probably one of the few times you would ever see Black Panthers and Upper East Side ladies mingling in an art gallery. The exhibition filled thirteen galleries and covered the history of Black Harlem, beginning with the first migrations from the South in 1900 and proceeding up to the present. There were massive black-and-white photos, slide shows, ambient sounds of people talking on the street, clips of recordings by singers like Billie Holiday and Aretha Franklin, and recordings of speeches by figures such as Marcus Garvey and Malcolm X. The major discovery of the show was James VanDerZee, a photographer who had taken wedding pictures and other photos of life in Harlem, such as portraits of musicians and other prominent figures, since the 1920s. His work was an amazing catalog of the cultural history of the area.

It was an impressive show, and I thought the book that Schoener put together—organized by decade and with dozens of photos and newspaper clippings—was exceptionally well done. But with all the controversy the exhibition had already stirred, the element that ignited everything came from an unexpected source.

Schoener had decided he wanted a fresh voice to write the introduction to the book and chose a high school student from Harlem named Candice Van Ellison, who had been assigned to work with him through the Ghetto Arts Program. Apparently, Van Ellison had let Schoener read an essay on the history of Harlem she had written for school. He'd been impressed and had asked her to redo it for the catalog.

As it appears in the book, Van Ellison's essay discusses the history of Harlem and the neighborhood's social and economic conditions. She then talks about relations between blacks and Jews, writing that the two groups are in constant contact because blacks have moved into the areas where Jews once lived. Van Ellison states that almost all grocery stores in Harlem are owned by Jews, allowing the Jews to exploit blacks by charging high prices. Jews, she writes, own a lot of the property in Harlem and serve as landlords, and she adds that many black women work as domestics in middle-class Jewish houses, leading to anti-Semitism. She wraps the section up by asserting, "One other important factor worth noting is that, psychologically, blacks may find that anti-Jewish sentiments place them, for once, within a majority. Thus, our contempt for the Jew makes us feel more completely American in sharing a national prejudice."

In his memoir of his time at the Met, Hoving writes that he fought with Schoener about these statements, but in the end he decided to let them go through because Schoener argued that they represented a truth. Because Random House was only distributing the hardback version, I don't think we did any of the editing. I never asked if we had, and I doubt that anybody had read the book very closely.

As soon as the catalog hit the street, all hell broke loose. At a press conference, reporters questioned Hoving about anti-Semitism as well as other inflammatory comments Van Ellison had made about the Irish and Puerto Ricans. The Anti-Defamation League came out against the book, and rabbis in the city started to denounce it. Soon, Mayor Lindsay was insisting that the catalog be recalled. By the end of January, the city council had passed a resolution urging the city to withdraw its funding of the Met unless the book was pulled. The Jewish Defense League protested outside the museum. I received a flood of letters accusing me of anti-Semitism and demanding that Random House recall the book.

As the situation degenerated, I went up to see Hoving at the Met. He was obviously under pressure. He'd had Van Ellison write a disclaimer that she had not intended to be racist, which he'd inserted in the books on sale at the Met. He had also publicly apologized. He refused, though, to remove the book from sale. I was against pulling a book under public pressure and told him so. I said that I understood he would have to make his own decision, but we agreed that he would call me if he decided to withdraw the catalog.

So I was blindsided a few days later when I got a call at about 4:30 in the afternoon from a *New York Times* reporter who told me that the Met was pulling the book. He wanted to know if Random House was going to follow suit. I asked for a little time, and the reporter told me he had about an hour before his deadline.

I began to feel a little panicked. If the Met recalled the book and we didn't, all the outrage would shift to focus on us. Jewish groups might call for a boycott of Random House. It was a potential disaster.

Not knowing what to do, I asked three executives to come into my office and asked for their opinions. The only one who was for keeping the book on the market was Jim Silberman. The others argued that now that the Met had caved, we could reasonably do so as well, getting us off the hook.

So many thoughts were running around in my head that I still didn't know what I was going to say when the reporter called back. In the end, I told him, "Random House will not withdraw the book. We feel that if you start withdrawing books under social pressures there will be no end to that, and I feel that whether the line is anti-Semitic or not, that the world—and certainly a city as strong as New York—can stand one anti-Semitic passage by a sixteen-year-old girl, if it is judged to be that. The precedent of withdrawing books after they've been published would be a far worse thing to happen."

I hung up, and I felt terrible. I went home and told Helen that I hoped we had both enjoyed my run as president because it might be over soon, and I remembered the line by Judge Learned Hand: "The spirit of liberty is the spirit which is not too sure that it is right." It was a sleepless night.

As it turned out, a couple of things got me off the hook.

The next day, the *Times*—which had been against the exhibition from the start—ran an editorial with the title "Harlem off Our Mind?" It was hardly complimentary. "The Metropolitan Museum of Art's misbegotten exhibit, 'Harlem on My Mind,' will continue into April; but the controversial catalogue with its racist introduction will be withdrawn from sale at the museum," it said, adding, "Neither the museum nor Random House, publisher of the catalogue, exercised any discernible editorial judgment in the project."

The *Times*'s editorial board backed the museum's withdrawal of the catalog, but it did not go as far as to keep coming after us. "But the matter ought to rest there," it said. "It would be a violation of every concept of free press for Random House to suppress the hardcover edition. That would be book burning without the flames, an even greater offense to American traditions than anything in the book."

Shortly after that, it was revealed that Van Ellison's inflammatory statement about hatred of Jews making blacks feel more American was actually taken from *Beyond the Melting Pot*, a 1963 book by the sociologists Daniel Patrick Moynihan and Nathan Glazer. It turned out that Van Ellison had originally included the comment in quotation marks, but Schoener had for some reason—probably to make it seem more dramatic—removed them.

The perception of the statement changed when people thought of it as coming from Moynihan and Glazer instead of Van Ellison. For some reason, it was suddenly less offensive.

Within a few weeks, the whole controversy had blown over. Random House—and my career—escaped. The *Harlem on My Mind* exhibition is now seen as something of a seminal event, when politics and culture collided at one of New York's most august institutions.

The New Press even reissued the catalog in 1995 with a foreword by Henry Louis Gates Jr., the prominent African American scholar, who called the book "one of the richest and most comprehensive records of the history of the African American in the twentieth century."

There was certainly no indication at the time there would be such a happy ending.

It was really the first time as president of Random House that I realized that whatever decision came down was not going to be on Bennett Cerf, but on me.

By the end of the 1960s, the Villard Mansion on Madison Avenue couldn't fit all of Random House. We had to rent office space in other buildings to accommodate everyone. At the Villard, desks were crammed into every nook and cranny.

I tried really hard to keep us in the Villard, but we were too late. It was a case where I think Bennett, who loved that building to death, ignored the problem until a move was unavoidable. When I became president, a new office building was going up next door. I had thought we could move some of our operations there while keeping the Villard as our main headquarters. But we waited too long and the building was sold out by the time we checked on getting space there. So, in 1969, we regretfully left the Villard Mansion and moved into fourteen floors of an uninspiring forty-floor office building on East Fiftieth Street and Third Avenue. RCA decided it wanted to get rid of the Villard space and sold it for $2.2 million, which in hindsight had to be the steal of all time for the buyer (it is now part of the Palace Hotel). I had suggested to Bobby Sarnoff that if RCA held on to the building, we could make it into New York's most spectacular bookstore. He wasn't interested.

It was around this time that I hired Christopher Cerf, Bennett's son, who started at Random House working directly with me. Chris was right out of college, where he had been the editor of the *Harvard Lampoon*, and having him in the firm kept the feeling of a family business.

Chris was not only immensely talented, but full of enthusiasm, and with his young *Lampoon* friends, who kept dropping in, a joy to have around. He was soon signing books on his own. One of his first authors was the radical "yippie" Abbie Hoffman. When he was working on his book, Hoffman often came into our office with his wild, unkempt hair and dirty jeans and walked around barefoot. One day, when Bennett was showing a visitor around, Hoffman was alone in Chris's office. Hoffman heard Bennett say, "Now this next office is my son's."

When Bennett opened the door, Hoffman was lying on the rug, his usual unkempt self. He looked at Bennett and said, "Hiya, Pop." Of course, Bennett being Bennett, he probably repeated the story more than anyone.

Not long after that, Chris came to me and said he was planning to leave Random House. He said he just couldn't work with his father anymore. When I asked him what had happened, he said: "I was sitting in my office with a young author I wanted to sign, and Dad sticks his head in the door and says, 'Can I interrupt you for a second?' I said, 'Of course, Dad.' And he says, 'If you want to get your laundry done this week, have it to our house by five.'"

Chris told me, "That's going to happen over and over again. There's no way of stopping Dad. I'm getting out." He soon left to take a job as a writer with *Sesame Street*, which was then just starting, and went on to a very successful career of authoring books and songwriting.

One of the saddest moments of my life came in August 1971, when I got a phone call telling me that Bennett had died.

Although Bennett was seventy-three years old, he had seemed to be in good health. It turned out that he had been in the hospital for abdominal surgery. The operation had gone fine, but he'd developed a blood clot in his leg. When he went home to recuperate, he had a hemorrhage that killed him. It was totally unexpected.

I called Chris and we began to talk about the funeral. Bennett was beloved, and his funeral was going to draw a lot of people. Since Bennett had loved Columbia University, his alma mater, I thought maybe we should have the ceremony at St. Paul's Chapel on the campus.

I didn't know the president of Columbia, but I called his office and told his secretary that Bennett's first love had been the school, where he'd gone with Richard Rodgers and Lorenz Hart and many other of his very close friends. I knew he would like his funeral service to be held in the university's chapel. Also, I knew it was nondenominational, and Bennett was not a religious man.

She said, "Well, there's a problem, because it has to have the president's approval and he's in Berlin." This was on a Thursday morning. I told her I needed a decision by later that day so the *Times* would have the correct information on the funeral. If we couldn't have it at Columbia, it was going to have to be in a funeral home.

She called back later in the afternoon and told me she hadn't been able to reach the president, but that she thought it was something he would support. She said she would take the chance and give us the approval of the president and to go ahead and put it in the paper. I thought it was really admirable for her to not get caught up in the bureaucracy.

The funeral was a mob scene. Some 1,500 people attended. Bennett was not only loved in the publishing world, but he also had a wide following from his television appearances, lectures, columns, and books. The mourners included Frank Sinatra, Danny Kaye, Ginger Rogers, Truman Capote, Richard Rodgers, Philip Roth, Dr. Seuss, and Elie Wiesel.

Eudora Welty sent in a tribute that read: "I wonder if anyone else of such manifold achievements in the publishing world could ever have had so many friends."

John Hersey: "His entire life, right into the 70's, was one long zestful, ravenous boyhood."

And James Michener wrote: "When the echo of the laughter is forgotten, that excellent row of books will be remembered."

5

POLITICS AND PUBLISHING

WE SIGNED MUHAMMAD ALI TO WRITE HIS AUTOBIOGRAPHY IN 1970. At the time, he was a focal point for all the divisions in the country. After he beat Sonny Liston in 1964 for his first heavyweight title, Ali—who had been talking intensively with Malcolm X—renounced his "slave name" of Cassius Clay and joined the Nation of Islam, a black separatist group.

Soon after his religious conversion, Ali was drafted into the army. He refused to enlist, declared himself a conscientious objector to the Vietnam War, and told reporters: "I ain't got no quarrel with them Viet Cong." In 1967, boxing commissions around the country revoked his title and his boxing license. A jury found Ali guilty of draft evasion and sentenced him to five years in prison, though he remained free while the case was on appeal. The Vietnam War at that time still had wide popular support, and people around the country vilified Ali for refusing to serve.

He had been out of the ring for almost three years by the time we announced his book deal in January 1970. To make some money while his prison sentence was on appeal, he opened a restaurant chain called Champburger.

Our signing of Ali got a lot of attention, and we decided to have a press conference—the first really big one I did as the head of Random House. I wasn't prepared for the number of journalists who showed up.

When we entered the Random House boardroom, it was like a

prizefight—there were twelve television cameras, twenty photographers, and around a hundred reporters. I handed over a ceremonial check for $60,000—part of the advance—and Ali, who was dressed in a black double-vested suit, took over.

"Writing is as good as fighting," he said, adding, "I can't wait to get started writing. I believe that this book will outdo all of them that's been written."

Ali, as usual, joked, gesticulated, rubbed his hand across his head, and preached to the reporters. I sat silently next to him and smoked a pipe. When it came around to me, the first question came from the sportscaster Howard Cosell, who asked, in his Brooklyn accent: "Mr. Bernstein, how does it feel to give such a big advance to a man who refuses to fight for his country?"

I thought for a moment and said, "I hope we don't live in a country that won't allow people to say what they want to say. If good publishers stop publishing controversial books, it'll be a bad day for democracy.

"Besides," I added, "the case is still on appeal, and my impression was that someone is innocent until proven guilty."

As it turned out, the Supreme Court overturned Ali's conviction for draft dodging in 1971. When the book finally came out four years after that, Ali had already made his amazing comeback, including wins over Joe Frazier in the Philippines (the "Thrilla in Manila") and George Foreman in Zaire (the "Rumble in the Jungle").

To me, the most memorable story in Ali's autobiography was about his return to Louisville, Kentucky, his hometown, after winning the gold medal at the 1960 Summer Olympics in Rome. Ali wrote that he went into a segregated diner, tried to order a hamburger, and was told that the establishment didn't serve blacks. Some thugs tried to beat him up for just daring to come in, and Ali took off running until he finally came to a bridge over the Ohio River. He felt his medal in his pocket and realized that even after winning the gold for his country he was still considered a second-class citizen. So Ali took the medal out, threw it in the river, and walked away.

* * *

I began to turn against the Vietnam War not long after Muhammad Ali made headlines for refusing to go. My reasons were at first mainly personal—I was very concerned that either Peter or Tom, who were born in 1951 and 1952, respectively, was going to be drafted and sent to be killed. I quickly realized that if I felt that way about my sons, I had to feel that way about all American soldiers.

Writing this many years later, I recognize that the decision of when to use force is an extremely difficult problem. Vietnam was complicated because it was clear that neither side in the civil war there was going to let the citizens have a say in determining their own fate. As we see today, with the damage that even small groups of extremists can exact, there is going to have to be some hard thinking by many more mothers and fathers in open societies about the world we want to live in, the values we want to preserve, and the price we will pay to preserve those values in other countries. As far as the Vietnam War, I don't personally think it met the threshold that would justify sending American troops to a foreign land.

The only time I ever cried in public was after Peter learned that his draft number was so high that there was almost no chance it would come up in the draft lottery. I was out at lunch with Tom Guinzburg of Viking Press when Peter called and told me, and I just burst out in tears. Until that point, I hadn't even realized how deeply emotionally involved I was. I still think about it when I see young Americans getting killed in Iraq and Afghanistan, especially knowing that many of them are there because of their economic status. If we need to go to war, perhaps every American family should be involved. If not, you have a situation where a small percentage of the population shoulders most of the burden.

By 1970, many people I knew had turned against the Vietnam War. At that year's meeting of the Association of American Publishers—which included almost all major American publishers—the membership passed a resolution calling for an end to the conflict, making it probably the first industry association in the country to condemn the war.

At home in Scarsdale, Tom, who was a senior in high school, had become a leader of the local antiwar movement. Every morning, Tom and about 150 other students would gather at the commuter rail station to protest the war, standing silently and holding up signs. Sometimes you would see a man in a business suit interrupt his trip to Grand Central to join them.

I met George McGovern in 1968, when we published his book *A Time of War, a Time of Peace*. We rushed the book into print that summer when McGovern, a senator from South Dakota, announced in early August that he wanted to be considered as a presidential candidate at the Democratic National Convention, which was to start at the end of the month.

McGovern's late entry into the race as the antiwar candidate came after the assassination of Bobby Kennedy two months earlier. McGovern lost the nomination to Hubert Humphrey, Lyndon Johnson's vice president, but the effort gave him national exposure. I got to know McGovern as his publisher, and I found him to be straightforward and by far the best choice to end the war. When he announced his intention to run for the Democratic nomination in 1972, I was an immediate supporter. Very early in the process, I convinced Bennett and Phyllis Cerf to throw a dinner party for McGovern and his wife, Eleanor.

The guests included several Random House authors, the most prominent being Truman Capote. Unfortunately, McGovern just didn't make it with these people, at least at that time. He was very articulate and a lovely man, but he came in a blue suit—not navy, but sort of teal—that made him look like a New Yorker's idea of a hick from South Dakota. His wife, Eleanor, who was both warm and charming, wore a dress that fluffed way out and had frills all over it, like a young girl's party dress. And here they were, totally earnest and nice, among these very sophisticated New Yorkers, all very chic. It was very uncomfortable, although maybe I'm attributing too much to the clothes, and the guests just didn't have as much enthusiasm for McGovern as I did.

My two older sons, Peter and Tom, became very involved in the McGovern campaign, working in the New York City office. In the fall of 1971, they published a co-written op-ed in the *Times* pointing out that the "archaic" New York State election law was going to make it hard for eighteen- to twenty-one-year-olds to register to vote in the presidential election (they wrote that they hoped the youth vote would help elect McGovern). Tom took a semester off from Yale in order to run the McGovern primary campaign in northern New Hampshire. On the night of the primary, Helen and I went up to help out, and Tom assigned us the job of taking hamburgers to all the campaign volunteers, which required many trips to McDonald's.

McGovern finished surprisingly strong in New Hampshire, coming in a close second to frontrunner Edmund Muskie. The momentum pushed him past Muskie to get the nomination. Tom, then nineteen years old, was selected as one of the youngest delegates to the Democratic National Convention, which was in Miami that year, and Helen and I went as well. At one point we overheard Tom telling another delegate, "Everyone and his mother's here, including mine."

McGovern's platform called for an immediate withdrawal from Vietnam in exchange for the return of American prisoners of war, amnesty for men who avoided the draft, and a reduction in defense spending to be put toward things like education and health care. He also supported the Equal Rights Amendment, which would have added protection of the rights of women to the Constitution. It was all very exciting at the time.

Of course, Richard Nixon, who was up for reelection, beat up on McGovern during his campaign. His surrogates characterized McGovern—who had won a Distinguished Flying Cross as a bomber pilot in World War II—as a crazed leftist. In the spring before the election, the conservative columnist Bob Novak wrote that an unnamed Democratic senator had told him: "The people don't know that McGovern is for amnesty, abortion, and legalization of pot."

I was so enthused that I didn't realize how badly the stars were lining up against McGovern. Soon after the Democratic convention, McGovern had to dump his vice presidential running mate, Thomas Eagleton, from the ticket after it was revealed that Eagleton had been hospitalized several times for mental illness and had received shock treatment. In addition, former Alabama governor and Dixiecrat George Wallace, who was expected to run as a third-party candidate as he had in 1968 and siphon southern white votes away from Nixon, dropped out of the race after he was paralyzed in a May 1972 assassination attempt.

Finally, even Nixon did himself a few good turns, enhancing his popularity with his Henry Kissinger–orchestrated trip to China and the signing of an arms-control agreement with the Soviets.

Before the election, I asked Claudette Colbert to come with me to a McGovern rally at Madison Square Garden. Claudette, who at the time was nearly seventy, was a lifelong Republican and a personal friend of Ronald Reagan's. I told her it would be fun, and to my surprise, she agreed to go. For the rest of her life, she always brought it up, telling me, "I don't know why I did that."

That was because McGovern got absolutely trounced. Nixon got 61 percent of the vote to McGovern's 38 percent. The only two places McGovern won were Massachusetts and the District of Columbia—he even lost his home state.

American publishing houses in the 1960s and early 1970s were, for the most part, small companies, and their relations with the government could vary. Most publishers wanted to publish interesting books regardless of which party was in power. Rarely in my career did the government get involved in having an opinion on a book, although there were some major exceptions.

Overall, we tried to find a balance. In the late 1960s, Bennett published a book by FBI director J. Edgar Hoover on the dangers of communism. Even though the full story of how Hoover's FBI illegally spied on Americans during his forty-year tenure wasn't fully revealed until after he died in 1972, it was still clear in the 1960s that he was abusing his power. When I asked Bennett why he wanted to publish the book, he told me that if you put out a book by J. Edgar Hoover, you can publish almost anything else political and then say, "Look, we publish on both sides—we published J. Edgar Hoover."

The Hoover book actually came in handy after one of our editors, John Simon, signed the Black Panther Eldridge Cleaver for his second book, which was to be a collection of his essays and speeches (Cleaver's first book, *Soul on Ice*, which we did not publish, had been a sensation). In 1968, Cleaver was a national figure, leading the Black Panthers and running for president as the representative of the Peace and Freedom Party. In April 1968, though, a few days after the assassination of Martin Luther King Jr., the Black Panthers got in a shoot-out with the Oakland police. Three officers were wounded, and Cleaver fled the country to Algeria.

Shortly after that, two FBI agents came to Random House, said they were looking for Cleaver, and asked if they could walk around our offices, which were then still in the Villard Mansion. I told them that he wasn't there, but they were welcome to see for themselves. They proceeded to go and have a look through all five floors. As I remember it, they even looked under desks.

When they were getting ready to leave, I told them, "We always like to give our visitors one of our books." I handed each of them a copy of J. Edgar Hoover's speeches. I tried to study their faces, but I saw no reaction. I always wondered what they thought about their boss sharing a publisher with Eldridge Cleaver.

Not long after the FBI agents visited Random House, I took my youngest son, Bill, on a trip to Washington, D.C., to see the sights. When we visited the FBI, Hoover came out to greet us personally, and Bill posed with him for a photo. Since Hoover was very short, one of his assistants brought out a little platform for him to stand on.

Publishing as a business can be full of many surprises. The authors are always the experts on their subject area, and the publisher generally makes three decisions—on the quality of the writing, sometimes on the value of the information presented, and to some extent on the marketability, which really depends on whether the author wants a lot of money in advance.

When you're publishing books about the government, it's usually to give information, which is, of course, very important in a democracy. It becomes difficult if the government wants to stop the publication of a book—when that happens, the government always gives the reason that it is trying to protect information that would be harmful to the country if it were known. The question then becomes: Is it harmful to the country, or does the government just want to cover up a decision or action that it would rather not be public?

Frequently, the book is presented to the publisher before the government knows about it, and the publisher might also have a judgment on whether the information could hurt the country. In almost every case, however, the publisher's inclination is to resist any kind of censorship.

Some times in American history have been tougher than others for free speech. When I became president of Random House, the memories of the McCarthy hearings of the early 1950s, when many people had their careers destroyed after being accused of having communist sympathies, were still fresh in mind. The early 1970s under the Nixon administration were not all that pleasant, either.

The biggest free speech case of the Nixon era was of course the Pentagon Papers, the forty-seven-volume, seven-thousand-page history of American involvement in Vietnam from 1945 through 1968. Compiled in the late 1960s by a thirty-six-member team of analysts on the orders of Secretary of Defense Robert McNamara, the report, which was never supposed to be released to the public, revealed that the U.S. government had been systematically lying to the American people about the Vietnam War. The papers showed that even while the Johnson administration insisted that the war would be easily won and the number of casualties limited, it knew that was far from the truth.

One of the analysts on the project, Daniel Ellsberg, leaked the report to the *New York Times* and the *Washington Post*, which both published excerpts from the report in June 1971.

The Nixon White House got injunctions to force the papers to stop publication. The two cases were joined into one—*New York Times Co. v. United States*. On June 30, 1971, the Supreme Court ruled 6–3 that the government had not met the "burden of proof" to show why publishing the Pentagon Papers would endanger national security and therefore could not exercise "prior restraint" on the newspapers' right to publish.

That is the most well-known part of the Pentagon Papers story. But there was also a second act that involved book publishers.

Ellsberg had given a third copy of the report to Alaskan senator Mike Gravel (Ellsberg had offered the Papers to George McGovern, who declined because he thought it might hurt his presidential campaign). Gravel, who was the chair of the Senate Subcommittee on Buildings and Grounds, called an emergency meeting of his committee and began to read the Pentagon Papers out loud. After three hours, he broke down in tears and could not continue. He had achieved his purpose, though—the report was entered into the public record.

Gravel wanted to have the Pentagon Papers publicly available in a book. He convinced Beacon Press, a small house in Boston that was the publishing arm of the Unitarian Universalist Association, to publish the report.

It was a brave decision. Soon after Beacon announced its intention to publish the Pentagon Papers, Gobin Stair, its editor in chief, got a call at home from Nixon, who asked him not to do it. After the call, two FBI agents visited Beacon's offices and asked Stair to return the Papers.

The harassment only hardened Stair's resolve to publish, and Beacon released its four-volume version of the Pentagon Papers in October 1971. A few months later, the government filed charges against the house, claiming that it had received and published stolen government property. The strategy was pretty apparent—even though the administration had lost in its case against the *Times* and the *Post*, it could still deliver a message by taking out Beacon Press. It was about making publishers and potential whistleblowers think twice in the future.

By the summer of 1972, Beacon had already spent $45,000 on legal expenses, a significant sum for a small imprint. That year, I was the chair of the Association of American Publishers. I thought that, as a group, we had to do something to show support for Beacon Press, so I called an emergency meeting at the Biltmore Hotel in New York that was attended by about two hundred publishers and editors.

I called the whole thing "a sad, shabby affair" and suggested a legal defense fund for Beacon of $100,000, to which Random House gave the first $2,500. At the time, I told *Publishers Weekly* that the industry had to send a message back to the government that no matter how miserable it wanted to make things for us, publishers were going to battle to defend our rights under the First Amendment. "It's very hard to fight this kind of thing and run a business at the same time," I said. "One dissipates so much of his creative energy just trying to hold on to freedoms one should be able to take for granted."

For a publisher, these types of fights can be disastrous. Not only are they very time consuming, but the government, which has unlimited overhead and free legal advice, does not have the same constraints as a business. There's a saying that the worst thing you can ever have to do is go to court against the U.S. government. Even if the government doesn't win, it can make it so that your business is no longer viable.

In the end, Beacon got a break. The Nixon administration's obsession with subterfuge and secrecy did it in. On June 17, 1972, five burglars were caught breaking into the Democratic National Headquarters in the Watergate Hotel. By 1973, it was becoming clear that the burglary had ties all the way up to the White House and the Justice Department. Nixon, of course, was forced to resign in August 1974 after it became apparent that he had been involved in the cover-up. The Beacon Press case never went to court.

At Random House, we were about to have our own run-ins with another part of the government where we, even in a democratic society, assumed there should have been some secrecy. The question was how much.

Our dealings with the Central Intelligence Agency began in 1964, when we published *The Invisible Government*, by the journalists David Wise and Thomas Ross. The book, which was edited by Bob Loomis, argues that since the CIA's beginnings in 1947, the United States had built a massive espionage apparatus the scope of which Americans were completely unaware. (In the belief that to win the Cold War something had to be done to counteract the KGB, the CIA at its founding had been officially exempted from many of the oversight procedures to which other government agencies were subject.) *The Invisible Government* was the first book to critically examine the actions of the CIA. Among other things, Wise and Ross documented the agency's role in military coups in Iran and Guatemala, the Bay of Pigs invasion of Cuba, and ongoing efforts in Vietnam and Laos.

When CIA director John McCone learned about the book, he approached Bennett and offered to buy the whole print run of ten thousand copies. Bennett said he would happily sell the government the first run.

"What will you do then?" McCone asked.

Bennett said, "Well, we'd be out of stock, so we'd have to reprint it."

As you may have guessed, that was not McCone's intention, and the deal fell through. After we published the book, I later learned, McCone assigned a CIA team to enlist sympathetic journalists to pan it.

By 1970, the CIA was nearly twenty-five years old and deeply involved in top secret operations around the world. Victor Marchetti, a CIA operative, was disturbed by what he saw around him. Marchetti had joined the CIA in 1955 after getting a degree in Russian studies from Penn State. He rose through the ranks to become executive assistant to the deputy director of intelligence, a position that gave him a broad overview of the CIA's covert activities.

Marchetti quit the agency in 1969. Two years later, he had finished a novel, *The Rope-Dancer*, which portrays the spy agency as bureaucratic and ineffectual. To comply with the terms of the secrecy agreement he had signed in order to work at the CIA, Marchetti gave a copy of the manuscript to the organization for review before publication. The agency found nothing that compromised security and cleared it to be published, but it placed Marchetti under surveillance.

Grosset and Dunlap published the novel, which didn't sell well. Marchetti then began to work on an article for *Esquire* magazine that was to reveal more about the CIA's covert activities. Before it was published, Marchetti met David Obst, a literary agent with leftist political sympathies, who told Marchetti to forget the magazine article and turn it into a book. Knopf bought the proposal for the book, *The CIA and the Cult of Intelligence*, at auction for $40,000.

The book was to tell the story of what the CIA was actually up to around the world. That included its front businesses, such as the airlines and radio stations it ran; its role in tracking down Che Guevara in Bolivia; its secret base in Peru; and its part in the Gulf of Tonkin incident. Marchetti's main point was that obsession with secrecy and meddling in the internal affairs of other countries had grown more important to the CIA than its original mission, which was supposed to be collecting and analyzing intelligence.

CIA director William Colby was extremely disturbed when he found out that Marchetti was writing the book. In April 1972, Marchetti received a court order, instigated by the CIA's lawyers, to submit the book to the CIA for censorship prior to publication.

CIA employees, then and now, have to sign secrecy agreements before starting work at the agency. These include the stipulation that anything written for publication must be submitted to the agency for vetting before it is given to a publisher. In 1972, the legality of the agreements had not been tried in court. Marchetti, represented by the American Civil Liberties Union (ACLU), challenged the agreement by claiming that the CIA was infringing upon his First Amendment rights—basically arguing that you can't sign away your freedom of speech.

The court disagreed. Marchetti would have to hand over the book to the CIA for censorship before Knopf could publish it. Dan Okrent, the book's editor, was not even allowed to see it before the CIA was done with it. The court decision basically formalized the government's right to enforce secrecy contracts with its employees.

That was round one. In the summer of 1973, Marchetti—who was working with co-author John Marks, a former State Department analyst—sent the 517-page manuscript to the CIA. It came back with 339 different passages—anywhere from a few words to several paragraphs—deleted. In total, about 20 percent of the book was cut.

So we had a manuscript that had been literally sliced up with scissors. The government was clearly exercising its power to censor, and the only judge of whether that power was being abused was the person who did the censoring. We decided to take the government to court for infringing upon our right to publish—never before in American history had the government censored a book prior to publication. We believed that even if there were secrets the government had to keep, there should be some oversight.

I called Floyd Abrams, a lawyer who had worked on the Pentagon Papers and has since become one of the most prominent First Amendment lawyers in the country. He estimated that taking the case to court would cost about $50,000.

Before we continued, I knew it would be wise to speak with RCA. When the company had purchased Random House several years earlier, David Sarnoff had stressed that we should make no compromises that we would not make if we were still an independent publisher. Nevertheless, I knew that one of RCA's major clients, as a defense contractor, was the government, and its defense business brought in a lot more money than we did. So I called the RCA vice president who was responsible for overseeing Random House and a couple of executives over to talk about it. I told them that as a publisher, this is what I had to do to defend my business. I also invited Aryeh Neier, the head of the ACLU, who talked to them about freedom of the press and the importance of this case. The RCA executives were nervous, but to their credit, they did nothing to interfere.

We filed the suit in October 1973. In the time before it went to court in February 1974, Marchetti and the lawyers met several times with the CIA to challenge the deletions. On several, Marchetti argued that the information was either already in the public record or he had gathered it after his employment at the CIA had ended. The idea was to show the CIA that we were going to fight over every word; even before the trial, the deletions were reduced from 339 to 168. To me, it showed how arbitrary the editing process was.

The case was heard in Alexandria, Virginia, by Federal Judge Albert Bryan Jr., the same judge who had earlier decided for the CIA's right to censor the Marchetti book. The five highest-ranking CIA officials appeared to testify. We argued that the CIA could not simply censor information at will on the basis of national security—it had to concretely show that the information in question was actually classified, not just deemed so by the assertion of the censor.

Judge Bryan released his decision at the end of March 1974. Of the remaining 168 deletions, Bryan ruled that the CIA had failed to show proper cause for 141 of them—that left only 27 of the original 339 cuts by the CIA, less than 10 percent of what it thought was too sensitive for the public to know.

It was a tremendous victory for us. But because the CIA immediately filed an appeal, we decided to go ahead and publish the book as it was, with the 168 deletions. However, so that the public would be aware of where the censorship had occurred, instead of bridging those spaces over, we left white space, so readers could see what was being discussed before and after and how much had been removed. We printed the sections that had been restored in bold ink, so people would know what the CIA had attempted to censor. We planned to fill in the rest after the appeal, when the book came out in paperback.

Unfortunately, it wasn't over just yet. On appeal, Judge Clement Haynsworth, whom President Nixon had unsuccessfully nominated for the Supreme Court a few years earlier, threw out Bryan's decision. Haynsworth's opinion was that a judge couldn't referee what was really secret and what was not. Besides that, Haynsworth found, Marchetti "effectively relinquished his First Amendment rights" when he agreed to the secrecy contract.

In the end, the book ended up with 168 deletions, and the CIA had established that its right to enforce the secrecy contract superseded a former agent's First Amendment rights. On balance, we won a few victories, but the government won the war.

Thinking about it years later, I believe that Judge Haynsworth could not have been right on both counts. There has to be somebody in a democracy other than the party committing the act who can pass judgment on it. Otherwise, anything can be covered up forever. We still have the same problem today with terrorism cases, where a high amount of secrecy is necessary, but there is still no independent oversight to counteract the government's inclination toward restricting information.

By the mid-1970s, the CIA was under a lot of scrutiny. In 1974, Seymour Hersh, who had published *My Lai 4* with us a few years earlier, reported in the *New York Times* that the agency had, in violation of the 1947 National Security Act, compiled at least ten thousand dossiers on Americans involved in antiwar activities. After Nixon's resignation that year, Congress began to assert its right to oversee the executive branch and government agencies such as the CIA, resulting in investigations into the CIA's operations by a committee led by Frank Church, a Democratic senator from Idaho.

Starting in 1975, the Church Committee found the CIA not only had a role in assassinations and coups—both successful and attempted—in places such as the Republic of the Congo, Cuba, Chile, and the Dominican Republic, but that the CIA had opened more than two hundred thousand pieces of domestic mail without a warrant or the knowledge of the U.S. Postal Service.

As a result of the committee's findings, President Ford issued an executive order banning the CIA from assassinating foreign leaders. The Foreign Intelligence Surveillance Act (FISA) and the Foreign Intelligence Surveillance Court (FISC), which are supposed to regulate wiretapping and spying within the United States, grew out of the committee's recommendations.

The Vietnam War was also reaching its end in 1975, and it was against this backdrop that more CIA agents began to write about their experiences. In 1975, Penguin published *Inside the Company* by Philip Agee, a former CIA agent who had developed Marxist views. Agee's memoir not only recounted various CIA misdeeds, but also included an index listing the names of 250 CIA agents in several countries. When the proposal for Agee's book came around to us, we didn't bid for it. We thought that Agee's actions in exposing agents in place were, if not illegal, then certainly dangerous and unethical.

Shortly after Agee's book was published by Stonehill, Richard Welch, the CIA's station chief in Athens, Greece, was assassinated. Welch had not been named in Agee's book, but he had been outed in *CounterSpy*, a magazine funded by Norman Mailer that was dedicated to investigating the CIA. Welch had also been named in the Athens press as a CIA spy.

Welch's assassination generated a backlash against the Church Committee recommendations and increased the CIA's drive to stop its agents from their writing endeavors. George H.W. Bush, who was director of the CIA for the last year of Ford's presidency, pushed hard after Welch's killing to pass the Intelligence Identities Protection Act, a law that makes it a felony to expose a CIA agent's cover. (Ironically, that law was the crux of the more recent case involving CIA agent Valerie Plame and accusations that George W. Bush's administration deliberately exposed her after her husband published an op-ed in the *New York Times* questioning the administration's case for war with Iraq.)

It was also during this period that we signed a book by Frank Snepp, another disgruntled CIA agent, though one with far different politics from those of Philip Agee.

A southerner from a patriotic family, Snepp had been recruited into the CIA in 1968 by one of his professors at Columbia University, where he was getting a master's degree in international relations. Within a year, the agency posted him to Saigon.

In Vietnam, Snepp compiled intelligence, interrogated prisoners, cabled reports back to Langley, and briefed the press. His disillusion began in the waning days of the war. As the North Vietnamese Army approached Saigon, Snepp began to produce reports calling for assistance for Vietnamese who had worked with the Americans during the war. If the United States did not come up with a plan to evacuate its Vietnamese collaborators, Snepp warned, their lives were very much in danger.

Snepp left Saigon by helicopter on April 29, 1975, one of the last Americans to exit as decades of U.S. involvement in Vietnam collapsed. As he flew out, he looked down with shame and a sense of betrayal at the Vietnamese crowding around the embassy below and begging for help. He also knew that the American bureaucracy in Saigon had failed to destroy files that the North Vietnamese could use to identify Vietnamese who had helped the United States.

Upon his return to CIA headquarters, Snepp called for an investigation into the treatment of our Vietnamese allies. He felt that instead of any serious consideration of what had happened, the whole affair was in danger of being swept under the rug. Through a friend who was a literary agent, Snepp submitted a book proposal about the last days in Saigon to Jim Silberman.

Snepp reasoned that since he didn't plan to reveal any secret information in his book—he said everything in it was already part of the public record—he was not bound to give the CIA his manuscript for censorship. Our in-house lawyer, Gerald Hollingsworth, reviewed the proposal and came to the conclusion that Snepp's position could be legally supported. I approved the project. Bob Loomis, who had edited *The Invisible Government*, signed on as the book's editor.

When word got out at the CIA that Snepp was planning to write a book, he was asked to sign an affidavit that he would let the CIA review any manuscript he produced. Snepp refused and resigned from the agency.

At Random House, we tried to keep the whole project under wraps. Silberman, Loomis, Hollingsworth, and I were the only people in the house who knew about it. Loomis and Snepp met at a park near Random House so that Snepp would not be seen in the office. We did no prepublication publicity. While the CIA knew that Snepp was writing a book, we weren't sure if it knew *who* was going to publish it. We didn't want the agency to take preemptive action, as it had done with Marchetti. Loomis really made an extraordinary effort. The flap copy was typed and photographed in-house and sent to the printer only at the last minute. We didn't announce the book in our catalog, so the sales team had to write a note to bookstores around the country telling them they were going to get a shipment of books they weren't expecting and not to send them back.

Without any prerelease publicity or copies sent to critics for reviews, we had to find a way to publicize the book. Snepp went to *60 Minutes* and arranged to have the show do a segment on him the day before the book was to be released in November 1977. Loomis knew about the deal with *60 Minutes* and let Mike Wallace, the correspondent, know that since there had to be some print publicity for the book as well, he had made a deal with Seymour Hersh to write a story about the book in the *New York Times*. Hersh's story would appear on the Monday morning the book came out, which would be after *60 Minutes* aired on Sunday night.

Without telling Loomis, however, Snepp also went to the *Washington Post* and *Newsweek* with the story. When Loomis found out, he had to tell Hersh that the exclusive deal they had made was off. Hersh said he was going to publish right away, which meant that the news would not be broken on *60 Minutes*.

When Wallace found out, he was livid. He called me, clearly very upset—I remember sitting in my office with the phone held away from my ear—and demanded I fire Loomis. Of course, I didn't do that. We thought that *60 Minutes* might kill the story, but it ended up airing the piece. It turned out to be the show's highest-rated episode up to that time—all the publicity had only generated more interest in the segment on the show, though I'm sure that didn't placate Wallace, who had lost his scoop.

So Snepp's book, *Decent Interval*, came out in a big way. It was, in retrospect, horrible timing. Not only had the CIA already suffered through the Marchetti and Agee books, but another former agent, John Stockwell, had just released *In Search of Enemies*, published by W.W. Norton, an exposé of CIA incompetence in Angola. For the agency, it was all extremely embarrassing, and CIA director Stansfield Turner decided to come down on Snepp as an example to other would-be whistleblowers.

The government sued Snepp for breaking his secrecy agreement. It also charged him with doing "irreparable harm" to national security. The government asked that Snepp turn over all his royalties from the book and that he be required to submit all of his future writings regarding intelligence activities to the agency for prepublication censorship.

I wasn't all that surprised when I heard about the lawsuit. Once again, I had to go to the executives at RCA and give them the unwelcome news that we were again going to get involved in a case against the government. In the meantime, we took out a full-page ad in the *Times* decrying the government's attempt to censor a whistleblower whom I felt was only calling attention to our country's shameful behavior as we made our hasty retreat from Vietnam.

Unfortunately, once Snepp's case got to court in August 1978, it was a train wreck. Snepp's lawyers argued to Federal Judge Oren Lewis that since the book contained no secrets, there was no reason for him to submit it for prepublication review. Lewis was not at all sympathetic to that line of reasoning. Following the Marchetti precedent, Lewis decided the case not on First Amendment grounds but on the basis of the secrecy contract Snepp had signed. Lewis ruled, as the government requested, that Snepp not only had to give the government all the money he made from the book—two years of work—but that in the future he would have to submit all his intelligence-related writing to the agency for review.

Snepp appealed and the case went to the Supreme Court, which reviewed it without taking any new arguments from Snepp's lawyers or the government. In an unsigned judgment, the justices ruled 6–3 to let the lower court's decision stand—the existence of the secrecy contract was enough to compel Snepp to submit his writing to the agency, the court found, regardless of whether he had revealed actual secrets.

In *Irreparable Harm*, Snepp's 1999 memoir, he detailed his research years later into the case files of Justices Thurgood Marshall and William Brennan. He found that Justice Lewis Powell, a military intelligence officer in World War II, drafted the judgment and was the animating force behind the majority ruling. Justice Powell was joined by Justices Harry Blackmun, William Rehnquist, Warren Burger, Byron White, and Potter Stewart.

In the dissent, Justice John Paul Stevens, who was joined by Justices Thurgood Marshall and William Brennan, wrote that since no secrets had been revealed in Snepp's book, "the confidentiality that Snepp's contract was designed to protect has not been compromised."

In the end, Snepp's loss resulted in secrecy contracts being instituted as terms of employment with dozens of other federal agencies. Many corporations now also require employees to sign similar agreements before they begin their jobs.

All in all, it was a terrible defeat for us, but even worse for Snepp, who was just crushed. He'd not only lost his career and all his royalties, but many of his old friends accused him of treachery and refused to speak to him.

With America today involved in wars in places like Iraq and Afghanistan, I still think about Snepp. It is to be hoped that Snepp, who has suffered from his decision to go public, has at least helped to make us aware of what can happen to those who help America after we leave a war. It is also likely, in my opinion, that because of Snepp's fate, fewer people will be willing to identify the problem as it exists, although in an open society there always seems to be a surprising number of people who will step up to what they think is right, even in tough situations.

I had only one more direct contact with the CIA while working at Random House. In the mid-1980s, I got a phone call at my desk.

"Bob, this is Bill Casey," a man said in a friendly voice.

"Bill Casey from the CIA?" I asked.

"Yes, Bob, Bill Casey," he said.

Of course I wondered why the head of the CIA was calling me. "What can I do for you, Mr. Casey?" I asked.

"Well," he said, "we hear that you're publishing a book, and in the book you might be committing treason. So I thought I'd tell you about it and maybe we could work something out to see if this was true or not."

He didn't identify the book so I asked which one he meant. It turned out it was Seymour Hersh's *The Target Is Destroyed*, which detailed the shooting down of Korean Airlines Flight 007 by the Russians in 1983. We were set to publish it in 1986.

Casey continued. "I just thought between you and me, Bob, that you could send me the manuscript," he said. "I'll read it or have it very confidentially looked over and let you know if there is any material in it that would later cause you trouble, and that way we can avoid it."

"We usually don't send out books in advance," I said. "It's called 'prior restraint.' Why don't you let me check on it? It's very kind of you to call, and if I can work it out, I'll get back to you."

I hung up, called Floyd Abrams, and sent Floyd the book. He said there was absolutely nothing in it that could be treason. I still don't know what Casey was worried about. The book did contain some details of U.S. intelligence activities, but nothing that was groundbreaking news.

We published the book, and I never heard from Bill Casey again.

For Random House, nothing good came out of the Nixon administration, even when I made my best effort.

In the early 1970s, I actually made several trips to the White

House to meet with Henry Kissinger, who had called me out of the blue to invite me to breakfast. We would share small talk, with Kissinger always filling me in on the gossip of the day. He'd then ask me about the state of publishing and the marketplace. I was delighted to tell him everything I knew and both flattered and interested in meeting with him. I knew he was thinking about writing his memoirs and hoped the visits meant that he would offer them to Random House first. I was surprised when I eventually got a call from Marvin Josephson, Kissinger's book agent and the head of ICM, who thought I would be delighted to know that Random House would be one of four publishers "authorized" to bid on Kissinger's memoirs.

For the most part I had the feeling that books by major political figures were important, but as they were almost certain to be published, a publisher should buy one based only on a projection of sales. I thought that the glamour of the authors frequently led to overbidding, and this certainly seemed likely to be the case with the Kissinger book. I also felt, perhaps with some arrogance, that Random House was a special place.

So when Josephson called, those feelings came together with a feeling that I'd been slightly used by Kissinger, much as I enjoyed our White House breakfasts. So without asking any other opinions, I told Josephson that there would be only three publishers bidding on Kissinger's book, and Random House would not be among them. I might today have done it differently and simply put in a bid for what I thought the book was worth and let it go at that. Kissinger's memoirs, which eventually came out in three volumes, were published by Simon & Schuster.

Then there was Kissinger's boss, Richard Nixon.

Not long after Nixon resigned, the legendary agent Irving "Swifty" Lazar, invited me to lunch to discuss a memoir that Nixon, his client, wanted to write. Swifty, who had represented authors from Lauren Bacall to Vladimir Nabokov, was quite a character. He was in his sixties, very short, and always wore extremely well-tailored suits and his signature thick, black-rimmed glasses. He was famous for the post-Oscar parties he gave every year in Los Angeles, which always included dozens of A-list names.

He was also known for making huge deals but not necessarily always telling the truth. I first met Swifty one day when I was at lunch with Bennett Cerf. Swifty was eating at another table, and, after the introduction, Bennett asked him why he was in New York.

"Well, Bennett, you know I'm Herman Wouk's agent," he said. "I sold his book *Marjorie Morningstar* to Warner Brothers. His lawyer is some damn professor at Columbia University and I can't get him to sign the contract. So I'm going up to see the professor to tell him, 'For God's sake, can you stop correcting papers and read this contract?'"

Swifty apparently didn't think the book was a great candidate for a movie, because he added: "If he doesn't do it, somebody at Warner Brothers is going to read *Marjorie Morningstar*, and we'll all be in trouble!"

One day a very excited Bob Gottlieb came in and said, "Swifty Lazar just offered me the third volume of Noël Coward's autobiography. He wants a $200,000 advance and I want to make an offer right away."

I told Bob that was fine, and he rushed away. A few weeks later, Bob walked down to my office and said, "Well, we're not getting the Noël Coward book."

"Bob, that's outrageous," I said. "What did Swifty do to you? You said you were going to accept his offer."

Bob said, "I accepted his offer right after I left your office."

"Then what happened?" I asked.

"Swifty just called me and told me that Noël Coward didn't really want to write a third volume!"

As far as our discussion of Nixon's memoir at lunch, Swifty asked if Random House would be interested.

Playing the wise guy, I asked, "Is it going to be fiction or nonfiction?"

Swifty wasn't in the mood to kid around—he was trying to get a big number to take back to Nixon.

I thought about it for a moment. Publishing can be a very intimate business. While that's not a big deal for a lot of books, there are certain books for which you should really admire the author if you are going to publish him, because you're going to be very involved with that person—he has to meet with the publicity people, you have to come up with a sales campaign, and you need to launch the book with a party or event. Back in those days—this is less true today—a house and its principals often became identified with the authors it published.

When I considered it, I had no problem telling Swifty that Random House would not be putting in a bid.

6

THE RUSSIANS

THE RUSSIANS CAME INTO MY LIFE IN OCTOBER 1970, WHEN I WENT to Moscow as part of a delegation representing the Association of American Publishers (AAP). The idea behind the trip was to have an exchange with the people running the Soviet publishing industry, make contacts, and learn about their business and tell them about ours. We also wanted to convince them to sign the Universal Copyright Convention. Back then, the Soviets just took any foreign book they wanted, had it translated, and published it without entering into a contract and without paying royalties to the publisher or author.

Brad Wiley, the head of John Wiley & Sons, one of the country's oldest publishing houses—the house had, for example, published James Fenimore Cooper's *The Last of the Mohicans* in 1826—was the motivating force behind the trip. He had already led a previous group to Moscow in 1962. In 1970, he was the chair of the AAP, and although I knew him only casually, he asked me to be vice chair of the organization, which is how I became included in the trip and started, what was for me, a wonderful friendship with Brad. Two other AAP officers—Mark Carroll, the head of Harvard University Press, and Edward McCabe, the head of the Grolier Society—plus Bob Frase, vice president of the association and its expert on copyright, rounded out our group.

To get to Russia, we first flew to Paris, where we switched to Aeroflot, and I got my first taste of the Soviet Union. I'm glad I didn't know at the time that Aeroflot would become notorious for its high number of plane crashes. Its customer service wasn't great, either.

We were practically the only passengers on the plane—there may have been three or four others. I quickly grabbed a whole row of seats so I could stretch out and sleep. A flight attendant soon came by and told me I had to move to the front. The attendants then roped off all the seats so that we had to sit three in a row just as though the plane were sold out.

I kept running into little things like that as I learned about the Soviet Union. For example, it was hard to get a waiter's attention in a restaurant, because there was no tipping. And it was almost impossible to get a taxi in the morning, because the drivers were not paid a percentage of the money they earned, but to show they were working they had to drive a certain distance every day, with or without passengers. So in the morning they were all out on the Moscow ring road treating it like it was a racetrack, piling up their mileage.

We landed in Moscow at six o'clock in the evening. Sheremetyevo International Airport was big, clean, modern, and nearly totally empty. Our welcoming committee consisted of a group of Soviet publishing officials and a few people from the U.S. embassy. As we drove into the city, there was hardly any traffic on the road even though it was what should have been rush hour.

They brought us to the Sovietskaiya Historical Hotel, which, we were told, was used to house very important dignitaries. It was a mammoth place, with a cavernous lobby, hallways that were wider than the suburban streets in Scarsdale, and, from what I could tell, very few guests. I was set up in a suite that had a living room with a microwave-sized shortwave radio, a black-and-white television, a lot of overstuffed furniture, a cabinet lined with tea sets and figurines, and a grand piano.

That evening, Boris Stukalin, the head of the Soviet publishing industry, hosted a dinner for us in one of the hotel's private dining rooms. It turned out that I would get to know Stukalin pretty well over the following years. At around five-foot-ten, he was a box of a man—thickset with a stolid demeanor. He could be quite charming when he wanted, although if you said something that upset him he could very quickly freeze you out. That first meeting was as friendly as we ever got with each other.

Stukalin and his subordinates had arranged an elaborate feast. We had several courses, starting with caviar and then moving on to cold meats, chicken Kiev, and ice cream, all washed down with white wine and many, many shots of vodka. Stukalin told us that he didn't expect our visit to turn us into communists, but he asked us to approach everything with an open mind. After he and Brad Wiley had given several toasts, Stukalin said that since the cult of personality was over in Russia, they should let the rest of us talk as well.

As there were no women at our dinner, one of the lower-ranking Russians held up his glass and proposed a round for our mothers. He told us, "In Russia, this is a toast we do not think about, we do not probe, we just drink." So we did.

The toasts went on for quite a while. Just when you would think they were ending, one of the Soviets would think of something else to say, and they would refill the glasses with vodka. We couldn't do anything about that, but when the toasts seemed to come to the end, Ed McCabe, the chair of Grolier, got caught up in the moment and decided he wanted to give still another one. I don't think any of us were pleased.

It didn't take long for it to become clear that while the Russians were going to roll out the red carpet for us, they weren't serious about signing the copyright convention. The deal they had going—taking our books and printing whatever they wanted—was working just fine for them. As I understood it, occasionally, if they liked an author, they would pay him something. For example, an American writer named Mitchell Wilson, who wrote a novel called *Live with Lightning*, was very popular in the Soviet Union, though he was little known in the United States. I believe the Soviets paid him royalties. (His daughter, Victoria "Vicky" Wilson, has for many years been one of the best editors at Knopf.)

We were in the Soviet Union for two weeks, and they kept us very busy, not only during the daytime but in the evenings. At night, however, Stukalin and the other higher-ups went home and had their apparatchiks make sure we all stayed together, taking us to the circus, or the opera, or some other event, and always plying us with vodka. During the day, we visited publishing houses and printing plants in Moscow, Leningrad (now Saint Petersburg), and Minsk.

As we spoke with Soviet publishers, I was surprised to find that at least a few regarded me almost as something of a pornographer, because Random House had just published Philip Roth's *Portnoy's Complaint*. The editor in chief of one state-owned publishing house did little to hide his contempt for me. When we had lunch with him, he said that it was the job of the publisher to protect the morals of the people, and that he thought the only reason I had published *Portnoy* was for profit. This was obviously something very distasteful to him. Books in the Soviet Union, I got the idea, were meant for education rather than entertainment.

In Minsk, we went on a tour of the city and were told about the fighting there during World War II. When the Germans invaded the Soviet Union in 1941, they took control of the city. Three years later, when the Russians were driving out the Germans, it was the site of intense fighting that destroyed nearly everything. Our hosts brought us to one of the only houses in the city that was still standing after the war. The rest of Minsk had been rebuilt in the Soviet style, so you had a lot of boxy concrete buildings and wide avenues. It made a big impression on me—being there, you could really imagine how much the Russians had suffered during the war and how little we really knew about it in the United States.

I also inadvertently learned a lesson about dealing with the Soviets in Minsk. One morning, they took our delegation to a printing plant. When we arrived, they gave us each a tumbler of vodka to drink, and I mean a *big* tumbler of vodka, not just a shot. It was before lunch, and the last thing I needed was a glass of booze. So when I thought nobody was looking, I poured it into a plant.

I wasn't as sly as I thought—the manager of the plant, a big, burly man, saw me do it. He marched straight over with the interpreter and said, "You have just insulted us. You have insulted the Soviet Union. You are not drinking with us. I saw you put the vodka in the plant."

I was shocked at his vehemence, but I responded very calmly, probably because when you are speaking through an interpreter, you want to be sure they get your words. I said, "You have just insulted *me*. I have traveled eight thousand miles to come here to try and improve publishing relations between the Soviet Union and the United States. Your government has given me a very heavy schedule for the day, with a lot of afternoon meetings, and you, the head of this plant, have given me a tumbler of vodka to drink. You must know that if I drink it all, it will be very difficult for me to carry out the schedule."

I added, "Because you have insulted me by trying to force me to drink your vodka, I don't think I want to have lunch with you. Please tell the group that I have gone out to the bus and will wait for them there."

When I finished, he completely changed his tune. All of a sudden, he was very nice. "I did not know your customs," he said. "I did not know you didn't drink at lunch, and please don't go out to the bus. I apologize."

I realized that when the Russians were being firm with you, it was best to treat them in the same manner. It was hard, though. With all the minders watching you, the sense of being controlled began to feel suffocating. I now recognize that this was the type of social control the Soviet authorities used over the whole society.

The Soviet Union was something of a mystery at the time, and I was happy for the chance to go there and see firsthand how communism was working. It didn't take long, though, before I started to feel a sense of isolation and paranoia.

In our hotel, there was a woman on every floor who sat at a desk. Her whole job was to keep an eye on things. Since there were hardly any guests, there was very little to keep an eye on. But every time you came back to your room, there she was.

I had been told that it was a good idea to bring some small gifts, so I carried over some records of classical music—Beethoven, Brahms, and so on (I didn't bring any Tchaikovsky as I figured the Russians had him covered). When I returned to my room after one of our first days in Moscow, I found the records exactly where I had left them, but the plastic wrap around them had been removed. It was pretty unnerving.

I mostly noticed how the Russian bureaucrats totally controlled publishing in the country. As the head of the publishing industry, Stukalin decided the amount of paper sent to printing plants. I learned that he didn't have to be heavy-handed and shut down publishing houses in order to censor—if he didn't like the books a house wanted to publish, he just cut off the paper supply.

It's like what the dissident Natan Sharansky, who was jailed and eventually immigrated to Israel, said many years later, when someone asked him, "Is it true they don't let people into bookstores in Moscow?"

"Of course they let people into bookstores," he said. "They just don't let in books."

To say that the Soviet Union had not been anywhere near the front of my mind before the trip to Moscow would be an understatement. At the time, I was totally overwhelmed with running Random House and trying to be a good father and family man—I coached my sons' soccer and basketball teams in Scarsdale and occasionally played tennis.

But when we returned from the Soviet Union, I found that I kept thinking about what it would be like to be a writer there, what would happen to you if you opposed the party line, and how tight and arbitrary that line could be.

I knew that I needed to learn more about the situation in the country, so I called Ed Kline, someone with whom I'd had a long history, though we didn't know each other very well. In the early 1950s, when they were both in their twenties, Ed had dated my first cousin Ann Bernstein. Ann became sick with terminal cancer. During the time Ann was in the hospital, Ed got to know her best friend, Jill Herman, who happened to be my secretary at Simon & Schuster. After Ann died, Jill and Ed eventually got together and married.

Ed was heir to a chain of department stores—Kline Brothers Company—that was located in the Midwest. After his father died, Ed took over the family business. He worked very hard, but I don't think he found retailing fulfilling. In the early 1960s, he started to study Russian literature as a hobby. He hired a Russian language tutor and began trying to read Russian books in the original language.

In 1968, he co-founded Chekhov Press with Max Hayward, a professor at Oxford who was a translator and perhaps the leading expert on Russian literature. The sole intent of the house was to publish Russian writers in English. Their first two books, which they released in 1970, were a collection of poems by Joseph Brodsky and *Hope Against Hope*, Nadezhda Mandelstam's terrifying account of life under Stalin in the 1930s.

Though Ed hadn't had a particular interest in human rights when he began the press, he soon found that many contemporary Russian authors were writing at great risk to themselves. When the news got out that our AAP group was traveling to Moscow to meet with the Soviet publishing authorities, Ed called and asked to speak with me.

I scheduled him in for a brief meeting right before we left. He looked and spoke every bit like an eccentric academic—with disheveled hair and a distracted, intellectual manner—and nothing like a man who made a living by selling underwear to ladies in the Midwest. He was very intense and obviously knowledgeable. I have to admit that I was so busy and preoccupied with other things that I didn't pay much attention to what he said.

When I returned, I immediately called Ed. "Why didn't you tell me about what's going on in Russia?" I asked.

"I tried," he said.

We set up a dinner and began to meet on a regular basis. It was the first step of a process that would go on for well over the next decade, as I learned about Soviet dissident writers, who have always amazed me. A few whom I would meet personally in the coming years included Vasily Aksyonov; Lev Kopelev and his wife, Raisa Orlova; Andrei Amalrik; Natan Sharansky; and Andrei Sakharov and his amazing wife, Elena Bonner. They were so determined to express themselves that many gave up everything—comfortable careers, homes, families, their country, and their health. Some even lost their lives.

* * *

At the time I first went to Moscow in 1970, the Soviet dissident movement was in its infancy.

While Stalin was in power, from 1929 to 1953, no dissent was tolerated within the Soviet Union—anyone who spoke out in the slightest was either executed or sent to the gulag. There is no consensus among historians as to how many people died under Stalin's regime, but estimates—which include deaths in purges, the gulag, and the famines that followed the forced collectivization of agriculture—run up to 60 million. (Let me say that figure again: *60 million.* It has always staggered me when people mention these huge figures—like the 36 million who died in China in the famine of 1958 to 1961, and the 72 million who died in World War II—especially when I consider that we are still living in a world where violence of this kind could break out again.)

Then, in February 1956, at the Twentieth Party Congress, the new premier, Nikita Khrushchev, gave a five-hour speech denouncing the "cult of personality" and the arrest and execution of Communist Party members during Stalin's reign. After the speech, as millions of people began to return home from the labor camps, a small window for discussion opened, but the government still had total power to suppress dissent, which it exercised at its whim.

For example, Boris Pasternak couldn't get *Dr. Zhivago*, with its underlying theme that the state can crush the will of the individual, published in Russia after he completed it in 1955. He had to smuggle the manuscript out of the country. In 1957, Giangiacomo Feltrinelli, an Italian Communist who ran a publishing house, published it in Russian and in Italian translation. (Pantheon soon published an English translation in the United States, where it was a bestseller.) When Pasternak won the Nobel Prize in Literature in 1958, the Soviet leadership was incensed and attacked the choice in violent language. The Soviet press called Zhivago "an infuriated moral freak" and Pasternak "a malicious literary snob." Though Pasternak had initially accepted the prize, he later wilted under the pressure—afraid he would be forced to emigrate—and refused it. He died two years later of lung cancer.

In 1962, however, Khrushchev, somewhat inexplicably, allowed the publication of *One Day in the Life of Ivan Denisovich,*

Aleksandr Solzhenitsyn's depiction of the brutality of life in Stalin's prison camps. The next year, though, the young Joseph Brodsky, who wrote poetry and was not considered a political writer, was arrested and charged with being a social "parasite." The accusation was that Brodsky had shirked "useful" work in order to write and translate poems. Further, he had never studied how to write poetry in school. In a famous exchange, the judge asked: "Who recognizes you as a poet? Who enrolled you in the ranks of poets?"

Brodsky replied: "No one. Who enrolled me in the ranks of humankind?"

He was sentenced to five years of internal exile and did two years of hard labor before the regime—which was embarrassed by the international publication of his trial proceedings—relented and let him return to Leningrad. (Brodsky was exiled from Russia in 1972; he moved to the United States and won the Nobel Prize in Literature in 1987.)

By the early 1960s, a new generation of dissidents was coming of age in Moscow, including many people I would in the following years come to know and publish. This loosely organized group included writers and dissidents such as Vladimir Bukovsky, the identical twin brothers Roy and Zhores Medvedev, Anatoly Marchenko, Larisa Bogoraz, Andrei Amalrik, Pavel Litvinov, and Valery Chalidze.

The relative thaw ended in October 1964, when Khrushchev lost power and was succeeded as Communist Party secretary by Leonid Brezhnev, who upped the level of state repression. The government signaled its change in position when it arrested and prosecuted the writers Yuli Daniel and Andrei Sinyavsky, who had both, using pseudonyms, published stories and novels in the West that mocked the absurdities of life under Soviet Communism. In one of Daniel's stories, for example, he describes a fictional "Public Murder Day" in which the state encourages citizens to kill one another. In another story, a man can ensure that he will have a son if he thinks of Karl Marx during sex.

The trial ended in early 1966. Daniel received five years of hard labor and Sinyavsky got seven. But instead of intimidating the dissident movement, as the prosecutions were intended to do, the case is now credited as being the start of a more organized opposition to Soviet repression. Acting against the expectations of the government, the Moscow dissidents signed petitions, attended the trial, and openly protested the treatment of the writers.

The Moscow dissidents communicated through samizdat newspapers. In 1968, they began to publish the *Chronicle of Current Events*. Compiled underground and released bimonthly, the *Chronicle* featured detailed descriptions of human rights abuses committed throughout the country, including dispatches smuggled out of the gulag. It was basically an extensive compilation of the state's crimes against its citizens.

The dissidents also sometimes protested publicly, at great peril to themselves. On August 25, 1968, eight members of the Moscow circle gathered at Red Square to demonstrate against the invasion of Czechoslovakia. They carried signs that read "Shame to Occupants" and "For Your Freedom and Ours." Within minutes, they were assaulted by the secret police and hauled off to jail. Almost all were sent to internal exile, labor camps, or psychiatric hospitals where they were "diagnosed" with conditions such as schizophrenia.

The biggest name to join the cause of the Moscow dissidents—and the most damaging to the regime—was the physicist Andrei Sakharov. A national hero, Sakharov was the brilliant young scientist who had led the team that developed the atomic and hydrogen bombs for the Soviets in the wake of World War II. As such, he was a testament to science in the Soviet Union—he was given the Hero of Socialist Labor award three times. Sakharov lived about as well as a person could in the Soviet Union, with a high salary, special housing, a chauffeur, bodyguards, and access to consumer goods available only to the Soviet elite.

By the late 1950s, though, he began to have doubts about the direction of the Soviet nuclear program. He wrote to Khrushchev to say that atmospheric nuclear tests weren't necessary—he feared the effects of fallout and an escalation in the arms race. He kept up a quiet campaign, urging the Soviet authorities to scale back their nuclear weapons program and to work toward a nonproliferation treaty with the United States. He lent his name to human rights causes by taking actions such as signing a petition that protested the trial of Yuli Daniel and Andrei Sinyavsky.

Sakharov finally went public in 1968 with the publication of his essay "Reflections on Progress, Peaceful Coexistence, and Intellectual Freedom," which was circulated openly in the West—the *New York Times* published the whole text—and by samizdat in the Eastern Bloc. In it, Sakharov wrote that the communist and capitalist worlds needed to work together to avoid the dangers of nuclear and environmental destruction. He called for tolerance between the two systems and respect for freedom of thought.

Sakharov made two main points in the essay. The first was that humans stood on the brink of disaster. "The division of mankind threatens it with destruction," he wrote. "Civilization is imperiled by: a universal thermonuclear war, catastrophic hunger for most of mankind, stupefaction from the narcotic of 'mass culture' and bureaucratized dogmatism, a spreading of mass myths that put entire peoples and continents under the power of cruel and treacherous demagogues."

Though written in 1968, those words could have been jotted down yesterday.

Sakharov's second argument in the essay was that "intellectual freedom is essential to human society" and "the only guarantee against an infection of people by mass myths, which, in the hands of treacherous hypocrites and demagogues, can be transformed into bloody dictatorship. Freedom of thought is the only guarantee of the feasibility of a scientific democratic approach to politics, economy and culture."

The Soviet leadership was shaken—its leading scientist and one of the country's biggest heroes had just very openly fallen out of lockstep. In the coming years, the government would tighten its grip on him even as he developed into one of the world's greatest advocates for peace and human rights.

As I learned about Sakharov and the other dissidents, I thought there was one obvious thing that Random House could do to help them: publish their books.

As it happened, Ash Green, an editor at Knopf, was in the process of editing *Let History Judge*, a history of Stalinism by Roy Medvedev, a Marxist historian who had become a scathing critic of the Soviet system. The book, which we published in 1972, explored the damage that totalitarianism wreaks on both individuals and society. Though some criticism of Stalin had been allowed after Khrushchev's 1956 speech, Medvedev went too far for the Soviet authorities. His book was barred from publication in Russia, and Medvedev was expelled from the Communist Party.

I brought Ed Kline to meet Ash Green, who had studied Eastern European history and had an interest in books from the area. I told Ash that he should publish the first five books that Ed recommended to him.

Before long, my personal life began to intersect with the dissidents.

In 1972, my son Peter graduated from Brown University and took a summer trip to Israel and then spent five weeks in the Soviet Union. While he was there, he happened to meet Vera Chalidze, who was the granddaughter of Maxim Litvinov, Stalin's foreign minister, and the wife of Valery Chalidze, a dissident at the center of the Moscow movement.

Like Sakharov, Valery Chalidze was a physicist, but he had also devoted himself to the study of Soviet law. As a human rights advocate, his approach was to point out to the Soviet government the areas where it had violated its own laws and constitution in its zeal to suppress dissidents. It was a controversial strategy—many other dissidents thought there was no use in trying to call the Soviet government to account. Chalidze, though, kept at it, and in 1969 he began to publish *Social Issues*, a samizdat journal devoted to questions of Soviet law and its relation to civil rights.

The following year, Chalidze, Sakharov, and another dissident named Andrei Tverdokhlebov founded the Moscow Committee for Human Rights. The purpose was to hold the Soviet government accountable for human rights violations, though the committee was also insistent that its actions were all within the letter and spirit of Soviet law—the organizers claimed that they were simply offering "consultative assistance" to the government on human rights issues. The committee also offered advice to Soviet citizens who felt that their human rights had been violated.

The committee was a major step forward for the dissident movement in Russia. As the first nongovernmental human rights organization within the Soviet Union, it was an attempt to establish the beginnings of a civil society. But as the committee took on causes such as compulsory confinement in mental hospitals and the trials of various dissidents, the regime didn't react well. Chalidze was forced to stop his work as a physics researcher.

Though Peter did not meet Valery Chalidze in Moscow in 1972, he had a good conversation with Vera, who told him that Valery had been invited to speak at some American universities. Peter told her that they should come and have dinner with the Bernstein family if they made it to New York.

As it happened, Valery Chalidze had received an invitation to lecture on human rights issues at Georgetown University, followed by one to speak at NYU. Normally, of course, the Soviet Union wasn't likely to let a nonconformist like Chalidze out of the country, so it was very surprising when he was granted a visa. The unspoken deal, it seems, was that Chalidze was more or less informed that he could accept the invitation and go abroad—with the high likelihood that he would never be allowed back—or stay in Russia and run the risk of being sent to the gulag.

When Chalidze and his wife arrived in New York, he arranged to meet me in my office at Random House. He came in on a day in December, and the first thing he told me, through a translator, was that he had just lost his Soviet citizenship. He said that a man from the Soviet consulate had come to his hotel room that morning and asked to verify his identity. When Chalidze handed over his passport, the man put it in his pocket and told him that the Supreme Soviet had decreed that he was stripped of his citizenship and barred from returning home.

I immediately took a liking to Chalidze. Darkly handsome and then in his mid-thirties, he was an outgoing and brilliant man. He was also very particular about doing things his way—for around the first three years he was in New York, he always spoke through a translator, because he didn't want to talk in broken English. When he finally began to speak English, he was quite fluent.

In exile in New York, Chalidze hooked up with Ed Kline and set up Khronika Press, a subsidiary of the not-for-profit Chekhov Publishing Corporation that focused on publishing Russian-language books by dissidents. He also founded *A Chronicle of Human Rights in the USSR*, a periodical devoted to recording human rights abuses in the Soviet Union as well as political reactions in the West. It was a counterpart to the *Chronicle of Current Events*, which was being published sporadically in Moscow as the Soviet regime worked on shutting it down.

I also signed Chalidze to write a book, *To Defend These Rights*, which was a rather technical analysis of the Soviet legal system. It is an interesting and important book, but didn't sell very well. I later concluded that it was perhaps too detailed for the American public to absorb.

In May 1973, shortly after Chalidze arrived in the United States, I went to Moscow for the second time with the same group of publishers that had gone three years earlier. The Soviets had let us know that they wanted to discuss the copyright convention further, and we went hoping to come back with some kind of deal.

It was a pretty dreadful trip. The Russians tried to keep us busy with all the same cultural stuff as they had on our previous visit, but the novelty was gone. During the day, our negotiations seemed to go on and on with no apparent progress. The question was pretty simple: Were they going to sign the document and pay royalties or not? But nothing could be done in a straightforward way with the Soviets. Most of our time was spent sitting around a table that always held a tray of terrible sandwiches and a bottle of vodka. In the end, the Soviets surprised us and announced they were going to sign the copyright agreement, and on May 27, 1973, they did.

It was a victory for our delegation, but it also turned out to be the start of many more problems—not only did things begin to get even worse for Soviet dissident writers, but, once the possibility of doing business in the Soviet Union became a reality, a split began to develop within American publishing that would worsen in the coming years.

Although the Soviets told us that they wanted us to publish their writers, it was apparent that they had every intention of determining exactly which ones. They did this in a simple and brutally effective manner—if they didn't like what someone had to say, they would harass him or, if that didn't work, imprison him until he was silenced. They couldn't stop us from publishing what we wanted, but they could make the writer pay a very high price.

One of the first cases that came up after the Soviets signed the copyright deal was that of Andrei Amalrik. Then in his mid-thirties, Amalrik had been writing and speaking out against the Soviet leadership since the early 1960s. In 1970, he predicted the eventual breakup of the Soviet Union in an essay titled "Will the Soviet Union Survive Until 1984?" The Soviets didn't think much of that forecast. They accused him of "defaming the Soviet state" and arrested him in May 1970.

In an attempt to avoid international attention, the trial was held in a court in the Urals, about one thousand miles from Moscow. Still, the statement Amalrik made to the court before his sentencing was published in the *Chronicle of Current Events*, and I was moved to tears the first time I read it.

Amalrik began: "The criminal prosecution of people for their statements or opinions reminds me of the Middle Ages with their 'witch trials' and indexes of forbidden books. But if the medieval struggle against heretical ideas could be partially explained by religious fanaticism, everything that is happening now is due only to the cowardice of a regime which perceives danger in the dissemination of any thought or any idea alien to the upper strata of the bureaucracy."

This was what Amalrik said as he was facing an unknown length of time in the gulag. He was sentenced to three years in a labor camp. But in the summer of 1973, at the end of his sentence, the Soviets arbitrarily tacked on three more years.

Having met the leadership of the Soviet publishing industry, I knew that one thing they hated was being called out on their actions. In reality, it was very hard to get American newspapers to publish stories on the struggles of Soviet writers—the press really wasn't that interested in the problems of people whom no one had ever heard of (which was one reason why Sakharov, with his higher international profile, was so damaging to the Soviets).

I thought that we somehow needed to call attention to what was going on, so I got several Random House authors and some other publishers to lend their names to something I called the Committee to Defend Andrei Amalrik. The writers included John Hersey, Robert Penn Warren, Harrison Salisbury, and Arthur Miller (who wasn't a Random House author but was very attuned to human rights issues). The other publishers were Brad Wiley; Bill Jovanovich of Harcourt, Brace; Mike Bessie of Atheneum; and Winthrop Knowlton of Harper & Row. We drafted a letter that we sent out to several newspapers and magazines.

The next year, we sent another letter to call attention to the situation of Vladimir Bukovsky, who came from the same Moscow dissident circles as Amalrik. Bukovsky had dedicated himself to exposing the way the Soviets used the mental health system against dissidents, basically diagnosing anyone who opposed the regime with a disorder such as schizophrenia (the thinking of Soviet psychiatrists was that if you confronted the regime, it proved you were crazy). In 1974, Bukovsky was in a prison camp, on limited rations, and deprived of the right to have visitors, mail, essential medical treatment, or legal counsel.

At the time, our actions felt totally inadequate, but they were the best we could do. Until I came up with something better, I thought the Soviets at least needed to know that people were paying attention.

After Valery Chalidze was set up in New York, Sakharov's work began to be smuggled to him through a network of Russian exiles. Ed Kline published Sakharov in Russian, and, working through Ed as an intermediary, I signed Sakharov to Random House. The first Sakharov book we published was *Sakharov Speaks*, a collection of his writing and speeches that came out in 1974. Sakharov spent the spring of 1975 working on *My Country and the World*, an extended essay in which he examined the Soviet government and its treatment of its citizens.

Neither Ed nor I had ever met Sakharov. But in the fall of 1975, Helen and I got a chance to meet his wife, Elena Bonner, who was as forceful a personality as her husband.

Elena had been born in Turkmenistan in 1923, the daughter of a Jewish mother, Ruth Bonner, and an Armenian father. Elena barely knew her biological father. Her mother married a high-ranking Armenian Communist Party official soon after Elena's birth. As her stepfather advanced in the party ranks, Elena grew up among the Soviet elite in Moscow.

Her parents were arrested in 1937 during Stalin's Great Purge—her stepfather was executed and her mother, who refused to denounce him, was sentenced to eight years of forced labor in Kazakhstan. Elena, who was fourteen years old at the time, took her younger brother and went to live with her grandmother in Leningrad. She finished her education and worked as a filing clerk in a factory and a cleaning woman. When World War II started, she enlisted in the Red Army as a nurse. She tended to the wounded on hospital trains and almost died in a bomb explosion.

After the war, she returned to Leningrad to study medicine and became a pediatrician. She married a fellow medical student, had two children, and later divorced in the 1960s. At around that time, she began to become involved in the Moscow human rights circle. Sakharov, as he recounted in his memoirs, was instantly taken with Elena Bonner when he first saw her in 1970. Sakharov's first wife had died in 1969, and he married Bonner in 1972.

It was no accident that Sakharov's international profile increased after he met Bonner. She was a fiercely smart, fiery woman, but she also helped to give Sakharov the fortitude to keep up with his dissident activities. She was fantastic at advising him on things like how to deal with the foreign press and the best ways he could get his message out. He loved her passionately, and as a pair they really played to each other's strengths.

By 1975, Bonner was going blind because of a degenerative condition related to the injuries she suffered in World War II. She was in a bind in Moscow—she was told in private that if she did have the operation there, she would probably wake up blind. One doctor who was a friend said he would do it, but it became apparent to Bonner that if he did and was successful, he would lose his practice and his career. She wrote to a close friend in Italy and managed to get an invitation to have the surgery done there. When her request to leave for medical care was denied, Sakharov and Bonner called a press conference. Finally, the Soviets backed down and allowed Bonner to travel to Italy.

Helen and I had a short trip to Rome planned in October 1975, so we took advantage of it to meet Bonner. She was immediately memorable, with striking eyes and an excess of energy. She also smoked like a chimney. Over tea, she told us about the different ways the Soviets were trying to silence Sakharov—he had lost many of his privileges by then and was under constant surveillance. She also made sure to point out that although her husband was the most recognizable name, many other dissidents were also suffering, but they didn't have the advantage of being able to get Western press attention when they needed it.

After we met, Bonner had the eye surgery, which was a success. While she was still in Italy, the Nobel Committee announced that Sakharov was to receive the Peace Prize that year.

As they had done when Pasternak and Solzhenitsyn had won Nobel Prizes for literature, the Soviets would not grant Sakharov a visa to attend the ceremony. Because Bonner was already out of the country, she traveled to Oslo to receive the prize on his behalf. She invited Ed Kline, me, and our wives to the ceremony—I was Sakharov's English-language publisher, and Ed published his books in Russian. Helen and I flew to Oslo with Ed and his wife, Jill.

The ceremony was held on December 10, 1975. The night before, we gathered in Bonner's hotel room. It was a very warm evening. She had invited a few friends who lived in Europe, including several Soviet exiles who were living in Paris and her Italian eye surgeon and his wife, a very charming couple. Also present was Alexander Galich, who was described to me as the Bob Dylan of the Soviet Union. Galich had started his career as a poet and playwright, but in the 1960s he became a bard, writing and singing folk songs about World War II and life in the labor camps after the war. As Galich became more political with his songs and plays, he was forced into exile in 1974.

Galich showed up with his guitar but said he couldn't sing much because his throat was very sore. Bonner urged him on, telling him, "Sing! We may never be together again." So for most of the night,

Bonner's smoky hotel room was packed with Russians singing Galich's Russian folk songs and draining bottles of vodka. (Two years later, Galich was found dead in his bath in his Paris apartment, clutching a television set—he appeared to have been electrocuted. There are still arguments over whether it was a suicide, an assassination, or an accident.)

The next day, Bonner read the speech Sakharov had written for the Nobel presentation ceremony. She called him in Moscow immediately after it was over only to find that he was not there—he had traveled to Vilnius, Lithuania, to attend the trial of his friend Sergei Kovalev, another human rights activist. The Soviets wouldn't let Sakharov and Kovalev's other supporters into the trial, so Sakharov spent the day that he was awarded the Nobel Prize outside the courtroom protesting with other dissidents while KGB agents looked on and taunted them.

After the ceremony, we flew to Paris with Bonner and the Klines. After we arrived and checked into our hotel, we went to have a drink at the home of Marie-Claude and Laurent de Brunhoff, the author of the Babar children's books (created by his father, Jean), with whom I'd worked from the start of my time at Random House.

It was getting late, and Helen and I were exhausted. When I suggested that we turn in for the evening, Bonner scoffed. "Are you crazy?" she asked. "How many nights do you think I'll be in Paris in my life?"

We didn't know what to do, and Ed suggested that we might go to the Lido cabaret show, which he had seen when he was in Paris as a teenager. Laurent was dismayed by the idea—he said that only tourists went to the Lido—but he went ahead and called to see if we could get reservations. When he got off the phone, he said that there weren't any tables for the eleven p.m. show, but there were some available for one a.m. Bonner really wanted to go, so we asked him to call back and book one.

I wasn't quite aware of it before we went, but the Lido was famous for its troupe of beautiful young women, naked from the waist up. I remember in particular one topless showgirl riding around on horseback. It was a loud, raucous, and smoky place, and the show included songs, dancing, and magic tricks. Bonner loved it.

* * *

In September 1976, I made my third trip to Moscow, this time as part of a twelve-member delegation of American publishers. The purpose of our trip was once again to meet with and get to know Russian publishers. I welcomed the chance to go back and extend my contacts with the dissidents. Spouses were also invited on this trip, so Helen came as well.

Since I had already been to Moscow twice, I wanted to see some new things. Before we went, I'd been put in touch with Peter Osnos, who was then the Moscow bureau chief for the *Washington Post*. I quickly learned that when Peter does something for you, he really does it.

I'd told Peter that I'd like to see the Jewish parts of Moscow, so he introduced Helen and me to a young dissident named Anatoly Shcharansky, who was then in his twenties. Shcharansky was already a refusenik—after his graduation from university with a mathematics degree, his application to immigrate to Israel was denied. So instead of leaving the country, he became Sakharov's interpreter for English-speaking visitors.

He is, of course, now known as Natan Sharansky, long ago successfully immigrated to Israel and now a well-known Israeli politician and writer. But back then he was just a charming, gregarious guy. He brought us to see an old synagogue in the Jewish quarter, and he also had some fun. At one point, he walked up to a man who he knew didn't speak English and smiled. The man smiled back at him and also at us. And then Sharansky said, "This man is a member of the KGB. He's going to offer to change money to try to entrap you. Don't do business with him. It's a very bad idea." And then he walked over to another man and said, "Now this man, if you want to change money, also changes money. But he's not a member of the KGB, and you're perfectly safe."

That was also the week I first met Sakharov in person, when we made the handshake deal that I would publish his memoirs, but there is one more part of the story.

At the end of the evening, Helen and I walked out of the dinner party with Sakharov and Bonner. As we stepped out of the building, there were several blinding flashes of light. It was totally disorienting—I had no idea if we were being shot at or what. Then two men jumped into a large black car, which peeled out and sped away like something out of a movie. I said that we should get the license plate number of the car, but when I looked I saw there was none. Sakharov just smiled, and then it occurred to me that it was just the KGB taking pictures.

Always the gentleman, he turned to Helen and said, "I apologize for the bad manners of my countrymen."

As was their custom, the Soviets had arranged a heavy itinerary for our group of publishers. The day after the dinner party, they had scheduled us to take the train to Leningrad.

When I told one of the bureaucrats in charge of our delegation that Helen and I weren't going, he acted very offended. "You really have to go with us," he said. "The whole group is going."

"What do you mean I have to go? You can't tell me where I'm going to go and where I'm not going to go. And I'm not going with you," I said.

"But we have already paid for your train tickets and your hotel room," he said. "If you don't go, we will lose a lot of money."

I said, "Tell me what the amount is. I'll be glad to repay you. I don't want you to have any financial loss on account of me."

"No, no, forget it," he said, giving up.

When they had gone, Peter Osnos picked Helen and me up and drove us out toward the suburbs of Moscow. After about an hour, we arrived at Peredelkino, which was an area that had been given to the Soviet Writers Union in the 1930s. The government had built about fifty dachas, or little cabins, there for the use of writers, and the area had been a retreat for authors and the intelligentsia ever since. The most famous dacha, which is now a museum, is the one where Boris Pasternak lived the last few years of his life after he had been forced to refuse the Nobel Prize.

It was a beautiful place, where the writers worked in secluded cabins set back in the forest. Peter took us around and introduced us to several, including Andrei Voznesensky, who was one of a handful of poets—Yevgeny Yevtushenko was another—who could fill stadiums of up to one hundred thousand people for public readings during the Soviet era.

The two people I took to most were Lev Kopelev, an author and gulag survivor, and his wife, Raisa Orlova. Kopelev, who was in his mid-sixties, was a big man with a beard down to his chest. Orlova, a few years younger, was outgoing and spoke English very well. They were both very friendly.

Their little cottage was warmed by the fire in the woodstove. Both had become active in the dissident movement in the 1960s, and though Kopelev had avoided getting sent to a labor camp for a second time, they were really walking a thin line. As we sat and drank tea, they talked about the different methods the Soviets had to silence writers.

After we had spoken awhile, I made an offer to Orlova. "You know," I said, "your government wants me to publish books. What American publishers do is get a scout in other countries to find books and writers that might be worth publishing. So I'll make you the scout of Random House, and we'll pay you a modest salary, and you'll look for books for us in the Soviet Union. If they want to arrest you, they'll be arresting the Random House scout."

She was surprised but accepted. I don't think we ever got any good leads from her for the little money we paid, but I was mainly looking for ways to support the dissident movement.

Now, when I think back on that trip, I see it as kind of a turning point in my own life, the place where my publishing and human rights careers really began to intersect. My own involvement with the human rights movement was going to accelerate in the coming years.

The lives of the Soviet dissidents with whom I was coming into contact were also about to make major turns, in most cases for the worse.

7

THE BIRTH OF HELSINKI WATCH

MY OPINION THAT AMERICAN PUBLISHERS SHOULD PRESS OUR SO-
viet publishing counterparts about their government's abuse of dissident writers was not universally shared within the AAP. For the
most part, the divide ran between trade and educational publishers.
The fact was, trade book publishers were doing very little business with the Soviet Union and felt freer to be critical of the Soviet
regime. Educational publishers, particularly of scientific, medical,
and other journals, however, were doing some business and didn't
want to jeopardize it. At the time, I thought that the stance of educational publishers was mercenary and was outspoken in my opposition. I admired Brad Wiley, who, while continuing to make sales
in the Soviet Union on the educational side, found a way to be critical, albeit he was not quite as confrontational as I was.

For educational publishers, the Soviet Union was a market, and
they took the position that doing business with the Russians would
lead to more openness in Soviet society. They argued that as the Soviets interacted with foreigners, the Soviets would gradually come
into line with international standards. These publishers said that
confrontation would be counterproductive.

My position, which was shared by several other trade publishers,
was that if you wanted to do business with the representatives of a
repressive regime, the least you could do was to keep pressure on
them about the way they were treating their dissident authors. After
my first visit to Russia in 1970, I realized that what was happening

with dissidents there was not getting much coverage in the press. The more I got to know Soviet dissidents who were fighting for their own freedom of expression, the more important it seemed to me to speak out for them.

It's a recurring debate—you hear the same dialogue now about the roles that U.S. companies such as Yahoo!, Microsoft, and Google should take when doing business in China. As China fights to censor the Internet, we see these firms—like publishers in the 1970s—making concessions. In the Internet age, these companies are really the major publishers of today, or at least distributors of knowledge, information, and opinion. Their decisions to cooperate with the Chinese government can have terrible consequences for dissidents in China.

As an organization, the AAP's main task was to lobby Congress for laws that would be favorable to publishers in general—things like copyright issues and discount rates for shipping books through the mail. The AAP did have a small Freedom to Read Committee, which worked mostly on not having librarians remove books from the shelves of public libraries in the United States. It was, overall, a pretty staid organization.

The Soviets, though, didn't treat it that way. Since their publishing industry was completely centralized, they looked for a similar structure to deal with in the United States. The AAP did have some influence as a lobbying group in Washington, D.C., but it really didn't have control of its membership, which was voluntary. The Soviets, however, seemed to regard anything that came out of the AAP with great importance.

After the 1973 copyright deal was signed, Boris Stukalin began to travel to the United States a few times a year to talk business with American publishers. I was usually not even aware he was in the country—naturally, he gravitated toward the publishers who treated him well and avoided those who didn't. Several American publishers would take him out to dinner in New York and roll out the red carpet.

As dissident writers became the leaders in the fight for free expression in the Soviet Union and were actually being sentenced to exile in Siberia—or worse still, to long sentences in labor camps—I found myself thinking about the situation more and more, so much so that it became a minor obsession. If my sons were talking to me at the dinner table and it was apparent that I was not hearing them, one of them would say, "Dammit, Dad's off talking to Stukalin again."

In 1975, the AAP finally made a small compromise. A group of publisher members of which I was a part convinced the organization that if it had a Freedom to Read Committee in the United States, then it should fight for the same principles internationally. That year, the AAP founded the International Freedom to Publish Committee. This group was a follow-on to the work I had started a few years earlier, when I had organized the letters in protest of the treatment of Andrei Amalrik and Vladimir Bukovsky. At the time, I had called it the Soviet-American Publishing Committee. Since the Soviets always objected to having a special committee taking shots at them, we came up with the new name. But when the Freedom to Publish Committee began, the main target was still the Soviet Union. Later, it spread out, particularly when Czech writers such as Václav Havel started to be imprisoned.

I was to be chair of this new committee, but other active members at the start included Winthrop Knowlton of Harper & Row and Larry Hughes of William Morrow.

As we fought our battles within the AAP, there were several broader international initiatives developing that would deeply affect relations with the Soviet Union.

The one that got the most press in the United States was the Jackson-Vanik Amendment, which linked American trade relations with a country's willingness to allow its citizens to emigrate. The legislation, signed into law in 1975, was motivated by the Soviets' decision to charge a "diploma tax" on anyone who wanted to leave the country. This fee, which the Soviets said was justified to pay back the government for the education it had provided, could add up to many times a person's annual salary. The intent was to stop the "brain drain" of scientists and other intellectuals from Russia. Since many of these were Jews who wanted to move to Israel or the United States, American Jewish groups lobbied strongly for the passage of the amendment and did a lot to call attention to human rights abuses in the Soviet Union.

The other thing that happened during that same period was at first greeted primarily with a shrug in the West. But the signing of the Helsinki Final Act in August 1975 turned out to be a key turning point in the movement for human rights in the Soviet Union.

Negotiation on the accords, which were a product of a détente between the Soviet Union and the West, had begun in 1973. Overall, thirty-five countries were involved in the discussions, including the USSR, the nations of Western and Eastern Europe, and the United States. The goal was to normalize aspects of the relationship between the Soviet Union and the West.

The Final Act contained a "Declaration on Principles Guiding Relations Between Participating States," which validated the territorial integrity and sovereignty of states and prohibited intervention in their internal affairs. These provisions were basically seen as recognizing the right of the Soviet Union to control the territories that it had gained at the end of World War II, notably the Baltic States—Lithuania, Latvia, and Estonia—and parts of Poland and Romania, and they were considered by many a big victory for the Soviet Union and its premier, Leonid Brezhnev.

The agreement also included three "baskets," which set a framework for cooperation on issues such as security and disarmament as well as collaboration in economics, science, education, and the environment. There were, in addition, a few human rights provisions. One was an affirmation of "respect for human rights and fundamental freedoms, including the freedom of thought, conscience, religion or belief" and a call on states to fulfill their obligations under the International Covenants on Human Rights. Another affirmed "equal rights and self-determination of peoples." But hardly anyone thought that the human rights and humanitarian provisions would mean much of anything—since the act required that all thirty-five signatories approve any action, it was assumed that the Soviet Union would just block anything it didn't like.

Pravda was one of the few papers in the world to print the entire Helsinki Final Act. Yuri Orlov, a prominent Soviet nuclear physicist and friend of Sakharov and Bonner's, read the text and had an idea: Instead of assuming the Soviets would disregard the human rights provisions, why not try to hold them to their word?

Orlov recruited ten other Moscow dissidents, including Natan Sharansky and Bonner, and in May 1976 launched the Moscow Helsinki Group with a press conference at Bonner and Sakharov's apartment. The group immediately began to compile reports on human rights violations within the Soviet Union, which they then publicized through press conferences that were attended by Western journalists.

Orlov and the other members of the group knew that the regime was not likely to tolerate their dissent for long, but they couldn't foresee the immense consequences that their actions would eventually have. Over the next few years, similar associations of dissidents began to spring up in other Eastern Bloc countries. In Poland, the Committee of Workers' Defense, a precursor to the Solidarity movement, formed to advocate for workers' rights under the terms of the Helsinki Final Act. In Czechoslovakia, Charter 77, a loose confederation of dissidents that included the playwright Václav Havel, came together to call for adherence to the human rights provisions in the accords.

These groups, which tried to force their governments to uphold the rights guaranteed in the Helsinki Accords, laid the foundation for the modern human rights movement, which is based around holding governments accountable to international agreements and laws.

Orlov's group would also inspire a counterpart in the United States, but that was still a few years away.

In the meantime, I was trying to get the International Freedom to Publish Committee off the ground. From the start, though, there were problems that I probably should have foreseen. The basic operations were fairly simple—the committee was a group of publishers who met on a regular basis to discuss cases of government censorship of authors and publishing houses. Once we came up with a list, we would send out letters to the governments in question, newspapers, and anyone else we thought could raise a fuss.

To do this, we needed a budget—the publishers on the committee didn't have the time to research cases around the world and still do their day jobs. I wanted to hire a staff person to do the legwork and make recommendations. We also needed money to send out our mailings. The AAP, though, didn't want to allocate any funds to the committee. I felt that it was just trying to sidetrack any real action.

My main adversary within the AAP was Martin Levin, who was the head of the Times Mirror Company's book group. He totally disagreed with my approach and argued that confrontation with the Soviets wouldn't achieve anything. He said that the protests weren't getting the dissidents out of jail, so what was the point?

Levin was generally supported by Townsend "Tim" Hoopes, who was the paid, full-time president of the AAP and a former Defense Department official. Hoopes and I did not get along at all. He always seemed extremely annoyed whenever I brought up human rights.

Things came to a head when Boris Stukalin came to the United States for a big meeting with American publishers, for which we all gathered at a mansion outside of New York City. The Soviets really wanted the AAP to sign a protocol that had something to do with ties between our two industries. It was really fairly worthless, but these types of formal pronouncements were important to the Russians, and Stukalin was very concerned with it. From my point of view, the desire of the Soviets to have their protocol signed gave us a small point of leverage, though many of the publishers at the meeting were not interested in using it.

Our Freedom to Publish Committee had a list of Soviet writers who were imprisoned, and our position was that the protocol should not be signed until they were released. We wanted to read the name of each author to Stukalin and ask him what he could do.

Hoopes was absolutely furious. He accused me and the publishers who supported the committee's position of stirring up trouble for no good reason and wanting to embarrass our "guests." There was ill will all around, and the meeting fell apart.

I realized at that moment that the AAP was not going to take any advice from the International Freedom to Publish Committee when it came to dealing with the Soviets. As it was, Hoopes and a few of the publishers doing actual business in Russia were the only ones who had contact with the Soviets, and they really didn't share their knowledge with our committee. Combined with the rapid growth of Random House, that led me to step down as chair of the committee in early 1977.

Getting away from the conflicts within the industry would also allow me the space to think of a new way to approach the issue. As for the Freedom to Publish Committee, Winthrop Knowlton succeeded me as chair, and it should be noted that the group continues to this day.

During this time, the members of the Moscow Helsinki Group had been active. They released their first report immediately after their formation in May 1976. It detailed the case of a Crimean Tatar activist who had been convicted of slandering the state.

Over the next year and a half, the Moscow group put out an additional seventeen reports. Each one was copied by typists using carbon papers and sent to the embassies and representatives of the countries that were signatories to the pact. People from around the Soviet Union began to travel to Moscow and show up at the apartments of Helsinki group members to report abuses they had suffered. Helsinki groups started up in Ukraine, Lithuania, Georgia, and Armenia.

Orlov and the members of the Moscow group were not naive—they expected that the government would act against them, and in early 1977, the KGB began to move.

On February 3, Alexander Ginzburg, one of the group's members, was arrested. They came for Orlov a week later. Later in the month, another founder, Lyudmila Alexeyeva, was forced to leave the country. Finally, on March 15, Natan Sharansky was taken into custody. He was charged with espionage and faced a sentence of fifteen years in labor camp.

It was at just this time the Soviets announced they were going to host an international book fair in Moscow to display books from publishers around the world. They scheduled it for September 1977.

It was unbelievable to me that a regime so engaged in jailing writers wanted to hold an exposition to celebrate books and believed that authors and publishers would not see how it was trying to manipulate public opinion, particularly in its own country. As soon as the Soviets sent out the guidelines for exhibitors, the wording made it clear that they reserved the right to ban any book they thought was inappropriate. When I saw that, I decided that Random House shouldn't participate in a book fair that would make it seem we were willing to cooperate with censorship.

Many other publishers chose to skip the event as well, but some took the position that attending the Moscow fair would help loosen things up in the Soviet Union. Martin Levin told the *New York Times*: "The question is, 'Can a closed state open up enough?' They're moving ahead slowly in adjusting to Western practices. Nobody is trying to make trouble or to embarrass the Russians. But we'll have to see how they supervise us, if all Russian citizens will be allowed in, if the public will be able to buy or order books directly, what treatment the Israeli publishers will receive. I think they'd rather loosen things up than make the fair a farce."

In the same article, I told the reporter, "You really can't talk to the Russians about publishing if you know that they turn around and put people in jail or take out their telephones or watch you if you're having dinner with a Soviet author."

Looking at it now, I think both of us were right, and that's one thing that makes an open society a powerful advocate for its own openness. Different ways to approach a problem are used by free people, and sometimes the combination is better than any single one. In this case, it was probably good to get the fair started so that Soviet authors had some access to the international book business, and it was also good that some publishers were willing to call the Soviets out and say that the book fair was censored.

My idea when I stepped down as chair of the Freedom to Publish Committee was that I would form my own independent organization to pressure the Soviets. I had absolutely no experience with nonprofits or any clue how to run or fund one.

So I started the Fund for Free Expression out of necessity. It was essentially a continuation of the work I had been doing as a publisher. The aim was to call attention to writers and dissidents in the Eastern Bloc and to press for their rights. I recruited a very distinguished board, including several Random House authors who were interested in civil and human rights, such as Toni Morrison, E.L. Doctorow, and *New York Times* op-ed columnist Anthony Lewis, as well as Kurt Vonnegut, who was published by Delacorte. Several other publishers joined as well, including Winthrop Knowlton of Harper & Row, Larry Hughes of William Morrow, and Roland Algrant of Feffer & Simons.

Once the board was in place, I knew exactly whom I wanted to hire as our first staff member.

I had first met Jeri Laber in December 1975 at a rally outside the Soviet consulate calling for Vladimir Bukovsky's release from prison. A crowd of several dozen people, all bundled up against the cold, gathered in front of the building on East Sixty-Seventh Street and began to march in a circle.

It was a strange mix, including members of the movement pushing for the freedom of Soviet Jews to emigrate, people from the local chapter of Amnesty International, and several actors. Dustin Hoffman was there as well as Celeste Holm, the movie star and Broadway legend whom I had seen—and loved—decades earlier when she played Ado Annie in *Oklahoma!* She was bundled in furs and perfectly made up.

At one point, I ended up walking next to Jeri and we began to talk. Several months later, we ran into each other again at a dinner party at Ed Kline's.

Jeri's father was a Russian Jew who had emigrated in 1906, and her mother was from a Jewish family that had fled from pogroms in Lithuania. Jeri was enrolled at Columbia University's Russian Institute when she was selected as one of the first four American students granted visas to visit the Soviet Union in 1954.

Upon her return, she married a New York tax attorney and had three daughters. For the next fifteen years, she raised her family while working part-time at an anticommunist think tank in New York and writing occasional articles about developments in the Soviet Union for magazines such as the *New Republic*. In the early 1970s, she became active in Amnesty International. She also happened to get a contract with Knopf to revise *The Fannie Farmer Cookbook*, so at the time we met she was, in a manner of speaking, already working for Random House.

Jeri, who was in her mid-forties, was quick-witted and had the somewhat dark sense of humor you would expect of someone who focused on Russia. Soon after Ed's dinner party, I went to lunch with her and asked her to come on as a staff member of the International Freedom to Publish Committee. In an odd bit of timing, I stepped down before the job details were finalized, and my successor as chair, Winthrop Knowlton, ended up finally hiring her.

When the Fund for Free Expression was up and running, I hired Jeri on a part-time basis, and she worked out of a small office at Random House. One of the first things we did was to become the American distributor of the British journal *Index on Censorship*, which published the work of censored writers. Later on, we contributed some of our funds to keep *Index on Censorship* solvent.

In March 1978, I got one of those phone calls that changes your life. McGeorge Bundy, the president of the Ford Foundation and a former top aide to President Lyndon Johnson, told me he had an idea he wanted to discuss with me.

Bundy, as national security advisor to both Presidents Kennedy and Johnson, had been one of the chief architects of the Vietnam War. By the time he called me, he'd been president of the Ford Foundation for twelve years. I had met him a few times when I went to the Ford Foundation to have lunch with Fred Friendly, who was very close to Bundy and was advising him on making the foundation one of the main backers of public television. Fred had taken a job there after he resigned from CBS News in 1966.

When we met for lunch, Bundy said that he'd been speaking with Arthur Goldberg, who was the American representative to the first Helsinki review talks, which were being held in Belgrade. The review talks were part of the Helsinki Accords process and were meant to ensure that the West and Russia continued to make progress toward the goals stated in the Helsinki Final Act.

Bundy told me that Goldberg—who was both a former Supreme Court justice and the U.S. ambassador to the United Nations—

was extremely frustrated. Goldberg was outraged by the treatment of dissidents such as Sakharov, Sharansky, Havel, and Orlov, but when he spoke out, he couldn't get any traction. He found European diplomats to be totally unreceptive. They were most interested in the talks about security, and no one wanted to get in a fight with the Russians over human rights.

Goldberg told Bundy that there should be a nongovernmental organization that could tell the story of Soviet repression, get stories into the press, and arouse public sympathy for the dissidents. He thought if that happened, he might have an easier time getting human rights issues on the table at the Helsinki talks.

I was certainly interested. In early April 1978, Jeri Laber and I met with Bundy and a few Ford Foundation staffers to discuss the idea further.

We were all enthusiastic, but I told Bundy I was worried that I would have to spend too much time fund-raising. "With my work at Random House and the time it's going to take to get this started," I said, "I don't think I'll have the time to raise money as well."

"Don't worry about it," Bundy said. "How much do you need?"

I thought for a moment. "Well, I think we probably need $200,000 a year to do it right."

"How about $400,000 to cover your first two years?" Bundy asked.

All we had to do was figure out how our new organization was going to do its job. We had several months and a small planning grant to get working on it.

Today, with universities across the country offering courses in human rights, it seems surprising that the term was hardly a household phrase when we met Bundy. At the time, however, there was no established international human rights "movement," though a number of factors were coming together to launch it.

The bedrock of the human rights movement lies in the Universal Declaration of Human Rights, which was adopted by the UN in 1948. A short document, the Universal Declaration lays out the basic rights of all humans, including freedom of speech, freedom of religion, freedom of movement, freedom from arbitrary arrest and detention, and freedom from torture. For the first thirty years after its adoption, though, the Universal Declaration remained basically dormant as the Cold War progressed.

The only large human rights group to emerge during that time was Amnesty International, which was founded in 1961 by Peter Benenson, a British lawyer, after he read a newspaper article about two Portuguese students who were sentenced to prison after making a toast to freedom in a Lisbon bar. Benenson wrote an article calling for an international network to defend political prisoners. That launched a movement that soon included thousands of volunteers organized in small groups around the world. They "adopted" political prisoners by writing to them in prison and publicly calling for their release.

The 1975 signing of the Helsinki Accords helped to dust off the Universal Declaration, as did the election of Jimmy Carter in 1976. Carter announced that respect for human rights was going to lie at the heart of U.S. foreign policy. He appointed Patricia Derian, a former ACLU lawyer, as the assistant secretary of state for human rights, a position created by Congress after it investigated Augusto Pinochet's 1973 coup in Chile and found that the CIA had played a role in it. The creation of the office turned out to be a very important development—it has given human rights groups in the United States a door into the State Department.

We looked at Amnesty International and decided that while its efforts were admirable, Amnesty's focus on letter writing was too limited. We felt that the Universal Declaration was a document that opened up the whole issue of governance and the relationship between governments and their citizens. We thought the Helsinki Final Act created the possibility to directly engage with and pressure the repressive governments of the Eastern Bloc. We also wanted to move the American political leadership to action, so that our own country would be a leader in fighting for human rights in closed societies.

The Ford Foundation grant was an opportunity to build something different from the Fund for Free Expression, which was doing very well but was based within the publishing world. Instead of expanding the Fund for Free Expression, I thought it would be better to start a completely new organization.

In order for our group to have a high profile, I realized that we had to have prominent people from every walk of American society, so I looked to put together a masthead that would lend weight to our reports and press releases. The original committee included more than forty people. We had authors such as Toni Morrison, Arthur Miller, Robert Penn Warren, and John Hersey; legal academics, lawyers, and judges; a number of Wall Street heavy hitters; representatives of unions such as the head of United Auto Workers; and college presidents from places including MIT, Columbia, the University of Chicago, and the University of California. Some played much bigger roles than others. When I contacted people, I let them know that if they didn't have the time to actively participate, their names could be very useful as it was a new organization and a new idea, and both needed stature and publicity.

Before long, a core group of people emerged as those who would really drive the organization.

Foremost among these was Aryeh Neier, an extremely analytical, methodical, reserved, and intellectual man with a fantastic understanding of the nuts and bolts of organizing a nonprofit. We had first met in the early 1970s, when Random House was going to court with the government over the Marchetti CIA book. At the time, Aryeh was the national head of the ACLU, which supported our position in the case.

Aryeh had been born in Berlin shortly before World War II and fled Nazi Germany with his family, eventually landing in New York City. After graduating from Cornell, he'd risen to become head of the ACLU while still in his early thirties.

He'd come into the national spotlight in 1977, when the ACLU represented a small group of neo-Nazis who wanted to march in Skokie, Illinois, then the home of many Holocaust survivors. The ACLU won the case on First Amendment grounds, but there was great disagreement within the organization about the wisdom of representing Nazis, and a lot of members withdrew their support. By 1978, Aryeh had stepped down and had taken an academic position at NYU. At our meetings, he quickly revealed a knack for planning, strategy, and organization. He was a perfect fit for our executive committee.

One of the strokes of good timing in my life came when a friend who lived in Scarsdale called and told me she knew a lawyer whom she thought would share my interest in human rights. That's how I first went to lunch with Orville Schell Jr., who was a partner at the Wall Street law firm of Hughes, Hubbard & Reed.

You usually don't think of corporate lawyers as passionate advocates for human rights, but Orville was. As the head of the New York City Bar Association from 1972 to 1974, he had been outspoken against the Vietnam War. He had also been to Russia on a mission for the Union of Councils for Soviet Jews.

Orville was a very businesslike, buttoned-up type of guy. He wore impeccable suits and carried a huge leather bag that was always stuffed with books and papers. He was an understated man but very firm when he believed in something. In meetings, he would quickly cut through any nonsense and get to the point. He loved the ballet, and as I got to know him, I learned that he had a place out in the country where he indulged his passion for beekeeping.

He had an air of authority about him and hardly ever lost his temper (though there was one memorable time, which I will get to later). And I felt that with his reputation and position as a leading New York lawyer, his involvement would give us a certain gravitas and respectability.

Several other people played key roles in planning our new organization. They included Ed Kline; Adrian DeWind and John Carey, who were both lawyers in New York; Jack Greenberg, who had headed the NAACP Legal Defense Fund; and Bob McKay, the head of the justice program at the Aspen Institute.

This group, along with Jeri Laber, met every week at Random House to hash out a plan for our American Helsinki group. We agreed that we would focus on abuses in the Eastern Bloc and work to publicize them at the next Helsinki Review Conference, which was due to start in Madrid in November 1980.

Our proposal to the Ford Foundation was approved, and the $400,000 for the first two years of operation that I had asked for began in January 1979.

Helsinki Watch was born.

We still had a few kinks to work out, however.

First, we had to hire an executive director. I wanted Aryeh Neier to take the position, but he passed on it when I asked—after leaving the ACLU, he didn't want to return immediately to running an organization. Instead, he recommended a colleague named David Fishlow.

I believe that because Aryeh recommended David, we did not interview David carefully enough about his beliefs as to what Helsinki Watch should be. It turned out that he wanted to focus primarily on human rights abuses in the United States, just as the Helsinki groups that had been organized in Eastern Europe kept tabs on their own governments.

While there are plenty of human rights problems in the United States, there were already several organizations that focused on them. I felt that we should place our emphasis on closed societies, which was where our help was really needed—and we had a unique opportunity to call attention to the plight of Soviet dissidents. David just didn't see it this way, and, after a few months, he left.

We began a search for a new director, and I received a letter from Jeri putting herself forward as a candidate for the job. We went to lunch to talk about it, and she convinced me she was the right person. She became executive director of Helsinki Watch in June 1979, and our organization took a critical step forward.

By that time, the second biannual Moscow Book Fair was fast approaching.

I had decided that I'd been wrong to skip the first one. The book fair, I realized, offered a rare chance to have some contact with ordinary Russians. I figured that instead of confronting the Soviets head-on, we would outsmart them.

I wanted to show Russians something about how people lived in the West and the differences between their system and ours. I wanted them to see the material wealth, cultural diversity, and complexity of the United States, but also to show them that there was the freedom here to criticize and to publish books the government did not like.

The way to do this, I thought, was to put together an exhibition of books to demonstrate that. I suggested the idea to the AAP and the publishers took it on. Kurt Vonnegut chaired a committee that included literary critics, editors, and librarians. They ended up choosing more than three hundred books for the exhibition, which I named *America Through American Eyes*.

The exhibit included Muhammad Ali's biography; a collection of Ansel Adams photographs; several picture books on American homes and architecture; fiction by authors such as Saul Bellow, Toni Morrison, James Michener, Philip Roth, Eudora Welty, John Updike, E.L. Doctorow, and Gore Vidal; books on the Vietnam War such as C.D.B. Bryan's *Friendly Fire* and Michael Herr's *Dispatches*; Bob Woodward and Carl Bernstein's *All the President's Men*; Richard Nixon's memoirs; Robert Pirsig's *Zen and the Art of Motorcycle Maintenance*; histories of the civil rights movement; and a *Reader's Digest* book of do-it-yourself home repair.

I asked the committee to put in plenty of picture books, because I knew that at a book fair most people would pick up and flip through whatever was there. We needed to have things that could be consumed quickly.

The New York Times Foundation gave us a grant to print one hundred thousand copies of the catalog, which was about the size of a small paperback book, five by eight inches and 124 pages. It listed all the books and had short summaries of each one in Russian and English.

In the months before the book fair was to start in September 1979, there was a mad scramble to get everything done. Jeri managed the project with the help of a wonderful woman named Sophie Silberberg, a retired librarian from the AAP. She was a calm presence who helped keep everyone around her on track. We later hired her to help run the office at Helsinki Watch, and she eventually became executive director of the Fund for Free Expression, which we kept going after the founding of Helsinki Watch.

I was excited to go to Moscow, not only to see how the *America Through American Eyes* exhibit was received, but to renew my ties with the group of Moscow dissidents—those who weren't in jail, at least. I should have known that it wouldn't be so simple.

In early August 1979, I got an interview request from a man who said he was a reporter for TASS, the Soviet news agency. When he came to my office, he was very nice, low-key, and understanding. As he asked me questions about my publishing philosophy, I began to expand on what I thought of the Soviet treatment of Sakharov and other dissidents. I guess I should have taken it as a clue that he had a notebook out but didn't write anything down. After he left, I became so worried that I called Jeri and told her I had probably been a bit too strident. The article never appeared in TASS. The Soviets had obviously sent the guy to see if I was going to be a loose cannon in Moscow.

Then, on August 23, Alexander Godunov, a twenty-nine-year-old Russian ballet dancer on a tour of North America with the Bolshoi Ballet, defected while the troupe was in New York. The problem was he had left the hotel without his wife, another Bolshoi dancer on the tour. When the Soviets discovered what had happened, they brought her to JFK International Airport and put her on an Aeroflot plane that was to leave for Moscow.

In the meantime, Ed Kline had become involved with the case through Joseph Brodsky. Ed had asked Orville Schell to represent Godunov, who wanted his wife to stay in America. Orville got the State Department to block the plane from taking off.

Negotiations began in the terminal at JFK. Godunov argued that the Soviets were removing his wife against her will. The Soviets said they would let the couple talk, but only on the plane. Godunov, understandably, didn't want to get on a Soviet airliner in the company of Soviet agents. The talks became international news as they stretched out over seventy-three hours. The plane remained on the tarmac, all the passengers stuck on board. In the end, the State Department allowed it to leave with Godunov's wife after she had been interviewed by Orville through a reliable interpreter and expressed her wish to return to Moscow. This assured that she would be greeted with a hero's welcome in Moscow. (Godunov went on to Hollywood, where he acted in several films, his most famous role being that of a terrorist in *Die Hard*.)

The drama at the airport landed Orville in the papers and on the evening news. I didn't have anything to do with the case, but I suspect the Soviets noticed Orville's involvement in Helsinki Watch.

At the end of August, I received a call from the State Department and was told that the Soviets had revoked my visa; I wouldn't be allowed to travel to Russia for the book fair.

I immediately protested. Townsend Hoopes at the AAP issued a press release but did little else. It was only when Cyrus Vance, the secretary of state, lodged a complaint that the Soviets started a negotiation.

The State Department called and told me that the Soviets had promised to reinstate my visa if I agreed "not to abuse Soviet hospitality." I said that sounded a bit vague and asked if the Russians could clarify what they meant. When the State Department called back, it said that the Soviets had decided I couldn't be trusted to abide by their conditions and had therefore rescinded the offer. I was banned from the Soviet Union.

I canceled the Random House delegation to the fair and arranged to have our books shown by William Morrow—I didn't think we should go, but I wanted our authors to be represented.

Jeri went to oversee the *America Through American Eyes* exhibition, which was a tremendous hit. For years later, I have been told, the exhibit catalog was circulated throughout Moscow, which, from my point of view, served the purpose of showing average Russians the wide range of publishing in an open society.

The Soviets, despite their promises before the fair, banned books they didn't like. These included Israeli prime minister Menachem Begin's *White Nights: The Story of a Prisoner in Russia*; a biography of Adolf Hitler (the Soviets had an official history of World War II that overlooked things like the nonaggression pact between Hitler and Stalin); several books by Aleksandr Solzhenitsyn; a biography of the ballet dancer Mikhail Baryshnikov, who had defected to the West; and even a book of editorial cartoons, because it included a caricature of Soviet premier Leonid Brezhnev.

The Soviet censors didn't have a chance to read everything before the fair opened, so they banned books as they worked their way through the exhibits. Some books simply disappeared at night with no word as to what happened to them. Jeri went from stand to stand and compiled a list of everything that had been pulled by the Soviets and distributed it to journalists, who reported it in the press.

Boris Stukalin explained to reporters that the censorship wasn't a question of freedom of expression, but "freedom of fascist pro-paganda." He said he could not allow books that "do not serve the spiritual exchange of mutual understanding between peoples, but encourage hostility."

Jeri also went about making contact with the Moscow dissidents, in part to let them know that our American Helsinki Watch group existed. She met first with Andrei Sakharov and Elena Bonner and then with Lev Kopelev and Raisa Orlova, whom I had met three years earlier at their cabin in Peredelkino.

Orlova helped to plan a dinner at a Moscow restaurant for So-viet writers, which was to be hosted by Larry Hughes, president of William Morrow and head of the AAP's Freedom to Publish Com-mittee. A few hours before the event started, it was denounced on Moscow radio. That evening, the restaurant was surrounded by plainclothes police. None of the establishment writers who had ac-cepted invitations showed up.

It turned out to be a once-in-a-lifetime gathering of Soviet dis-sidents, many of whom would be imprisoned or exiled shortly af-terward. The attendees included Sakharov, Bonner, Kopelev, and Orlova, as well as more than forty other dissidents, such as Vladi-mir Voinovich, Vasily Aksyonov, and Anatoly Marchenko and his wife, Larisa Bogoraz.

On the day she was scheduled to fly out of Russia, Jeri met with the Moscow Helsinki Group in Sakharov and Bonner's apartment. Many of the original members, including Yuri Orlov and Na-tan Sharansky, had been imprisoned or expelled from the coun-try. Those who remained were mostly women too old to be sent to prison. Jeri told them about the existence of our group in New York and our intention to help them any way we could. She promised that we would try to keep their names and their fight in the eyes of the world.

Over the next decade, we would struggle to do that, though sev-eral disheartening years were to come.

Far left: Showing an early interest in books, around 1928

Left: Jacob Bloch, maternal grandfather, who arranged immigration of sixty-eight German Jews, 1935

Getting commended while serving in the U.S. Air Service Command in India, 1945

Top left: Bernstein family portrait with parents, Alfred and Sylvia, and sister, Barbara, 1946; *top right*: with Helen and our parents on our wedding day, 1950; *above*: with author and entertainer Kay Thompson, illustrator Hilary Knight (*second left*), and singer Andy Williams (*right*) celebrating the publication of *Eloise*

With Bennett
Cerf, Donald
Klopfer, and Lew
Miller after the
announcement
that Bernstein
would become
Random House
president,
December 1965

"Good God. Kay Thompson's
been here again!"

Hilary Knight's
depiction of
Bernstein's first
day at Random
House

Left: With Muhammad Ali, 1970

Below: With Donald Klopfer at Klopfer's retirement from Random House, 1972

With ACLU founder, Roger Baldwin, 1970s

Top: Supreme Court Chief Justice Earl Warren speaks at the publication of Justice William Douglas's book, 1974; *above left*: Claudette Colbert giving a toast in Barbados, 1970s; *above right*: with the family in China, 1976

Left: Protesting in New York, 1975

Below: With Helen and members of the Association of American Publishers, 1976 (*from left*: Peter Neumann, Michael Foyle, Townsend Hoopes, Brad Wiley, and Ted van den Beept)

Toasting with the Sakharovs, 1976

Dinner in Leningrad, now Saint Petersburg, 1986, with Peter Osnos, Andrei Sakharov, John le Carré, Elena Bonner, and Helen

With dissident author Andrei Amalrik, late 1970s

With Ted Geisel (Dr. Seuss),
1977

Letter from Ted Geisel, 1981

Dear Robt:
Re your moscow-
Book-Fair piece
in the N.y. Times,
I thought you hammered
and sickled them
properly... and very
fairly.

Dr. Doesteffsky

Sesame Street renews its contract with Random House, mid-1980s

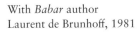

With *Babar* author Laurent de Brunhoff, 1981

Alfred A Knopf

PURCHASE *New York* 10577

December 13, 1982

Robert L. Bernstein, Esq.
C/o Georgian Suite
1A East 77 Street
New York, NY 10021

Dear Bob:

The year 1968 was a very important one for AAK Inc., even if I did not realize it at the time, for somehow during that year you stopped asking me what I thought of a plan of yours (I was cool to it) until one day, believing I needed them, you ushered into their jobs Tony Schulte, Bob Gottlieb and Nina Bourne. Bob and Tony soon assumed all the authority and responsibility which I could and should no longer carry, continuing to make our list one of the best and best known of publishers. So, dear Bob, to you I am forever grateful and only sorry that I cannot be here this evening to pay you honor.

Yours devotedly,

AAK:ah

Letter from Alfred A. Knopf, 1982

With James Michener, 1980s

Helen and Jacobo
Timerman, 1983

Speaking with the
committee planning
the Moscow Book Fair
catalog, chaired by
Kurt Vonnegut (*third
from left*), 1985

Top: *Peanuts* cartoon given to Bob by Charles Schulz after working together, 1980s

Above: Helen with Robert Fulghum, author of *All I Really Need to Know I Learned in Kindergarten*, early 1990s

Left: With Chinese dissident Harry Wu, 1990s

With Chinese
dissident Wei
Jingsheng and
his sister after
Wei's arrival in
the United States,
1990s

Left: With Sharon
Hom, executive
director of Human
Rights in China,
1990s

Below: Helen
with Bard College
president Leon
Botstein and his
wife, Barbara
Haskell, 1998

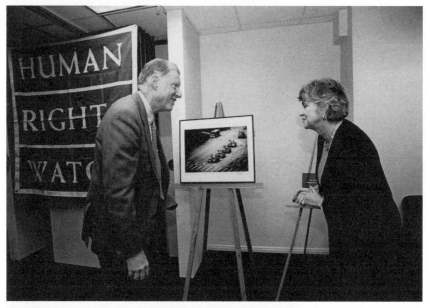

Top: With Fred Friendly, 1996; *above*: with Jeri Laber after stepping down as chair of Human Rights Watch, 1998

Left: With Soviet dissident Yuri Orlov and author Bob Moskin, 1998

Top: With the other winners of the first Eleanor Roosevelt Award for Human Rights, *from left*: Bette Bao Lord, Dorothy Thomas, and John R. Lewis, presented by President Bill Clinton and First Lady Hillary Clinton, 1998; *above*: Bernstein family at the fifteenth anniversary of the Robert L. Bernstein Fellowship program at Yale Law School, 2014 (*top row, from left*: Elisabeth, Will, Drew, Amy, Andi, Bill, Alexander, Nicholas, and Sam; *bottom row, from left*: Lori, Tom, Helen, Bob, Lee, Peter)

Above: Bernstein family in Martha's Vineyard, 2010 (*top row, from left*: Peter, Amy, Michael, Elisabeth, Alexander, Nicholas, Tom, Andi, and Bob; *bottom row, from left*: Sam, Laura, Lee, Bill, Lori, Helen, Allison, and Will); *below*: laughing with youngest grandchild, Jack Bernstein, 2015

8

FROM RCA TO NEWHOUSE

HUMAN RIGHTS WORK TOOK UP MORE AND MORE OF MY TIME, BUT I still had to run Random House. A lot of my job came down to dealing with our corporate parent, RCA. That relationship became increasingly tricky as RCA began, in the early 1970s, what would turn out to be a long, slow, and terminal decline.

At the start, though, I thought things might work out. Right after our sale to RCA in 1966, I had a meeting with General David Sarnoff. When I asked him what he expected from Random House, he was succinct: "Run it like a publishing house."

Shortly after that, we were set to publish *Due to Circumstances Beyond Our Control*, Fred Friendly's memoir about the early days of CBS News. Because the book included sections about Sarnoff's rival, William Paley, I thought that Sarnoff would love to read it. I also figured that it wouldn't be a bad idea to keep the General interested in his new acquisition, so I sent over a galley.

I soon got it back with a note that really impressed me: "I'm very interested in reading this, but I want to wait until it's a finished book. If people start seeing galleys in my office they'll think I'm trying to influence Random House editorially. You and I know that's not what I'm trying to do, and we don't want to give that impression."

At the end of the 1960s, Sarnoff's health began a rapid decline. In 1968, he was stricken with shingles, which damaged his nerves, contorted his face, and slurred his speech. He was hospitalized for a long period and then sent home to his Upper East Side town house for bed rest. Several operations followed, but the General never again entered RCA's headquarters at Rockefeller Center. He died of cardiac arrest in December 1971, a few months after Bennett.

In the meantime, Bobby Sarnoff had taken over as RCA's president, and the company had begun to slide. Bobby had been dead set on making RCA a player in the computer industry, investing hundreds of millions of dollars in development, but it never really challenged IBM, which was so dominant in the field. The company finally had to dump the whole division—including 7,500 employees and a $490 million write-down—in 1971. It was a total debacle.

RCA was also struggling to oversee a growing empire of unrelated businesses. In addition to Random House, it had acquired several other companies in the late 1960s and early 1970s in an attempt to boost its profits. Our corporate siblings included the real estate firm Cushman & Wakefield, a carpet and furniture manufacturer, and the Hertz car rental company, among others. With so many holdings, it was difficult for RCA's management to focus on any one thing.

The sale of the computer business, of course, negated the reason RCA had bought Random House, which was supposed to be the content provider for its computers. So by the early 1970s, there was absolutely no reason for RCA to own us at all.

It was also a rocky time in publishing—a headline in the *New York Times* put it simply: "Book Publishing: Industry in Turmoil." The "book boom" of the 1960s had led to several corporate acquisitions of publishing houses besides RCA's purchase of Random House (there were thirty-eight mergers and acquisitions in American publishing in 1968 and thirty-three in 1969). With the money of larger corporations available, firms hired more staff, signed authors for bigger advances, and published more books than they could successfully market. Inevitably, profits began to shrink—especially when the recession hit in the early 1970s—leaving the new corporate owners none too happy with their investments.

At the same time, the growth and influx of money led many houses to lose their small mom-and-pop feel. Editors, once expected to stay for life, were quitting firms to take higher salaries, leaving authors under contract, who were not free to move with them, high and dry. Publishers who could not hit profit targets were replaced by a younger generation that often had an accounting rather than a literary focus.

At Random House, we managed to do reasonably well. One main reason, I think, was the structure that allowed our imprints and divisions enough autonomy to retain the feel of much smaller firms. Each imprint—Knopf, Random House, Ballantine—was run pretty much as an independent publishing house, and I tried to be a firewall between our editors and the profit demands of RCA.

Our saving grace, though, was that we were making money. On our fiftieth anniversary in 1976, we had our highest sales ever—$114 million—and pretax profits of $8 million. Our adult trade imprints, which had a mix of bestselling authors and literary superstars, were both profitable and prestigious. Our juvenile division—with Dr. Seuss, the Berenstain Bears, and Roald Dahl, author of such titles as *James and the Giant Peach* and *Charlie and the Chocolate Factory*, among others—was minting money.

Despite Random House's growth, I tried to keep the lighthearted tone that Bennett and Donald had established so well.

One of our new bestselling authors in the 1970s was the journalist Nora Ephron, who published two books with Knopf that decade—*Crazy Salad: Some Things About Women* in 1975 and *Scribble Scribble: Notes on the Media* in 1978. Of course, she later went on to even greater renown as a screenwriter of movies such as *When Harry Met Sally . . .* and *Sleepless in Seattle*, which she also directed.

At a cocktail party, Ephron came up and began to chat with me. When it was clear that I didn't recognize her, she half-jokingly said, "This is the third time we've met. If you don't remember my name next time, I might just quit Random House."

I decided I didn't want that to happen, so I took one of her book jackets, cut out the author photo, mounted it on cardboard, and set it on my desk where I could see it every day, and every morning I came in, looked at my desk and said, "Hi Nora." I figured that would solve the problem.

Apparently, the story got around Random House, because before long the assistant to Ephron's editor came up to my office. She said they'd heard I had a picture of Ephron on my desk and wanted to check if it was true. I confirmed that it was.

Regrettably, all of my picture training went for naught. I never met Nora Ephron at an event again, and she became so famous that I don't think I would have needed the practice.

Sometimes a book just doesn't sell. One of those was the memoir of Meyer Weisgal. A Polish immigrant, Weisgal, as a young man in the 1920s, had become one of the leaders of the American Zionist movement. From 1949 to 1966, he chaired the Weizmann Institute, Israel's great scientific university and research center. He was an irrepressible, energetic man, and he proved to be a terrific fund-raiser—his ability to bring in money really got the Weizmann Institute off the ground.

We published Weisgal's memoir in 1971 with the expectation that it would do well—Weisgal had told us that there were thousands of members of Hadassah, the Women's Zionist Organization of America, and he said all of them were sure to buy a copy of his book.

When the book didn't sell, Weisgal came in to Random House and called a meeting with members of the publicity team and me. "Girls," he said to them, "you're just not doing it right. But it may be too late. I may just have to write a new book."

"Meyer," I said, "you're almost eighty years old. You've written your autobiography. How will you do it all over again?"

"Very simple," he said, "I've already got the title: *I Left the Best Part Out.*"

Over the years, RCA several times assigned Random House to an executive to whom I would report. Usually, this executive had other, much larger units reporting to him as well, and in most cases, he had no previous experience of any kind connected with publishing. At one point, I reported to the executive who ran RCA's satellite division. He told me he had no idea why he had been given the assignment, said his other work would keep him more than busy, and told me to keep him posted as best I could.

The main focus of RCA executives was that Random House show

growth in profits. They began to ask for "five-year plans." These were supposed to detail the growth of the business in the coming years, ideally with a predictable jump in earnings every quarter. They didn't find it funny when I told them in one meeting, "In publishing, no five-year plan ever beats straight muddling through."

A big chunk of our profits depended on bestsellers, and you couldn't tell James Michener—not if you wanted to keep him at your imprint—to hurry up and finish his next book because we needed a bump in the second quarter. Publishers like Bennett, Donald, and Alfred Knopf didn't have a great need to turn huge annual profits. They knew that when they published a popular book, it would have a value that would pay off over decades as it continued to sell, and they would make their money when they sold the backlist years later, which is of course exactly what they did, each becoming quite wealthy. As a corporation, RCA simply had other priorities—even if RCA executives understood the concept, they couldn't go and tell Wall Street what a great backlist we had going and how Dr. Seuss would still be producing royalties at least twenty years in the future.

In 1974, when I needed a new vice president for finance, RCA sent me three candidates. Two were older men who had been with RCA for decades, and I knew right away that they were trying to find a place for executives who for one reason or another were not usefully employed. The third was a man named Sandy MacGregor, then thirty-two years old, whom RCA had hired from Ford Motor Company, where he had been one of their "whiz kids," a concept that had been started by Robert McNamara years before. Sandy was very bright, and the chemistry between us was apparent. The decision was an easy one, and Sandy and I worked together closely for the next sixteen years.

Sandy also helped me deal with the five-year plans. The reason there were so many small publishers, and the reason that publishing was looked at as being somewhat different from other businesses, is that publishers market creative work, not a product that comes off an assembly line. While many books came out, the majority of them were not large moneymakers; in fact, only a small group of authors regularly turned out bestsellers. That was why the backlist—books that sold year after year—was so important.

Sandy understood this perfectly, but he told me, "You're never going to sell it to a public company like RCA, which measures its success by the growth of its stock, not improving the foundation of the company."

He also explained that it was only actually important what you did in the existing year and the rest was blue sky. Putting that all together, he said, "The key thing is to write a plan that shows steady growth over the five years, so we'll show a ten percent growth every year."

That's what we did and it worked fine, because as I discovered, not only were many divisions of RCA not growing 10 percent a year, but some were losing fortunes. We more or less operated in our traditional way, which was to be always somewhat profitable, but erratically so, depending on when our leading authors finished their works. We did far better than most because the combination of Knopf and Random House gave us a very impressive group of writers.

In addition to the business differences, the cultural gap between the two companies varied depending upon which single executive at RCA had been assigned to oversee Random House.

Most of the executives understood that a publishing house has its own rules and acted more or less in a friendly but hands-off manner. To explain the range, however, one time I very excitedly called the RCA executive to whom I reported on a Monday morning, to ask him if he had seen the *New York Times* bestseller list. I told him that Random House not only had the number one fiction and non-fiction books, but, as I remember it, more than a third of the books on the list. The call didn't really have much of an impact when he explained, "I don't take the *Times* on Sunday."

On the other hand, in the early 1970s, I began to report to an executive named Andy Conrad, who was exactly the opposite. He was not only a voracious reader—I think he actually read more books than I (and most other people at Random House) did—but he was also very interested in the book publishing industry. He seemed actually to understand what the business was about, and his thoughts were always given in a self-deprecating way that let you know he was trying to be helpful but not the least bit threatening. Unfortunately, his time at the company was cut short.

There were a few times when individual acts of powerful RCA executives were difficult to deal with. I learned that frequently these were not company policies but directives coming from little power bases within a large corporation. Nevertheless, some could be very destructive.

One example happened in the early 1970s, when RCA's legal department would not allow us to buy a profitable paperback house because it thought the deal would be blocked by the Federal Trade Commission. It turned out to be not only a wrongheaded decision, but also one that made for severe complications at Random House for many years.

Another more personal incident came in 1975, when Donald Klopfer announced he was going to retire as chair of Random House. I can't say enough times how extraordinary Donald was. Looking back, he taught me more about handling people—which in a creative business is so vitally important—than anyone else. Donald understood many things, among them that there was no substitute for making yourself available and taking the time needed to hear out any disputes. He also really believed that letting the younger and less important people in the company know that they were valued was critical. About two or three times a year, he would hold a breakfast for all the new employees. The breakfast would start at 8:30 and would go until at least 10:00, and he would tell the history of Random House and talk about some of its most important books. He told the new employees that staying at Random House meant that we had an investment in them, so that their happiness at the firm was important, and if they were unhappy in their job, let us know before looking elsewhere. He realized that people coming into publishing frequently just wanted to be in the industry and started wherever they could. I completely embraced this policy and later continued it and even expanded the talk, particularly the part about telling people that I understood that they might start as secretary when they really wanted to be editor in chief.

When Donald retired, he made three requests. The first, he said, was that he'd like to keep an office at Random House. He referred to the columnist and writer Harry Golden, who had had the line "A man needs a place to go in the morning." His other two requests were for the half-time use of a secretary and for a $7,500 yearly expense account to lunch and entertain the many authors he knew from his fifty years in publishing. In Donald's way, he asked me if I thought those requests were reasonable. I said they not only seemed reasonable, but it was a very cheap price to have him around to talk to the authors and editors who were so used to his golden touch.

I put through a brief note to RCA personnel to say that Donald was going to retire but that we were lucky he would still be involved. George Fuchs, the head of the RCA personnel department, came over to my office and told me that the company policy was that after a person retired, to have him still coming to work could be counterproductive. He said that people might continue going to Donald with their problems, and he asked that I find a way to ease Donald out.

I don't remember if I quoted Emerson—"A foolish consistency is the hobgoblin of little minds"—but I patiently explained that whatever the policy, Donald should be an exception. Fuchs was quite insistent, so much so that I finally said that the day Donald left Random House not of his own will was the day I would leave. The conversation ended and I never heard another word about it. Donald came in to Random House almost every day until his death in 1986.

The Sarnoff era at RCA ended in 1975. The company's profits had been declining for several years—not only was there the fiasco with its computer division, but sales of televisions and radios were also taking a hit. In 1975, Bobby Sarnoff reportedly demanded a raise from the board—he'd made around $500,000 the previous year—and then took off for a vacation in Asia and Australia. When he got back, the board told Bobby it wasn't going to give him more money, and Bobby resigned.

RCA decided to promote from within the company and picked Andy Conrad, the executive vice president who had been overseeing Random House as well as several other divisions. Reporting to him had been such a pleasure that I had mixed feelings when it was announced he was to become president. I realized that with his responsibilities I would see little of him, though I kept sending him books.

Conrad had run RCA for a little less than a year when the IRS came after him. It turned out that he hadn't filed an income tax return in five years. Nobody, including me, knew what he was thinking—it turned out that practically all of his taxes had been paid through withholding on his earnings at RCA and he owed the government very little money. So his main crime wasn't avoiding tax payments, but not filing a return. The board, spurred on by a smart but overzealous head of the legal department, asked for Conrad's immediate resignation, got it, and in effect fired him.

I was upset enough by the whole incident that I found out where Conrad was staying and impulsively went over to see him the night his resignation was announced. He was all alone in a hotel room, his home being in Maryland. I told him I just wanted to let him know how appreciative all of us at Random House were that he had been around. Conrad soon hired a prominent tax attorney and, as I heard, the matter with the IRS was quickly settled.

We were not as fortunate with Conrad's successor, Ed Griffiths, who had started at RCA as a bill collector and risen through the accounting side. He was still an accountant to the bone. His nickname within the company was "Bottom Line Ed."

Griffiths took it as his job to try to get things in order at RCA. Quarterly earnings growth became more of a focus than ever.

One thing that really sticks in my mind about Griffiths is that he lived in the suburbs on the south side of Philadelphia and commuted two hours by chauffeured car every day to midtown Manhattan. It was known all over RCA that he had to be home every night by six o'clock to have his evening martini, sit with his dogs, and watch the news. So if you were in a meeting with him and it was getting close to four, he would get up and say, "Gentlemen, I have to leave." This didn't bother me too much because I rarely met with Griffiths, but it was a strange way to run a giant corporation.

Griffiths had no feel for or interest in publishing. Soon after he became president of RCA in the fall of 1976, he got an offer from the Times Mirror Company—owner of several publishing imprints as well as the *Los Angeles Times* and other newspapers—to buy Random House. The Times Mirror executive in charge of the merger was the head of its book group, Martin Levin. At the time, Levin and I were engaged in a fight within the AAP over how to best deal with the Soviet publishing industry.

I could not imagine any way that Random House would thrive if it entailed my having to interact with Martin Levin. At the time, I asked Sam Levin, one of our best salesmen and Martin's brother, about Martin's feelings toward me. As I remember it, he told me more with his facial expressions than with any words. The matter, however, was out of my hands.

Several executives from RCA as well as Sandy MacGregor and I flew to Los Angeles to meet with the Times Mirror people, including the president, Robert Erburu, to discuss the details of the deal. I was sure that it was going to happen.

The next thing I heard was that Martin Levin had gone to RCA headquarters for the final signing and that he tried to get RCA to drop the price by a million dollars. RCA thought the deal had been agreed upon and evidently took this as a breach of faith and called off the whole thing.

I'm quite sure that Random House would not have prospered under the large, more hands-on corporate structure of Times Mirror. Looking back, I realize how much I was being torn back and forth between the "good old days" of publishing and the idea that it could be big business.

After the flirtation with Times Mirror, I had a good but very limited working relationship with Ed Griffiths. With his attention directed at other aspects of RCA, I felt that as long as I kept Random House profitable and running well, we'd be one less problem on his agenda.

With the failed Times Mirror deal behind us, I asked Griffiths at one of our meetings to please let me know in advance if he was going to put Random House on sale again, so I wouldn't be surprised. He said he would. It turned out we had different ideas about what being told in advance meant.

One morning in September 1979, Griffiths called and asked me to meet him in his office at one that afternoon. I told him I had a lunch date. He said, "I'm sorry. It's rare that I would ask you to do this, but you have to be in the office at one. Either change your lunch date or have an early lunch. I'm sorry."

Of course, I wondered what was so urgent. When I went over, he told me, "Bob, the reason you had to be here at one is because I promised I would tell you before we put Random House up for sale. At two o'clock we're putting Random House up for sale and announcing it over the tape at the stock market."

"Well, that's not exactly what I meant by getting advance notice," I said, "but thanks for telling me."

Later that day, I found out we were not the only RCA subsidiary that had been put up for sale. The company was also getting rid of Banquet Foods, a frozen food and chicken-processing company. I don't think it mattered much to the world, but from my point of view, the public relations of announcing the sale of what I was absolutely sure was one of the finest publishing companies in the world in conjunction with a chicken-processing company lacked a certain sensitivity.

Our sale was placed in the hands of RCA's two investment banks, Lehman Brothers and Lazard Frères. The banker for Lehman was Steve Schwarzman. A few years later, Schwarzman left Lehman Brothers and, with Peter Peterson, founded the now famous Blackstone Group, one of the largest private equity firms in the United States.

Schwarzman's big candidate to buy us was the Hearst Corporation. I went over to Hearst and had lunch with its head, Frank Bennack, who later became even more prominent as the chairman of Lincoln Center. He introduced me to the man who ran Hearst's book divisions, which really weren't much—they consisted of Avon Books, a paperback publisher, and a few minor imprints. Bennack said I would be reporting to this vice president, and Random House would be just another subsidiary under Hearst's book publishing division. This didn't appeal to me at all. I felt that it might be difficult for me to operate while having a vice president in charge of book publishing who would have the final word on business decisions.

After that meeting, I don't remember seeing Schwarzman again. My guess is that he wasn't particularly interested in making the deal and this suited me just fine.

The banker for Lazard Frères, Donald Petrie, came in to talk to me about Random House and to see what the company was about. He was friendly, informal, and had a great sense of humor. It came through quickly that he had a great respect for Random House. One of his opening lines was "I don't want to sell Random House to any company that you and your editors don't want to go to."

He then went on to explain to me that he had been told to sell both Random House and Banquet Foods. Then, with a big smile on his face, he said he really didn't think he could do both at the same time, so he wanted me to know why he was going to work on Banquet Foods first. "You have to understand, Bob, there are ten thousand chickens walking in every day and having their heads cut off, and they have to be shipped out someplace. That's a lot of dead chickens," he said. "So I think you can see that we can't have them all piling up. What I'm trying to say is that the Modern Library is not moving that fast."

Petrie soon called and told me he had lined up a potential buyer—Advance Publications, a privately held chain of newspapers, magazines, and television stations. The owners, Donald and S.I. "Si" Newhouse Jr., wanted to have lunch with me.

At the time, the Newhouses were not well known, even in the Manhattan media world. I had heard of them, but that was about it. When I did some research, I learned that their company had been built by their father, S.I. "Sam" Newhouse Sr. The son of Jewish immigrants—his father was from Russia and mother from Austria—the young Sam Newhouse took a job as a clerk to a lawyer in Brooklyn to help support his parents and siblings. When his boss saw how competent Newhouse was, he asked him to oversee a failing newspaper he owned in New Jersey, the *Bayonne Times*. Newhouse turned out to have a knack for the newspaper business—he brought in a raft of new advertisers and made the newspaper profitable. In 1922, when he was twenty-seven years old, Newhouse borrowed money and bought the *Staten Island Advance*, just a few years before Bennett Cerf and Donald Klopfer founded Random House.

Newhouse had a reputation as a frugal and hands-on manager

who always kept a careful eye on costs. He began to acquire other papers, including the *Newark Star-Ledger*, the *Cleveland Plain Dealer*, and the *St. Louis Globe-Democrat*. His chain eventually included almost thirty papers. They were known for being of varying degrees of quality but extremely profitable and, unlike Hearst, not having a single national political view. They were local newspapers trying to represent the cities where they were published.

In 1959, Newhouse's wife, Mitzi, asked for a fashion magazine for their thirty-fifth wedding anniversary. He paid $500,000 for Condé Nast, whose publications included *Vogue*, *Glamour*, and *House & Garden*. With his monopoly newspapers churning out cash, Newhouse saw the lower-margin magazines as something to give his wife a thrill.

The acquisition also gave Si Newhouse, who was then in his early thirties, a newfound purpose in life. While his younger brother, Donald, had taken to the newspaper business, Si was drawn to the glossier world of magazines.

Sam Newhouse died in August 1979, right before RCA put Random House up for sale. His death left his sons fully in charge of the family media business. When I began to ask around, I found that the Newhouses had a pretty good business reputation. Some people liked them, some didn't. They seemed to keep a low profile and run their companies well. In general, though, people knew very little about them, which was interesting in itself. From what I'd heard, as long as they made money, they pretty much kept out of the management of their properties. They sounded like they might be better owners for Random House than Hearst.

I met Si and Donald Newhouse for lunch in the Sky Club, which was at the top of the Pan Am Building on Park Avenue. I liked them. They were both short, well dressed, and friendly, though Si was a bit reserved. In our meeting, Si—who would take on Random House as one of his responsibilities if they bought it—did most of the talking.

The brothers told me that they were a family business, dedicated to building on their father's legacy. They said once they bought a business they never sold it. And nobody working for them ever had

to retire; you could work there forever—they even had an accountant in his nineties who was still at one of their papers. They said
they liked to make profits, but were not profit-driven—they were
patient and built their businesses slowly, for the long haul. Finally,
they said they were both very interested in becoming book publishers, but that they would remain hands-off with the day-to-day operations. They asked me to check with the staff, as they only really
wanted to acquire us if they had not just my approval, but also the
approval of what I considered the major staff.

It sounded great. I really liked the idea of having private ownership. It's particularly important in a publishing business, because
writing down unsold books—which is necessary and certainly gives
a more accurate value of a publishing business—cuts taxes, but cuts
profits as well, which corporations don't like. Publishing houses
therefore can grow more naturally with private ownership.

I talked to a few people at Random House, but they seemed to
feel the decision was in my hands. So I informed Donald Petrie, who
let the Newhouses know that Random House would be happy to be
bought by them.

In February 1980, they closed the deal, buying Random House,
as the newspapers reported, for $70 million in cash. Si told the
Times that he planned "absolutely no changes" at Random House
and that it would operate as an independent unit.

Mitzi Newhouse, Si and Donald's mother, threw a lavish dinner
party to celebrate the deal. Amid all the good feelings, there was
one thing that gave me pause: Roy Cohn was the only guest at the
dinner not associated with Random House or the Newhouses' publishing concerns. Cohn, I later learned, had been close friends with
Si Newhouse since they attended prep school together. Though he
had become a prominent New York lawyer, Cohn was still most
famous for his role as the bullying lead counsel for Senator Joseph
McCarthy during the communist witch hunts of the 1950s. To put it
bluntly, no liberal liked Cohn. That evening, though, he was seated
next to Helen, and to be fair to Cohn, he was perfectly charming.

The dinner was a kind of launch party for Si, who would not only
become increasingly involved with Random House over the next
decade, but in that time would also build Condé Nast into what

it is today, resurrecting *Vanity Fair* magazine in 1983, purchasing the *New Yorker* in 1985, and building *Vogue* into an international fashion powerhouse. By the end of the 1980s, Si Newhouse would no longer have a low profile in the Manhattan media world.

At the time of Mitzi Newhouse's dinner party, the 1980 presidential campaign was just beginning to gain steam. It wasn't until later that year, after the election of Ronald Reagan, that the 1980s would really begin in earnest, bringing in monumental changes for both Random House and the world of human rights.

9

FINDING OUR FOOTING:
HUMAN RIGHTS, 1980–85

ON JANUARY 22, 1980, KGB AGENTS PULLED OVER ANDREI SAKHA-
rov's car as he was on his way to lecture on theoretical physics at
the Russian Academy of Sciences in Moscow. They took him to
the prosecutor's office, where he was told that the Presidium of the
Supreme Soviet had decided to banish him from Moscow. He was
to be confined to the city of Gorky (now Nizhny Novgorod), about
250 miles to the east, where he would be barred from contact with
foreigners. Elena Bonner would be allowed to go with him. Immediately after Sakharov called to let her know, her phone went dead.
A few hours later, agents knocked on her door. That evening, the
couple was put on a plane and sent into internal exile.

Sakharov's punishment appeared to be a reaction to his statements on the Soviet invasion of Afghanistan, which had begun
in December 1979. The Soviets claimed they were coming to the
aid of the country's communist leader, Hafizullah Amin, in a fight
against guerrilla forces that were attacking from Pakistan. Once
they reached Kabul, however, the Soviets executed Amin and set up
a puppet regime. In interviews with Western journalists, Sakharov
had denounced the invasion as "expansionism." He predicted that
the occupation would go horribly wrong and called for a boycott
of the Summer Olympics, to be held in Moscow, if the Soviet army
did not withdraw.

The banishment of Sakharov turned out to be part of a larger
Soviet crackdown on dissent motivated by several forces. First, the

Soviets wanted the upcoming Olympics to showcase their society without meddling from dissenters. At the same time, several minority groups within the empire—including Jews, Germans, Armenians, and Pentecostals—were getting increasingly vocal in their demands for exit visas. Furthermore, détente with the United States had cooled—the U.S. Senate failed to ratify the SALT II arms treaty, a major setback in cordial relations between the superpowers, and there were increasing concerns about human rights in the Soviet Union. Finally, it was also the last days of the Brezhnev regime—he would be replaced by Yuri Andropov in 1982—so there was quite possibly some jockeying for power going on within the Kremlin.

Between the fall of 1979 and the summer of 1980, some 150 dissidents in the Soviet Union—many active in the various Helsinki groups throughout the Soviet empire—were arrested or brought to trial. Others, such as Lev Kopelev and Raisa Orlova, the couple I had met in 1976 in Peredelkino, were stripped of their citizenship and forced out of the country. Some dissident authors were simply expelled from the Soviet Writers Union and effectively blocked from publishing.

With that as a backdrop, it was a dispiriting time to be trying to get Helsinki Watch off the ground even though it made our work more urgent than ever. Sometimes it seemed like our activities were limited to putting out press releases as yet another of our dissident contacts was exiled or put in prison. It was certainly hard to be upbeat in the face of the Soviet crackdown. At times, we wondered if we were doing anything useful at all.

The first years of the 1980s, however, were also exciting ones for our organization. There was very little hierarchy, and the dedication and passion of both our small staff and our board were invigorating. Without any kind of road map as far as how to build an effective human rights organization, we improvised. Many of the techniques and methods that would become integral to our style emerged and began to gel. We began to find our voice.

Our first office was on Forty-Fourth Street, in midtown Manhattan, and before long, it became a hangout for exiled dissidents from all parts of Russia and Eastern Europe. They came in to use the photocopier, to see who else was around, and to chat with Jeri Laber and Lyudmila Alexeyeva, a member of the original Moscow Helsinki Group who had moved to New York after her expulsion. The exiles brought us news of the latest developments from their home countries—I never quite understood the complex networks through which news and gossip flowed out of the Soviet bloc—and their presence was a constant reminder of why the work we were doing mattered.

We met every Wednesday in the Random House boardroom, where we sat around a massive conference table and had what were, in hindsight, incredibly freewheeling discussions about the direction and strategies of Helsinki Watch. I thought that the setting conferred a gravitas on us that would have otherwise been lacking for a new organization. It was especially useful and impressive when visitors such as exiles and prospective donors—which included anyone from the then budding philanthropist and financier George Soros to Norman Mailer to George Konrad, a dissident Hungarian novelist—sat in on our meetings.

One of the principal reasons the Ford Foundation had funded Helsinki Watch was to establish a presence at the Madrid Helsinki Review Conference, which was set to start in November 1980. The conference was called by the nations that had signed the Helsinki Final Act five years earlier to monitor progress toward its resolutions. It was at this time that we really came to life.

Jeri suggested that we establish an office in Madrid for the duration of the conference, where we could monitor the meeting, lobby participants, and speak with reporters. It was a brilliant move. Before the conference started, we met with Max Kampelman, a Washington lawyer whom Jimmy Carter had appointed to succeed Arthur Goldberg as American ambassador to the Helsinki talks, and spoke about human rights abuses in the Soviet Union. He said he was going to do everything he could to give human rights a more prominent place on the agenda. We knew, however, that this would be challenging—the United States had other interests, such as disarmament; many other countries were not eager to address human rights; and, of course, the Soviets were adamant about blocking interference in what they regarded as their internal affairs.

The Madrid Helsinki Review Conference, from the start, had a completely different vibe from that of the one in Belgrade, which had ended just two years earlier. In the interim, various groups with interests in pressuring the governments of the United States, Western Europe, and the Soviet Union had figured out that these meetings were their best bets. So in Madrid, émigré groups from countries around the Soviet empire rubbed shoulders with others who were there to press their cases, such as Afghan mujahideen and Native American groups.

The Soviets made their attitude toward all this quite clear. Even after the Madrid conference started, they continued to arrest and jail Helsinki monitors. Their primary concern was disarmament in Europe. Our mission was to keep the issue of the dissidents in the public eye and to make sure any talks about disarmament were linked to human rights discussions. I flew over at the beginning of the conference and, along with Orville Schell, held a press conference to call for the release of all the jailed Helsinki monitors in the Soviet Union.

Over the course of the talks, Jeri and Ambassador Kampelman formed a strong working relationship. He not only took the information we gave him about imprisoned dissidents and raised it at the meeting, but he also shared details about the talks with us. That, in turn, gave us an edge with reporters, who came to us to find out how the discussions were going. Our office became something of a news center.

The Madrid conference would eventually stretch out over several years. It's worth noting one tragedy that happened right before it was set to begin.

On his way to the meeting in Madrid in November 1980, the Russian dissident Andrei Amalrik, who had lived in the Netherlands since his exile in 1976, died in a collision after he pulled out to pass another car on the highway. The other three people in the car, including his wife, emerged from the accident with only slight injuries.

In 1982, Knopf published Amalrik's final book, *Notes of a Revolutionary*, his memoirs of his life as a dissident. He had finished it just before leaving for Spain. In the preface, Amalrik wrote: "The philosophy of totalitarianism is still spreading through the world. But in the land where it first triumphed, the process of overcoming it has begun. . . . The theme of these memoirs is the conflict between the individual person and the system in a country where the individual is nothing and the system is everything."

I think it's fair to say that Madrid was the start of a process that has become prevalent in the human rights movement, which is to attend international meetings of every kind to highlight and embarrass governments that are abusing human rights. As often as possible, human rights groups actually use the rules of the organization holding the meeting—such as provisions allowing nongovernmental organizations (NGOs) to speak at the meetings—to push for human rights goals.

I think today that this technique has been most effective with China, where rule of law and an independent judiciary are not only leading human rights goals, but also important to foreign companies doing business in China. Not only do corporations want to make sure that their investments in China are secure, but no business wants it revealed that their products have been made by slave labor. This has given human rights groups an opening to bring up subjects such as Chinese labor practices at meetings of international groups such as the World Trade Organization and the European Union.

I was always surprised at how touchy Soviet bureaucrats became when they were called out on their human rights abuses. You would think that as representatives of an oppressive regime, they would have fairly thick skins. But I found that an apparatchik like publishing boss Boris Stukalin came to international meetings with his peers from other countries and not only wanted to be regarded as a man of letters, but also mix and converse with writers and intellectuals as though he were one of them. I guess it is human nature to want to be liked, but I always thought they would have been better off if they had just ignored us.

The irritability of the Soviets motivated me to keep thinking of ways to embarrass them. At the time, I was more than busy with Random House, but I always had in mind that it was extraordinary to be in a position to make publishing stand for the values that I believed were so important to society, values that I thought without which publishing could not exist. I was also very conscious of the fact that the issues we followed at Helsinki Watch—which involved people with very important ideas getting imprisoned all over the world—were not getting nearly enough press attention, which was one of the only things we could do that might ease the lives of those in prison and even get them released. Up to this day, I have never understood why it is so difficult to get the media to really highlight and stay on cases where everything, including torture, is occurring.

So, with this in mind, I would listen at the meetings very closely to try to pick up incidents that might generate the interest of reporters, though I was frequently disappointed when we would contact a journalist covering the country and get little, if any, result. I learned that one of the reasons was that media organizations balance their own interests—such as not getting kicked out of a country—and make judgments about how far to push things.

I had one advantage as far as getting attention, and that was the fact that I was president of Random House. If I called a press conference, there was a good chance that at least a few reporters would show up. So I tried to think of things that would grab media attention.

For example, *Time* had its well-known "Man of the Year" feature (the magazine only changed it to "Person of the Year" in 1999). I suggested Helsinki Watch select a "Forgotten Man of the Year," highlighting the case of a person of tremendous bravery in a closed society who had been put away, and explaining why it was particularly important for the world to try to keep him or her as much as possible in the public eye.

The idea was to make an image that looked like a *Time* magazine cover, with the red border, that could be mailed out and made into a poster. Our first "Forgotten Man" was Yuri Orlov, who had been imprisoned since 1977 for organizing the Moscow Helsinki Group. We announced the choice at a press conference, and I thought the unveiling of our "Forgotten Man" (or woman) could become an annual event. But not only did *Time* magazine not promote this idea, which I was foolish enough to think it might, but I received a letter from its lawyer telling me that the use of the red border infringed upon its copyright.

We didn't continue with the concept, I believe, because we felt we didn't get enough out of it. As I sit here today, I realize I missed a great opportunity. We should have done it again and possibly *Time* would have sued us, which would have helped a lot.

We did take the "Forgotten Man" idea and make calendars, with each month featuring a different dissident and a short biography. Overall, you had twelve forgotten men and women. We mailed the calendars to all the government participants in the Helsinki process, reporters, and anyone else we thought might take notice. Recently, Human Rights in China, the human rights group with which I am now very involved, did the same thing, making a calendar that features a different imprisoned Chinese lawyer for each month. (We used a similar idea when we started our annual fund- and friend-raising dinners for Human Rights Watch. We always had an empty chair on the podium that represented someone who couldn't make it because he or she was in prison.)

The idea that generated the most publicity at the time, however, centered on the 1981 Moscow Book Fair, which was scheduled to run for a week in September.

Since the Soviets had banned me from Russia two years earlier, I decided if they wouldn't let me go to their book fair, we could have one of our own at the same time. They had forced so many writers into exile that it wouldn't be hard to gather a good group. I thought we could call it the "Moscow Book Fair in Exile."

I called Vartan Gregorian, who was then the head of the New York Public Library, and asked if we could hold it there. He was very enthusiastic. Jeri, who by that time had also been barred from the Soviet Union, took on the task of organizing the event.

We set up an exhibition of banned books in the library and arranged for eighteen exiled Russian writers to come to a September 14 dinner. The *Times* gave the event enough publicity that it attracted an overflow crowd. The writers in attendance included Andrei Sinyavsky, Vladimir Voinovich, Joseph Brodsky, Vladimir Bukovsky, and Vasily Aksyonov.

It was a warm evening, with plenty of wine, vodka, and Russian food and music. Many of the writers stood up to give brief remarks. Lev Kopelev, who came with Raisa Orlova, said: "Books are as necessary for some people as bread. For us, the word is also our weapon in resisting brutal tyranny; we cannot decide the problems of armament and big politics, but we can defend peace by working for human rights. Our freedom in speaking and publishing which we now enjoy is also our duty."

The Soviets reacted predictably—they denounced the event as a sham in the Soviet press. That, of course, only drew more attention to their treatment of dissident writers. I was glad that we were getting to them, but the whole thing was also tinged with sadness.

For one, the Soviets kept arresting and sentencing writers to prison camp and exile, so it was hard to know what effect our efforts were having. Also, I saw what exile did to the writers who had been kicked out of their country. Many had based their lives on speaking out against Soviet tyranny. While they faced difficulties, that struggle had animated them and provided meaning. In the United States or Western Europe, they were free to say what they wanted, but they did not have the same audience. It was very difficult for a lot of them to adjust. I think this is something the Soviet regime understood very well.

This continues to be a huge problem—exile today is still an effective way to silence people. In exile, dissidents regain their ability to speak, but only in rare cases are they able to be as eloquent as they were or, even if they are eloquent, to get the press to recognize it. For example, when the Chinese dissident Wei Jingsheng posted his call for democracy on a wall in Beijing in 1978, he drew more press than anything he was able to write after he arrived in the United States eighteen years later, although he continues to speak eloquently and to travel all over the world.

The dissidents who have had the most impact—Sakharov, Havel, Nelson Mandela, Aung San Suu Kyi—have remained in their own countries.

Just as my involvement with dissidents in the Soviet Union and Eastern Europe was increasing through Helsinki Watch, I received a visitor who got me interested in a completely different part of the world.

Rabbi Marshall Meyer came to see me at Random House in 1979. Rabbi Meyer, who had been born in America and educated at Dartmouth, had moved to Argentina in 1958 to take a position as an assistant rabbi in a temple in Buenos Aires. He ended up staying and later founded a rabbinical school and led his own large congregation.

After years of instability, political violence in Argentina began to mount in the early 1970s, as left-wing insurgents clashed with Isabel Perón's increasingly repressive government. The situation worsened after the military staged a coup d'état in 1976 and began an all-out effort to destroy its opposition. Over the next seven years, the government arrested, tortured, killed, and disappeared thousands of people, mainly members of trade unions, activists, and, most of all, students. Anyone who was seen as potentially sympathetic to the insurgents was a target.

The junta had a way of killing people that I've never heard of before or since, it's so horrible. It was reportedly used mostly for young people and students, who would be tortured in order to get the names of their friends. When the officers thought they could get no more names from them, they were given large doses of Valium, stripped naked, loaded onto aircraft, flown out over the ocean, and pushed into the sea. Young women who were pregnant were kept alive until their babies were born, because many in the military wanted to adopt, and they were then given the children.

An organization called Mothers of the Plaza de Mayo, which consisted of mothers of adult children who had been disappeared, was formed in 1977. Every Thursday, they would march in one of the central squares of Buenos Aires and demand to know what had happened to their children.

Rabbi Meyer, at great danger to himself, used his position to denounce the military junta's abuses of human rights. He repeatedly went to the prisons and demanded to see political prisoners. He probably saved hundreds of lives this way.

When Rabbi Meyer came to see me, he was in New York on a short trip to try to mobilize prominent American Jews to speak out against Argentina's military regime. One of the prisoners he spoke to me about was the journalist Jacobo Timerman, a man who would have a profound personal effect on me.

Timerman was born to a Jewish family in Ukraine on January 6, 1923, which made him exactly one day younger than I was. In 1928, his family fled Eastern Europe to escape from pogroms and settled in the Jewish quarter of Buenos Aires. Early in life, he became a committed socialist and a Zionist. Timerman said he was a born journalist, and he landed his first job as a reporter in 1950. He soon became one of Argentina's leading political analysts, appearing on radio and television in addition to print. In 1971, he launched his own newspaper, *La Opinión*.

La Opinión was an intellectual, left-of-center paper modeled after *Le Monde*, and it soon achieved a wide circulation. In the early 1970s, as Argentina's political situation deteriorated, Timerman drew death threats from both the Right and the Left by denouncing the indiscriminate killings committed by each side. After the 1976 coup, he began to print the names of the disappeared on the front page of the paper. In his editorials, he assailed the madness infecting the country.

The junta had him arrested on April 15, 1977. He was imprisoned for over a year, during which time he was brutally tortured. His interrogators beat him, applied electric shocks to his genitals, and put him in solitary confinement. When he was finally released from jail, he was confined to house arrest. He was never specifically accused of a crime.

Rabbi Meyer was vital in mobilizing an international push for Timerman. Patricia Derian, Jimmy Carter's assistant secretary of state for human rights, called for his release. Henry Kissinger, Aleksandr Solzhenitsyn, and the Vatican were among others who made statements denouncing Timerman's treatment.

This publicity eventually paid off. In September 1979, after thirty months of prison and house arrest, the junta revoked Timerman's citizenship, confiscated his newspaper, and sent him into exile. Timerman planned to move to Israel with his family, but before he went, he came to New York.

When Timerman arrived, I met him with a small group of people who had worked for his release. He was a large man, quick-witted, and, with his journalistic mind, intolerant of overstatement and insincerity of any kind. He was the kind of man who people felt strongly about. You either liked him a lot, as I did, or you didn't. People, of course, were interested to know the details of his story and how he had endured the more than two years of imprisonment. My memory is that, when he was under house arrest, he was kept in his bedroom in his pajamas, while in the rest of the rooms of his apartment, soldiers were allowed to party and have their girlfriends up though they were theoretically guarding him.

When we got a moment alone, I told him, "This is awkward, but my experience with people like you is that you arrive penniless and nobody thinks about it. I'm going to give you a check. It's not my money, it's Random House's money, and it's an interest-free loan. It's not a payment on any kind of book. We'll bid for the book when you want to write one, and I'm sure you will."

He said, "I have no idea if I'm going to write a book."

"Well, I know you are," I said.

"How do you know that?" he asked.

"Because you have a great story to tell, and you're a writer," I said. "But at that time we'll bid with everybody else. You return the money whenever it's convenient for you. It's to get you through this moment."

He said, "Thank you, and you are absolutely right. I think I have $12 in my pocket. Everything has been confiscated."

A few weeks later, Timerman came to see me at Random House and told me I was right, he wanted to write a book. I told him that since he probably didn't know much about publishing contracts, perhaps we should get him an agent. He said that wouldn't be necessary, that if Random House wanted to publish the book, he would like that. In the discussion, I suggested that I pretend he had an agent and think about how much I would bid for the book. He said that would be an interesting idea. So I thought about it a few minutes and said I think I would bid $75,000, maybe higher if pressed. He laughed and said, "You're not being pressed—$75,000 is fine!"

* * *

By the late 1970s, Argentina was just one of many Latin American countries with a military leadership that abused human rights. Though far from perfect, the administration of Jimmy Carter had at least kept human rights issues on the table when negotiating with these regimes. And Carter had placed the very vocal and effective Patricia Derian in the job. That policy was reversed with the inauguration of Ronald Reagan in January 1981.

Jeane Kirkpatrick, a professor of government at Georgetown University, laid the intellectual groundwork for this change. In November 1979, Kirkpatrick published an article in *Commentary* called "Dictatorships and Double Standards," in which she drew a distinction between "totalitarian" and "authoritarian" regimes. She argued that totalitarian governments, like that of the Soviet Union, exercised total control over every aspect of their citizens' lives and therefore never changed. Authoritarian governments, like the one in Argentina, tolerated competing institutions such as the church and private business ownership, she wrote, and therefore could sometimes evolve into more democratic societies. Her conclusion was that, because of this difference, the United States should therefore fully oppose left-wing totalitarian regimes but engage with right-wing authoritarian ones. It was basically a Cold War justification for sorting out, tolerating, and doing business with any regime, no matter how oppressive, as long as it wasn't communist.

The article resulted in Kirkpatrick becoming one of Reagan's chief foreign policy advisors during his presidential campaign. After his election, Reagan appointed Kirkpatrick to become the American ambassador to the United Nations.

At Helsinki Watch, we were appalled by the Kirkpatrick doctrine. As an organizing principle for foreign policy, it didn't leave much room for human rights concerns when dealing with right-wing military governments such as that of Argentina. Kirkpatrick's ideas would also be influential in American policy toward other Latin American countries such as Chile, Guatemala, El Salvador, and Nicaragua.

After Reagan's election, we began to kick around ideas in our weekly meetings about how to respond. Eventually, we agreed that it made no sense to be against oppressive governments that were communist and not be against oppressive governments like those in Latin America. We believed that the Universal Declaration of Human Rights should be universal, and that it would lose validity if it was used only against communist governments. We believed that human rights could not be more or less regarded depending on the political system of a country.

This all came together in 1981, and we founded Americas Watch.

We knew that our new offshoot was going to have to navigate rougher political waters than Helsinki Watch. While our work to expose human rights abuses in the Soviet Union often dovetailed with established American foreign policy, doing the same thing in Central and South America would directly challenge the Reagan administration.

It was clear to me that Orville Schell, with his businesslike manner and Wall Street résumé, would be the perfect person to preside over the new organization—as a stoic, rational figure of the establishment, he could hardly be accused of being pro-communist. I was delighted when he accepted the position as chair of Americas Watch.

I also thought that we needed an executive director who could oversee both Americas Watch and Helsinki Watch, someone with both business and organizational ability, and hopefully with some fund-raising skills, which we desperately needed. I asked Aryeh Neier, who was then still at New York University and was very involved on our board and executive committee. It had been a few years since he had stepped down as the head of the ACLU, and he now said he was ready to do something more active than his teaching role. Needless to say, he was not happy with American foreign policy in Latin America.

Juan Méndez became the first staff member of Americas Watch. He was a young Argentine lawyer who had begun to represent political prisoners during the regime of Isabel Perón. For his efforts, he was thrown in jail and tortured.

It happened that Juan had been a high school exchange student in Iowa. After his arrest, his former host family began a campaign to get him released. They convinced members of Congress to protest directly to the Argentine authorities. The noise they made may have saved his life. As Juan recalls, he was one of a group of young attorneys in Buenos Aires who protested torture and defended political prisoners; at least seven of his colleagues were killed. The junta sent Juan into exile in 1977. He ended up in Washington, D.C., where he worked for a civil rights law group and did pro bono work for human rights cases in Latin America. We set up an office in Washington for him, which gave him the great advantage of being able to meet with members of Congress, and it also gave Helsinki Watch a Washington office whenever Jeri or Aryeh needed to go down for a meeting.

Jeri Laber still headed Helsinki Watch, and I remained as the chair. As executive director, Aryeh looked after the strategic direction of both divisions. Aryeh, with his huge experience at the ACLU, fit naturally into the role. In the early days, when we had very little staff, he did everything from press relations to some fund-raising, as well as pushing to develop considerably our research and reporting techniques.

I saw Americas Watch being added to Helsinki Watch more or less the same way I saw Knopf joining Random House. While both had obviously separate functions, the organization was strengthened by having two strong, complementary arms. This also marked the beginning of the overlap in approaching governmental agencies and the press that would eventually lead to Human Rights Watch.

Our first conflict with the Reagan administration came right after we established Americas Watch.

We had worked with Patricia Derian, the assistant secretary of state for human rights under Jimmy Carter, on several occasions in our first few years, and she was dedicated to keeping human rights issues on the diplomatic agenda of the United States. We were less than thrilled when the Reagan administration announced that it had nominated Ernest Lefever as Derian's replacement.

Lefever, an academic and the head of a little-known right-wing think tank, had written that the United States had no right to "promote human rights in other sovereign states." His policy, he made clear, would be to denounce publicly the human rights violations of communist governments, but to work behind the scenes with right-wing dictators friendly to the United States. He had also written that he did not believe that military and economic aid given by the United States should be linked to human rights concerns. He had essentially swallowed, enhanced, and regurgitated the ideas espoused by Jeane Kirkpatrick.

We concluded that the appointment of Lefever would be a disaster for human rights causes around the world. It would be particularly devastating in Latin America, where the dictatorships were using more and more violence against their citizens. His approach could have really destroyed the whole idea of human rights if America stopped condemning the outrages of these governments while pretending to care deeply about the same abuses in the Soviet Union. One of the main parts of our strategy was to lobby the United States to include human rights issues as part of its diplomacy. Since Lefever had renounced that approach, he seemed a horrible pick to be the State Department's lead person on human rights.

We also knew that it wouldn't be easy to block Lefever's appointment. His position was considered by the Senate to be a minor nomination, and the tendency was to go ahead with whomever the president recommended, as the Senate had more important things to attend to.

In a fortunate bit of timing, the Lefever nomination brought the publishing and human rights sides of my life together. It turned out that Lefever's hearing before the Senate Foreign Relations Committee was scheduled for May 1981, the same time that Random House was preparing to publish Jacobo Timerman's memoir of his imprisonment in Argentina, *Prisoner Without a Name, Cell Without a Number.*

As soon as I got the galley and read Timerman's book, I knew that he had written a work of incredible power. As I read it, I had something of an epiphany—I saw what we could do if we brought the advantages of a book publishing house with national and international contacts and hooked it up to the human rights movement. I realized that I was in an incredible position to do that by making the decisions on what to publish without having to sell the ideas to other publishing houses, because the projects were frequently very speculative. These authors, who were so important in dramatizing and humanizing the human rights struggle, would have the imprimatur of a major publishing house, which could work to make sure the authors' stories were heard.

In his book, Timerman wove the facts of his own imprisonment and torture together with everything else he had witnessed. He wrote about hearing a whole family—father, mother, and daughter—tortured in front of one another: "Suddenly an entire culture based on familial love, devotion, the capacity for mutual sacrifice collapses."

He detailed the anti-Semitism of his captors, from the torturers who chanted "Jew, Jew, Jew" as they did their work to his appearances before military tribunals in which the first question he was asked was always if he was Jewish, as if that were a sufficient crime in and of itself.

Looking back at his experience, he wondered how the rest of the world went about its business without making an attempt to intervene. "If you add up all the victims and victimizers, they form such a small percentage of the world population," he writes. "What are the others engaged in? We victims and victimizers, we're part of the same humanity, colleagues in the same endeavor to prove the existence of ideologies, feelings, heroic deeds, religions, obsessions. And the rest of humanity, the great majority, what are they engaged in?"

As it turned out, Timerman's book showed how the combination of book publishing and human rights could influence the political process. The publication of the book gave Timerman a platform, and he was a man who knew how to use it.

With his book about to be published, I got the idea that he would be the perfect person to speak against Lefever's appointment. Timerman, of course, was eager to get the United States to become a forceful voice against the atrocities of Latin American governments. He credited Derian's vigorous advocacy on his behalf with helping to secure his release, so he knew how important it was to have someone in the State Department who would use the position to speak out and advocate.

When we opened our Washington office, along with Juan Méndez, Aryeh had hired Holly Burkhalter, a former staffer for

Congressman Tom Harkin of Iowa, who was particularly effective as a liaison to Congress. It was apparent right from the beginning that she was a person of great ability. She combined good judgment with adept writing skills, was able to speak forcefully in public, and had a personality that endeared her to almost everybody she met.

For a month or two before Lefever's confirmation hearings, Holly set up a series of meetings for Orville, Aryeh, and me with most of the seventeen members of the Senate Foreign Relations Committee. When we spoke with the senators, we made a point to bring up Timerman's story and Derian's role in his release. If Lefever had been in charge of the human rights policy at the time, we said, Timerman might still be in prison, or worse.

Many of the senators were sympathetic to our argument. They included the head of the committee, Charles Percy, a Republican from Illinois, and the ranking minority member, Claiborne Pell, a Democrat from Rhode Island. After our meeting with him, Pell read *Prisoner Without a Name, Cell Without a Number* and was appalled by its depiction of torture and anti-Semitism.

The night before the Lefever hearings were set to begin, I hosted a dinner in Washington to celebrate the publication of Timerman's book. Many of the senators on the Foreign Relations Committee attended and spoke with Timerman.

The next day, Aryeh, Juan, and I went to the hearing with Timerman. It was an electric moment when we walked into the Senate hearing room. Senator Pell stopped the meeting to welcome Timerman, and the crowd gave him a standing ovation. I knew then that we had succeeded in making the hearing a contest between two men's views of how the United States should advocate for human rights—Lefever's and Timerman's.

Lefever had said that, when dealing with Latin American military regimes, he favored "quiet diplomacy" over public shaming. At one point in the hearing, Senator Percy asked if Timerman wanted to say anything. He got up, went to the microphone, and told the senators: "Silent diplomacy is silence. Quiet diplomacy is surrender."

The Senate Foreign Relations Committee voted 13–4 against Lefever's confirmation, and the Reagan administration withdrew the nomination.

* * *

In the fall of 1981, Jeri made her first research trip to the Eastern Bloc. The idea was that she would meet with dissidents and gather information about their treatment. This firsthand knowledge would then add to our credibility in our talks with reporters and government officials.

When Jeri applied for visas, she put her occupation down as "housewife" and listed the purpose of her trip as "tourism." In Prague, she visited with people involved in the Charter 77 dissident movement, which was then under intense political pressure—several members of the group, including Václav Havel, had just been jailed. She spoke with Solidarity leaders in Warsaw before moving on to Budapest, where she met with dissident intellectuals there. To avoid having her notes confiscated at the airport, she wrote them in tiny script and crumpled them up before placing them in her pockets. She also developed a system, which I never understood, of writing in code, so she could list phone numbers in a way that only she could read.

I saw what was involved in Jeri's work a few years later, when Helen and I went to Prague on vacation. We met Jeri, who was there for work, and we went to visit a Czech novelist, Ivan Klima. I remember the extreme care we had to take. First we went by bus, then took a trolley, and then walked around the block a few times to make sure no one was following us.

Jeri, like me, had been barred from Russia, but we hired a fearless woman named Cathy Fitzpatrick to do on-the-ground research there. To visit one dissident imprisoned in a mental hospital in Moscow, Cathy went on the weekend, when she knew the regular guards would be off duty. She gained entrance by claiming that she was the dissident's cousin visiting from Latvia, which she figured would explain her accent. She did this successfully. It's the kind of thing when you're running an organization that you don't want to know about until it's over, because the consequences of her getting caught could have been quite horrible. It's one of the reasons I've always admired people doing human rights work.

In early 1982, we also began an effort to cobble together an international federation of Helsinki groups. The idea had originated with the Moscow group that formed in 1976, but for obvious reasons—several members were in prison—the group didn't have the luxury to pursue it. My thought was that we could have all these letterheads from Helsinki groups in different countries, and when we wanted to call attention to something, we could send a letter from all these different places—the Helsinki groups in Finland, England, Spain, and so on. It seemed like a way to multiply the pressure that we could exert.

There were a couple of big problems. The first was that there simply weren't Helsinki groups in a lot of Western European countries, and the second was that there was absolutely no way to raise funds for several new groups. So building a network of new Helsinki groups had to be done on a tight budget, and it really only came about because of the sheer perseverance of Jeri Laber and later the federation's executive director, Gerald Nagler, who didn't let the idea die.

Jeri spent several months on the road in Europe, visiting cities such as Madrid, Milan, Vienna, Brussels, and Stockholm in order to find people who were interested in heading local Helsinki groups. She eventually recruited representatives from eighteen countries. They included scientists, academics, lawyers, and writers—anyone she could find with a genuine interest in human rights and the potential to do something about it. It was all done on a volunteer basis.

Aryeh got the Rockefeller Foundation to fund a September 1982 meeting at its Bellagio Center on Lake Como in Italy, where we agreed to launch the International Helsinki Federation for Human Rights. I don't remember much about the conversation, but the comfort and location of the conference center was something very rare for human rights meetings. It's almost worth trying to figure out something to meet about just so you can go to Bellagio.

We did succeed in agreeing to get the international federation going, and the group began to take shape.

In the meantime, Americas Watch quickly came into prominence. It had to, because the human rights situation in Latin America was deteriorating as various dictatorships, with their usual brutal methods, took power throughout the region.

In El Salvador, an American-supported military government was fighting off a leftist insurgency. The government's tactics included "death squads" comprising out-of-uniform members of the military who kidnapped and killed the opposition, real or perceived. In 1980 and 1981, death squads assassinated Catholic archbishop Óscar Arnulfo Romero as he was giving Mass; kidnapped six opposition politicians from a press conference and murdered them; raped and killed three American nuns (two Maryknoll and one Ursuline) as well as a lay worker; assassinated two American land reform advisors from the AFL-CIO; and killed John Sullivan, an American freelance journalist who disappeared from his hotel room hours after his arrival in the country and was later found in a shallow grave. In the worst atrocity, government troops in December 1981 massacred more than 800 civilians in the village of El Mozote as part of their efforts to stop peasants from supporting the leftists.

In Nicaragua, to the south of El Salvador, the four-decade-long, American-supported military dictatorship of the Somoza family had been overthrown in 1979 by the left-wing Sandinistas. Upon taking office, Reagan denounced the new Nicaraguan government and, through the CIA, began to fund an insurgency by Somoza loyalists, known as the Contras. The result was a horrible civil war.

Guatemala was in the middle of its own prolonged civil war, which ran between 1960 and 1996 as the country's military government clashed with a left-wing guerrilla insurgency. That war took an estimated two hundred thousand lives.

In all these conflicts, Reagan's administration supported the right-wing military forces with scant regard for human rights. I did the best I could to keep informed, but I was very glad that Orville Schell, board member Steve Kass, and the low-key but indomitable Juan Méndez were deeply involved.

There were some tense moments with the American government—so tense that even Orville lost it at one point.

After Jeane Kirkpatrick's appointment as U.S. ambassador to the UN, Orville and I set up a meeting with her before she was to take a trip to Argentina. On some issues, such as calling out the Soviets on their treatment of dissidents, Kirkpatrick agreed with our positions. This, however, was not one of those cases.

Our purpose was to convince her to meet with the Mothers of the Plaza de Mayo. We wanted her to make a visible show of American support and to send a message to the Argentine junta that the United States was concerned about the disappearances and helping the mothers find out what had happened to their children.

Kirkpatrick simply refused to consider it. She didn't give a reason. While admittedly it could have been a long discussion, we really didn't even have a very satisfactory short discussion. Orville—in my view one of the most reasonable of men and someone who could find ways to make strong points graciously—became increasingly frustrated at the meeting. Before long, he was banging the desk and saying, "I just can't believe this! It's outrageous!"

We accomplished nothing. Kirkpatrick did not meet with the Mothers of the Plaza de Mayo, and in Chile she sent her number three person to a human rights meeting, which was a clear signal to General Pinochet that he didn't have much to worry about from the United States.

After Reagan's election, Congress passed a law that required the president to certify that El Salvador was making progress on human rights in order for U.S. military assistance to continue to flow into the country. The certification was required every six months. We knew that the Reagan administration was going to overlook human rights abuses in order to support its Salvadoran allies, so we scrambled to publish our own research before the first certification was due in January 1982.

The 275-page report, a joint effort with the ACLU, documented six hundred disappearances in El Salvador as well as repression of the Catholic Church and the suspension of freedom of the press. It made the case that the military government was a serial abuser of human rights. Nevertheless, Reagan, as expected, certified the Salvadoran government, saying that it was making a "concerted" effort to improve human rights conditions.

Our report was a well-documented, carefully researched challenge to the administration's version of reality in Central America and it received a lot of press attention. It was also the first shot in what would be a running battle between Americas Watch and the White House.

We hired more staff members to fund research in Latin America. Every six months, right before the presidential certification was due, we published a report detailing abuses in El Salvador. The administration, in turn, tried to cast doubt on our methods and to brand us as communist sympathizers. One would think that our work on the Soviet Union would make it hard to discredit us as being left-wing, but that contradiction did not seem to occur to them.

At Americas Watch, we felt that even though the Reagan administration was going to keep insisting that El Salvador was making progress on human rights, our efforts to shine some light on the situation might result in officials quietly pressuring their Salvadoran allies to cool things down.

If nothing else, however, the constant scrutiny of the Reagan administration helped us to perfect our methodology. We knew that everything we did would be open to attack, which made us extremely careful in our reporting. I should add that we had an extraordinarily competent researcher in El Salvador, Jemera Rone. I never got to know her very well, but I admired her enormously and many times found myself worrying about her security; her flaming red hair made her easy to spot.

In the early 1980s, the Nicaraguan Contras were a pet cause for Ronald Reagan. The president, in arguing for funding for the Contras, called them "freedom fighters," "the moral equal of our founding fathers." The Sandinistas, in his rhetoric, took their place among the most odious regimes on the planet.

In March 1985, we released a report on the situation in the country. We found that the Sandinista government was indeed guilty of a large number of human rights abuses. At the same time, the Contras had an even higher rate of atrocities.

Our researchers found, for example, that the Contras had killed a whole wedding party of six—including the bride and groom—in order to strike terror into civilians in the countryside. They documented cases of rape, mutilation, kidnapping, torture, and murder. As an insurgent group, the Contras deliberately terrorized civilians—the point was to show them that the U.S. government could not offer protection.

Nicaragua, in short, was a place where there was certainly no easy solution. If the U.S. government couldn't stop the Contras from committing atrocities, we felt that the least it could do was to not arm them. Our position was that our government should not further inflame a terrible situation with aid to the insurgency.

At the time, Congress was considering whether to cut off funds to the Contras—it eventually did, leading to the Iran-Contra arms-for-hostages scandal, in which the Reagan administration clandestinely sent arms forbidden by Congress—and our report was not welcome. In testimony before Congress, Secretary of State George Shultz attacked us, saying that our research didn't accord with the U.S. government's intelligence on Nicaragua.

In the end, a lot of our mainstream credibility as an organization came from Orville Schell's position as a Wall Street lawyer and mine as the head of Random House. Because the staff was getting so much heat over its reporting on El Salvador, we decided that we should go to Nicaragua and see things for ourselves.

So in the spring of 1985, Orville and I flew to Managua, Nicaragua, with Juan Méndez, who had set up a number of meetings for us. We spoke with the family that owned one of the major newspapers in the country, who turned out to be pro-Contra. A prominent Spanish Jesuit priest, Juan Hernández Pico, told us the Sandinistas hadn't been great, but they had accomplished two things: they had stopped torture in police stations and forbidden the military from raiding farms and stealing the livestock. He said these were pretty good advances in Nicaragua.

We also had a long meeting with Daniel Ortega, the Nicaraguan president. His goal was to tell us all he could about the human rights violations committed by the Contras. We also pressed him on reports about Sandinista abuses, asking him about specific cases. Juan asked to see the government's interrogation centers, a request that he would make for years before it was finally granted.

Our sense of Nicaragua was that there was a corrupt government on one side engaging in a civil war with a vicious guerrilla force on the other. From a human rights standpoint, it was a mess. And the United States had certainly not picked savory allies in the fight.

The most memorable part of our trip came when we drove into the countryside, to the north near the Honduran border. We rented a Jeep and driver, and we were stopped upon entering the area and asked by the Nicaraguan soldiers whether we wanted a military escort to go near the border. We had a discussion among ourselves about whether a military escort would offer more or less protection. While the escort might be able to defend us if we were attacked, it also could attract an attack as well.

I remember thinking it was the kind of discussion I never thought I would have in my life. I think it was Juan who convinced us against taking the military escort, his reasoning being that without it we'd be just another car driving around the country. Also, we had been told that most of the attacks happened at night, so if we got out before dark, we'd be okay.

It was a very hilly region, not far from Managua but difficult to reach because of the bad roads. The Contras, who were based over the border in Honduras, were very active in the area. Most of the farmers there had been organized into collective farms as part of the Sandinistas' agricultural policy, and also, for safety—at least on the farms some of your fellow farmers were armed and you could defend yourself. Still, the collective was often not powerful enough to fend off guerrilla attacks by the Contras, who would kill the farmers, rape the women, and destroy the local school before they left.

My memory of one farmer is particularly vivid. He told us that when the Contras attacked his farm, he had fallen to the floor and his son had draped himself over him. The farmer showed us a bullet scar on his neck, where they had shot at him but missed. His son had been shot in the head and killed. The farmer told us he had blacked out. When he woke up, he saw the family dog lapping up his son's blood from the floor.

I realized that what was happening in Nicaragua was much more terrible than our government was letting on.

* * *

In the early 1980s, the human rights field was still something of a cottage industry, so people who were dedicated to the issues and wanted to have challenging work tended to come into our orbit. Our early staffers were generally young, in their twenties and thirties, and the majority of them were women. It's impossible to say exactly why that was, but there were a lot of very smart, highly motivated women who found their way into jobs with us, including Jeri Laber; Cynthia Brown and Jemera Rone, who were Latin American researchers; Holly Burkhalter, our liaison with Congress in Washington; Cathy Fitzpatrick, the Russia researcher; Dorothy Thomas, who founded our women's rights division; and Susan Osnos, who took a leadership position when she and her husband Peter Osnos returned from the Soviet Union.

Our staff was augmented by a motivated and involved board that included people with high levels of interest in human rights issues. Some of the most involved board members were Alice Henkin, Steve Kass, Bruce Rabb, Marvin Frankel, Jack Greenberg, and Bill Carmichael. George Soros attended many meetings and was also an early funder. A lot of ideas came out of board meetings, and it wasn't unusual for board members to go into the field with researchers. The line between the staff and the board was not as fixed as it would later become, especially as the organization began to rely on board members as fund-raisers. In the early days, Aryeh and I did all the fund-raising in individual meetings with foundations.

Aryeh was very dedicated to building the organization and its reputation step by step. We met every week for about two hours to go over every facet of the organization. I was always amazed at the amount of information Aryeh was able to keep in his head ready for instant recall—he knew everything from what each field researcher was doing and the details of individual reports to the latest on our advocacy strategy in Washington.

With both Watch groups well established, we began talking about expanding to cover other parts of the world. To enlarge the organization, though, we needed funding.

I was thinking about how to drum up more money when I got a call, totally out of the blue, from a man named Thornton Bradshaw, who was the chairman of RCA. Bradshaw had taken over the company in 1981, a year after it had sold Random House. He told me he thought Random House was a real jewel and that RCA had been stupid to unload it. When he invited me to breakfast, I was happy to accept.

So we met for what I assumed would be just a social conversation. After we chatted for a bit, Bradshaw asked me about my interests outside of Random House. He seemed really interested when I started to tell him about Helsinki Watch and Americas Watch, which was unusual for a businessman. When I finished, he asked what I wanted to do next.

"Well," I said, "we'd like to expand to cover the rest of the world. We'd like to start Asia Watch, Africa Watch, and Middle East Watch."

"How much do you think that will cost?" he asked.

I said, "At least $250,000 for each committee annually for three years, so, overall, $2,250,000."

He thought for a moment, and the next thing out of his mouth blew me away. "I think I can get it for you," he said. "I'm chairman of the board of the MacArthur Foundation. Let me see what I can do."

Bradshaw was true to his word. The money that came out of that meeting paid for us to cover most of the world by the end of the decade.

It also set the template for how fund-raising went for much of my time as chair of Human Rights Watch. Many large donations came from private foundations whose founders, board members, or program staff were introduced to me or I met at social functions.

The specific stories tell it best. Leon Levy, who managed a series of mutual funds, was a wonderful personal friend who was always great to talk with because his interests were so varied. Leon was one of our early and consistent funders. He also founded an economic institute at Bard College to honor his father, and when he invited me to the opening, he sat me next to a friend of his, the banker Herbert Sandler. I told Herbert and his wife, Marion, about Human Rights Watch, and they became interested. They got to know

Aryeh and his successor as executive director, Ken Roth, and have been big supporters ever since.

One year I won an award at Barnard College, the Barnard Medal of Distinction, and was seated next to the businessman Donald Pels. Not only did he become a substantial funder of Human Rights Watch, but he also married the brilliant Wendy Keys, who developed the sensational programs of the Lincoln Center Film Society and joined the Human Rights Watch board.

In the late 1980s, a woman named Irene Diamond started coming to our Human Rights Watch board meetings with her friend Dorothy Cullman, who was also a big supporter. Irene had led an interesting life. She had started out as a script editor in Hollywood, and one of her discoveries was a much-rejected, unproduced play called *Everybody Comes to Rick's*. She urged Warner Brothers to take a chance on it, so we can thank Irene for the movie *Casablanca*. In the early 1940s, she married a New York real estate developer named Aaron Diamond, who later became quite rich. The couple set up the Aaron Diamond Foundation, and right before Aaron's death in the early 1980s, they decided to give away all of the foundation's money over the next decade—$220 million.

Irene started by giving $50,000 a year to Human Rights Watch, and over time we became friends. Irene was greatly disturbed by the way those afflicted with AIDS were treated in the early days of the disease, so she used a lot of the foundation's money to pay for a lab to try to come up with a cure. The then unknown young scientist she found to head the organization, David Ho, turned out to be a superb choice as he pioneered the use of antiretroviral therapy, which has saved an untold number of lives.

One day, when we were at lunch, Irene asked me what Human Rights Watch really needed to secure the organization's future. I told her that one of our most consistent concerns was our yearly overhead, and I'd love to build up a cash fund to pay for it. She asked how much we would need.

Not really thinking about it, I came up with the figure of $30 million. To my shock, she told me she wanted to make a donation for that amount. It gave us a solid base for many years.

10

THE SOVIET UNION IMPLODES: HUMAN RIGHTS, 1985–90

DURING THE FIRST HALF OF THE 1980S, IT WAS IMPOSSIBLE TO know if we were making any headway with the Soviets. No matter how much attention was directed at their human rights abuses, nothing seemed to deter them from jailing or exiling anyone they wanted.

The Madrid Helsinki Review Conference, which started in late 1980, dragged on for three years, until the summer of 1983. The main result of the negotiations was a carefully worded thirty-five-page document in which all sides agreed to participate in a series of further meetings. The Soviets succeeded in watering down all the human rights provisions. For Helsinki Watch, the main usefulness of the conference was that it had provided a venue to publicize the plight of dissidents. By the end, though, the Madrid conference was overshadowed by Soviet-American tension over Reagan's plan to base more intermediate-range nuclear missiles in Western Europe.

It was also a time of substantial turnover in the Soviet leadership. In November 1982, Leonid Brezhnev died of a heart attack. Yuri Andropov, who had been the KGB head responsible for crushing both the Prague Spring in 1968 and the dissident movement in the 1970s, succeeded Brezhnev. Three months after taking charge, in February 1983, Andropov suffered total kidney failure and died a year later. He was replaced by Konstantin Chernenko, who had been Brezhnev's right-hand man. Chernenko had health problems from the start and died in March 1985. His replacement was Mikhail Gorbachev.

At age fifty-four, Gorbachev was younger and more energetic than his immediate predecessors. Though he was a lifelong Communist Party apparatchik, he recognized that economic reforms were necessary to revive the Soviet Union's stagnant economy. He took office with promises of "New Thinking."

At Helsinki Watch, we were skeptical. Despite the rhetoric, there were no immediate changes after Gorbachev took power. In July 1985, after his first one hundred days in office, I published an op-ed in the *Times* titled "Under Gorbachev, the Old Repression."

I noted that since April, there had been no news of Andrei Sakharov and Elena Bonner—their house in Gorky was dark and shuttered. The rumor was that Sakharov had been placed in a hospital for force-feeding after he began a hunger strike to protest the authorities preventing Bonner from getting the medical care she needed.

Yuri Orlov, the founder of the original Moscow Helsinki monitoring group, had been released from prison camp but was in internal exile in a provincial town, where he had just been beaten up by a group of hooligans. Photos smuggled out of Russia made it clear that he was in terrible shape.

After thirteen years in exile in the United States, Valery Chalidze was still hoping that his sister would get a visa to leave the Soviet Union. After applying to emigrate, she had lost her job as a scientist and was working as a maid. Although he had tried for years, Chalidze was unable to get his mother out of Russia, and she had died of cancer while waiting.

Finally, I wrote in the op-ed, Natan Sharansky was in his seventh year in a prison camp, where his health had dangerously deteriorated.

It was a bleak summary. Fortunately, things were about to take a turn.

During Andrei Sakharov and Elena Bonner's exile in Gorky, Elena's heart problems had worsened. She was always worried that if she went into the hospital in Russia, she wouldn't come out again, and

Andrei had been calling for her to be allowed to go abroad for medical care.

It turned out that the rumors that had reached us in New York were true—in the spring of 1985, Andrei went on a hunger strike and the Soviets forced him into the hospital, where he was fed through a tube rammed down his throat. He was released in July, but wrote a letter to Gorbachev to tell him that he would go back on hunger strike in two weeks if Elena did not receive permission for medical leave.

No word came from Gorbachev—instead, Soviet agents simply took Andrei back to the hospital. Elena's two children, Alexei and Tatyana, lived in Boston, and in August Alexei began a hunger strike in front of the Soviet embassy in Washington. That led to a congressional resolution protesting the treatment of Andrei. In October, while Gorbachev was on a state visit to France with his wife Raisa, permission was suddenly granted for Elena to travel abroad.

She came to New York in December 1985 and we met in my office. She arrived with her usual determination and purpose. After some talk about Andrei and life in Gorky, she got down to business. She said that she was scheduled to have heart surgery in Boston, but that after the operation, she'd have a six-week recovery period during which she wanted to write a book.

"Don't you think you'll be too weak?" I asked.

"No, no," she said, "I'll be able to do it. I'll be sitting there with nothing else to do."

"Well, have you ever written a book?"

"No, but I'm absolutely sure I can do it," she said. "It's going to be the story of Andrei and me in Gorky. I get a lot of interest in that. And the reason I have to write is because my two children are living in the same house together and they fight all the time. I have to buy another house so they can be separate."

She told me that she'd already picked out a house to buy in Boston. She wanted to close on it before her operation, which was in three days, so she needed an advance on the book right away.

"Well, we do give advances," I said. "It's usually part on signing and part when the whole manuscript is handed in or published."

"I need the advance all at once, before I begin the book," she said.

"Why?" I asked.

"Because I need to buy the house for my kids."

"Okay," I said, "I'll give you a small advance."

"It can't be a small advance," she said. "It's an expensive house."

At this point, Anne Johnson, my assistant who was very friendly with Elena, came into my office. I asked Anne to stay and listen to the negotiation.

I asked Elena how much she wanted.

Without a pause, she said, "$250,000."

I was absolutely thrown. It was, to say the least, a lot more than I had been thinking about paying. Anne stood behind Elena, emphatically shaking her head no and giving the thumbs-down signal.

Elena continued: "I need the money now, before I leave today, so I can close on the house. I promise you, you'll have a book that you can publish. I'm absolutely sure of it or I wouldn't do this."

I thought a minute, turning over in my head everything Andrei and Elena had been through as well as our chances of making the money back. I also remembered that we had Andrei's autobiography under contract, for which we had paid a reasonable amount.

Finally, I said, "Okay, we'll do it. Anne, go downstairs and tell them that Mrs. Sakharov is in my office, and I'm buying a book from her. We'll do the contract later, but I'm giving her an advance of a quarter of a million dollars against the book about the story of Andrei Sakharov and Elena Bonner in exile in Gorky."

Anne looked at me like I was crazy and then went down and got the check. I gave it to Elena, who thanked me and said that I would have a manuscript in six weeks.

Looking back now, it strikes me that Andrei and Elena were pretty good negotiators. With our handshake deal, Andrei had guaranteed that I was going to bend over backward to be fair to him financially, and Elena, with her urgency to get money for a house for her kids, spurred me in the moment to be more generous than perhaps was wise. But knowing the couple well, I figured it would work out in the end.

After Elena left, Anne came back into my office. "Well, what are you going to do now?" she asked. "You just blew a quarter of a million dollars."

I didn't exactly know, but I immediately called Carol Janeway, who sold foreign rights for Knopf, and told her, "I just bought this book by Elena Bonner. Here's what I want to do with you. Let's put together a list of foreign publishers and tell them we bought it blind and they have to buy it the same way if they want it. Let me know how much you think we can get from each country. I paid too much for it, but it's the Sakharovs and I felt it was the right thing to do."

So she went to work. My memory is that we recovered more than $150,000 by selling the rights in countries such as Germany, Japan, and Italy, which made our final investment under $100,000.

Elena had sextuple bypass heart surgery. As she promised, she worked on the manuscript during her recovery. For part of the time, she went to the Virgin Islands with Ed Kline, where she locked herself in her hotel room, chain-smoking and typing late into the night. When the guests in the next room complained about the noise, she reluctantly agreed to stop by ten p.m., though she didn't quite see the problem—she had paid for the room, she said, so why couldn't she do what she wanted in it? We published the book with the title *Alone Together*. It was well reviewed, generated favorable attention for the couple's plight, and sold modestly.

In February 1986, Natan Sharansky, then in his ninth year in prison camp, was released. He was not pardoned in any way, but exchanged for two Soviet spies. Still, it was a small victory for the human rights movement, including Helsinki Watch, the Jewish human rights groups, and, above all, Sharansky's wife Avital, who had dedicated her life to getting him released. We regarded the fact that we had made a dissident important enough for the U.S. government to trade two spies as a step forward. Reagan, we learned, had taken a personal interest in Sharansky.

In a scene out of a John le Carré novel, Sharansky was brought to a bridge in East Berlin, where he was allowed to cross into the West. Avital was waiting for him on the other side.

Nine years earlier, when Avital had left Russia for Israel, the plan had been that Natan would follow a week later. Instead he had been arrested and imprisoned. When he reached Avital on the other side of the bridge, Natan's humor, which must have been part of what

sustained him during his horrific experience in prison, was still in-
tact. When he touched his wife's hands for the first time in nine
years, his first words were "I'm sorry I'm late."

During the years he was in prison, Natan Sharansky had become
an international symbol of the struggle of Jews to emigrate from
Russia. Jewish students in New York, for example, had demon-
strated in front of the Soviet consulate to press for his release. As a
result, there was a substantial amount of interest among publishers
in his story, so I decided to preempt it. Natan and Avital had gone
from Germany to Israel, so in April I flew there with Peter Osnos,
the *Washington Post* reporter who had introduced me to Natan in
1976 and whom I later hired as an editor at Random House. We
met with Natan and spoke with him about writing a memoir about
the refusenik movement and his time in prison. We then met with
his agent, Marvin Josephson, who named a price. I think he was
surprised when I immediately accepted it. We published the book,
Fear No Evil, two years later.

In May 1986, Natan came to the United States, where he was to
be honored by Congress and scheduled to meet with Ronald Reagan. He arrived in New York before going to Washington, and we
held a press conference for him at Random House. He was joined
by Elena Bonner, still in the country following her heart surgery,
and Lyudmila Alexeyeva, another original member of the Moscow
Helsinki Group who had been working with Helsinki Watch following her exile. It was the tenth anniversary of the founding of the
Moscow Helsinki Group and the first time the three of them had
been together in nine years.

They met briefly in my office before going out to speak with
the reporters. The emotion of the moment was overwhelming. Although dissidents such as Elena and Lyudmila always came across
as extremely tough, they also knew that when friends such as Natan
were imprisoned, there was a chance they would never come out.

At the press conference, the trio spoke about Yuri Orlov and the
other Helsinki monitors who were still jailed in Russia. Elena described the harassment the group had faced before it disbanded in
1982. "So many were arrested that when it was national political
prisoners day, I spent it by myself," she said.

Natan displayed his typical humor. At one point, a young, aggressive *New York Post* reporter pointed his finger at him and said, "Tell us, Mr. Sharansky, when you meet with President Reagan on Monday, what will you say to him?"

Sharansky paused. He seemed very tired. He made a show of looking down and then up at the ceiling, as if he was thinking it over. Finally, he said, very slowly, "You know, I think President Reagan should be the first to hear what I am going to say to him." The whole room broke out in laughter.

Gorbachev, the Soviet bureaucrat, and Reagan, the Cold War warrior who unwittingly joked into an open microphone about bombing Russia, turned out to be unlikely partners. The pair had their first summit meeting in Geneva in 1985. The second was to be held in Reykjavik, Iceland, in October 1986.

About a month before the meeting in Iceland, Jeri Laber traveled to Washington to meet with State Department officials. While she was there, Jeri had a private discussion with Rozanne Ridgway, the assistant secretary of state for European and Canadian affairs. Jeri told Ridgway about Yuri Orlov, explaining how he had started the Moscow Helsinki Group and how he had been in prison followed by internal exile for nine years. Jeri said that Orlov's health was failing and stressed that something should be done to get him out immediately.

A few weeks later, Ridgway called to say that the Soviets had agreed to release Orlov in exchange for a Russian spy. She asked that Helsinki Watch look after him when he arrived in the United States.

Orlov landed at Kennedy Airport on October 6, 1986. He was a small, white-haired, soft-spoken man with an understated sense of humor. He told the reporters gathered at the airport he was grateful for his freedom but also very sad.

"I left behind my homeland, my beloved culture, my language, my friends and dear ones," he said. "This, of course, is not easy. And maybe the hardest part is that I left behind people who are still serving time. I suppose I feel some guilt over this. Why am I here and they there?"

Ed Kline and Lyudmila Alexeyeva took in Orlov and began to introduce him to other Russian émigrés. For me, it was hard with many of the dissidents, because I didn't speak Russian and always had to communicate through a translator. My role, I realized, was more as a facilitator than a friend—I was a person who could pull levers and get things done.

Helen and I hosted a dinner for Orlov in our apartment, and when he and I had a chance to speak with each other, I found him to be very humble. He told me that the years in prison camp had been terrible for his health, and he felt especially bad that his teeth had rotted because of lack of care.

I thought that was a problem I could do something about. I called my dentist, Dr. David Hendel, and asked him to see Orlov and to send the bill to me. Orlov came away with a new set of teeth. When I asked Dr. Hendel how much I owed him, he told me not to worry about it. "It's the least I can do," he said.

I later learned that Dr. Hendel happened to be Ed's dentist as well. After Dr. Hendel worked on Orlov, Ed sent several other Russian dissidents to him, and Dr. Hendel donated his time to do their dental work. After he saw how bad their dental care was, he actually made several trips to Russia to train dentists there in modern techniques.

Many years before Dr. Hendel worked on Orlov, I had been given a small, framed aphorism that I treasured. I always thought that someday I would like to have an award given to the person who most emulated the sentiment in the saying—that is, somebody who performed an act that makes a difference to someone else with absolutely no thought of personal gain of any kind. The sign read as follows: "There is no limit to the good a person can do if he or she doesn't care who gets the credit." David Hendel would certainly be a recipient.

As for Orlov, shortly after his arrival in the United States, he headed to Western Europe with Cathy Fitzpatrick, our Russia researcher, for a series of meetings with presidents, prime ministers, and diplomats. A very determined man, Orlov pressed them to call for the release of all political prisoners still locked up in the Soviet

Union. When he returned to America, he took an academic position as a nuclear physics scientist at Cornell. He remains there today.

The Soviets were sending so many mixed messages that it was impossible to know what they were up to. They had released both Orlov and Sharansky, but also stripped their citizenship and forced them into exile. Was this signaling a new direction, or were they just getting rid of a couple of headaches?

On December 8, 1986, Anatoly Marchenko, the indomitable author of the prison memoir *My Testimony*, which created a stir when it was published in the West in 1969, died in the gulag of a cerebral hemorrhage. During the previous years, he had suffered numerous beatings, had been placed in solitary confinement, and hadn't been allowed to see visitors. In the months before his death, he had been on a hunger strike to call for better conditions for prisoners. He was forty-eight years old when he died. Overall, he spent around twenty years of his life either in prison or internal exile.

His death brought a wave of international condemnation, and it must have scared the Soviets into thinking that Andrei Sakharov and Elena Bonner might die in exile. A week after Marchenko's death, at ten at night, the doorbell rang at the couple's apartment in Gorky. Andrei and Elena opened the door to find two electricians and a KGB agent. They said they had orders to install a phone. The next day, Gorbachev called. He told Andrei that the banishment was over and that he would be transported back to Moscow.

During the six years he spent in Gorky, Andrei had worked on the memoir we shook hands over in 1976. I've been told that he always carried the latest part of the manuscript with him. Once, when he went to the dentist, they put him under anesthetic without his consent; when he woke up, he found the manuscript had disappeared, and he had to start that section over again. As he finished portions of the manuscript, Elena would bring them to Moscow. They were smuggled out of the country from there, eventually making their way to us in New York, where Ed Kline and Ash Green, the book's editor, had them translated and waited for more to arrive.

* * *

By early 1987, Gorbachev had started the reforms that were meant to keep communism viable in the Soviet Union. *Perestroika* was gradually supposed to open the economy, and *glasnost* was to allow more freedom of speech. I don't think anyone had any idea where it all was headed.

At that time, I began to notice some changes in the behavior of Soviet publishing officials. In the summer of 1987, when Boris Stukalin and his cronies came to the United States for meetings, they accepted a list of one hundred imprisoned writers that Jeri and I had put together for the AAP's Freedom to Publish Committee. Instead of acting offended, they simply said they would look into it. It was a noticeable shift in attitude. They also promised that the Moscow Book Fair, set for that September, would be held in the spirit of *glasnost* and specifically invited me to come.

Though I had been banned from the Soviet Union since 1979, my visa for the book fair was promptly approved. Oddly enough, the Soviets at first denied Jeri's visa. They reconsidered after Roland Algrant, then chair of the Freedom to Publish Committee, threatened to boycott the fair if Jeri was not allowed to go.

Helen and I were looking forward to going back to Russia. When our friend Claudette Colbert, who would turn eighty-four that year, heard about the trip, she asked if she could come along as well. She said she had wanted to go to Russia for a long time, and this seemed like the perfect opportunity. I thought, "This is going to be interesting."

By this time, we had known Claudette for more than twenty years. Since I'd first rented her apartment in 1966, Helen and I not only became her friends, but even more than that, she practically adopted our children and gave them the most lavish presents imaginable every Christmas. And we had traveled with her before—once, for example, on a family ski trip to Austria.

Helen and I visited her in Barbados every winter, sometimes with our kids. We usually slept in a wonderful cottage that she originally had built so that Frank Sinatra and Mia Farrow would have a place to stay on their 1966 honeymoon.

Having dinner with Claudette was a really wonderful thing. Claudette had strong opinions and did not hide them, and almost every action in her life spoke to her belief in the freedom of the individual. She was a delight, very social and interested in art, ballet, music, and film. Though she was a staunch Republican and was close to Reagan from their days together in Hollywood (so close, in fact, that President Reagan and the First Lady once visited her in Barbados, but not when we were there), Claudette rarely talked politics. But if someone at the table started off on some political thing that Claudette did not agree with, she would grab whoever was sitting next to her and whisper in his or her ear a line that I think is one of the greatest I've ever heard: "When you're born dumb, it's for a long time."

Claudette always had very interesting guests. During one Barbados visit, Helen and I stayed with her at the same time as the playwright Lillian Hellman. At one of the lunches in the beautiful pavilion that Claudette had built down by the sea, Claudette and Lillian started to discuss food, which they both knew quite a bit about. The food at Claudette's was always superb—she had sent her Barbadian cook to culinary school in Paris.

Claudette and Lillian went back and forth, with Claudette saying why she thought French food was the best, and Lillian, who was from New Orleans, making the case for her hometown's cuisine. Right then I got the idea that the two of them could write a charming book together, alternating between chapters of Claudette championing French recipes and then Lillian praising New Orleans food. Both women said, "Oh, Bob, what a really wonderful idea! We have to do that."

Later in the afternoon, Lillian asked if she could speak to me alone. I strolled over to the cottage where she was. "Bob," she said, "of course I had to be enthusiastic about your idea. But I'm a writer and Claudette is an actress. What would I need Claudette for if I were going to write a cookbook? If I did, I would just write it and my name alone would carry it."

"Of course, Lillian," I said, "how foolish of me."

A little later, Claudette said, "Bob, dear, come up and let's have a chat." So we went to the little terrace attached to her room, where she usually spent the afternoons answering her mail and doing other little chores. She said, "Bob, I couldn't say anything at lunch.

I might love the idea of doing a little book on French cuisine. And I love having Lillian as a guest; she's charming and interesting and wonderful. But can you imagine trying to do a book with her? Are you out of your mind?"

Needless to say, the book never appeared.

Unfortunately, from almost the minute we landed in Moscow, Claudette hated the Soviet Union.

The first problem was that we couldn't get reservations at the National Hotel, which was the nicest place to stay. We ended up at the Intourist Hotel, a drab place that was a far cry from Claudette's usual standards. While Helen and I were unpacking, our phone rang. "Bob," Claudette said, "what kind of hotel have you booked us into? They don't have room service!" I couldn't believe that I had to explain to this very intelligent woman that not having room service was one of the least of the problems that she was going to encounter in the Soviet Union.

The next day, Helen, Claudette, Peter Osnos—who was along as an editor with the Random House delegation—and I went to have a meal at Andrei and Elena's apartment. It was a tiny place, and we were crowded into the living room with them and Elena's mother, who had survived a stay in the gulag during the Stalin era. Elena cooked up a wonderful multicourse Russian meal and the family was very warm and welcoming, but both Elena and her mother were chain-smokers, and her mother had a hacking cough. It was only our manners that prevented us from saying, "For God's sake, stop smoking!" It wouldn't have helped, for both Elena and her mother were not good at taking other people's advice.

That was the high point as far as Claudette's time in Moscow. After three days, it was clear that the trip wasn't working out for her. Moscow is very large, but Claudette was absolutely overcome with claustrophobia, as if she were in a cage. She despised everything about being in a closed society, from the drab surroundings to the women "minders" who sat on every floor of the hotel. It didn't help that a favorite brooch was stolen from Claudette's room and nothing could be done about it.

Claudette basically shut down. She was so miserable that we decided we had to get her out as soon as possible. Unfortunately, even something as simple as changing a plane ticket turned out to be very time consuming.

Peter, who spoke fluent Russian, managed to sort everything out. When we finally got Claudette to the airport, Peter tried to get her through customs quickly and easily. Despite his strenuous attempt to accomplish this, the Soviet border agents searched through Claudette's luggage and gave her a hard time about the missing brooch, which she'd had to declare on her customs form when she arrived. Claudette broke down in tears before they let her through.

For the rest of her life, whenever the trip came up, she just shuddered.

Despite Claudette's reaction, things were actually loosening up in Moscow, at least a bit. For one, the atmosphere at the book fair was somewhat relaxed. The Soviets still censored books, including ones by Lev Kopelev and Vasily Aksyonov, but the usual heavy-handedness was overshadowed by the feeling of change. Many of the writers on the list of prisoners that Jeri and I had prepared earlier that year had actually been released. Even the usually dour Soviet publishing officials seemed in positive spirits, as if they were at least debating what could and could not be said, and not just assuming that they could say nothing.

While we were in Moscow, Jeri and I also did some Helsinki Watch business. We went to meet a journalist named Lev Timofeyev, who had recently been released from prison. He had started a group called the Glasnost Press Club, and we were thinking about asking the group to join the International Helsinki Federation for Human Rights as the Moscow representative.

We knew that Timofeyev wanted to publish a samizdat, so we brought over a laptop computer to give to him. At the time, laptops were fairly bulky, very expensive, and very heavy. In the taxi on the way to Timofeyev's apartment, I asked Jeri where she had put the computer.

"It's in the bag right under your legs, Bob. When we get there, just take it out and bring it up to Timofeyev's apartment," she said.

I said, "Jeri, you know that when we get there, the apartment's going to have KGB outside. How are we going to do this?"

She said, "Well, you're going to pick it up, and they won't stop you, because you're president of Random House."

"Jeri, how are they going to know that?" I asked. "Did you send them a letter?"

As it turned out, we arrived at Timofeyev's apartment and carried the computer up without a problem. A few years later, when the KGB came to confiscate it, they asked Timofeyev where he got it. He said he'd bought it secondhand in downtown Moscow.

That week, the AAP hosted a reception and dinner for Russian writers. Unlike the one in 1979, where dissident writers had to pass through a cordon of police to get in, this one was attended by not only dissident writers but also mainstream Russian authors as well as Soviet publishing officials.

At the end of the trip, Helen, Peter, and I flew to Leningrad to spend a weekend sightseeing with Andrei and Elena. We found that we could go everywhere and no one recognized Andrei—even though he was famous in Russia and around the world, his photo had never been published in the Soviet press. One night we went to dinner at a newly opened private restaurant—Leningrad's only one at the time—where we were joined by David John Moore Cornwell, more commonly known by his pen name, John le Carré. A Knopf author, le Carré was in the country doing the research for his book *The Russia House*.

Over caviar and vodka, le Carré and Andrei talked about spies. Just a year earlier, such a conversation would have been unimaginable.

Three months later, in December 1987, Gorbachev came to Washington for another summit meeting with Reagan. The trip got a lot of press—by this time, Americans were intrigued with Gorbachev and his wife Raisa. Unlike the previous Soviet premiers, he was charismatic and charming, and people wondered if Russia was really changing.

Gorbachev had said he wanted to speak with the leaders of various American industries, and I was part of a group of publishers that was invited to the Soviet embassy to meet with him. It was meant to be something of an informal chat.

As we all sat around the conference table and shared small talk over coffee, it became obvious to me that absolutely nothing was going to come out of this. Here were the top book, newspaper, and magazine publishers in America—people such as Katharine Graham, the owner of the *Washington Post*—and they were asking questions like "How are you finding your reception in the United States?" Clearly, most of the group had decided that this was a social moment and not a time to engage Gorbachev.

We were each allowed to ask one question. In the group of twenty, I was in the last ten, and I remember thinking quite hard about whether I should go down the social path. Finally, I thought, "This is the only time in my life I'm ever going to have a chance to ask Gorbachev a question." I also thought that if nobody asked him about the writers and others still in prison for expressing their thoughts, he would assume that the issue wasn't high enough on our agendas to engage him.

Gorbachev had just had his book published by Harper & Row, so when it came my turn, I started by saying, "Mr. Gorbachev, you've just had your first book published here, and I hear it's doing very well. I'm certainly jealous that Harper is publishing it and not Random House, and I hope we get a chance to bid on your next one."

Gorbachev beamed.

I continued. "I also want to congratulate you on being the first Soviet leader to attack the problems of those imprisoned for their ideas in your country. I've been told that in your first two years, you have released half of the dissidents. That leads to the obvious question: When are you going to release the other half?"

As Gorbachev looked at me for a long moment, a transformation came over him. All the cheer went out of his face and you could tell something was building up. Then he exploded in an absolute rage—his face turned red and he began to scream at me. "I think you have problems enough in your own country, with your homeless, your prisons, and keeping Mexicans out with machine guns at your border! Why don't you look into that?"

Everyone in the room was completely taken aback. I hadn't expected such a strong reaction. I had just felt that he needed to know that this was a problem that was not going to go away. I had expected Gorbachev to make some statement like "We're going to look into their cases" and move on to the next question. His reaction was a total surprise.

After the meeting, some of the other publishers clearly thought I had made a mistake. They felt it was Gorbachev's first visit to the United States and that he should be received as a guest and allowed to express his views, and he should leave feeling good about the United States. I've thought about it a lot since. I think if this had been the beginning of a potentially longer relationship with Gorbachev, they might have been right. But in view of the fact that I never expected to see him again (and never did), I think, for me at least, that I did the right thing.

We realized something new was going on in Russia when the Soviets, in the fall of 1987, invited the International Helsinki Federation, which we had organized five years earlier, to visit Moscow for a week to discuss human rights issues.

By this time, the International Helsinki Federation had grown into something sizable. The group was based in Vienna and headed by Gerald Nagler, a retired Swedish jeweler. It was chaired by Karl "Kary" von Schwarzenberg, the descendant of a family of Czech aristocrats who had lost their property to the Communists. The family had relocated to Vienna, where it owned a baroque palace called Palais Schwarzenberg. Kary Schwarzenberg and his family lived in one wing, and another section had been turned into a magnificent five-star hotel. Schwarzenberg once told me that in the Middle Ages his family had owned ninety-nine castles throughout Central Europe. When I asked him why they didn't just make it one hundred, he said there was a very good reason: anyone who owned a hundred castles had to field his own army.

Jeri Laber and Nagler had done a great job of organizing the federation. As we had planned, it had become a way for protests about Soviet human rights abuses to come from groups located all around Europe, thus giving the impression that our movement was broadly based.

There was definitely an agenda behind the Soviets' invitation. A year earlier, at the start of the Vienna Helsinki Review Conference—the successor to the Madrid meeting—Soviet foreign minister Eduard Shevardnadze shocked the gathering when he announced that the Soviet Union wanted to host a human rights conference in Moscow. The idea was, to say the least, met with skepticism in the West. The invitation for the Helsinki Federation to visit Moscow seemed to be an attempt by the Soviets to build their credentials as being sincere about human rights.

At Helsinki Watch, we were of differing opinions about making the trip. I thought it might all turn out to be a sham, while Jeri argued that it would be an opportunity to meet with Soviet officials—at their invitation—and press for the release of political prisoners. I eventually came around to her way of thinking.

Overall, our delegation consisted of twenty-one people from ten Western countries. Some of the members were active in human rights work. They included František Janouch, a Czech physicist and dissident who had been forced into exile in Sweden; Irwin Cotler, a human rights lawyer from Canada (he later became Canada's attorney general and minister of justice and now sits on the board of Advancing Human Rights, a new organization in which I'm involved); Eric Siesby, a professor and head of the Danish Helsinki group; Ole Espersen, a Danish parliamentarian and former justice minister; Max van der Stoel, a former Dutch minister of foreign affairs; Gerald Nagler, the director of the International Helsinki Federation; and Kary von Schwarzenberg, the chair of the federation. The American contingent was made up of Jeri, Cathy Fitzpatrick, and me.

It was apparent after we landed in Moscow that some things had changed and some things hadn't. As we went through customs, I was approached by Soviet security agents who said they wanted to take me aside for "questioning." They said everyone else could go to the hotel, but they wanted to keep me there. Thankfully, Jeri stepped up and told them, "None of us will go anywhere without Mr. Bernstein." After a few tense minutes, the Soviets relented.

It was the last week of January 1988, and it was snowy and bitterly cold. On that first night, I called Andrei and Elena and they extended an invitation to come to their apartment. I went with František Janouch, and we stayed until one in the morning, learning about developments in Moscow and filling Andrei and Elena in on our trip.

That week, our group of International Helsinki Federation members traveled together to meet with Soviet bureaucrats, including officials from the Ministries of Justice, Internal Affairs, and Foreign Affairs. We used the opportunity to present them with a list of four hundred political prisoners, ask for the release of all dissidents, and stress the importance of freedom of speech. The Soviets gave us almost the same answer at every stop. "We really have our hands full," they said, "but we'll see what we can do." Their unofficial mantra was, "We want cooperation, not confrontation."

You could tell that change was happening, but no one knew how far it would go. The officials we met with were themselves trying to figure out which way the wind was blowing.

The most interesting part of the trip had to do with the Glasnost Press Club, the group organized by Lev Timofeyev, the journalist and recently released political prisoner to whom Jeri and I had delivered the laptop a few months earlier. Timofeyev had put together what was essentially the successor to Yuri Orlov's original Helsinki Group; the Glasnost Press Club focused on publicizing the Soviet regime's violations of its own laws. We had invited the association to become the Russian affiliate of the International Helsinki Federation.

After we arrived in Moscow, Jeri and I, along with several members of our delegation, went to Timofeyev's apartment to meet with the group. When we arrived, we saw a big black car parked outside with two men standing next to it. Very loud, amplified voices were coming out of speakers inside the car. We quickly realized that the men were listening to a conversation coming from Timofeyev's apartment.

We proceeded up to the meeting, where we told Timofeyev about the men. He said, "Good! We want the Soviets to know what the human rights problems in the country are. That's what we're here for."

It signaled a remarkable change for Timofeyev, who had already been imprisoned, to feel he could say that. The change was also brought home by the fact that around two dozen people had gathered in his apartment to meet with our group of Americans and Western Europeans. They included the two other leaders of the

Glasnost Press Club: Larisa Bogoraz, the widow of Anatoly Marchenko, the recently deceased dissident author, and Sergei Kovalev, a
biologist and longtime friend and ally of Andrei and Elena's.

As Jeri vividly recounts in her memoir, *The Courage of Strangers*, they had also invited representatives of many other independent
groups, including Ukrainians, members of an association for the
handicapped, former camp inmates, Hare Krishna, Jewish activists, and congregants of the Russian Orthodox Church. The room
was so crowded that several people had to sit on the floor. Once we
were all settled in, we began to talk about human rights conditions
in the Soviet Union.

Before long, the phone rang. When Timofeyev answered, a man—
Timofeyev later said it was probably the KGB—started to ask him
very pointed questions about why he did not have a job and was
leading the life of a "parasite." While it was, of course, an attempt
to intimidate Timofeyev, it also let us all know that the meeting was
being monitored. It showed the willingness of the Soviets to keep
you off-balance, so that you never knew what harsh methods they
might use if you stepped over the line (and, because the line moved
back and forth, you never knew exactly where it was). For the members of our delegation who hadn't experienced Soviet intimidation
firsthand, I think this blunt approach came as a shock.

The Soviet government had recently set up its own human rights
group, called the Public Commission for International Cooperation
on Humanitarian Problems and Human Rights. The Soviets told
us that they now understood about NGOs, that this was one of
their first, and they were going to be happy to discuss human rights
problems with us. I decided it should not be called an NGO, but a
"GONGO"—a government-organized nongovernmental organization, a phrase I think I invented.

The high point of our trip was to be a daylong meeting of the
International Helsinki Federation with the Soviet group, which
was headed by a bureaucrat named Fyodor Burlatsky, an aide to
Khrushchev and later Gorbachev. Without saying anything, we invited Lev Timofeyev, Larisa Bogoraz, and Sergei Kovalev to meet us
at our hotel on the morning of the meeting, as their group was the
new Russian affiliate of our federation. We decided that no special

discussions had to occur with the Soviets, as clearly they had invited us, and the Glasnost Press Club was one of the members of our group.

What occurred over the next few hours is so typical of what happens in closed societies, when hours can be spent on issues so small you can't conceive they're going to matter.

Timofeyev, Bogoraz, and Kovalev met us at our hotel and got on the bus with us to go to the meeting. The bus driver got off, and a few minutes later he came back with the two men who had been assigned to take us to the meeting. They said that the trio could not ride with us. We made it clear that, as far as we were concerned, none of us would go if they couldn't come. The men then had a discussion among themselves and allowed all of us to go. In my view, they were just passing the problem down the line, which is exactly what happened.

When we arrived and entered the meeting hall, things had been arranged in the following manner: at the front of the room there was a long table with about seven or eight Soviets sitting at it, all members of Burlatsky's committee. A U-shaped table was out in front of it, which was where all of us, the representatives of the International Helsinki Federation, were to sit. We invited the three members of the Glasnost Press Club to join us at the table.

Soviet agents immediately came up and said that not only could Timofeyev, Bogoraz, and Kovalev not sit at the table, but they could not remain at the meeting, either. So of course we decided if our Soviet members could not be at the meeting, there would be no meeting.

Jeri got into a big discussion with Burlatsky, and Burlatsky made the first of what were to be several phone calls he made during the meeting. This all played out in front of the cameras of Soviet and international news organizations, which the Russians had invited to report on the meeting.

After some tense moments, Burlatsky acquiesced. He made a regal gesture with his arm and announced, "Let them sit."

So the meeting began, in front of an audience of about fifty people: a mix of Jewish refuseniks, Hare Krishna, and Soviet and international press.

After some introductory back-and-forth between the groups, Irwin Cotler spoke. He made some brief remarks and then said he'd like to cede the floor to Timofeyev, explaining that the Russian knew more about the issues of human rights in the Soviet Union than he did.

The place became totally silent. Finally, Burlatsky said: "What are we up to? What do we want? A scandal, a confrontation? A show? I did not mind the presence of all those who wanted to come. But this is an open meeting of the delegates of the Helsinki Federation and our Soviet Human Rights Commission, and not a meeting with all organizations existing in Moscow. It is our prerogative to meet with those whom we invite. This is a meeting of the commission and allow me to kindly request that you follow our procedure."

He gave the floor to another committee member. After that, Kary von Schwarzenberg spoke in favor of letting the Glasnost Press Club speak. Burlatsky ignored him and turned it over to another Russian. Then I spoke, saying I didn't understand what the problem was. "Frankly, I am baffled," I said. "It seems to me that they are not just any group. They are members of our organization. Why is it such a big matter, now that they already are here at the table? They will speak responsibly."

During all this, Jeri kept trying to interject with a point of order, but Robert's Rules of Order were totally lost on the Russians. Finally, a member of the Soviet delegation got up from the table and left, and there was an intermission in the proceedings.

When we all came back, Burlatsky announced: "I do not think that this will be such a calamity. Since I have spent some time in China, I would like to quote Mao Zedong. The sky will remain clear, the birds will go on flying, the fish will keep swimming in the river, if Timofeyev speaks."

He concluded: "Well, let the cameras roll—everyone on Timofeyev!"

After all the buildup, Timofeyev was allowed to speak freely. He very calmly asked that Burlatsky's commission work with independent groups like his to further human rights in Russia. Before he finished, he passed on a list of political prisoners his group had compiled.

The meeting went on for another hour without incident. When it was over, the Hare Krishna circulated through the crowd and passed out homemade candies to everyone, including a couple of KGB officers.

It's comical looking back on it, but at the time little things like getting Timofeyev to speak were a big deal for us. We felt it was very important to help establish independent human rights groups in Russia. We wanted Russian society to open to the point where its own citizens could speak for themselves. If we could do that, then our organization wouldn't even be needed.

Burlatsky turned out to be quite an operator. It became quickly apparent that he had a long checklist of things I could do for him, and I quickly realized that we would never get to my list.

At the end of the meeting in Moscow, despite the drama with Timofeyev, Burlatsky suggested that our delegations meet again in a few months. We agreed, mainly because with the changes under Gorbachev, it seemed like Burlatsky might be an important person in the new Soviet Union—he certainly did everything he could to promote that impression. When we asked where and when he wanted to get together, he suggested Paris in the spring.

So our groups met in France that May. From the start, it was obvious the Russians had no intention of discussing anything serious. They also showed up with no money. We ended up taking them to restaurants for a week, where they ordered the most expensive food and wine and thoroughly enjoyed themselves. It reminded me of the movie *Ninotchka*, in which three Russian officials are sent to Paris after the 1917 revolution to sell confiscated jewelry, but instead find themselves enjoying the comforts of capitalism a little too much. Greta Garbo plays a Russian envoy sent after them to find out what's taking so long and to complete the sale. Instead, she falls in love. I remember thinking that it was sad we got Burlatsky instead of Garbo, but we certainly had the three sidekicks along.

When I got back to the United States, Burlatsky, who was also a writer, started to send me parts of a manuscript that he wanted Random House to publish. I kept sending them back and telling him that the translation wasn't good enough and it just didn't read like English.

He got angrier and angrier in his responses, telling me, "Get me a big advance! You're not doing your job."

In the end, Burlatsky's group disappeared from the scene as soon as Gorbachev lost power.

Not long after our trip to Moscow, the whole Soviet and Cold War apparatus began to unravel at a shocking speed. By the end of 1988, all but 140 of the Soviet political prisoners we tracked had been released. Russia also eased its emigration restrictions, and people began to flow out of the country. At the same time, Gorbachev pulled back soldiers and arms from the empire's satellite states.

Once it started to disintegrate, it just picked up speed. Poland, Hungary, and Czechoslovakia went first, and then East Germany, Romania, Bulgaria, and the Baltic States, and then finally the Soviet Union itself.

In November 1988, with the assent of Soviet officials, Andrei Sakharov made his first trip to the United States. During his two-week stay, he visited Elena Bonner's son and daughter in Boston and went on to New York and Washington for meetings with scientific and human rights groups, including Helsinki Watch. He also had a twenty-minute conversation with Ronald Reagan.

In addition to calling for the release of all remaining political prisoners, Sakharov warned that Gorbachev's program of *perestroika* could go wrong. He stressed that Russia must continue to move toward democracy and that the process would be fragile. If great care wasn't taken, he said, Russia would remain an autocracy.

A few months later, in March 1989, Sakharov was elected to the new Russian parliament, where he became a leader in the democratic opposition. It seemed as if he would continue to be a key figure in the emerging Russia, but, on December 14, 1989, he died of a heart attack at the age of sixty-eight. It was a huge shock. In Russia, thousands gathered for his funeral. In New York, we were just putting the finishing touches on his memoir. He had been disappointed that it was taking so long to publish, but the translation and editing—especially of the science sections—had proven to be difficult. I think Russia would be a different place today if Sakharov had lived long enough to help guide the transition away from communism.

Random House published his memoirs in 1990 to general acclaim. In a review, the *New York Times* called it an "extraordinary work," commenting: "One learns, sometimes in embarrassing detail, about the stubbornness of this man, who went on hunger strikes to get his wife a visa to receive medical treatment abroad, who seemed utterly fearless and who never lost his sense of outrage at man's indecency to man."

In February 1990, Václav Havel came to the United States after becoming president of Czechoslovakia (Kary von Schwarzenberg, the chair of the International Helsinki Federation, became his chancellor). His first stop in New York was the Human Rights Watch office, where he said words that made a huge difference to us: "I feel I'm here as a friend among friends," he told our staff. "I know very well what you did for us, and perhaps without you, our revolution would not be."

It would be nice to believe Havel's assessment, but it's hard to say exactly what role human rights activism played in the dissolution of the Soviet Union.

The towering figure, to me, is Andrei Sakharov, and beside him, his remarkable wife, Elena Bonner, who was never afraid to express her opinion or to quote him when he was silenced. It amazes me that with all the efforts the Soviets made to silence the couple—including having the KGB on top of them every minute of the day and their five-year exile in Gorky—they still managed to have their voices heard. I think the Soviet Union was bound to come apart for economic reasons, but the combination of Gorbachev's political leadership and Sakharov's intellect was conceivably a reason that the change was not a violent one.

Of course, Sakharov and Bonner were part of a movement that included many people whose names are now forgotten, people who died or had their lives ruined at the hands of the Soviet authorities, all out of a desire to be free to speak their minds.

People who work in human rights are always trying to evaluate what, if any, difference their work makes. The main role of Helsinki

Watch, I think, was to support the Soviet dissidents and let them know that people on the outside were fighting for them. We helped get some of them out of prison and helped others to avoid going. The advances I paid for their books at Random House helped several of the dissidents through terrible financial times. But the most important thing was to try to foster enough openness inside Russia so that dissidents would be able to speak for themselves. One thing that working in human rights has taught me over and over again is the importance of protecting free speech, even with all its faults. It really is the most basic of rights, and the one without which all others become endangered.

During this time, our own organization grew and took shape. By the end of the 1980s, we had started new divisions that covered Asia, Africa, and the Middle East. In 1988, we adopted the name Human Rights Watch and moved into new offices on Fifth Avenue, right across from the New York Public Library. We were becoming a big, influential organization and would soon struggle with the speed of our own growth.

In the meantime, rapid changes were also under way at Random House.

11

RANDOM HOUSE IN THE 1980S:
THE NEWHOUSE YEARS

AT THE START OF OUR RELATIONSHIP, SI AND DONALD NEWHOUSE proved to be everything I'd hoped for as owners of Random House. As we had discussed before the sale, Donald kept his focus on the Newhouses' newspaper, television, and radio interests. Si added Random House to his portfolio.

While interested in Random House, Si did not interfere in its operations, and for the first several years he really devoted himself to learning about how book publishing worked. He made it clear—in both our personal conversations and newspaper interviews—that he intended for me to have the freedom I needed to run the company. He told me, quite reasonably, that he wanted to learn everything he could about the business side of publishing, things like production, distribution, sales, and marketing.

So Si and I began to meet for lunch every week at a booth in the Grill Room of the Four Seasons, on East Fifty-Second Street between Park and Lexington Avenues. Si was a very punctual man, and our talks always lasted exactly an hour and fifteen minutes. During our allotted time, he peppered me with questions about our operations and took notes on a yellow legal pad. At the end of our meetings, he always told me what he wanted to talk about in the next one—the warehouse, Knopf, finance, et cetera—so I would have a chance to get all the material together.

Before long, I realized that instead of answering his questions about our divisions myself, I might as well bring in the various department heads. So if Si, for example, wanted to know about our textbook operations, he could ask the person directly responsible. I didn't see any reason for everything to be centralized through me—I thought it would be better for Si if he got several different takes on the business and also got to see the quality of the executives who worked for him, of which I was very proud. There was also one huge advantage to my new policy. When just Si and I met, Si's short questions and my necessarily longer answers brought us to the end of the hour and fifteen minutes with Si having had a fine lunch and most of mine still sitting in front of me. So my new policy had gastronomic as well as business advantages.

These meetings with Si, in hindsight, also signaled a huge change in my job. Ever since RCA had bought Random House in 1966, I had spent a lot of time trying to keep executives who knew absolutely nothing about publishing from tampering with us. Though Si didn't know much about the book business initially, he was a quick study and very much a publisher in his own right. And throughout the 1980s, he was usually willing to invest in new opportunities for the business, some of which were my ideas and some his. The result was that the company expanded exponentially. One consequence of this growth was that a lot of my time was spent working to integrate the new divisions into our company.

The Newhouses had bought Random House at the beginning of a period in which publishing was undergoing rapid change. The consolidations that had begun in the 1960s gradually gained even more momentum. For generations, publishing houses had been owned by publishers who were in some respects also the editors in chief—the books the houses published reflected their owners' individual interests, and these owners often knew their authors personally. As corporate ownership increased in the 1970s and 1980s, this model virtually disappeared.

Random House led the way into this new era but clung to the old model at the same time. For the most part, even though they didn't own the company the way Donald and Bennett had, most of the key executives at Random House, including me, knew their authors well and shaped their publishing lists to reflect their personal interests. As the house grew larger, publishing over a thousand different authors, it was obviously impossible to keep in contact with all of them, but I maintained warm relationships with as many as I could, including James Michener; E.L. Doctorow; Toni Morrison; Robert Penn Warren and his wife, Eleanor Clark, also a talented writer; John Hersey; Tom Peters; Barbara Taylor Bradford; Richard Condon; and David Halberstam, among others.

Si was a figure in this transition, too. While he was an individual owner, it was on such a large scale that he represented both sides of the equation. I found that when he took an interest in one part of his empire, he would focus on it almost as if that were his only venture, tinkering with it until he felt he had gotten it right before he moved on to another part. Because enough of the Newhouses' businesses were making money, particularly the television and cable operations, Si could afford to take chances and develop a long-range view. It helped that, unlike a publicly held corporate owner, he didn't have to meet quarterly earnings projections. At the same time, Random House was just one part of a very large portfolio, so Si's personal involvement was also limited.

The biggest financial headache Random House had in the early 1980s stemmed from a bad business decision made a decade earlier, to which we finally discovered an unlikely solution. In 1973, I'd told the management at RCA that we really needed to add a mass-market paperback imprint in order to keep up with changes in publishing—keeping our most successful books in-house instead of selling off the paperback rights to a paperback publisher would make us a lot more money.

There was one big problem: RCA's chief lawyer, Robert Werner, was worried that if we bought a profitable paperback publisher, it would create antitrust problems with the Federal Trade Commission. Since most of our competitors already owned paperback houses, I didn't see how that was at all possible. Still, he told us to buy an imprint that was actually losing money. I disagreed, but I wasn't able to change his mind or override him.

I decided that we had to take a chance and buy a paperback house anyway. We settled for Ballantine, which had been founded by Ian

Ballantine in 1952. While we knew that Ballantine was in bad shape and losing money, we gambled on being able to turn it around. That turned out to be impossible for us to do. Ian had been buying books that just didn't sell, and since paperbacks are 100 percent returnable to the publisher, we soon found that we were receiving back 60 percent or more of everything we put out.

The bright spot in the company were the editors Judy-Lynn del Rey and her husband, Lester. Judy-Lynn, especially, had a genius for science fiction, and she was a huge fan. Her biggest coup was securing the rights to publish the *Star Wars* books from George Lucas before the first movie came out in 1977. I can't imagine how much money that one deal made Random House.

Overall, though, Ballantine only caused us problems, so we jumped when CBS contacted us in January 1982 to let us know that it wanted to sell its Fawcett paperback division. Fawcett had also fallen on some difficult times, but it was a much better imprint than Ballantine. I told Si that if we bought Fawcett, we could turn it around. Putting it together with Ballantine would be even better, because then we'd have enough volume and could combine the sales staffs, saving on overhead. He said to spend whatever was needed. Our conversation was over in less than an hour, and it showed once again the difference between individual and corporate ownership.

After the negotiations started, Sandy MacGregor came into my office and told me that the CBS lawyers who were handling the deal didn't know anything about the book business. They had simply been told by William Paley, the founder and head of CBS, to sell Fawcett. Everyone knew that when Paley wanted something done, he didn't want to hear anything more about it. The lawyers were under pressure to finish the deal.

Sandy said that one thing the CBS lawyers didn't realize was that a lot of the books that go out to bookstores come back and the publishing house is responsible for picking up the tab. Sandy said we could propose to CBS that it should be responsible for the books Fawcett had already put out and would pay for anything that came back for the first year and a half. CBS agreed to that condition, and we bought Fawcett. The condition on returns saved us a substantial amount of money and made it a highly profitable deal for us.

Over the course of the negotiations, Susan Petersen, Ballantine's marketing director, really took the lead. Then in her early thirties, Susan was very hardworking, very smart, and very energetic. She came up with a plan for the acquisition and recommended several ways to get the most out of the merger.

I decided then that I had to give Susan a chance to run the combined imprint. There is no adequate way to explain why you make certain changes in a creative business—I learned that it is something you just do, and if it works out, you look like a genius, and if it doesn't you have to try again.

Susan turned out to be a brilliant publisher. She worked extremely hard and motivated her staff to do so as well, and she made great hiring decisions, such as keeping Leona Nevler, Fawcett's editor in chief, to oversee the combined imprints.

Susan also had great instincts for books and read a lot of submissions herself. An example of that is one time when she came to me and said she wanted to pay a million dollars for the paperback rights to a new author who was going to be published by Putnam, then an independent publisher. This was pure speculation, as the hardback book had not yet been published. Because it was Susan, I immediately went along with it. The book was *The Joy Luck Club*, by Amy Tan, which was a runaway success.

The acquisition of Fawcett was the first major step in a decade of rapid growth. Soon after, we bought Times Books from the New York Times Company, founded the Villard Books imprint, and acquired some minor college textbook lines. We also took over distribution for several publishers, including Reader's Digest Press, Grove Press, and Warner Books. Si made business decisions quickly, which resulted, I believe, in huge savings.

For example, when I told him that we needed a new warehouse at a cost of around $9 million, he just said, "Go do it." In contrast, it would have been an endless negotiation with RCA, which would have brought in site experts and figured out in great detail the trucking costs to various parts of the United States, and would have probably been several years until we could have actually started the warehouse. Sandy MacGregor did all of this on his own, and about a year later we had a new modern warehouse built and running, a model for the whole industry. I don't think Sandy ever got enough credit for this because it's not exactly the glamorous part of publishing, but it made a big difference in the speed of our handling of orders and therefore getting our books into bookstores.

Our revenues were rapidly growing. When I took over in 1966, we were doing about $40 million in annual sales. By the mid-1970s, we topped $100 million. By 1985, we were at around $500 million.

At this time, agents were really coming into their own. They were convincing authors to be businesspeople, so increasingly getting a new big author required a large advance. Especially with political and showbiz figures, this involved risks that might not work out, not because the books wouldn't be good and valuable, but simply because you had paid too much money to publish them.

I looked at these deals with the view that I had to make money for Random House. I also wanted Random House to retain its reputation for books that I considered worthy of the imprint. In retrospect, of course, this is a matter of judgment. My policy was that editors should come to me with any book that required a large advance, but also any book that could pose any legal or taste problem.

The one time I had a real difference with Susan Petersen was when she published a book called *Truly Tasteless Jokes*, which included what I considered to be mean-spirited gags about the handicapped, blind people, dead babies, blacks, Jews, Poles, gays, and so on. When I asked Susan why she had not brought the book to my attention, she said it was humor and didn't involve any threat to Random House, particularly because it was being published by Ballantine/Fawcett in paperback, where the standards were to publish what the public wanted. It was a onetime discussion. The book sold more than 2 million copies, and I didn't stop Susan from publishing *Truly Tasteless Jokes Two* and *Three*. There wasn't a word of protest from anywhere about the first one, and I wanted the business.

Si was a very structured, serious businessman who kept to an exacting schedule. Every morning, he arrived at the office at five, and I found that if I wanted to speak with him, it was best to go around seven, before he was caught up in an extremely busy day.

As Si learned more about Random House, he wanted to use some of the ideas that had worked for him in the magazine business. He was attracted to the intersection of celebrity, glamour, and buzz for two reasons: he thought it made for good business, and he enjoyed it. After a few years, he made it known that he would like us to publish more books along these lines. I was skeptical but went along.

Si's interest in big "buzz" books, however, did not limit our ability to publish books simply because they were important. For example, in 1986 I received a phone call from a monsignor in Brazil. He told me that the Catholic archbishop of the São Paulo diocese, Cardinal Paulo Evaristo Arns, had commissioned a study of the incredible torture and brutality inflicted on political prisoners under the military regime that ruled Brazil from 1964 to 1985. A team of researchers, beginning in 1979 and working in secret, had compiled an extensive report drawn from thousands of military records they had obtained.

The monsignor said the book had been published by a Catholic press in Brazil and was garnering a lot of attention, but the church was receiving pressure from the government over the publication. He told me that it would help immensely if there were an American version published in English, as the church could then say the information was out there and there was nothing the government could do about it. I knew it was not going to be a big seller for us but immediately agreed to publish it in the United States. It was one way that a publisher in a country with a free press could back up others who were fighting for that privilege.

Ted Geisel and I remained very close throughout the 1980s. We had a lot of special occasions together, and each time he was absolutely amazing in the way that he came through with something unique. In 1982, the company threw a party for me on my twenty-fifth anniversary at Random House. Ted came to the party and read aloud a special Dr. Seuss verse he had written:

HAIL TO OUR CHIEF!
(AND I DON'T MEAN RONALD REAGAN)

Since that memorable day
back in Nineteen Five Seven,
most witnesses, long since
have packed off to heaven.
But to those who still breathe
the great memory's still fresh
of the wild wind that blew
with a woosh and a wesch
when Bob Bernstein showed up
in his fine freckled flesh.

Like Gandhi
he brought to our souls newborn hope.
Like Einstein
he broadened our breadth and our scope.
To the restrooms
he brought better paper and soap.
He brightened our darkness!
He gave us more rope!
He became, with acclaim,
both our Kaiser and Pope.

So . . .
Fill full your glasses
and raise them aloof
in salute to the Fiddler
on the Random House roof!

The following year, when Ted turned eighty, I arranged a party at the New York Public Library. He arrived with a poem to read, and I found I had been, in Ted's eyes, demoted. It was titled: "On an Occasion Such as This I Maintain That My Late Father Is of Much Greater Importance Than Even Robert L. Bernstein":

If my Daddy hadn't have
met up with my Mommy,
I'd have missed this fine party tonight.

If my Daddy had shacked up
with some lady else . . .
just supposing, for instance,
Miss Abigail Schmeltz . . .
    Or Patricia MacPhee . . .
    Or Louella McGee . . .
I would not have resulted. I wouldn't be me!
There'd just be no telling who the hell I might be!

For example, had he foolishly eloped
    To South Wooster
with some floozy named Florabell Frakenstein
    Flooster,
I might now be writing for Simon and Schuster
and this party could never have been.

Nor could it have been
if he'd shacked up in Chelsea
with Carolyn Baumgarten Crinoline Kelsey
or wedded some frump named Felicity Frink.
Then who would I be . . . ?
Oh I shudder to think.

I'd quite likely be writing
under the name of Dr. Gussler
for the National Enquirer *. . .*
or maybe even the Hustler.

In which case, Bob Bernstein,
though a most generous soul,
wouldn't have touched tonight's banquet
with a 15 foot pole.

So I thank you, dear Daddy
for doing things right
or I wouldn't be here
with my good friends tonight.

When Ted and I discussed various issues, sometimes quite serious, but were trying to be not so serious, Ted would say, "If we can't settle this, I'll have to take it to my lawyers." I could never remember the name of his "law firm," which was one of the best Geisel names in history, so I always kept on my desk a card in Ted's handwriting, which I have here in my hand as I write this. The name of the law firm was "Grimalkin, Drouberhannus, Knalbner and Fepp." It got to be too much for me when, on July 12, 1991, I received the following letter from Ted.

Dear Robert,

I would not wish to be quoted on this and I have absolutely nothing whatever against G, D, K and F, but as the Supreme Court moves further and further to the right, I am placing more and more of my litigation into the hands of Abernathy, Arbutnot, Proudfoot and Cadwaller.

Very Confidentially,
THEODOR

I could never master the name of the second "law firm," but I don't think he ever actually made the switch.

Ted died a few months after writing that letter, in September 1991. Toward the end of his life, he was invited to speak at the annual meeting of American booksellers, which was being held in Anaheim, not far from his home in La Jolla. Unfortunately, he became ill and couldn't make it. He didn't want to disappoint the crowd, though, so at the last minute he sent me a poem and asked me to read it. He titled it "A Rather Short Epic Poem (Size 6 and ⅞)":

Oh . . .
I would that I were in Anaheim
in this early morning room.
How I would that I were in Anaheim
with Maurice Sendak and Judy Blume

and with all you friendly Booksters
and beautiful Bookster-esses
to discuss, as old friends, the sad state of the world
and other lugubrious messes.

But . . .
I languish far from Anaheim
with a bad case of the Hyper Sty-mar-ees,
an optical malady caused by reading
much too much junk
about the Presidential Primaries.

And being unable to be here
and to do it myself today,
I have asked Mr. Bernstein,
who is an excellent blesser,
to bless you all and to say
that in a country where Illiteracy is on the rise
and the Economy is slinking low,
and the Chastity is out of the window
it is comforting to know
that, though the frost is on the pumpkin
and civilization is on the skids,
You guys are fearlessly working underground
smuggling books into the hands of kids!

As the 1980s progressed, each Random House imprint developed
in its own way.

Pantheon, under André Schiffrin, published many books with a
liberal slant. It was by far the smallest of the divisions, but Bennett
and Donald had bought it, and it added to the range of publishing
we were doing.

For example, in 1974 André approached me about a textbook,
Mississippi: Conflict and Change, which Pantheon wanted to publish. It was written primarily by James Loewen, a professor at Tou-
galoo College, a historically black college in Jackson, Mississippi,
that my son Peter had attended for a semester. Loewen's textbook
was the first to counter the overtly racist history textbook that was

then used in the state's public schools, which, for example, lauded the Ku Klux Klan. Loewen was having a difficult time with it because textbook publishers were worried they would lose all their business with the state if they took his book.

André wanted to publish it at Pantheon, but he knew there was a potential problem because the people at L.W. Singer, the textbook company that we had bought, were opposed to putting out the book. André came with the Singer salespeople to discuss it with me. Of course we decided to publish it.

The state of Mississippi would not purchase the book for its school system, but it turned out that hundreds of teachers were interested in using it. The state pressured them not to adopt it, threatening their jobs if they did. Several years later, the NAACP took a case to federal court, arguing that the state had violated the teachers' First Amendment rights. In 1981, it won the decision, which finally opened up the Mississippi school system to textbooks that presented a more accurate version of the state's history.

Loewen, it turned out, went on to become a bestselling author. In 1995, he put out *Lies My Teacher Told Me: Everything Your American History Textbook Got Wrong*, which has sold 2 million copies. Interestingly, it was also published by André, who by then had founded and was running The New Press.

At Pantheon, André's profits, if they existed at all, were small. He always complained that he was being assigned too much overhead, and this hurt his numbers. He liked to remind me that Pantheon had sold over a million copies of *Dr. Zhivago* at a time when it had only two salespeople and said the imprint didn't need the sales force for which he was being charged. Besides that, he always said he could move the imprint into smaller offices in the Village and save money. It was an ever-going argument, but as Random House grew larger and larger, and Pantheon wasn't losing a lot of money, I always instinctively protected André.

Bob Gottlieb, at Knopf, was really the most outstanding editor I worked with during my publishing career, a man with an astounding set of talents. He was able to attract big books over a wide range of subjects and edit them himself when necessary. He hired smart people around him and kept up an esprit de corps at the imprint that was truly admirable. Bob did whatever was necessary to get the best book possible out of an author. I remember when Lauren Bacall was having trouble with her memoir, and he invited her to move into Knopf and work in an office near him, so that he could help her get through the tough parts. He was equally good on important books like Robert Caro's impressive multivolume biography of Lyndon Johnson and Toni Morrison's novels, which he edits to this day. He could switch from that to working with the Muppets on Miss Piggy's book, from which Bob picked up one of his favorite expressions: "Pretentious? *Moi?*"

I don't think Bob and I ever really clashed on anything. Although he would clear large expenditures he wanted to make with me, I don't remember ever challenging one. He had a certain need to show his independence, which always amused me, though I was perfectly comfortable with it. But sometimes at staff meetings, he would react to something I said in a dismissive way, so much so that I remember at one meeting saying to him, "Bob, could you do me a favor?"

As usual, when faced with a question like that, he tilted his head and sort of barked back: "What?"

I said, "Could you say behind my back the things you say to my face?"

Unlike Pantheon and Knopf, the Random House trade imprint in the early 1980s did not have clear leadership. Jim Silberman, who had headed it for years, left to run his own imprint at Simon & Schuster. He was succeeded by Jason Epstein in 1982.

Like Bob Gottlieb, Jason's range was truly extraordinary. Jason had helped to found the *New York Review of Books* and later started the Library of America, which publishes the anthologized work of great American writers. When he worked at Doubleday, before coming to Random House in 1958, he had also started Anchor Books, one of the first imprints for serious paperback books. A very erudite man, he was also a gourmet cook and a lover of antiques. I always envied his ability to discuss just about anything with assurance.

I had wanted to go outside the company after Jim Silberman left, but since Jason wanted a chance at being editor in chief, I went against my instinct and chose him. My feeling was that Jason was really good at whatever he wanted to be—when he was editing, he was a very good editor, and when he was developing one of his business ideas, he was a good businessman. I don't think he ever really wanted to be a good editor in chief. He did not seem to have an interest in nurturing a staff. It became apparent pretty soon that it wasn't working out for anyone, and in 1984 he went back to being a senior editor.

Si then suggested that I hire Howard Kaminsky, who was then running Warner Books, to replace Jason. Howard had been successful publishing mass-market bestsellers such as a Richard Simmons diet guide and *Megatrends* by John Naisbitt.

Si and Howard were on the same wavelength as far as acquiring "big books." And for a while I reluctantly went along. After Howard came on, Si really began to pursue Donald Trump, who was then known in New York City but not nationally. With the help of Si, Trump was getting there, though. In 1985, *GQ*, a Condé Nast magazine, put Trump on its cover. When Trump finally decided to do a book, he came to Random House. Si bought the book himself. The result, *The Art of the Deal*, which we published in 1987, was a bestseller and helped to make Trump a household name. I think it also convinced Si that he had ability in acquiring books, which, at times, he undoubtedly did.

In the meantime, Howard continued to press for paying huge advances for a few books, which we did. Some sold well, such as the autobiography of Speaker of the House Tip O'Neill. Others, such as Nancy Reagan's memoir and Trump's second book, did not earn back their advances. Howard then also began to pay large advances to sign writers of popular fiction such as John Jakes and Barbara Taylor Bradford. Jakes, as it turned out, had already written most of his big books by the time we signed him; Bradford, on the other hand, continued her success. All in all, Howard's track record was decidedly mixed.

The judgment about these authors was really a money judgment. I had allowed those decisions (up to our agreed-upon advance level) to be made by editors who I thought had a combination of literary sensibilities and business judgment—editors like Bob Gottlieb,

Jason Epstein, André Schiffrin, Bob Loomis, Judith Jones, Albert Erskine, and many others. But I never really had that kind of confidence in Howard Kaminsky. It was a difficult situation for me to be in—I knew that Si was attracted to big celebrity books and also had a personal relationship with Howard. Finding an editor in chief for Random House had been extremely difficult, and Howard was the choice that Si wanted.

At one of our lunch meetings, Si asked me how I thought Howard was working out. I told Si I didn't think Howard was doing very well in managing the staff. Si said that if I felt that way, I was free to make a change. It was clear between us that I would let Howard go.

I went back and talked to Howard. I told him that we weren't making it together and that I thought he ought to look for another job, but that he could take several months to do that. We agreed that Howard should talk to Si. Shortly after he left my office I got a call from Si telling me he had spoken with Howard, and that was that.

One day in 1987, Si came to my office and asked how I would feel if he were to offer Bob Gottlieb the position of editor at the *New Yorker*. He asked me if I thought it would hurt Knopf too much. I instantly realized that this was not a conversation I could have. I answered very quickly, saying, "Si, once you've told me that, there's no way that I can even consider what I think. I would never want to be in the position of having denied Bob Gottlieb the chance of being editor of the *New Yorker*, if that's what he wanted to do. So by all means offer him the job, and we'll do the best we can if he takes it."

Si, who had bought the *New Yorker* in 1985, had just abruptly dismissed the magazine's longtime editor, William Shawn, a move that had caused shock and dismay in Manhattan literary circles. Shawn had been at the helm since 1952 and was thought to be inseparable from the magazine.

Since Bob Gottlieb was a great editor and beloved by the people who worked for him at Knopf, I think Si must have decided that Bob could ease some of the unrest Si had caused by firing Shawn, and that Bob's flair would bring some new life to the *New Yorker* and make it a better magazine.

A common American idiom is that nobody is indispensable, but Bob Gottlieb was pretty close. I understood why Si wanted him at the *New Yorker* to replace Shawn, but he left a hole at Knopf that didn't seem in any way good for Random House. I was very worried that Bob's departure could spark an exodus of talented editors from Knopf.

I had just hired Joni Evans, who had come over from Simon & Schuster, to replace Howard Kaminsky as the publisher of the Random House trade imprint. Joni also had an attraction for hugely commercial books, but I had much more confidence in her judgment. I wasn't sure whom to hire at Knopf, so I asked Bob his opinion. He suggested Sonny Mehta, who was then the publisher of Pan Books in London.

I had always thought highly of Sonny but realized that I had previously handled him in a way I shouldn't have, when I had almost hired him to become editor in chief of the Random House trade imprint three years earlier. We were in talks and almost to the point of having a deal when Jason Epstein told me he really wanted the job. I felt I had to give Jason a chance. I called Sonny and told him that I couldn't offer him the job.

In 1987, though, we did hire Sonny to head Knopf. At first it was a rough transition, because Sonny's management style was so very different from Bob's. While Bob was paternalistic and took an intense interest in his staff members and the books they were working on, Sonny was not nearly as hands-on. He spent a lot of time in his office with the door closed, reading manuscripts. He also failed to return the calls of prominent literary agents, which created problems, given that these are generally people with very healthy egos of their own. I found myself on the phone more than once trying to smooth things over. For much of the staff, Bob's departure was like a bucket of cold water dumped over their heads, and several editors came to me with their complaints.

My initial worry was whether Sonny's style and the culture of Knopf would eventually come together, which, in the end, they certainly did. Sonny's track record in London showed he was a brilliant publisher and he's done just as well over here. Most of the key people at Knopf stayed after Sonny's arrival, including, for example,

Jane Friedman, who had been one of Bob's closest deputies. (Jane would eventually leave and become the president of HarperCollins, but that was in 1997, long after she had been comfortably and enthusiastically working with Sonny for many years.) Sonny is still at Knopf today and, more than two decades later, seems as indispensable as Bob Gottlieb once seemed to me.

Bob's tenure at the *New Yorker* was brief. He was succeeded by Tina Brown. When he left the magazine in 1992, Bob took an office at Knopf and he still edits major projects for the imprint, such as Bill Clinton's memoir. In personal style, Sonny and Bob couldn't be more different, but both have one thing in common: their judgment about what to publish, at which they both have excelled.

After a number of years of just listening, Si, quite understandably, began to form his own opinions about various aspects of our business. I learned then that when Si decided to make an acquisition or sell a division, he made up his own mind about pricing, often without much internal consultation. For example, at one of our weekly lunches, Si said he wanted me to sell our elementary–high school (elhi) and college textbook divisions, which were very much separated from other parts of the company. The elhi division had started small when Bennett and Donald bought L.W. Singer in the early 1960s, and it had never really gained a big market share. The college division, while also small, was distinguished.

Overall, Si felt educational publishing didn't fit Random House. Left to my own devices, I probably would have let the divisions continue as long as they weren't losing money, but I had no strong feelings about being in the educational publishing business one way or another.

Si told me that he had talked to Goldman Sachs, which told him the divisions were worth $80 million.

That number, I said, seemed low.

Si seemed a little surprised that I would challenge the Goldman Sachs estimate. I explained that, of course, I wouldn't do that on anything except a book publishing business, in which I felt I had some expertise and experience. In this one specific situation of evaluating Random House's school and college divisions, I had a very different opinion from the investment bankers.

To Si's credit, he said, "I don't want to muddy the waters for Goldman Sachs, but why don't you take your best shot at selling the divisions and see if you can do it in one month."

At the time, McGraw-Hill had announced that it wanted to expand its school and college division by 20 percent. Since we had the only divisions up for sale in educational publishing with plenty of books in the pipeline, it seemed likely the company might be interested in an acquisition.

We decided that we would approach McGraw-Hill and that Siebert Adams, head of our college department, and George Rosato, the head of the elhi division, would make the pitch. We set the price at $200 million. McGraw-Hill accepted and bought the two divisions. Siebert and George went to work for McGraw-Hill as part of the deal.

While we were getting out of educational publishing, however, we were expanding elsewhere. We began to look into the British market to increase our distribution and bought a London-based publishing group comprising Chatto & Windus, Jonathan Cape, and the Bodley Head—all prestigious and well-respected English publishing houses with many wonderful authors.

In 1988, just a year later, Si broached the idea that he wanted to buy the Crown Publishing Group, which had been founded by Nat Wartels and Bob Simon in 1936. Wartels and Simon had built the business on remaindered books, buying them up from publishers for very low prices and then reselling them to bookstores for their bargain tables. They later added a trade paperback division and a direct-mail company called Publishers Central Bureau, which sold books and records through a widely distributed catalog. Si wanted to get into direct marketing and Publishers Central Bureau was the main reason he was interested in Crown.

Crown was a big publisher, and when Sandy MacGregor and I started to conduct due diligence on the company, we found that its accounting was in disarray. Simon had died, and Wartels, who was eighty-six years old in 1988, was famous for insisting that he sign every check the company sent out, no matter how small the amount. His filing system was to stack all his papers on his desk so high that you could barely see over them. He seemed to have an amazing ability to pull out the right piece of paper when needed.

That system, however, made it impossible for us to figure out if Crown was making or losing money. We had to keep asking Wartels for more financial information. Si didn't want to wait—he had a feeling that someone else was going to step in and buy the company. Sandy and I didn't agree with him on that. We sensed that acquiring Crown would mean an enormous amount of work and in the end would not be worth it. Nevertheless, Si went ahead and bought the publishing house.

It soon became obvious that Crown was losing more money than anyone had guessed. As the new owners, we did the only thing we could do at that moment—we went to work restructuring Crown, separating its divisions very carefully so that we knew what was what and working through the problems one by one.

At the same time changes were sweeping through publishing houses, there were significant structural changes at the retail level as well. Independent bookstores, which when I started in publishing accounted for more than 80 percent of book sales, were on the decline and finding it harder to stay in business. These were wonderful stores where the owners and many of the staff were book readers, and publishers and customers alike relied on their judgments—the publisher tried to get the bookstore personnel interested in a new author or book, and the customers in many cases trusted that the staff knew them well enough to make personal recommendations. We sometimes went so far as to distribute galleys widely among bookstore clerks for titles that we thought would need word of mouth to get started.

But with the advent of the shopping center, big chain bookstores, like Barnes & Noble and Borders, began to get more and more of the business. They started to discount bestsellers, which the independents didn't want to do because they were the main source of their profits. The big stores also became more sophisticated in marketing, in some cases even starting to charge publishers for prime display space in the store. As smaller bookshops started to disappear, small publishing imprints started to disappear too, as many merged into larger publishers.

Amid all this change, certain patterns in publishing remained timeless, particularly the sudden emergence of bestselling inspirational or self-help books.

One of those books, which I got to know intimately, was by an unknown author named Robert Fulghum. His essay "Everything I Need to Know I Learned in Kindergarten" had appeared in newspapers around the country. An agent, Patricia van der Leun, read it and sought out Fulghum, who was a schoolteacher in Seattle. She asked him if he had any more pieces like the one that had appeared in the paper. He told her that he was a Unitarian minister and had for years given a sermon every Sunday, and he had hundreds stored away. She asked him to pick out fifty or sixty of the best and send them to her, and told him that if he wanted her to become his agent, she thought she could sell a book of his essays.

Villard, a new imprint we had formed at Random House to give a few young editors a bit more freedom, signed it. My memory is that we paid a $60,000 advance, and that the hardback edition of the book, which we published in 1988, sold 2 million copies and the paperback 5 million. Fulghum earned millions of dollars from it and found himself quite wealthy.

Fulghum—he always went by his last name—and I became close friends, and he asked if Helen and I wanted to go down the Colorado River on a raft trip with him. I think he was very surprised when we accepted. We had a wonderful time, but when we were about two hours down the river, the principal guide announced that he had forgotten the tents. There was nothing we could do about that, so we were lucky there was only one day of rain. There was one hike in a canyon where you had to walk on a ledge about four or five feet wide, with a drop of several hundred feet. I have a fear of heights so I didn't go. The group was late getting back, so I started to worry about Helen. Fulghum thought he was reassuring me when he said, "Oh, don't worry about Helen, she's with Mac." Mac was the guy who had forgotten the tents.

A great thing about publishing is that you're introduced to so many ideas and receive knowledge from so many places because of the range of books you publish. At the same time, to be a good publisher, you have to find a way to share the authors' interests rather than your own. While Fulghum never talked about human rights, he made his point in the most dramatic way—by giving all the royalties of his book *Words I Wish I Wrote* to Human Rights Watch.

I had been at Random House a long time, and Si and I had talked about finding a successor, but I had a hard time thinking about who was to succeed me. I valued many of our people very highly, but I think I underrated them in the sense of not choosing one or two who could have risen to the job, which was what Bennett Cerf did with me twenty-four years earlier. Susan Petersen, for example, went on to head Viking Penguin for many years. Jane Friedman had a very successful run at HarperCollins. Sandy MacGregor, I'm convinced, would have done a great job. Before he went to the *New Yorker*, Bob Gottlieb could certainly have stepped in.

At sixty-six years old, though, I didn't feel any great sense of urgency about resolving this dilemma. I loved my job and was in good health, and I knew that many of the top executives at the company were happy and fulfilled in their work as well. So I wasn't expecting anything when Si came into my office in October 1989. I was surprised when he sat down and said he thought it was time for me to retire. He suggested that January 1, 1990, should be the day, and reluctantly I had to agree.

Even now, after many years, I'm still somewhat jarred when I pick up the *New York Times* from November 2, 1989, which I kept (and is now, in any event, easily accessible online), and read "President of Random House Out Abruptly After 23 Years." Nor did the *Times* leave it at that. A few days later, Edwin McDowell, the paper's publishing reporter, wrote a follow-up story under the headline "Random House Swept by a Rash of Rumors." And while my feelings were rawer about the turn of events at the time, reading some of McDowell's words now is comforting and reaffirming:

About the only thing insiders agreed upon is that, whoever the successor, the events of the last five days are likely to change Random House irrevocably.

"If this could happen like this to Bob, it could happen to any of us," said one Random House executive, who assumes that Mr. Bernstein was forced to resign.

Under Mr. Bernstein, Random House has been a large and usually harmonious empire, comprised of semi-autonomous fiefdoms, presided over by a benevolent emperor.

With the benefit of time, I can see that Si had let go of a few other longtime executives shortly before: William Shawn, who edited the *New Yorker* from 1952 to 1987, and Grace Mirabella, editor of *Vogue* from 1971 to 1988. Soon after the news about my leave-taking became public, Si parted with Bernard Leser, the president of Condé Nast, who had been with the company thirty-five years and was very close to Si.

Over the twenty-four years I headed Random House, we grew from revenues of $40 million to nearly $900 million. Through all that change, I feel we managed that growth in a way that stayed true to the ideals of our founders, Bennett Cerf and Donald Klopfer.

I am most proud of the stellar list of authors who stayed with us for years. I am thankful that I was able to use my position to call attention to dissidents like Andrei Sakharov and Jacobo Timerman.

When news of my departure from Random House after more than two decades as chairman and president hit the newspapers, the only recognition from Washington came through a phone call. My very alert eight-year-old granddaughter, Elisabeth, was on the line. "Bobby," she said, "you're on the front page of the *New York Times*! Can I use you in current events?"

Si reached out to Alberto Vitale, the head of Bantam Books, to be the next president of Random House. I didn't know Vitale. He had a business background, coming into publishing only after Istituto Finanziario Industriale, the Italian conglomerate where he worked, bought Bantam in 1975. He had a reputation as a financial executive.

After the announcement was made, Vitale came in to see me. He was a short, stocky man and very energetic. He treated me with great deference and told me quite frankly that he was completely aware of what a delicate situation I was in, but that he would appreciate my help. I tried.

Vitale began to make changes as soon as he was in charge. In one of his first actions, he told André Schiffrin, the head of Pantheon, to cut his list by 40 percent (this is according to André's account). André refused and ended up resigning, as did all five of Pantheon's senior editors. About three hundred people, including authors such as Studs Terkel, Kurt Vonnegut, and Barbara Ehrenreich, took to the streets outside of Random House's office to protest, which was certainly a first in book publishing.

What really surprised me as the years went on is that André Schiffrin, who was portrayed as a publisher with no business ability, put together The New Press, which has been around now for more than twenty years (and is now publishing this book). André believed in the value to a democratic society of publishing good but noncommercial books, and he convinced enough foundations to support his new house and the idea of publishing in the public interest.

I was very surprised when Vitale soon let go some other key people, including two whom I really held in the highest regard. He fired Susan Petersen in 1992, but, as it happened, Susan had a favorable clause in her contract. She took a year off to spend time with her son, who was in high school, and traveled in Europe. When she came back, the head of Putnam, the very astute Phyllis Grann, immediately asked Susan to start a new imprint for Putnam called Riverhead. When Putnam was bought by Viking Penguin, Susan was named president of Viking Penguin, which she led brilliantly for more than twenty years. In 1994, Vitale dismissed Sandy Mac-Gregor, who chose an entirely different life, moving to Santa Fe, New Mexico, where he has thrived.

In 1998, the Newhouses made an unusual decision for them, as they seldom if ever parted with businesses they acquired, and sold Random House to Bertelsmann, the private German media conglomerate. Newspapers reported that the Newhouses had bought Random House in 1979 for $70 million and reportedly sold it less than twenty years later for more than $1 billion.

Even before its 2013 merger with Penguin, Random House was the world's largest trade book publisher. While it is certainly a long way from the place that Bennett and Donald had envisioned when they started, or that I thought it would end up, Random House continues to flourish.

There is no question that book publishing is thought of much more as a business today than it used to be. However, the real value of book publishing is much greater than anything on a balance sheet. Its real worth is in conveying new ideas, greater understanding of the human condition, awareness of the past, scientific knowledge, and much more, even to our youngest readers.

Despite knowing all of this, it's amazing how you constantly hear about the demise of books. I remember so well when I was just beginning in publishing how the Book of the Month Club was going to end bookstores. After that, television was going to take all of people's leisure time, and no one would read books anymore. And then computers and the Internet were definitely going to end books as we know them. With the tremendous overflow of information coming at us today, books seem to me even more important in helping people understand their own lives as well as the world they live in.

Today when people ask me my thoughts about books and publishing, I tell them there will always be publishers, because there will always be authors. Publishers are the vehicle to help them get their work into the world. And because books fill so many needs, there will always be readers. How they're published and what form they appear in may change, but I can't imagine a world without books.

12

CHINA

As the 1990s began and the Soviet Union started to allow dissidents the freedom to speak their minds, I realized that my efforts there weren't going to be much needed anymore. For example, with Václav Havel becoming president of Czechoslovakia and Andrei Sakharov getting elected to the Russian parliament, it was clear that things had changed beyond anything we at Helsinki Watch could imagine even a few years earlier.

At that point, Aryeh Neier and I started to talk about what I was going to do next. I had recently departed from Random House but didn't want to spread my human rights efforts too thin—I thought it would be best to really focus on one area. He said, "Bob, I don't know exactly what's going to happen, but the next really big human rights issue is going to be China. Maybe you can look into what's going on there and give it the extra push it needs."

At the time, most of what I knew about China came from what I had picked up from Human Rights Watch's Asia division and a trip I had taken there nearly fifteen years earlier. That had come about only because of an impulsive letter I had written as president of Random House.

After the Communist takeover of mainland China in 1949, the United Nations had recognized the Nationalist forces of the Republic of China, which had retreated to Taiwan, as China's legitimate government. The People's Republic of China did not have a seat at the UN until 1971, when the UN General Assembly voted to reverse the situation, granting China recognition and choosing to revoke Taiwan's membership.

China's first delegate to the UN was a man named Huang Hua. As a youth in the 1930s, Huang had been a translator and guide for the American journalist Edgar Snow, who wrote *Red Star over China*, the first major account of Mao Zedong and the Chinese Communist Party, which had been published by Random House. The Chinese Communists loved *Red Star over China*, and Snow had been back to China several times over the years to interview Mao as well as Zhou Enlai, China's second in command.

A few years after Huang arrived in New York, I wrote him a letter. I don't know exactly what inspired me to do it, except that Pantheon was publishing a lot of books about China and I was interested in the country. I said that I was president of Random House, the publisher of Edgar Snow as well as several other books about China, and asked him if he would like to come and see Snow's publishing house and have lunch with me and some of our editors. He was delighted.

This led to an invitation, in 1976, for my whole family to visit China. If we paid for our tickets to get there, the government offered to pick up everything else. We jumped at the chance. China back then was just emerging from the Cultural Revolution—Nixon had made his historic trip there in 1972—and it was still barely accessible to Americans.

So Helen, Peter, Tom, Bill, and I arrived in China in June 1976. It was a strange time to be there, because Mao—who would die that September—was on his deathbed. His demise would unleash many of the forces that would result three years later in Beijing's Democracy Wall movement, though at the time of our visit a push for human rights in China seemed far-fetched. When we were there, it seemed that everyone was on edge, both because Mao's real condition was a closely guarded secret and because nobody knew what was going to happen when he died.

As for our visit, it was clear from the start that the Chinese were going to do their best to be good hosts, setting us up with a full schedule of activities. In Nanjing, they took us to a hospital, where we were shown around by several doctors. They arranged for us to see a surgery. We were given robes and masks and brought into an operating room, where a man was laid out on the table having heart surgery. The patient had a board fitted down around his neck so that he couldn't see what was going on, but he was wide awake and able to speak with us through the interpreter. The staff told us that the only anesthesia they had used was acupuncture.

I was extremely interested in acupuncture. Several years earlier, I'd met Dr. Felix Mann in England, who had published a book on the technique when it was still quite unknown in the West. I'd bought the rights from the English publisher and published it in the United States, but it didn't sell well at all. However, when the *New York Times* columnist James Reston went to China with Nixon in 1972, he got appendicitis while there and was treated with acupuncture for his pain. He wrote a column about it, which raised American interest in the method. When we republished Mann's book in paperback, it sold well.

In the operating room, Helen and I stood on one side of the operating table and Peter, Tom, and Bill on the other. Helen and I were so absorbed in the operation that when we looked up there were only two boys, Peter and Bill. Tom was missing. We learned he had fainted. The hospital staff had actually carried him out on a stretcher, and he was taken to another room. When we went to see how he was doing, we found him relaxing on a bed, attended by two very attractive Chinese nurses. When he saw us, Tom put us on the defensive: "How could you stand there and see that happening and not be affected by it? What is the matter with you? I can see that I'm the only sensitive one in this family."

We stayed in China for sixteen days, also visiting Guilin, Shanghai, Suzhou, Xi'an and Beijing. In Shanghai, the waterfront, which is so built up today, was totally run-down, and we went to visit the neighborhood where some twenty thousand Jews had found shelter during World War II. In Nanjing, we had dinner with the mayor, who told us all about the Rape of Nanjing in 1937–38, when the Japanese occupied the city and killed perhaps as many as three hundred thousand people in six weeks. She also took us to a bridge and explained to us how the Russians had come to teach the Chinese how to make bridges, but their relationship changed when the bridge was half built. She was very proud to tell us that the Chinese had been able to complete the bridge on their own.

Bill had studied tai chi when he was at Brown University, so in Guilin he went out on a public square to practice a little bit. At that time, very few, if any, Westerners had been to Guilin. Within minutes, what seemed like thousands of people were all staring at Billy. It was a little disconcerting, as we were completely surrounded, but it turned out that everybody was very friendly and, I think, delighted to see a Westerner who had learned a Chinese discipline.

Despite the hospitality, we were aware of the Chinese's guarded answers to our questions. At the beginning, Tom, Peter, and Bill became irritated with their interpreters, because when they asked specific things about the country, the answers were always vague, very carefully worded, and almost identical—to the word—when the same question would be asked of another interpreter. As the trip went on, we all realized that not only the interpreters, but also most of the people we met, were plainly afraid to talk to us.

A visit to a Chinese music conservatory was one of the rare times when we were not treated with courtesy. The head of the institution attacked us for admiring the music of Mozart, Beethoven, and Brahms, which he called bourgeois crap. It was quite startling but drove home in a very concrete way the complete inanity of some Communist thought.

Thirteen years after that trip, in March 1989, a group of Chinese graduate students and scientific researchers working in the United States approached Aryeh and asked for his help in forming an organization that would call attention to the plight of political prisoners in China. Aryeh said he could give them guidance and offered them office space at Human Rights Watch. The office was just a big open space, like the newsroom of a newspaper, so the Chinese working there blended in with everyone else. They named their new organization Human Rights in China. Sometimes I would stop by to see what they were up to, and they began to fill me in on the dissident movement in China.

Though the world would watch as the Tiananmen Square protests unfolded in Beijing that spring, I learned that the Chinese free speech and democracy movement had really started a decade earlier, when the Democracy Wall—a long brick wall where people were allowed to put up posters—was set up in November 1978 on a street in central Beijing.

The wall, at the start, was supported by Deng Xiaoping, who was trying to consolidate his power as the leader of China and to introduce economic reforms. Many of the early criticisms posted on the wall took aim at the Gang of Four, the group of Communist Party officials—including Mao's wife—who were perceived to be responsible for the worst excesses of the Cultural Revolution. The Democracy Wall movement—which also included pamphlets and hastily produced journals—was at first seen as generally supporting Deng's calls for radical economic change, which included his "Four Modernizations" of agriculture, industry, science and technology, and defense.

But, of course, there is a reason that authoritarians crack down on freedom of speech—once it gets started, it can be hard to rein in. The person who really took things a step further in the Democracy Wall movement happened to be a very bright and determined twenty-eight-year-old electrician at the Beijing Zoo named Wei Jingsheng. In December 1978, Wei posted his essay "The Fifth Modernization: Democracy" on the wall. He argued that real change could not come to China with only economic reform. He wanted political change and the introduction of democracy.

"We want to be masters of our own destiny," he wrote. "We need no gods or emperors. We do not believe in the existence of any savior. We want to be masters of the world and not instruments used by autocrats to carry out their wild ambitions. We want a modern lifestyle and democracy for the people. Freedom and happiness are our sole objectives in accomplishing modernization. Without this fifth modernization all others are merely another promise."

It's hard to believe that a lone article pasted on a wall in Beijing, well before the day when everything could be spread on the Internet, could reach so far and bring such consequences.

Wei also published an article titled "Do We Want Democracy or a New Dictatorship?" in an underground journal, *Explorations*, in which he wrote that Deng could become a dictator if his power wasn't checked. This was too much for Deng, who had Wei arrested on March 29, 1979. A few months later, Wei was tried for treason and sentenced to fifteen years in prison. Though Wei would be horribly mistreated during his incarceration, Deng had not heard the last from him.

For the moment, though, as Deng gained the upper hand over his rivals for control of the Communist Party, he shut down the Democracy Wall movement. The government stayed its hand for a brief period, but in 1981 it made another move to silence dissent. Several other dissident leaders were arrested at that time, including the chief editor of the pro-democracy journal *April Fifth Forum*, a man named Xu Wenli, whom I would later come to know very well.

Those actions managed to tamp down outspoken dissident activity for most of the 1980s. But just as Human Rights in China was setting up in our offices, China itself was a few months away from the largest, most disruptive democracy protest in its history.

The beginnings of the Tiananmen Square protest can be traced back to early 1989, the same time period during which Gorbachev's reforms in the Soviet Union were taking hold. On January 6 of that year, Fang Lizhi, a leading Chinese astrophysicist who had spoken out for reform of the Communist Party for years, chose to send an open letter to Deng Xiaoping calling for the release of Wei Jingsheng from prison. Over a hundred other Chinese intellectuals followed Fang's lead and wrote to the party, asking for pardons for Wei and other political dissidents.

A few months later, on April 15, Hu Yaobang, a former Communist Party general secretary, died. Because Hu had been forced to resign his post after calling for party reform, he was a hero to many Chinese who wanted political liberalization. Within hours after the news of Hu's death became public, students began to assemble at Tiananmen Square in Beijing to mourn.

Thus began an ongoing round of protests. On April 21, the day before Hu's funeral, around one hundred thousand students marched on the square. From there, the protests mounted, as thousands of students occupied the square and began to call for democratic and economic reforms and freedom of speech. Students from around

Beijing began daily marches in support and were joined by thousands of workers. Protests soon erupted in other cities all around China. The international press, which converged on Beijing in May for Gorbachev's historic visit to China, televised the demonstrations around the world.

Behind the scenes, there was an enormous battle within the Communist Party among Deng Xiaoping, the de facto leader of China; Communist Party general secretary Zhao Ziyang, who supported reforms and wanted to go to the square to speak with the students; and Premier Li Peng, who wanted to take a hard line. The hard-liners eventually prevailed, and Zhao Ziyang resigned as the decision was made to move on the protestors.

On the evening of June 3, 1989, the Chinese army, which had massed around Beijing, rolled into the city, smashing through barricades set up on the way to the square. It is impossible to know how many people died in the violence as the troops rolled through the streets of Beijing because the Chinese government has never provided a legitimate accounting, but it was probably several thousand.

The violence, of course, shocked the world. Within China, the government got serious about putting dissenters in their place.

Deng placed Zhao under house arrest. Zhao remained there for the rest of his life, until his death in 2005, barely allowed to communicate with the rest of the world. Overnight, the voice of one of the most powerful men in China was silenced.

Bao Tong, a Communist Party official who had worked closely with Zhao, including writing his speeches and editorials, was put in prison after Tiananmen. Bao's son left China to come to the United States, where he worked with Human Rights in China to try to secure his father's release. The Chinese kept Bao Tong in solitary confinement for seven years before finally releasing him from jail in 1996. He has been under house arrest ever since, with his phone tapped, security cameras around his house, and his visitors limited. From there, he continues to write and get out articles calling for political reform, despite the ever-present threat that he might get sent back to prison. As always, the will of individuals to speak in the face of power amazes me.

After Tiananmen, the Communist Party became even more committed to economic growth, betting that a higher standard of living might dim the population's demand for political reform. The party also built up its police state, working especially hard to limit the amount of information the average Chinese citizen can obtain about the country.

The Tiananmen Square massacre is one thing the Chinese government doesn't want people talking about. The iconic image of the event is, of course, the picture of the young man standing silently in front of a tank, getting across the message that the only way forward was for the tank to kill him. To show how effective the Chinese government has been in squashing the memory of the Tiananmen massacre, in 2006 the PBS documentary show *Frontline* went to Peking University—the same elite school many leaders of the 1989 protests had attended—and showed four students the "tank man" photo. None of them could identify what he or she was seeing.

The Tiananmen Square massacre also spurred major policy changes at Human Rights Watch. Sidney Jones, the head of our Asia Watch division, was an extremely smart and competent woman. Her area of expertise, though, was Indonesia. As a result, since its beginnings in 1985, many of Asia Watch's resources had gone toward that country. Indonesia certainly had its share of human rights problems, but after Tiananmen, we realized that we needed to shift more of our attention toward China.

One thing that became clear was that, like the Soviet Union in the 1970s and 1980s, the Chinese government was locking up an immense number of political prisoners in either prisons or work camps.

Some amazing stories also emerged of dissidents trying to get out of China. For example, Fang Lizhi, the Chinese astrophysicist who had spoken out for Wei Jingsheng, realized that he was in great danger of being arrested. On the night of June 5, 1989, one day after the Tiananmen massacre, Fang and his wife, Li Shuxian, took refuge at the U.S. embassy in Beijing. They remained there, living in a converted closet, for a year, while the United States negotiated with the Chinese government. Fang and his wife didn't leave the embassy until the United States had assurances that they would be allowed to go to the airport and leave the country. The negotiations eventually included the White House. I've never been able to figure out what was in the minds of the Chinese government officials that made them fear so much this man leaving the country.

There were many stories of young students fleeing and some getting caught. One of the most dramatic was that of Li Lu, who was one of the leaders at Tiananmen and found himself number sixteen on the Chinese most wanted list when he was hiding in Beijing. He had a few hundred dollars and somehow contacted the Chinese equivalent of the Mafia, which he paid to smuggle him down to the south of China, which it did, at night, using the same methods as the Underground Railroad. (A number of the student leaders of the Tiananmen demonstrations were able to escape from China in this way and it became known as Operation Yellowbird.)

Finally at the bay facing Hong Kong, Li was placed on a boat and told he was going to be taken out to a buoy, where a boat from Hong Kong would be to pick him up. When they arrived at the buoy, the boat wasn't there. Li was told they couldn't bring him out again, so he should wait. They left him there, and Li sat on the buoy for three or four hours until the boat arrived. He came to New York from there, where I soon met him and where his story would take some fantastic turns.

When the Gulf War started in early 1991, the Chinese government used the diversion to sentence a large group of prominent activists to prison, including Wang Juntao and Chen Ziming, a journalist and economist, respectively, who had founded the Beijing Social and Economic Sciences Research Institute, a think tank that had been a main source of ideas about how China could open its society. In the aftermath of Tiananmen, the government blamed Wang and Chen for being two of the "black hands" behind the uprising. Student leaders such as Liu Gang and Wang Dan were also arrested and thrown into prison. They joined many of the Democracy Wall activists, who were still locked up after being sentenced more than a decade earlier.

From New York, there seemed to be very little we could do to affect the situation. Just two years after the Tiananmen massacre, it seemed that hardly anyone cared about Chinese dissidents or their problems. I think this lack of interest was exacerbated by the fact that the Chinese came from a country that, to the average Westerner, seemed even more foreign, opaque, and exotic than Russia. The Chinese also had names that were hard for English speakers to remember and get straight. I worked very hard on learning all these Chinese names—I had to, as I was meeting them every day. I got them down so well that years later, at the time of life when you start to forget names, Helen explained to a friend of ours that I had a very strange form of Alzheimer's—I could only remember Chinese names.

It seemed to me that one thing I could do was to try to raise the profile of Chinese dissidents in the West, so that when people read about them, there would be some kind of personal connection. I thought if people—both average citizens and politicians—came to know more about the Chinese dissidents, then they would be more likely to speak out. This, of course, had been my experience with Soviet dissidents such as Orlov, Sharansky, and Sakharov.

In early 1991, we formed a group within Human Rights Watch that we called the Committee to End the Chinese Gulag. I chaired it along with several co-chairs. They included Fang Lizhi, the dissident astrophysicist who had just arrived in the United States and taken a research job at Arizona State University; Cyrus Vance, former secretary of state during the Carter administration; Liu Binyan, the exiled dissident Chinese journalist; and Yuri Orlov, the Moscow Helsinki Group founder who was by then teaching at Cornell. As far as the membership of the committee, it was the same idea as when we started Helsinki Watch—we got high-profile people such as Arthur Miller and the opera singer Beverly Sills to add their names to the masthead.

We chose Richard Dicker, a Human Rights Watch staff member, to lead the committee. Richard, in my view, is just about the prototypical human rights activist—he is passionate, smart, and extremely dedicated, and he has an incredible work ethic. As Richard and I spoke about the work of the committee, we decided that one of the best routes to raise awareness of imprisoned Chinese dissidents would be to contact various professional associations and ask them to make statements for dissidents who were in the same professions.

Since many of the Chinese dissenters were scientists, this meant that Richard developed a lot of contacts at the New York Academy of Sciences. Richard and Fang Lizhi also wrote articles about the plight of dissident Chinese scientists and published them in scientific journals. Once we started to get some attention, we got several Nobel laureates and other prominent scientists to sign statements calling for the release of prisoners such as Liu Gang, the student leader at Tiananmen who had been studying physics. Although these efforts were not visible to the general public, we thought they were one way to pressure the Chinese government.

Just as we were starting to get our footing, China announced its desire to host the 2000 Summer Olympics, which were to be awarded by a vote of the members of the International Olympic Committee (IOC) in September 1993. We thought China's bid could be an opportunity to call attention to the government's human rights abuses. Our position was that unless China dramatically changed its treatment of its citizens, it didn't deserve to host the Olympics.

Richard and I set up a series of meetings with newspaper editorial boards to press the case, but we found that we had the most traction not with the editorialists, but with sportswriters. They were the only journalists closely tracking the Olympic bidding process, and we found that a lot of them already had negative feelings about the opaque—and allegedly corrupt—practices of the IOC. We told them not only about Chinese treatment of dissidents, but that when China hosted the Asian Games in 1990, it used the occasion as a reason to round up "undesirables" and put them in prison.

Eighty-nine member countries belonged to the IOC, and we began to lobby any of them that would listen to us. I also sent an open letter to seventeen corporations that had been sponsors in prior Olympics and warned them that if the games were held in Beijing, their images could be tarnished by the association.

There was a lot of pushback from the Chinese government. It spared no expense in wooing members of the IOC, wining and dining them on their visit to Beijing. For the Chinese leadership, the Olympics obviously presented an opportunity to showcase their country and to erase the memories of Tiananmen. But they didn't help their cause by choosing Chen Xitong as the head of their Olympic bid—he was the man who, as mayor of Beijing during the Tiananmen massacre, had authorized martial law and strongly pressed for the use of force to end the protests.

We found that the IOC had reasons to prefer Beijing. A lot of members on the committee, which was then headed by Juan Antonio Samaranch, saw holding the Olympics in Beijing as a great business opportunity—they thought the exotic location would draw more viewers, which would enable them to charge the sponsors more. There was also a sense that awarding the games to China was a way to make history—several committee members argued that holding a major world event in Beijing would bring China to the world stage and force it to clean up its human rights record.

The tension notched up ahead of the September 1993 IOC meeting, which was to be held in Monte Carlo. Richard testified to Congress about China's human rights record, and the House of Representatives passed a resolution opposing Beijing's candidacy for the games. Less than two weeks before the vote, China suddenly released Wei Jingsheng from prison, a move that was obviously meant to garner a few extra votes and to wrest the games away from Sydney, Australia, the other main contender.

Richard went to Monte Carlo for the meeting, where he spent the whole time lobbying IOC members, one by one. We stayed in contact over the phone, and Richard kept a running tally of how many votes he thought we had.

It ended up being as close as it could possibly have been. There were four rounds of voting, and in the first three, the other contending cities—Istanbul, Berlin, and Manchester—fell out of contention. That left only Beijing and Sydney. On the day of the final vote, I was chairing a Human Rights Watch board meeting when somebody came into the room to give me the phone. The person said, "It's Sydney." Thinking that it was Sidney Jones, the head of Asia Watch, I said, "Tell her I'm in a meeting, I'll call her back."

It turned out that Sydney, the city in Australia, had edged Beijing out 45–43 in the last round.

* * *

The Tiananmen Square massacre proved to be only a small speed bump in the commercial relations between the United States and China. Although President George H.W. Bush announced his intention to impose sanctions on China days after the event, six months later he sent National Security Advisor Brent Scowcroft and Deputy Secretary of State Lawrence Eagleburger to Beijing for friendly talks with Chinese officials. Many people inside the American government began to make the same arguments that some of my colleagues in publishing made in the 1970s in regard to the Soviets—by doing business with the Chinese, they said, we would bring about changes through mutual contact.

Less than three years after the 1989 Tiananmen incident, Secretary of State James Baker visited Beijing, signaling that relations between the United States and China were pretty much back to business as usual. The administration of George H.W. Bush—and later that of Bill Clinton—followed a policy of "constructive engagement," in which human rights concerns were put on the back burner to avoid angering the Chinese leadership.

The overarching human rights fight with China in the 1990s concerned China's status as a "most favored nation" trading partner with the United States. Though China had been granted MFN status in 1979, it was not permanent and was subject to renewal. If it were lost, the country could face higher tariffs, which could harm its export-oriented manufacturing economy. After the Tiananmen Square massacre, human rights concerns were increasingly part of public discussion over whether China's MFN standing should be renewed.

Human Rights Watch's position was that China's MFN approval should be tied to its human rights record. In 1991, we released a report based on documents obtained by our China researcher, Robin Munro, that showed that many of the products China exported to the United States were made in prison camps. This labor force included people who had not received trials and others who were political dissidents. The issue became headline news for a brief period—the television show *60 Minutes*, for example, did a segment on prison labor in China—but even though Congress voted to deny China's MFN status that year, President Bush overrode the decision.

For a few years in the early 1990s, the debate over China's MFN status flared each June when it came before Congress, with our side arguing that tying trade to human rights concerns would force China to change its practices. Corporations, on the other hand, insisted that doing business in China would help build the country's middle class, which in turn would lead to more "openness." The word "openness" was actually used by corporations, though they didn't actually define the word. If you mean freedom of the press, freedom of religion, freedom of assembly, freedom to travel and return to the country, or freedom in the arts, then it certainly wasn't applicable. But if you meant freedom to do business, then you had an argument.

As part of the yearly MFN ritual, China would release a few dissidents in the months before the vote. These actions would be held up by business interests as proof that China was easing up on dissent. We saw the actions of the Chinese government as proof that MFN approval could be a lever to pry human rights concessions.

We basically lost the fight in 1994, when President Clinton "delinked" MFN renewal from human rights concerns. In 2000, China was designated as a country with permanent normal trade relations with the United States, effectively ending the debate. Of course, in the decades since Tiananmen Square, China's financial power has only grown, so much so that the United States no longer has the economic leverage to raise human rights concerns when dealing with the Chinese government.

In March 1991, a little over a year after I left Random House, I took a position with John Wiley & Sons as a publisher at large. Up until that point, Wiley had mainly published technical, educational, and business books, and it had decided it wanted to do more trade publishing. I'd had a very warm relationship with Brad Wiley, and that had continued with his successor, Charles Ellis.

The first book I published at Wiley was *Black Hands of Beijing* by Robin Munro, Human Rights Watch's China researcher, and

George Black, a columnist for the *Los Angeles Times*. The book detailed China's democracy movement from the late 1970s through the 1980s and profiled several of its most prominent members—the people the Chinese government called "black hands" and accused of manipulating the masses to participate in the Tiananmen protest.

Not long after I signed *Black Hands*, I was introduced to an incredible man named Harry Wu, one of the most determined people I have ever met.

Harry had been born in Shanghai in 1937, the son of a wealthy banker. The comfortable life he lived as a child ended in 1949, when the Communists won the Chinese Civil War and his father's properties were confiscated. Though his family was no longer rich, Harry supported the Communists, believing that they could end the country's rampant corruption and bring economic equality. When he was eighteen years old, he left Shanghai to study geology and engineering in Beijing, where he would make the mistake of stating his opinion, a decision that would cost him years of his life.

In 1956, the Communist leadership started the Hundred Flowers Campaign. The stated intention of the campaign—which was promoted by Premier Zhou Enlai and supported by Mao—was to encourage China's intellectuals to voice their criticisms of government policies in an attempt to open up a conversation in Chinese society. At first, people were understandably wary of saying anything; in 1957, though, Mao sent orders that he wanted to hear more "healthy" criticism.

Harry, then twenty years old, stood up at a Communist Party meeting. He said he thought the 1956 Soviet invasion of Hungary was wrong; then he said that he objected to the way that Communist Party members had privileged places in society compared with everyone else.

As it turned out, the Hundred Flowers Campaign soured very quickly. It seems that once criticism started coming in—people said they wanted democracy and that the Communist Party should relinquish power—Mao didn't appreciate it. He quickly ended the experiment and began to persecute those who had spoken out. Some 550,000 people were labeled as "rightists" and suffered retributions such as job loss, public humiliation, imprisonment in reeducation camps, torture, and even execution.

Harry was labeled a "counterrevolutionary" and put under surveillance. His family was made to denounce him. Harry knew that the blacklisting meant he wouldn't be able to get a good job after graduation from university. He began to make plans to escape into Burma, but in 1960, he was arrested.

Harry did not have a trial. He was sent to a forced-labor camp, where he was told that, because of his bourgeois ways and lack of repentance for his counterrevolutionary views, he would live out the rest of his life. When Harry's stepmother learned about his imprisonment, she committed suicide by overdosing on sleeping pills.

For the next twenty years, Harry was forced to work seven days a week in a series of jobs in various prison camps, including a chemical factory, brick factory, iron mine, coal mine, steel factory, and farm. The idea was that hard labor could "reeducate" people like Harry and teach them how to be good socialists. The Chinese named this system of reeducation camps the "laogai," which translates to "reform through labor."

After Mao's death in 1976 and the ascendance of Deng Xiaoping, the Chinese government began to release many old prisoners. Harry walked out of prison in February 1979, at the age of forty-two. He'd been locked up for nineteen years, almost half his life.

After his release, Harry got a job as a university geology lecturer and, afraid that at any moment he could be sent back to prison camp, kept his head down. In 1985, he landed a position as a visiting scholar at the University of California at Berkeley, and he ended up staying in the United States. He didn't have a penny to his name. For a brief time, he was homeless. He worked night jobs, first in a doughnut shop and later as a clerk in a liquor store in order to save money.

When the 1989 Tiananmen Square massacre put human rights in China in the headlines, Harry was called to testify before Congress. In 1991, he published an academic book that described the workings of the laogai, and he went back to China with *60 Minutes* to help the show's report on slave labor in China's prison system. In

1992, Harry realized that he couldn't walk away. He left his academic job to work full-time for human rights in China. His goal has been to create a historical record and call attention to the laogai, so that other people will not have to suffer as he did.

I met him just as he was transforming from academic to human rights activist. Helen and I had him over to our apartment for dinner, and as Harry told me about his time in the laogai, I realized he had an incredible story. We both agreed that it should be a book, and I bought it for Wiley.

The result, *Bitter Winds*, co-written with Carolyn Wakeman, a China expert and journalism professor at UC Berkeley, is a personal and harrowing description of the dehumanizing conditions of the Chinese prison system. After its publication in 1994, it became a critical success and, more surprisingly for a book with such a grim subject matter, also sold reasonably well.

Harry has continued with his work. In 1996, I was his agent for his follow-up book, *Troublemaker*, in which he wrote about his three trips to China between 1991 and 1994, when he snuck inside prison camps in order to get video footage. When Harry tried to reenter China in 1995, he was stopped at the border, arrested, and tried and convicted on charges of "stealing state secrets." He was sentenced to fifteen years in prison and was released and expelled from China only after protests from the U.S. government.

The laogai can really be thought of as the Chinese equivalent to the gulag. It always bothered Harry that Solzhenitsyn, with *The Gulag Archipelago*, had made that system well known, but no one had heard of the Chinese version, which has locked up an estimated 50 million people.

A few years ago, Harry called me and told me he had accomplished one of his life's main goals—he had gotten the word "laogai" into the *Oxford English Dictionary*. But he went even further than that.

In early 2008, Harry called again. He said he'd gotten a huge grant—he hinted that it was between $10 million and $20 million—from Yahoo!, the Internet company. The money was to set up a museum dedicated to the laogai.

Yahoo! had funded the museum for an interesting reason. In 2004, the company allowed the Chinese government to look at some of its records, which enabled China to determine that a journalist, Shi Tao, had sent an e-mail to Human Rights in China—the group of Chinese working out of the Human Rights Watch office—detailing the government's orders to downplay the fifteenth anniversary of the Tiananmen Square protests. Shi was tried for "illegally providing state secrets to foreign entities." He was sent to prison and was released only in 2013, after eight and a half years—all this for simply writing an e-mail that Yahoo! had let fall into the hands of the Chinese government. The museum was an interesting way for a large company to try to make amends.

I went to the opening of the museum in Washington, D.C., in the fall of 2008. Harry gave a brief talk, saying that while the Holocaust was horrific, it was over, but there were still more than 3 million people in the Chinese laogai. Jerry Yang, the co-founder and president of Yahoo!, was supposed to appear, but he bowed out at the last minute. Instead, a Yahoo! vice president spoke and said how proud the company was to be financing the museum.

As I've learned, there are always surprises in dealing with Harry Wu. The next speaker was the wife of Shi Tao, the imprisoned Chinese journalist. She announced that under U.S. law she was suing Yahoo! for turning over her husband's e-mail to the Chinese government.

I thought that perhaps Jerry Yang had been wise to skip the opening.

In the spring of 1994, Helen and I planned a trip to Vietnam, Cambodia, and Hong Kong. When I spoke about it with Robin Munro, he said we should also go to China. After our previous visit to the mainland back in the 1970s, Helen had no desire to return, so I made plans to go a week early to visit Beijing with Robin.

The main purpose of the trip was to speak with Wei Jingsheng, the Democracy Wall dissident who had been released from prison in September 1993, just before the International Olympic Committee voted on the location of the 2000 Summer Olympics.

During the fourteen years Wei spent in prison, he had kept his focus in an amazing manner. Although he had been locked up in solitary confinement and suffered from arthritis, high blood pressure, headaches, depression, and the loss of his teeth, Wei wrote a series of letters to Chinese officials and his family. Many were addressed directly to Deng Xiaoping. When the Chinese wanted to release him, Wei said he would leave prison only if they gave him the file of his letters, which he knew they had kept. The Chinese acquiesced, and as soon as Wei got out, he had several copies made. Word of the letters made it to Human Rights in China, and from what I'd heard about them, Wei had not backed down from his demands a bit, even in prison.

When Robin and I arrived in Beijing in February 1994, we were met by Liu Baifang, whose husband, Orville Schell III, was a China expert and the son of Orville Schell Jr., the lawyer and founding Helsinki Watch board member and the first chairman of the Americas Watch committee. Orville thought Baifang, who was born in China, could be very helpful as an interpreter. He said that she also knew many people in the literary world and could arrange for me to speak with them, and she could also make phone calls for me when Robin was off on other business.

Baifang took me around to meet some magazine editors and other intellectuals. We also went to speak with the wife of Chen Ziming, the imprisoned "black hand" who, with Wang Juntao, had run the Beijing Social and Economic Sciences Research Institute think tank prior to the Tiananmen Square protests.

One night, Robin called me from the lobby of the hotel and told me he was downstairs having dinner with a close friend, Xu Wenli, who, after Wei, was probably the most well-known dissident in China. During the Democracy Wall movement, Xu had co-published a pro-democracy magazine, the *April Fifth Forum*. He'd been arrested in 1981 and sentenced to fifteen years in prison for "counterrevolutionary" activities. I later learned that for five years he was kept in solitary confinement in a nine-by-three-foot cell for twenty-three hours a day. Like Wei, Xu had been released in 1993, a bit before the end of his sentence, because of China's bid for the Olympics.

When I met Xu at the hotel, I could tell the years in prison had been hard on him. He had almost no teeth left and he looked very worn. At the same time, he was also very talkative and had an amazing enthusiasm and vigor as he told his story. What came through as Xu spoke was the enormity of the punishment he'd suffered. He'd not only been in prison, but he had been treated miserably while he was there. All this was simply for the act of publishing a small magazine that had a very low circulation. Life for me has rushed past too quickly, and I've never really found an answer as to why totalitarian governments are so terribly afraid of these publishing attempts by individuals with no organization, no money, and no power.

When I asked Xu if there was anything I could do for him when I got back to the United States, he immediately grabbed my arm and said, "Yes, there's one thing. I have this wonderful daughter, and she and my wife have suffered a lot because of me, because I've been in prison the whole time she's been brought up."

He continued: "She's very bright, but the Chinese won't let her go to college because I'm a dissident. I'm determined to get her educated. She speaks English. If you could somehow get her into an American college, that's what I would ask of you."

I told him that I couldn't guarantee anything, but I would try. When I got back to the States, I called Leon Botstein, the dynamic president of Bard College, whom Helen knew very well—she had attended Bard and graduated class of 1948, the first to allow women. I told Xu's story to Leon and said I hadn't met his daughter, Xu Jin, but I'd heard she was bright. I said that Helen and I could help her a bit financially, but that we couldn't pay the tuition. Without a moment of hesitation, Leon said, "We'll give her a full four-year scholarship."

It was the start of a long relationship with Xu Wenli and his family, but, unfortunately, his time in the Chinese prison system wasn't yet finished.

The other dissident I met on the trip was Wei Jingsheng. Robin and he arranged to meet in a hotel bar some distance from my own hotel. Even though Wei was consistently followed by security department thugs, Wei and Robin felt that this meeting place would allow us to have some privacy. When we got there, I saw that the bar was decorated like a German beer garden.

Wei was solidly built, with thick black hair that was combed down across his forehead, and he wore a black leather waistcoat. He had a warm smile and was very direct, not much for small talk. He soon got down to telling Robin and me about his time in prison. He didn't know if he was going to be sent back or not. He told us he wanted to publish what sounded like a very theoretical book about the nature of democracy. Robin and I both impressed upon him that the first thing people would want to know about was his experience in prison and raised the idea of a book of his letters. He gradually came around to the idea.

Before long, Wei suggested that we continue the conversation back at his office, which was located in his brother's house in the northern part of Beijing. This surprised me. I asked him, "Isn't it bugged?"

He shrugged and said, "Of course it is, but I'm a free man, for the moment. I'm not plotting to overthrow the government or anything like that. I just want to have my letters published, so we'll go back and talk about my book."

We left and got in a taxi. As we drove away, Wei, who is always humorous, looked back and said, "You must be very important men."

"Why?" I asked.

"Well, usually I have one car following me," he said. "Now there are two. You must have your own."

I came to understand that the government was keeping a very close eye on him and, to my surprise, me.

When we arrived at his brother's house, we sat down to hammer out the details of his book. "If you're going to be my agent," Wei said, "shouldn't we have a contract?"

I said, "Well, you don't really need a contract. Let me tell you what I did with Andrei Sakharov. We shook hands, and he said, 'Work out the contract,' and that's what it was."

Wei thought for a moment and said, "No, I want a written contract. You know enough about a publishing contract that you can dictate one right here, right now, and my assistant, Tong Yi, who speaks English, will take notes."

I told Wei that I would take a 10 percent commission, but that I would donate the money I received to Chinese human rights causes, though not necessarily the ones he chose. When we had gone through everything, Wei said that Tong would translate it all and write it out, he would sign it, and then she would bring it to me at my hotel. The night before I was set to leave, she arrived at my door at around eleven in the evening with two copies of the contract and a huge smile on her face. I could tell that she was very happy to have gotten it done and in my hands.

In the coming weeks, Tong typed up Wei's prison letters and put them onto computer discs. Liu Qing, the president of Human Rights in China, arranged for them to be smuggled out of the country.

It wasn't until I was back in New York and I saw a few of the translated letters that I realized the unbelievable quality that Wei had in him: a belief that no person or prison could stop him from saying what he wanted to say. Imagine a man who had been in solitary confinement for almost ten years at the time of Tiananmen handing a prison guard a letter to send to Deng Xiaoping, the head of state, from his cell in prison, and saying the following:

June 15, 1989

Dear Deng Xiaoping:

So, now that you've successfully carried out a military coup to deal with a group of unarmed and politically inexperienced students and citizens, how do you feel? If the impression I got from the brief scenes I saw on television is correct, you are not quite as relaxed and self-congratulatory as Li Peng. Your head is a bit clearer than I had originally thought and you're not so muddled that you're blind with success; you can still understand the heavy political price you've paid by initiating this bloody coup. That's more appropriate behavior for an old statesman like yourself, so I'm not too disappointed. But other than this, everything else you've accomplished can be described as nothing less than complete chaos.

Going down in infamy for carrying out a military coup doesn't sound too good to you, does it? . . . Several years ago I told you that you were small-minded and lacking in vision. And now, not only have you managed to miss an extremely good opportunity to stand together with the people; what's more, after finding that it's difficult to get off a tiger's back once you're on it, you just kept going. You refused to give in, so in the end you not only damaged your reputation, but you also harmed your own initiatives and turned yourself into a person who will go down in history as a laughingstock.

When I thought about which publishing house I should bring the book to, Viking Penguin was my first choice. Susan Petersen had finished the year's vacation given to her by Alberto Vitale and had been immediately hired by Viking Penguin upon her return. Not only that, one of her star editors was former Pantheon editor Wendy Wolf, who was so good that when Vitale fired André Schiffrin, he unsuccessfully tried to keep Wendy. Wendy enthusiastically bought Wei's book and we set about translating it.

Not much later, I read in the paper that an American journalist living in Japan was going to do a book on Chinese dissidents and he was going to use the letters of Wei Jingsheng, who had been thrown back in prison and was impossible to contact. I called the journalist's agent and said he couldn't use the letters because I had a contract with Wei. He was incredulous and asked me to send the contract. I said I wouldn't send it but he could come over and I'd show it to him. He did come, looked at the contract, and said he would stop his author from using the letters.

I never knew what it was in Wei that made him say he wanted a written agreement when a handshake was good enough for Andrei Sakharov, but it turned out to be a wise decision. I also thought that even after twenty-four years as president of Random House, I could still learn a thing or two about the value of contracts from a Chinese dissident.

During the time that my interest was shifting to China, our Watch committees were continuing to grow at a surprisingly fast rate. After adding Americas Watch in 1981, Asia Watch had followed in 1985, Africa Watch in 1988, and Middle East Watch in 1989.

By 1988, we realized that having all these separate committees was starting to cause some problems. For one, the press got very confused when dealing with us—reporters didn't know if we were one organization, which we were, or some kind of loosely affiliated group. Aryeh and I also found that the effectiveness of each Watch committee depended on the strength of its director and its board. Some committees were very well run, and others were having problems getting off the ground. Some kind of centralization seemed to be needed.

We made the decision to reorganize the committees under the name "Human Rights Watch," which officially placed all the divisions under Aryeh. Some directors of the individual Watch committees protested the change because they saw the reorganization as a diminution of their power—which, in truth, it was—but we were getting so large that, in my opinion, it was an absolutely necessary step. In the years since, we have added many more divisions and special projects under the Human Rights Watch umbrella, including ones on the United States, children's rights, and women's rights.

I always liked the name "Human Rights Watch" because like all good titles, it tells you exactly what it is.

It would be hard to overstate the role that Aryeh Neier had in the development of HRW. He excelled at finding and hiring great people, setting directives, and establishing high standards. From the beginning, Aryeh insisted that our credibility depended on our reports being accurate and thorough. When we found that we had made errors, Aryeh had them corrected immediately and made sure that the corrections were publicly announced.

Aryeh was also extremely important in advancing the human rights movement beyond the letter-writing mandate established by Amnesty International and into many other aspects, including discussions of how the movement could promote not only civil and political rights, such as voting and free speech, but also social and economic rights, such as freedom from hunger, which are also included in the Universal Declaration of Human Rights.

In 1993, Aryeh told us he was leaving Human Rights Watch to head George Soros's Open Society Foundations. With his departure set, we formed a search committee to find a replacement. It was headed by Jonathan Fanton, the president of the New School for Social Research and, since 1989, my successor as chair of Helsinki

Watch (at that time, I became chair of Human Rights Watch). After vetting many candidates, we ended up picking Ken Roth, a former federal prosecutor who had been working at Human Rights Watch since 1987.

For the next several years, Ken and I, as executive director and chair, respectively, worked very closely through what was a very tough time for Human Rights Watch, including our 1998 move into much bigger offices in the Empire State Building. Ken began to change Human Rights Watch's organizational structure—whereas before almost everything had been held inside Aryeh's head, Ken added new management positions. It made the hierarchy of the organization much clearer but also more bureaucratic. Ken made it known from the beginning that he did not like as much board participation as had been customary, which also began to change the nature of the organization.

Many members of the original board valued not only their involvement in policy matters, but also in some of the activities that inevitably occur in a human rights organization, such as appearing before congressional committees and actually making trips into the field. Under Aryeh, the board met on a regular basis, but there were also many special meetings and opportunities for the board to play an active role. Ken saw the organization as much more staff-run. The board began to switch from an advisory role to a fund-raising one, and as more people with money joined, others who had been involved for their expertise but not necessarily their bank accounts began to fall off. The people who stayed were more content with an oversight position similar to the board of a corporation.

Overall, we were transitioning from being a start-up to an established organization. The changes were necessary to encompass our growth and for the organization to survive, though I know many people were disappointed that the loose, improvisational nature of the early years was lost.

When it was clear that Human Rights Watch was on solid footing, I announced that at the end of 1998 I was going to step down from my position as chair. I had been the organization's chair for twenty years and I thought that, at age seventy-five, it would be good to have an orderly transition. In the back of my mind, I also understood that my fund-raising powers had waned as I moved out of the business community, which is where so much of the networking you need to raise money is.

But, to my surprise, I was soon once again actively involved in helping to guide and fund-raise for a human rights organization: Human Rights in China.

13

A NEW ORGANIZATION, A NEW APPROACH

HUMAN RIGHTS IN CHINA (HRIC) WAS FOUNDED IN EARLY 1989 BY Fu Xin-yuan, a postdoctoral fellow in microbiology at Rockefeller University (he is now a professor and director of international relations at the National University of Singapore School of Medicine). He was joined by several other Chinese graduate students and scientists who had come to the United States for their studies and work (at the time, 39,000 Chinese students were enrolled at U.S. universities). As I've mentioned, Aryeh provided them with space inside the Human Rights Watch office.

At first, their goal was to support the 1989 democracy movement that was building in China. After the bloody crackdown in Tiananmen Square and other cities in China, they worked to support the political dissidents and others who had been detained or forced into exile.

In 1991, a man named Xiao Qiang became executive director of HRIC. Xiao had come to the United States in 1986 to pursue a PhD in astrophysics at Notre Dame (in China, Xiao had studied under Fang Lizhi, the prominent astrophysicist who had been forced into exile after 1989). Xiao was living in a trailer in the Indiana woods and studying the sky when the Chinese military marched on Tiananmen Square in June 1989.

Xiao was horrified and immediately flew back to Beijing. In the aftermath of the massacre, he collected stories from people who witnessed the event. When he came back to the United States, Xiao hooked up with HRIC and changed the focus of his life from science to human rights. He was tall, thin, and somewhat debonair with his mane of long hair. Xiao was also very hardworking, very smart, and charismatic, and he was still in his twenties when he became executive director.

Xiao was soon joined in the leadership of HRIC by an amazing man named Liu Qing. An architectural engineer, Liu co-founded—along with Xu Wenli—the pro-democracy journal *April Fifth Forum* and was a leader of the 1978 Democracy Wall movement. After Deng Xiaoping cracked down on the movement in 1979 and had Wei Jingsheng and others arrested, Liu organized protests and was even able to get a recording of Wei's October 1979 trial, which Liu typed out and published. When Liu went to the Beijing police to request the release of other democracy activists, he was detained as well. He was initially sentenced to three years of *laojiao* ("reeducation through labor"). While he was there, Liu wrote an account of the horrible conditions in Chinese labor camps and had it smuggled out. After his report was published in the West, he received an additional eight years in the laogai.

The Chinese authorities spared nothing to punish Liu. He was beaten relentlessly and then held for more than five years in isolation, during which he was forced to sit on a stool and stare at a wall, totally silent and motionless, for twelve hours a day. The guards were changed every few hours so that they wouldn't develop too much sympathy for Liu, whom they were ordered to beat if he moved or spoke. After he tried to commit suicide several times, the guards also shackled Liu to an iron "tiger chair" so that he couldn't move at all.

Liu served his whole sentence and was released in early 1990. He was invited to Columbia University as a visiting scholar, but the Chinese government denied him permission to leave. It relented only after Liu's case received international attention and generated pressure from various Western governments. Upon his arrival in the United States in May 1992, Liu began to work with HRIC and became its second president.

The third member of the trio that ran HRIC throughout the 1990s was Sophia Woodman, an American specialist on China who headed the group's research efforts and later opened the Hong Kong office in 1996.

From its inception, HRIC played a special role. First, many large international human rights organizations had not paid all that much attention to China. For decades, the country had been hard to access and simply off the radar to most of the human rights world.

HRIC also had the distinction of being primarily staffed by Chinese who had great access to channels of information from inside the country. In essence, the work of HRIC was very similar to that of Helsinki Watch in its first days, except HRIC was staffed by dissidents from the country. Instead of making trips into the field—as Jeri Laber had done in the Eastern Bloc—the information on China was gathered and sent out of the country through technology: phone, fax, and Internet.

In 1997, after I had announced my intention to step down as chair of Human Rights Watch at the end of the coming year, Liu Qing and Xiao Qiang asked me if I would become more involved with HRIC. They said they were having a lot of problems with organizational matters and needed help.

After speaking with them, I realized that they had great connections inside China, but not much idea about how to develop, manage, or sustain a human rights organization in the United States. Basically, they didn't know the press, and they didn't know fund-raising.

It also occurred to me early in my work with them that if we could build the organization into a meaningful one, it would be a significant step for human rights organizations in that it would be an indigenous group—not outsiders—trying to change their own country. In the ensuing years, I grew to feel that this was extremely important if human rights were to take hold in closed societies. Having a group run by Chinese dissidents was particularly important in China, where the country's history with foreign interference meant that the Communist Party could turn the Chinese against outside human rights organizations by appealing to Chinese patriotism. This would be harder to do when the people sending the message were Chinese.

I did all the things with Liu Qing and Xiao Qiang that I'd been doing for years with Human Rights Watch, introducing them to journalists and the editorial boards at the *New York Times* and the *Wall Street Journal*, and teaching them something that I had painfully learned: that even though you were in New York with the story, you frequently had to get it back to the foreign bureau of the newspaper—in this case, Beijing—to get it published.

I also took them to meet people at the MacArthur Foundation and other organizations. Raising money for a Chinese human rights group as China's economic power grew proved to be extremely complicated and difficult. Many foundations were scared that giving money to HRIC might impact their own programs in China and access to the country.

As I became enmeshed in Chinese human rights issues in the 1990s, I found myself personally involved with many recently exiled dissidents. Though some were fortunate to land academic jobs as scientists at universities, many of them arrived in the United States penniless and with no support network. Some have adapted amazingly well, and others have struggled.

One of the first to arrive in America after Tiananmen was Li Lu, the student leader who had been smuggled out through Hong Kong after waiting several hours on a buoy. I got to know him soon after he arrived in New York, and it was immediately apparent that this man—who hardly spoke English—would somehow make it in America. Helen and I first met him at an Italian restaurant on Third Avenue in the East Sixties. At the end of the meal, Li had to leave to go up to Columbia, where he had been admitted as a student. I offered him taxi money to make things a little easier, and Helen and I were a little taken aback when he said, "No, no, I have a car waiting." I didn't know it then, but in life, Li would always have a car waiting.

We subsequently had him up to our house in Bedford, which has a terrace overlooking a small lake. Again, he hardly spoke English, but Li was adapting quickly to the United States. He looked at Helen and myself, looked at the lake, and a big smile came to his face. He said, "Ah, *Golden Pond*," referring to the movie, starring Henry Fonda and Katharine Hepburn, about an older couple living their last years at a lakefront. Helen and I preferred to think Li was comparing us with Fonda and Hepburn, rather than the elderly bickering couple they portrayed in the film.

Li lived at Columbia, and before we knew it, he was graduating, but not just from the college—he was also getting degrees from the law school and the business school as well. He had done all three in just six years total. We were honored when we were asked to be at his graduation, and we decided to throw him a party. A few weeks before it was scheduled, Li came to see us and told us that one of the richest Columbia alums had heard about him and wanted very much to give him a party. Li asked if we would be hurt. We meant it when we told him we wouldn't be the slightest bit hurt, especially when we heard the man was the billionaire John Kluge. There was that car again.

Li was the main speaker at the law school graduation. He gave a deeply moving speech, saying how much he owed to the United States and to all the people who had been so kind to him and had financed him, but he also felt that he owed something to the troubled country of his birth, China. He ended by telling the dramatic story of how he left China, recalling the moment when he was floating on a buoy in the South China Sea.

"As I sat there," he said, "I remember thinking, 'Who am I, and where am I going?' As I graduate today from this great law school, I have the same thought, 'Who am I, and where am I going?'" His delivery was very dramatic, and people rose from their seats in applause.

Where he went immediately, thanks to Kluge, was to a job at Donaldson, Lufkin & Jenrette, then a hugely successful Wall Street brokerage firm. Within a few years, Li was earning a great deal of money. Several years later he went out on his own and started Himalaya Capital, then moved to California, where Charles Munger, Warren Buffett's partner, became one of his major investors and a friend.

In April 1994, the Chinese arrested Wei Jingsheng once again, only a month after I had met him in Beijing and spoken with him about publishing a book of his prison letters. The Chinese were outraged that Wei had met with John Shattuck, the American assistant secretary of state for democracy, human rights, and labor, when Shattuck was in Beijing. Wei had told him that the United States should deny most favored nation trading status to China on human rights grounds. The Chinese arrested Wei a few days after the meeting.

The strangest thing about Wei's arrest is that he was basically disappeared—although it was known that the Chinese had taken him into custody, they denied it for over a year and a half. Finally, at the end of 1995, the government admitted that it had him locked up and gave Wei a sham trial. Despite protests from governments and human rights groups around the world, Wei was sentenced to another fourteen years in prison. (As I previously mentioned, he had been imprisoned from 1979 to 1993 for his writing on the Democracy Wall, so this was his second fourteen-year sentence.) Even though I had just met him during my one-week trip to Beijing, Wei was not a man you forget. My friend was in jail.

In prison, Wei's health deteriorated. The Chinese government must have become worried that he would die behind bars, because on November 16, 1997, three years into his term, they took him from his cell and drove him to a guesthouse near the Beijing airport. Wei's brother, sister, and father were brought there to urge him to take a deal the Chinese government had offered to let Wei leave the country on "medical parole." His family was worried that Wei would soon die if he didn't get out of China. In the end, Wei relented, and the next day he boarded a Northwest Airlines flight for Detroit.

At HRIC, we got the news when everyone else did—at the last minute. We were told that Wei had asked for Xiao Qiang and me to meet him at the airport, so we both immediately headed to Detroit.

It was a rather unusual experience. Wei was run-down and haggard when he arrived, so the State Department put him in a hospital for a few nights for rest and examination. Wei later told us that while he was there, a Chinese American doctor came into his room and spoke to him in Chinese, telling him that even though he was now in the United States, he should be careful what he said and that he shouldn't speak out against the Chinese government.

When Xiao and I got back to our hotel after meeting Wei at the airport, Xiao found that someone had entered his room and taken all his papers. We went down to talk to the hotel manager, and he was horrified. He said nothing like that had ever happened before. He told us the hotel would take precautions to see that it never happened again. I think he meant well, but what precautions could he take? Obviously not many, because the next night when Xiao came back to his room, the notes he had made from the trip and a few other things had also been removed.

The harassment continued. After Wei checked out of the hospital, we flew with him to New York. On arrival, the bags he had checked were missing. A few days later, Wei got a call from a Chinese journalist who said there must have been some mistake at the airport, because he had Wei's suitcases. Wei took it all in stride. He said, "Look, it's just the Chinese government going through my baggage."

Wei's remarkable book of prison letters, *The Courage to Stand Alone*, had been published by Viking Press a few months before he arrived in the United States. The book had received a lot of attention and helped to increase Wei's profile. When he arrived, there was a brief flurry of press, including a Q&A in the *New York Times*. The day after we landed in New York, a press conference we arranged for Wei in a room at the New York Public Library was packed with reporters.

Wei, who at age forty-seven had spent nearly a third of his life in prison, relished the back-and-forth with the journalists. "I have waited decades for this chance to exercise my right to free speech," he said, "but the Chinese people have been waiting for centuries."

He called for the world to keep pressing China for democratic reforms and announced that he had been invited to speak with President Clinton. He also vowed that he would someday return to China. Almost two decades later, that still hasn't happened.

Wei had no place to live, so Helen and I invited him to stay at our house in Bedford, an hour north of New York City. He moved into a small cottage on the property. After the trouble we'd had in Detroit, I called the New York City Mayor's Office and told the staffers that Wei was being watched by the Chinese government. When I asked if that might be a problem, much to my surprise they said it definitely was. They assigned a group of officers to provide security for Wei, so for a few months a policeman sat in a car outside our house in Bedford and traveled with Wei when he went to the city.

Wei and I got along very well, especially when we had someone to translate for us—he was quick with a joke and fun to be around. During the time he stayed up in Bedford, I taught him to drive in my car, and we practiced with him going up and down the long driveway. A few years later I learned that Wei had ten speeding tickets but no accidents. Wei believed the Chinese government would kill him in a way that could not be detected: through an automobile accident. So when he thought someone was tailing him, he would speed, which was his way of discovering if he was being followed. Ten times it turned out not to be the Chinese but the American police.

One day, Wei insisted that he cook a Chinese meal for Helen and me. We took him to the store, and he went in and bought everything he needed, which must have included about seventeen different types of vegetables. He then sequestered himself in the kitchen and cooked a delicious meal. It was all great until later in the evening. After Wei went back to the cottage, Helen went into the kitchen and let out a cry. When I followed, I saw that Wei must have used every single pot, pan, and dish that we had, and they were all piled up on the counter and in the sink.

Of course, we needed to get Wei set up somewhere. I called Michael Sovern, who had been very helpful to dissidents during his tenure as president of Columbia University from 1980 to 1993. Though he had gone back to teaching full-time, he was extremely cooperative as always and arranged for Wei to have a two-bedroom apartment in a Columbia faculty building as well as an office, and even the rights to use the restaurant on top of the faculty building. It was a truly wonderful arrangement. I just had to raise the money to get a translator who could work with Wei, who did not speak English and to this day still does not.

The deal at Columbia worked out for several years, and I heard only one complaint from the university. Wei is a chain-smoker, and there was no smoking allowed in the office building where Wei worked. Officials at Columbia explained to Wei many times that he couldn't smoke inside. Wei took the position that he was living in a democracy and that it was his office, and that if it was a true democracy he should make the rules for his office. He was perfectly serious about this, and I must admit every time Columbia asked me to get him to stop smoking, I thought, "You don't survive fourteen years in a Chinese prison without being a very stubborn person." I have no idea if in the end Wei stopped smoking in his office or Columbia stopped complaining.

After several years, Wei moved to Washington, D.C., and started the Wei Jingsheng Foundation, which he still runs. I receive several of the foundation's updates in my e-mail every week, and every time I look, it seems that Wei is somewhere in the world speaking out about human rights in China. He is still calling for the "Fifth Modernization," democracy, his addition to the four that Deng Xiaoping listed in 1979.

When I met the pro-democracy activist Xu Wenli in Beijing in 1994, Xu, who had just been released from prison, asked me to help his daughter, Xu Jin, get into an American college.

Jin—who is known by her nickname, Jing Jing—turned out to be a wonderful young woman. At Bard, she did very well in her classes and worked any job she could in order to send money to her parents in China. She saved for a long time and finally bought her father a laptop computer and somehow got it to him in China. He was delighted with it and was learning how to use it when Jing Jing got a note that the Chinese government had taken it away from him for inspection. A subsequent letter told how officials returned the computer, saying there was nothing wrong with it. When Xu Wenli tried to use it, however, he found it was filled with sand.

When Jing Jing graduated, I was concerned about her getting a job. Before I had much time to be worried, she called me and said she had arranged for a teaching fellowship and was getting her master's degree in fine arts at Boston University. When she graduated a year later, I again wondered what was going to happen, but not for very long. She called and told me she'd been hired as head of the art department at the Holderness School, a small prep school in New Hampshire. After two years, she called me and said, "Bob,

I'm bored. There's nothing here but a town with six pizza shops."
She told me she was going to look for another job. Again, in short
time, she landed a very good teaching job in the art department at
the Moses Brown School in Providence, Rhode Island. The only
part of the job she didn't like, she told me, was supervising girls'
field hockey in the afternoons, which she hated.

In the meantime, things had not gone well for her father. After
we met in February 1994, Xu continued with his pro-democracy
work and, in 1998, established the China Democracy Party. He
was arrested, convicted of "incitement to overthrow the state," and
was sentenced to thirteen more years in prisons—he had already
been jailed from 1981 to 1993—which many thought he could not
survive.

There was a huge outcry over Xu's arrest, but the Chinese were
obstinate. Jing Jing took it on herself to try to gain his release. She
wrote letters to members of Congress and went to Washington for
meetings with some of them, including Nancy Pelosi.

It got really interesting when the Chinese premier, Zhu Rongji,
came to the United States on a visit in April 1999. He was scheduled
to speak at Harvard, and Jing Jing wanted to be in the audience. She
asked me if I could try to arrange it so that she would be called on
during the Q&A period.

Since I'd gone to Harvard and thought it was the most open of
schools, I called the president's office and ended up talking to the
professor who was head of the Harvard Committee to Welcome
President Zhu Rongji. I asked him if the questions during the Q&A
were going to come from the floor, in which case Zhu would have
to expose himself to a true democratic experience.

He told me they were not; the questions were going to be submitted beforehand, and he would go through them, select a representative choice, and read them to Zhu. I discussed with him if there
would be any way to make it known that Jing Jing was in the audience and she had submitted a question. He said, "I'm sorry, we
don't do it that way."

That was that.

Zhu next spoke at MIT, which decided it would only let in students and faculty to his talk, though there would be an open Q&A.

Since she was not a student and could not gain entry, Jing Jing stood outside protesting. She arranged for a friend, who was an MIT student and part of Amnesty International, to ask Zhu about the state of human rights in China and the status of her father.

Zhu responded that human rights in China were improving "from one day to the next" and then declined to discuss individual cases.

It was not much, but in human rights work, it was a small victory that there was a chance to even ask the question. Jing Jing, through her friend, had registered her father's name in the mind of the Chinese premier. Of course, he was smart enough to know that a great university had allowed that to happen, and that Xu Wenli was at least not below the radar in America.

The thing that really helped, in the end, was my son Tom's connection to George W. Bush. After graduating from Yale Law School, Tom had started his career as a lawyer at the New York law firm Paul, Weiss, Rifkind, Wharton & Garrison. In 1983, he left and joined his friend and former colleague at the law firm Roland W. Betts. Together, they launched Silver Screen Partners, financing a slate of HBO feature films and then the first seventy-five films created by the new management of the Walt Disney Company. It happened that Bush had been a friend and Yale classmate of Roland's, and Roland asked him to join the board of Silver Screen.

In 1989, Bush put together an ownership group that bought the Texas Rangers, recruiting Roland and Tom as the lead owners. Bush became a general partner and the public face of the ownership group. This was several years before Bush became governor of Texas and started his career in politics.

Tom happens to be a Democrat, but he and Bush have been great friends for more than three decades. While Bush was president, Tom always admired his deep commitment to human rights activists around the world. In 2002, Tom told President Bush the story of Jing Jing's fight to get her father, who she thought was very ill, out of prison. Bush was moved by the story and took a personal interest in getting Xu Wenli free, just as Reagan had acted in working to free Natan Sharansky many years before.

To do this, President Bush enlisted the support of the U.S. ambassador to China, Clark T. "Sandy" Randt. At the president's suggestion, Ambassador Randt met with me in New York City. It was immediately obvious that he was personally invested in working to free Xu. He told me he knew what Xu had been through and that he would be in touch from Beijing to let me know how he was doing.

A few days before Christmas, Ambassador Randt called to tell me that Xu would be freed. My son Tom recalls that I got a second call from Ambassador Randt letting me know that Xu's plane had cleared Chinese airspace and he was a free man. I can't emphasize enough the importance of the involvement of Ambassador Randt—even though Xu is just one person, I believe the ambassador's vocal work on his behalf also helped make the Chinese government aware that other imprisonments might not go unnoticed.

On Christmas Eve, the State Department followed up, calling and telling me that Xu would arrive the following day. I think the Chinese authorities planned it this way, as they knew most Americans would not be paying much attention to international news at that moment. The woman calling from the State Department also let me know they hoped I would take care of Xu and his wife.

"Exactly what do you mean?" I asked.

"Well, we hope you'll find them a place to stay and arrange for him to get some money. He doesn't have any," she said.

I found myself having an amusing conversation about which was larger: the assets of the United States or my personal assets and whatever I could conjure up. The U.S. government convinced me that if I didn't do something about it, Xu would starve in New York City. There was nothing to do but to prepare for the arrival of Xu and his wife, He Xintong.

Since it was Christmastime, I had trouble finding a hotel room. I ended up calling my friend Jim Ottaway, who was then senior vice president and a director of Dow Jones and chairman of the World Press Freedom Committee. If you're Jim's friend, or even if there's just a situation that he is sympathetic to, you know you can ask him for almost anything. He doesn't always agree, of course, but it's never a difficult conversation. In this case, I knew he had a pied-à-terre in New York that he wouldn't be using at Christmas.

So Xu, who had just been escorted under guard from a Chinese prison and turned over to the United States at the door of an airplane—he had not even been told that his wife was going with him, a final act of cruelty, but found her in the seat next to him in the airplane—spent the first week of his life in New York in the apartment of the senior vice president of Dow Jones. Jim even went so far as to buy a new rice cooker.

From there on, the serendipity of life took over. My son Peter, a graduate of Brown University, was a trustee of the school at that time. Jing Jing was teaching at the Moses Brown School in Providence, so the obvious thing was to try to get Xu involved with Brown University, just as we'd gotten Wei Jingsheng involved with Columbia. Brown University came through magnificently, making Xu an adjunct professor at the Watson Institute for International Studies, where he taught and continued his writing and his work with the China Democracy Party. He remained there until he retired in 2013, when he turned seventy years old.

At the end of Xu's first year at Brown in 2003, he was given an honorary degree. Part of Brown's commencement ceremony is held in one of the oldest chapels in the United States, the First Baptist Meetinghouse. Only the graduating class and a handful of guests can fit in the chapel, but huge television screens are set up on the lawn outside, so the service can be viewed by a larger audience. There are two pulpits inside, one on the stage and another about twenty feet above it. Our oldest grandchild, Elisabeth Bernstein, was graduating from Brown that year, and Helen and I had wonderful seats in the chapel.

Xu walked in with a wide smile—like all survivors of long prison terms, he had spent hours in a dentist's chair getting his mouth put back together again. Walking right behind him was Jing Jing, in a traditional Chinese dress with a headpiece. She went up to the high pulpit. Her father stood right beneath her, and she acted as his interpreter. He then told his story, speaking to the students about the importance of democracy. It was impossible not to be caught up in the emotion of the moment. As he spoke, the graduating class was visibly moved by his words, totally understanding what this man had gone through because of the simple act of espousing his pro-democracy views in China.

With his speech completed, Xu marched with the class up to the College Green, where Ruth Simmons, the first black president of an Ivy League university, who had grown up as the youngest of twelve children in a poor family on a farm in East Texas and faced a different kind of battle for freedom, presented an honorary degree to a man who had fought for everything she believed in and to whom she had now given a home in a great university.

In 1999, I became co-chair of Human Rights in China along with Fang Lizhi. Fang had been through a lot in China—including the year he'd lived in a closet with his wife at the American embassy in Beijing—and he really wanted to get back to science. It took a lot of persuasion to get him to become co-chair. It was amazing to me that I seemed to be the only one who thought it strange that a seventy-six-year-old American Jew was co-chairing a Chinese organization.

In 2001, Sharon Hom, a tenured law professor at the City University of New York who was born in Hong Kong and raised in the United States, took a two-year leave of absence to work at HRIC. Sharon, who is very energetic and capable, had been attending our board meetings for a few years and came in, at the suggestion of Xiao Qiang, to help refine HRIC's direction.

Xiao had headed HRIC since 1991 and kept it going on spit and string and the sheer force of his personality. He'd succeeded in making it a name in the international human rights world. To my mind, though, after a decade in charge he was getting tired and finding it hard to adjust to the more structured atmosphere that was needed as the organization grew. As Human Rights Watch had already done, HRIC was expanding its mandate from mostly working on dissidents to becoming a presence at world meetings, from those of the World Trade Organization to the many UN committees. It was clear that to have a greater impact, HRIC needed to develop a more effective strategy for both individual cases and raising systemic human rights problems. Sharon, with her legal background, including training Chinese lawyers and teachers in China and her decade of work on women's rights issues, was well equipped to take on the challenges. In 2003, she became executive director when Xiao left HRIC to take a position teaching at the journalism school at UC Berkeley.

As Xiao moved on, we took the chance of moving into bigger offices in the Empire State Building. For years, the Chinese officials
had refused to meet us in our offices, preferring instead to talk in
the coffee shop downstairs. As the Chinese government grew a little
bolder, officials and "researchers" began to come up—unofficially
in their "personal capacity" of course—to the actual office. I felt
that the more impressive space increased the stature of the organization in their eyes and made it apparent that it was not going away.

I stepped down from the chairmanship of HRIC in 2005, though
I have remained involved with the organization. After working on
China for more than two decades, I have come to see that it presents
some particular hurdles when it comes to human rights work. I often go back to *The Burning Forest*, a 1983 book by Simon Leys, the
pseudonym of a Dutch author who wrote extensively and insight-
fully on China. In the book, Leys argued that ever since the colonial
era, the Chinese have been seen by Westerners in a way that deval-
ues their humanity.

"Chinese were different, even physiologically; they did not feel
hunger, cold and pain as Westerners would; you could kick them,
starve them, it did not matter much; only ignorant sentimental-
ists and innocent bleeding-hearts would worry on behalf of these
swarming crowds of yellow coolies," Leys wrote. "Most of the ra-
tionalizations that are now being proposed for ignoring the human-
rights issue in China are rooted in the same mentality." He posed
the question: "If Soviet dissidents have, on the whole, received far
more sympathy in the West, is it because they are Caucasian . . . ?"

That question is more than three decades old, and while many
would challenge it, in my opinion there is no other way to explain
the fact that prominent lawyers, intellectuals, writers, and artists
can be arrested in Beijing, disappear for weeks, and come back and
say they were tortured, and even though there is reporting of it,
there is little outrage. If this happened in any part of the Western world, there would be real shock. I've always been amazed by
the ability of diplomats at places like the UN, or world leaders at
the Davos meetings, to talk to highly intelligent, often charming,
and certainly well-educated Chinese officials and, as far as I know,
never ask them how they can live with it.

In July 2015, there was a massive crackdown on hundreds of Chinese human rights defense lawyers and a vicious propaganda campaign against some individuals and groups of lawyers. Perhaps this event will be a wake-up call, as it has generated wide international concern and attention.

There are some people who think China would never have made the economic progress it has if it were a democracy, and some argue that the Chinese have a different culture and different values. I have to believe that it is possible to make progress without torturing people, locking them up, and destroying the lives of those who dare to speak unpopular thoughts.

When I stepped down as chair of Human Rights in China, I thought I would ease into an emeritus role in the human rights world. The last thing I expected was that I soon would be in a very public fight with Human Rights Watch, the organization I founded, over the direction the human rights field was taking.

14

SOME THOUGHTS ON THE FUTURE OF HUMAN RIGHTS IN THE MIDDLE EAST

MY INTEREST IN VARIOUS ASPECTS OF HUMAN RIGHTS CONTINUED to evolve as I grew older and the human rights situation changed around the world. Though I of course maintained my interest in China, at the turn of the new century I also found myself involved in some of the most vexing—and in my mind, worrisome—issues confronting the human rights community today. One of these issues was human rights in the Middle East and, specifically, the treatment of Israel. A second but related issue is government-sponsored hate speech. How these issues are resolved, I believe, will have a tremendous impact on the role of human rights in world affairs for the rest of the twenty-first century.

In 2000, the board of Human Rights Watch was presented with a policy resolution regarding the right of return of Palestinian refugees to Israel. I had stepped down as chair in 1998 and, at the time, was not at all involved with Israel or the Middle East.

I had been to Israel several times, the first visit being especially memorable as it came the week after the 1967 Six-Day War ended. Helen and I went at the invitation of our friend Larry Tisch. Larry, who was co-chairman of Loews, a growing, highly successful conglomerate, was a neighbor in Scarsdale. In the 1980s, he became even better known when Loews bought a minority stake in CBS and he became CEO.

Larry had great connections in Israel and I felt that, for me, it would be a much-needed educational trip. It was June 1967. Helen and I planned to spend the week prior to our trip to Israel in London. Right after we arrived in England, war broke out between Israel and Egypt, Syria, and Jordan. Larry canceled his trip, and we did not plan to go, either. But, as it turned out, the war lasted only six days, with Israel winning a decisive victory.

I knew a lawyer in London named Stanley Berwin who had connections with the Rothschild family. He called Lord Rothschild in Israel, who told him that, amazingly, everything was calm and that it was hard to believe there had been such a game-changing war. We decided to go.

Through Larry, I'd been introduced to Teddy Kollek, who was the mayor of Jerusalem from 1965 to 1993. He was a charismatic and thoughtful man, liked and respected by both Jews and Arabs. He was the only contact I had in Israel. When I called and told him we were still coming, he said, "You're arriving Saturday? Come by the house for lunch on Sunday. I'll have some of the boys over."

We found out that "the boys" meant much of the Israeli military and political high command. It was an amazing group of people to meet two days after a major war. There was Moshe Dayan—with the black patch he wore over his left eye—who was at the time the defense minister. There was Abba Eban, the foreign minister. There was Ezer Weizman, the head of the air force. There was Yigael Yadin, who had been chief of staff of the Israeli army and had then become a prominent archaeologist. And there was Yigal Allon, who was at the time the deputy prime minister.

All of them had fought and commanded in the 1948 Arab-Israeli War and played large roles in the founding of the country. After the Six-Day War, Israel was suddenly in control of all of Jerusalem, the Sinai, the Golan Heights, Gaza, and the West Bank. My memory of the lunch was that they were all ecstatic and somewhat amazed at how it had turned out.

I had been president of Random House for a year and a half, and, though I wished I knew more about the political scene inside Israel, it was not hard to realize that this was a publisher's goldmine. Several books came out of the visit, including Abba Eban's *My People:*

The Story of the Jews as well as his following works and Yigael Yadin's *Masada* and his subsequent histories. I can't remember if Chaim Herzog—a general, lawyer, and, in the 1980s, president of Israel—was at the lunch or if I met him later through Eban, his brother-in-law. Random House published Herzog's much-praised book *The Arab-Israeli Wars.*

After that trip, I'd been back to Israel a few times for the Jerusalem Book Fair, but did not follow the day-to-day politics of the country as so many American Jews did. Most of my attention was consumed by an expanding Random House. In human rights, I was focused on freedom to publish in the Soviet Union, the brutalities of the Latin American military rulers, and, as time went on, China. Also, though my parents observed the High Holidays and I was bar mitzvahed, I have never been an observant Jew.

In 2000, after further wars, peace agreements with Egypt and Jordan, and the Oslo Peace Accords, President Bill Clinton convened a series of peace talks at Camp David between Israeli prime minister Ehud Barak and Palestinian Authority chairman Yasser Arafat. The goal was to create a two-state solution to the Israeli-Palestinian conflict.

One of the most contentious issues during the talks was the right of return of Palestinian refugees, which is at its core a political issue. During the 1948 war over the founding of Israel, around seven hundred thousand Palestinians left or were forced from their homes in what is now Israel. They ended up in the West Bank, Gaza, Syria, Jordan, and Lebanon. The UN General Assembly at the time passed a resolution stating that "refugees wishing to return to their homes and live at peace with their neighbors should be permitted to do so at the earliest practicable date, and that compensation should be paid for the property of those choosing not to return."

Other Palestinians later fled their homes during the 1967 Six-Day War and the 1982 Lebanon War. Though there are perhaps only fifty thousand of the original 1948 refugees still alive, the total number of Palestinian refugees, mainly descendants at this point, is around 5 million. Many have lived in shantytown refugee camps for generations—though Jordan has finally granted Palestinians some citizenship rights, the other Arab states have generally refused. At the same time, it should be noted, after 1948 some nine hundred thousand Jews left Arab states, many because they also were forced to do so.

The various interpretations of "right of return" have filled books. Palestinian negotiators have demanded that any Palestinian refugees or their descendants who want to return to Israel should be able to; Israel has refused—not only would millions of refugees returning all at once destabilize the country, but it would also mean the end of Israel as a Jewish nation. This has been and remains one of the most contentious political issues in any negotiations.

A large part of the 2000 peace talks involved discussions over the right of return. Negotiators on both sides sought to find a mutually acceptable political solution to the problem; one that was on the table would have allowed a modest number of Palestinians to return and a payment of $30 billion in compensation to the other families.

Some staff members at Human Rights Watch did not acknowledge the political nature of this issue and instead sought to treat the right of return as an inviolable human right that should not be abridged. They wanted the organization to make a public statement to that effect. Given the controversial nature of the issue, it was brought to the board for discussion.

One board member, Sid Sheinberg, strongly objected. Sid, who had become president of MCA/Universal Studios in 1973—he is credited with discovering Steven Spielberg and green-lighting movies such as *Jaws*, *E.T.*, and *Jurassic Park*—pointed out that delicate negotiations were under way that had the possibility of finally bringing peace. Why, he asked, would a human rights group jump in with a statement on one of the most contentious issues while the negotiations still had a chance of success? He believed a political solution, based on a negotiated set of compromises, was better than sticking with an ideological imperative and seeing the talks fall apart.

I suspected he was right, and I know several other board members agreed with him, but I didn't know much about the issue at the time. Jonathan Fanton, a former associate provost at Yale and president of the New School, had succeeded me as board chair. When Jonathan took over, I thought I should stand back as much as possible, as Bennett Cerf had done with me at Random House. I also didn't want to be seen, so soon after stepping down as chairman, as going against the staff.

The resolution for Human Rights Watch to take a position in favor of the right of return passed, with only Sid voting against it. As the peace talks continued, Human Rights Watch put out a statement advocating that all the Palestinian refugees should have the right to return to their homes if they wanted.

Shortly afterward, the negotiations collapsed and the Second Intifada was launched. Around one thousand Israelis died in suicide bombings in buses, cafés, and discos, and three thousand Palestinians perished as the Israeli army responded to stop the bombings. Since then, there have been wars in Gaza, fights over settlement expansion, and the grave situation we witness today.

Obviously, the peace talks did not fail because Human Rights Watch made a statement. But the issue of the right of return had been on the table for fifty years by the time of the negotiations. It was obvious there was going to have to be some adjustment on all sides for it to be settled. In retrospect, I see Human Rights Watch's attempt to insert itself into the peace negotiations as evidence of a desire—tinged, I would say, with a certain amount of hubris— that has allowed it and other human rights organizations to wade into political questions that go well beyond clear human rights principles.

The vote on the right of return was an indication of the several changes that human rights work had undergone that now made it very different from what it was in its initial stages some decades earlier.

In those early years, a significant number of volunteer human rights advocates associated themselves with organizations such as Helsinki Watch and later with the other regional Watch committees because, for one reason or another, they had passionate interests in various regions of the world. There were very few paid staff members, and for most of us this was not something we did for a living. Increasingly human rights work has become a profession. Today students study human rights in college and in graduate schools, intern at organizations such as Human Rights Watch and Amnesty International, and aspire to careers in the field.

At the same time, the field has become increasingly law based and legally oriented. This shift toward law was influenced by the international response to the atrocities of the 1990s. These included, among other horrors, the Rwandan genocide, in which eight hundred thousand Tutsis were murdered—many with weapons as simple as machetes and clubs—over the course of three months in 1994; and, in July 1995, the slaughter of eight thousand Bosnian men and boys by Serbian forces in Srebrenica.

In the aftermath, the international community and the Western powers were shamed for their inaction in the face of these crimes—while the world had vowed after World War II that genocide would "never again" happen, once more it had stood by as it did.

It was a frustrating time for Human Rights Watch. We had researchers in both countries who tried to raise alarm at what was happening, but we failed to influence government policy.

In the aftermath of the wars, however, as the reality of Yugoslavia and Rwanda sunk in, the UN Security Council established international courts to try those responsible for genocide and war crimes in both countries.

Human Rights Watch forcefully supported the founding of these tribunals, which were followed by courts for war crimes in Cambodia and Sierra Leone and later the International Criminal Court, which came into existence in 2002 with jurisdiction in countries across the globe. Looking back now, one could write volumes on how these courts have not been as effective as they were intended to be—in essence, because there is a lack of political will globally to enforce their actions. Among the general public, few people know what these courts do, if they are even aware of their existence. As a result, getting the courts to work involves a tremendous amount of political maneuvering.

In practice, the establishment of these courts has had a few effects. First, it has speeded the professionalization of the field as people working at places like Human Rights Watch now need to have specialist education in human rights law. And the courts have also encouraged human rights organizations to expand the scope of their work on both human rights law and international humanitarian law, otherwise known as the "laws of war."

Human rights law has its roots in the 1948 Universal Declaration of Human Rights and nearly a dozen international treaties and accords that have been adopted since then. It is concerned with governing the rights of citizens in relation to the state. For example, human rights laws address things such as freedom of speech, the rights of women, and religious freedom. These rights, known as "civil and political rights," were our focus when we started Helsinki Watch to advocate for Soviet dissidents. (The Universal Declaration also includes "economic, social, and cultural rights," such as the right to food, clothing, housing, and medical care, which have been much more problematic for human rights groups to apply in practice.)

International humanitarian law has foundations in the creation of the International Committee of the Red Cross in Switzerland in 1863 and later the adoption of the Hague Conventions of 1899 and 1907 and the four treaties of the Geneva Conventions in 1949. These can be seen as a set of rules governing how wars are fought. One of the core principles of international humanitarian law is that it is concerned with how war is fought (*jus in bello*) but not the reason for war (*jus ad bello*).

Historically, the Red Cross has been the guardian of international humanitarian law. The Red Cross strives to maintain public neutrality so that it can administer medical care to civilians and visit prisoners of war on both sides. The organization monitors the conduct of war and engages with all participants in a conflict, but it presents its findings privately to the armed forces involved.

Since the 1980s, a number of human rights organizations have broadened their missions to include monitoring for violations of international humanitarian law during conflicts, a dramatic expansion of their mandates that has not been analyzed adequately in the media or in public debates about these issues. Such work requires, for example, teams of researchers who are available to go into conflict zones during hostilities and more systematically after they have ceased.

Both Human Rights Watch and Amnesty International, the two major human rights organizations now working in this area, have stated that they take the same position as the Red Cross in monitoring war crimes—in the words of Human Rights Watch, it maintains "strict neutrality" in order to call out both sides of a conflict if the organization believes the rules of war have been violated. These organizations are explicit that they never take a stance on whether one side in a war is right or wrong, no matter how the war happened to start or how belligerently aggressive one side might have been.

Though these human rights organizations now monitor both human rights law and the humanitarian laws of war, these two sets of laws operate from different premises that don't always mesh. The most prominent of all rights in human rights law is the "right to life." The laws of war, however, start from the premise that war has broken out, and both soldiers and civilians will be killed. Given these circumstances, international humanitarian law attempts to mitigate the violence, especially for noncombatants, and lays a groundwork of rules under which armies may operate.

I have always felt that the imprisonment and torture of those who exercise their right to dissent from government policy is a clear violation of human rights, both morally and legally. By contrast, international humanitarian law often involves very difficult and subjective judgments about conduct on the battlefield that seems to me a much more complicated terrain for human rights groups.

For example, if a group of soldiers is in close proximity to civilians and a bomb intended for the soldiers kills the civilians, that may be deemed legal. If a group of civilians is bombed and it is later determined they were not near a military target, then a number of judgments must be made after the fact: Was there cause to think the group was a legitimate target? Did the side that did the bombing make adequate efforts to determine if it was? What were the rules of engagement? What was the intent of the side that did the bombing? Was the use of force necessary and proportionate to the situation?

These types of questions can be extremely difficult to answer, especially while combat is continuing or has just ended. It can often take months or even years for forensic evidence to be examined, witnesses and military personnel to be interviewed, and for the essential facts to emerge—if they ever do, given the incentive and opportunities for combatants to hide and fabricate evidence.

In any case, modern warfare is far from the technologically aided, exact science one might get from reading the reports put out by human rights groups. Though it is impossible to come to exact numbers, it is estimated that in modern conflicts between 50 and 90 percent of the people killed are civilians. In some wars, civilians have been intentionally targeted as part of military strategy. In many others where civilians are not intentionally targeted, it is still the case that much of the fighting takes place in towns and cities among the civilian population, and officers have to make split-second decisions on which their lives and the lives of their troops depend—is that person looking out the window at you an enemy sniper or the father of a family checking to see what is happening on the street? It's even more difficult to make these decisions when your enemy is not in uniform. In these circumstances, terrible things are guaranteed to happen. They can often be very difficult to sort out after the fact.

During wars, in contrast to the more circumspect approach taken by the Red Cross, human rights groups often call out violations of international humanitarian law as soon as such violations are reported to have happened. These human rights groups have come to see themselves as trying, in effect, to referee wars. The idea is that they will monitor war crimes and call out each side in a conflict when they determine there has been a "foul."

In the Middle East, human rights groups frequently release statements on possible war crimes while the battle is ongoing and monitors from the groups haven't had a chance to get on the ground. Their positions are often based on reports from local contacts in the areas, and these reports can be wrong. In the case of the conflicts between Israel and its enemies, such as Hamas and Hezbollah, this has led to allegations against Israel that have been later proven false.

One prominent example occurred during the 2006 war in Lebanon between Israel and Hezbollah. The war started when Hezbollah indiscriminately fired rockets into Israel and crossed the border, ambushed Israeli troops, and captured two soldiers. Hezbollah demanded that Israel release Hezbollah prisoners to get the soldiers back; Israel refused and launched an invasion of southern Lebanon, which included air strikes.

Human Rights Watch reported that one Israeli air strike, on the village of Srifa, had killed "an estimated twenty-six civilians." Moreover, the organization stated that the attack was totally unjustified because there were no Hezbollah forces present in the village. The claims made headlines around the world and contributed to the idea that Israel was conducting the war recklessly.

The claims were hotly contested at the time, especially since the *New York Times* and many other news organizations had reported interviewing Hezbollah fighters based in Srifa.

In response to these criticisms, the executive director of Human Rights Watch wrote a published letter that vehemently denied any possibility that Human Rights Watch's reporting might be wrong. He went as far as to raise the number of estimated deaths in Srifa to "as many as 42 civilians," stating that the bombing should "generate outrage." He accused Israel of attacking Lebanese civilians in Srifa either "by design or callous indifference." Moreover, he asserted, the Israeli military had treated southern Lebanon as a "free-fire zone."

It was a strident defense. A year later, however, Human Rights Watch released a follow-up report that significantly altered its findings. It found that the bombing of Srifa had killed seventeen Hezbollah fighters and five civilians. "Eyewitnesses were not always forthcoming about the identity of those that died, and in the case of Srifa, misled our researchers," Human Rights Watch reported. "After the conflict, a visit to the graveyard made it possible to establish that most of those killed in Srifa were actually combatants because they were buried as 'martyrs,' not civilians."

Human Rights Watch claimed that these visits to cemeteries "provided an important safeguard against potential misrepresentations by witnesses." But it didn't mention that the organization had been relying on these "misrepresentations by witnesses" for the prior year to accuse Israel of "indiscriminately" killing civilians, and that the executive director had attacked those who raised questions about the veracity of the reports that were eventually found to be false.

Every war in which Israel is involved receives intense scrutiny from international organizations such as Human Rights Watch and from the media, even more than the horrible conflicts in places such as the Democratic Republic of the Congo and Sudan, where the levels of violence are much greater. In Israel or elsewhere, every statement made by a reputable organization such as Human Rights Watch is a potential tool for the political players in these conflicts. Set in these highly political environments, pronouncements and allegations of war crimes become part of larger propaganda wars. I believe that it is imperative that human rights groups refrain from contributing to this incendiary climate.

We started the Middle East division at Human Rights Watch in 1989. For many years, it hadn't been one of Human Rights Watch's most effective—it was really difficult for our researchers to get into many countries in the Middle East, and when they did, they were followed so closely that people were scared to talk to them.

After the 2000 statement on the right of return for Palestinians, two changes in 2004 altered the direction of Human Rights Watch in the Middle East. First, Jane Olson succeeded Jonathan Fanton as board chair. Jane became involved in human rights during the Cold War, when she took part in an interfaith group that worked to stop the nuclear arms race. In 1989, she co-founded the Southern California chapter of Human Rights Watch. Since then, she had gone abroad on humanitarian and fact-finding missions.

Jane was married to Ron Olson, a partner at Munger, Tolles & Olson, a California law firm started in 1962 by Charlie Munger, who is also Warren Buffett's partner in Berkshire Hathaway. Jane made it very clear when she became chair that she did not see it as her role to advise on policy, but instead to support the staff in its work. In hindsight, she was part of the larger shift toward the board being primarily a fund-raising, rather than a policy-making, organ.

That same year, Human Rights Watch hired a new director of its Middle East division, Sarah Leah Whitson. She had a Harvard law degree and had worked at Goldman Sachs. She had also been a board member of the New York chapter of the American-Arab Anti-Discrimination Committee.

We went to breakfast soon after she was hired. Whitson seemed energetic and passionate about the region. I thought she would definitely shake up the Middle East division. I joined its advisory board, which met with the staff three times a year. I saw firsthand how the organization responded as it became apparent that there was very likely going to be a war in Gaza between Israel and Hamas. Israel, which had occupied Gaza since the end of the Six-Day War in 1967, unilaterally withdrew its military forces and settlers from the territory in 2005. The following year, the Islamist group Hamas won the local Palestinian elections in Gaza. Hamas, an offshoot of Egypt's Muslim Brotherhood, was founded in 1987. Its charter states: "Israel will exist and will continue to exist until Islam will obliterate it."

There is no reason to think Hamas has changed its mind. To cite just one of dozens of quotes, Khaled Meshaal, the leader of Hamas, said in 2006, "Before Israel dies, it must be humiliated and degraded."

In 2007, an internal war broke out in Gaza between Hamas and Fatah, a rival Palestinian party. After hundreds of casualties—including many summary executions—Hamas drove Fatah from Gaza. Hamas then announced that it would not recognize the agreements signed by Israel and the Palestinian Authority, including ones designed to keep arms from entering Gaza through its border with Egypt. Hamas began to fire missiles from Gaza into southern Israel on a daily basis, resulting in multiple deaths and injuries. In response, Israel imposed a land and sea blockade.

This resulted in a horrible situation. In Israel, thousands of civilians were in danger of daily rocket attacks. In Gaza, ordinary Palestinians suffered terribly from the blockade.

Hamas's policy of lobbing rockets into Israel was a flagrant violation of law, and I thought that anyone who cared about the well-being of Gazans had to be very vocal that it had to stop. If it didn't, there was going to be an Israeli response, and it was apparent the response would be as severe as Israeli security forces determined it needed to be to stop the bombing. Besides costing the lives of civilians, it would also certainly destroy any chance for the economy of Gaza to prosper. Without jobs, young people would be left with few options and more likely to resort to violence.

At the time the Gaza blockade started, I felt that those concerned about human rights around the world, when looking at this situation, should in the most urgent, forceful, and persistent way possible call international attention to the need to pressure Hamas to immediately stop the rocket attacks.

While Human Rights Watch did call on Hamas to end the bombing, it placed a greater emphasis on denouncing the Israeli blockade of Gaza. Both Human Rights Watch and Amnesty International characterized the blockade as an illegal act by an occupying power, rather than a state's response to terrorism at its border. The NGO's reasoning was that even though Israel had withdrawn its military forces and settlers from Gaza, Israel still controlled Gaza's borders and airspace and was therefore an "occupying power." Under international law, a blockade by an occupying power can be seen as "collective punishment" of the population, which, characterized this way, is in violation of international law.

This approach struck me as wrong for two reasons. First, it placed greater scrutiny on the blockade than the causes of the blockade, which were the rocket attacks and the importation of arms into Gaza by Hamas. I believed that as harmful as it was to the Palestinian people, the blockade was a legal and justifiable response to indiscriminate cross-border bombing. I also felt that, in the absence of meaningful steps to stop the bombing, ending the blockade would allow Hamas to import more weapons and intensify the shelling, which would almost inevitably lead to war.

I believe all sides in a conflict should be held responsible for deliberate attacks aimed at civilians. I also think there is a fundamental difference between a state acting in self-defense to protect its citizens and an armed entity like Hamas deliberately shelling civilians in order to provoke a confrontation. To my eye, Hamas's indiscriminate bombing of Israeli civilians was a fundamental and clear-cut violation of international humanitarian law. It seemed to me that human rights groups should try to focus significant attention on this.

Second, as I looked into international law, I found that the interpretation that Israel was an "occupying power" and the blockade therefore "collective punishment" was just one opinion, and one with serious political implications—many others examined the situation and determined that Hamas was in control of Gaza and therefore Israel was within its rights to impose the blockade. This was not just the argument of "pro-Israel" groups—in 2011, a special UN commission on the blockade determined that it complied with international law and was "a legitimate security measure."

What human rights groups say about issues such as the blockade of Gaza matters. Much of the war between Israel and groups such as Hamas and Hezbollah involves a battle for international opinion. If Hamas and Hezbollah can provoke Israel into military action and then have that action condemned as a violation of international law, it results in a publicity victory—one of the main goals of these groups is certainly to isolate Israel in the international community. Hamas and Hezbollah understand this game, and unfortunately some in the foreign press play along, uncritically covering the reports of human rights organizations without closely examining the merits and political repercussions of their assertions.

In January 2009, Israel invaded Gaza with the intention of debilitating Hamas and ending the rocket attacks, of which there had been more than six thousand since 2005. The war lasted three weeks. Around 1,200 Palestinians were killed; the exact number of those who were Hamas fighters was bitterly contested. Three Israeli civilians and six Israeli soldiers were killed.

When the fighting stopped, Human Rights Watch sent in a small team of researchers to try to figure out if there had been violations of the laws of war. In a situation such as Gaza, this is a complicated task.

The Israeli Defense Forces employs a team of experts in international law to advise its military strategy and rules of engagement. In Gaza, the defense force took actions such as calling residents of houses and apartment buildings known to be Hamas weapon depots and warning them to get out. In addition, every soldier in its army is trained in the IDF Code of Conduct, a set of guidelines that draws from Jewish tradition, Israeli law, and international law.

Hamas could not win on an open battlefield, so once the conflict started, its fighters hid among the civilian population. Places that would be off-limits as targets under international law, such as hospitals and mosques, were used as command centers and for weapons storage. Hamas also used civilians as human shields, firing at Israelis from houses, farms, and schools that were occupied by civilians.

It was, in other words, an asymmetric war, one in which a uniformed army was fighting one that made up for its inferior military capability by using the civilian infrastructure to hide. It is a very difficult kind of war for a conventional military to fight, as any engagement threatens the lives of noncombatants. On the other hand, the closer army forces get to their targets in attempts to distinguish between fighters and civilians, the more their own lives are in danger. In the case of Gaza, an added complication was that there is tremendous pressure on Israel to fight a war in which none of its troops, not even a single soldier, is captured because Hamas does not allow the Red Cross to see prisoners of war. This is a point human rights groups have not emphasized.

The job of the human rights researcher in the aftermath of this was to go in and determine which civilian casualties in the war were "legitimate" and which were not. In the case of the 2008–9 Gaza War, Human Rights Watch received international press attention over the issue of Israeli use of white phosphorus, a chemical that creates a thick white smoke screen. Under international law, the use of white phosphorus is allowed if it is employed to mask troop movements; its use is restricted in civilian areas as it causes terrible burns if it comes into contact with the skin.

Human Rights Watch and Amnesty International both contended that Israel had improperly used white phosphorus in civilian areas. Israel claimed the use of the chemical was within the laws of war. Marc Garlasco, a Human Rights Watch researcher—before joining the organization, he had been chief of "high-value targeting" at the Pentagon during the Iraq War, a résumé point that Human Rights Watch stressed to bolster his credibility—appeared on several international news broadcasts to explain what white phosphorus was and what it does. Human Rights Watch issued a report immediately after the war that claimed that Israel had "deliberately" and "recklessly" used white phosphorus in "indiscriminate attacks."

In all, Human Rights Watch reported that it found twelve civilian deaths stemming from the use of white phosphorus. The organization demanded an international investigation, claiming that an Israeli Defense Forces investigation into the allegations would be "neither thorough nor impartial."

The report garnered a lot of coverage for Human Rights Watch—reporters were eager to latch on to a possible Israeli "war crime." It was, in reality, an argument over the appropriate use of military tactics, a point the media did not explain well. I think white phosphorus use is terrifying. I also think it is terrifying to be bombed.

I think it's very hard for an advocacy group such as Human Rights Watch to parse and report accurately on a situation such as this one—determining whether an army used white phosphorus "indiscriminately" or to create a legal smoke screen. The tendency to speak out in public before all the facts are straight is just too strong, and there is also an internal pressure within the organization to garner media attention.

When Garlasco, the Human Rights Watch researcher, returned from the Gaza War, he expressed reservations about Human Rights Watch's treatment of the issue of white phosphorus. As has been reported in the *New Republic,* Garlasco felt there were questions about Israel's bombing campaign that needed to be investigated, but that Human Rights Watch had placed too much emphasis on white phosphorus. Though Human Rights Watch had stated in a report that the IDF's use of the chemical "indicates the commission of war crimes," Garlasco did not believe what he had seen in the field supported that assertion.

Nevertheless, Human Rights Watch's allegations about Israel's use of white phosphorus were reported around the world and used in many quarters to bolster claims that Israel had run amok in Gaza. The media, for the most part, viewed Human Rights Watch researchers as experts and reported their assertions with little added analysis. So statements made by Human Rights Watch about issues such as white phosphorus very quickly became mainstream consensus and did enormous damage.

* * *

Another instance where I felt the human rights community acted in a counterproductive way was with respect to a UN commission set up to investigate war crimes in Gaza. While the UN can be useful at times, I believe that human rights groups should maintain their ability to step back and criticize the organization when it missteps. In the case of Israel, I think this was especially important.

After the Gaza War, the UN Human Rights Council announced a special commission to investigate human rights violations committed during the war. The commission's mandate was problematic and biased from the start, characterizing Israel as an occupying power and calling for an "international fact-finding mission . . . to investigate all violations of international human rights law and international humanitarian law by the occupying Power, Israel, against the Palestinian people," with no mention of investigating possible wrongdoing by Hamas. The four members of the special commission to investigate the Gaza War were to include Christine Chinkin, a British professor of international law who co-signed a letter published in *The Guardian* during the war that condemned Israel's actions. This special commission hardly had the appearance of neutrality.

The head of the commission was Richard Goldstone, a respected South African judge who played a leading role in that country's truth and reconciliation commission as well as the war crimes tribunals for Yugoslavia and Rwanda. He agreed to join the effort after the president of the Human Rights Council agreed informally to allow the commission also to look into possible war crimes committed by Hamas, although the wording of the mandate was never changed. Goldstone was the head of Human Rights Watch's policy committee, which he left to serve on the UN commission.

Despite the problems with the Goldstone Commission's mandate, many human rights organizations and international NGOs lobbied for its creation, including Human Rights Watch. Human Rights Watch's executive director praised Goldstone as the right man for the job. "We have strongly criticized the Human Rights Council in the past for its exclusive focus on Israeli rights violations, but Justice Goldstone is committed to an independent and impartial investigation into alleged wrongdoing by Israeli forces and Palestinian armed groups alike," he said. "He has the experience and proven commitment to ensure that this inquiry will demonstrate the highest standards of impartiality."

But given the Human Rights Council's record, the composition of the Goldstone Commission, and the wording of the commission's mandate, I could not see how the commission could possibly come back with anything but an unbalanced condemnation of Israel. The propaganda value of the commission was clearly seen by Ahmed Yousef, a Hamas political advisor, who predicted to a reporter that its report would be "like ammunition in the hands of the people who are willing to sue Israeli war criminals."

I wrote to Judge Goldstone, expressing my admiration for his accomplishments but also my concern that he was lending his name and reputation to a fundamentally flawed effort. I told him I thought it would end badly.

At the same time, I tried to persuade Human Rights Watch to distance itself from the commission and to adjust its stance on the Middle East. I wrote to the board, laying out my concerns, and attended a meeting, where I made it clear that I planned to publicly distance myself from the organization and its policies. There was heated debate—some board members said I had the right to say whatever I wished; others said I didn't have the right to speak out if it might harm the organization.

After many years of trying to sway opinion from the inside, it was clear to me that I had failed. The issue was tormenting me. I felt I had to put my opinion on the record, as much as it pained me to speak out against the organization. On October 20, 2009, I published an op-ed in the *New York Times* titled "Rights Watchdog, Lost in the Mideast."

Several years later, I stand by the arguments I made in the op-ed— that Human Rights Watch and several other major human rights groups are missing the big picture and allowing themselves to be used cynically as propaganda weapons by groups such as Hamas and the autocratic leaders of neighboring Arab countries. By participating in this way, they are undermining human rights throughout the region and helping to turn Israel into a pariah state. In addition, the reports of Human Rights Watch and some other groups continue to be problematic in the ways I've noted—ways that are seldom closely examined in the media or in our public discourse. As a result, I believe these human rights groups have contributed to a serious misunderstanding of the very difficult issues at play in the region.

After I went public with my criticisms of the role of human rights groups in the Middle East, I heard from many people who had been involved in human rights and supported my views, as well as others who had issues with other human rights policies and needed help in getting their arguments heard.

The latter included a retired lawyer named Stuart Robinowitz, who had been a prominent attorney at the firm Paul, Weiss, Rifkind, Wharton & Garrison. I didn't know him well, but he had been active with Human Rights Watch for decades, having participated in fact-finding trips to places such as El Salvador. Stuart told me he had grown worried about anti-Semitic hate speech in the Middle East. It was something that increasingly alarmed me as well.

This is how appears to me: in 1923, Julius Streicher started a paper in Germany called *Der Stürmer* that was meant to appeal to the country's working class. Over the following years, during Hitler's rise to power and the start of World War II, he published virulently anti-Semitic articles and cartoons, repeating every vile anti-Jew trope there is. He called Jews "bloodsuckers and extortionists" and wrote that the "Jewish problem" would be solved only when "world Jewry has been annihilated." He was captured at the end of the war and put on trial in Nuremberg in 1946, charged with helping to incite the hatred of Jews that made the Holocaust possible. His actions were taken very seriously. He was convicted of crimes against humanity and executed.

Several decades later in Rwanda, similar hate speech was directed against the Tutsi minority. Radio Télévision Libre des Mille Collines (RTLM), a private radio station, followed Streicher's playbook—it helped to arouse Rwanda's Hutu population to perpetrate a genocide less than a year after the station was founded in 1993. It aired constant denunciations of Tutsis, referring to them as "cockroaches" and urging that they be "exterminated" in a "final war." It should be noted that heavy weaponry or a system of gas chambers wasn't even needed in Rwanda—all it took was for a large part of the Hutu population to pick up everyday tools such as machetes and clubs for eight hundred thousand people to be slaughtered over the course of three months.

RTLM was so instrumental in riling up and inciting the population that the UN force commander in Rwanda said that jamming the station's transmissions might have saved countless lives. The International Criminal Tribunal for Rwanda later convicted the station's top two executives of incitement to genocide. They received prison sentences of thirty and thirty-two years, respectively.

I've seen the bitter fruits of hate speech here in the United States, in the South while I was stationed there during World War II. Later I heard the hateful rhetoric of public officials such as Alabama governor George Wallace, who in the early 1960s declared "segregation now, segregation tomorrow, segregation forever." I have no doubt that this kind of speech not only enabled the racist system in the South to keep functioning, but helped incite murders such as those of civil rights workers James Earl Chaney, Andrew Goodman, and Michael Schwerner in 1964, among many other acts of violence during that era.

It should be noted that there is a profound difference between the treatment of hate speech in the United States and in countries in the rest of the world. U.S. constitutional law, under the First Amendment, gives people the right to express hatred, the only exception being if that speech directly incites violent action. An example of the way the United States treats hate speech was Aryeh Neier and the ACLU's successful defense of neo-Nazis to march in Skokie, Illinois, in 1977. The Supreme Court ruled that even though the community included a large number of Holocaust survivors, the march and even the display of swastikas could not be regarded as a direct incitement to violence. In the United States it is believed that it is better that such toxic ideas are aired and then refuted in a free press rather than left to fester in the dark.

Most of the rest of the world does not share this opinion. The international view, which is contained in various human rights treaties such as the International Covenant on Civil and Political Rights, goes much further in barring speech that can incite discrimination, hostility, or violence.

This is a difficult issue. There is no doubt about the harm that hate speech can do. At the same time, governments have often used laws that ban hate speech to simply shut down any speech they don't like by labeling it "hate speech."

In the United States I believe we have a robust enough public discourse to tolerate hate speech, as detestable as it is. But my position has shifted over the years, and I am not as absolutist as I once was. For example, I think of Theodore Bilbo, who was a U.S. senator for Mississippi from 1935 to 1947. He was a Ku Klux Klan member and virulently racist toward blacks and Jews. Among his many, many terrible statements, in 1946, while still in the Senate, he called for "every red-blooded Anglo-Saxon man in Mississippi to resort to any means to keep hundreds of Negroes from the polls in the July 2 primary. And if you don't know what that means, you are just not up to your persuasive measures."

This statement came at a time when African Americans were in fact being killed for trying to vote. Given the horrendous amount of violence that was done to African Americans during that era, I think this is an example of hate speech by a public official that should have been stopped.

Similarly, when I look at the Middle East, I view government-sponsored anti-Semitic hate speech as a very serious issue that human rights groups need to address. Seeing as what happened in Rwanda took only a year, it's apparent it's going to take a very aggressive campaign to reverse more than sixty-five years of such speech in the Middle East. It has astonished me that many human rights organizations have not addressed this as a major issue, but have actually found ways to minimize its importance.

For example, Saudi Arabia has for decades published textbooks riddled with hate speech that have been distributed for free around the Muslim world. In Pakistan there are an estimated twenty thousand madrassas (religious schools for children). The majority of them use Saudi textbooks, which include passages such as "God will punish any Muslim who does not literally obey God just as God punished some Jews by turning them into pigs and monkeys," and "the Apes are the people of the Sabbath, the Jews; and the Swine are the infidels of the communion of Jesus, the Christians."

These books have also been distributed to religious schools around the Arab world and others countries, such as Afghanistan, Nigeria, Somalia, and even Britain and the United States. It's estimated that over the last thirty years the Saudis have spent $100 billion to spread Wahhabism, their particularly extreme version of Sunni Islam, which preaches that Christians, Jews, and even Shiite Muslims are to be hated, persecuted, and even killed. This export of hate has helped to incubate a radical generation of Islamists around the world.

This is a well-known problem. A 2012 State Department report looked at the content of Saudi textbooks and reported that it found that the Saudi government had not taken steps to rid the textbooks of their hateful content. We don't know exactly what else the report had to say, but it can only be devastating, as the U.S. government has suppressed the report out of fear of upsetting the Saudi government, which it needs for oil and as an ally on other problems in the Middle East today. It's amazing to me that human rights organizations, free of the restrictions of a government, are failing to pursue this issue.

The Saudi textbooks are only one aspect of hate speech in the region—it is also abundant in Gaza, the West Bank, and Lebanon. Hassan Nasrallah, the leader of Hezbollah, has stated, "If we searched the entire world for a person more cowardly, despicable, weak and feeble in psyche, mind, ideology and religion, we would not find anyone like the Jew." Khaled Meshaal, the head of Hamas, prays of Israel that "Allah willing, we will make them lose their eyesight, we will make them lose their brains." In the West Bank, Palestinian media has alleged that Israel poisoned Yasser Arafat; spreads AIDS, drugs, and prostitution among Palestinians; and plans to destroy the Al-Aqsa Mosque. One educational magazine funded by the Palestinian Authority printed an essay by a teenage girl in which she presents Hitler as a hero, appearing to the girl in a dream and telling her: "I killed [the Jews] so you would all know that they are a nation which spreads destruction all over the world."

If there is to be a two-state solution to the Israel-Palestine problem, it's apparent that those states will still be very intertwined. It is hard to see how this will be accomplished unless the Palestinian leaders stop telling their people that the first step is to get a state and the next is to then eliminate Israel.

These hateful sentiments have been echoed by senior Iranian officials. The Ayatollah Khamenei, Iran's supreme leader, has called Israel a "cancerous tumor that must be removed" and declared that there is "justification to kill all the Jews and annihilate Israel, and Iran must take the helm." Iranian officials have called Israel and Jews "bloodthirsty barbarians," "filthy bacteria," "wild beasts," "cattle," "cancerous tumor," "criminals," "a blot," "a stain," and "wild dogs." This all of course goes with the usual claim that the Holocaust never happened but was invented by Jews for their own nefarious purposes.

I'd brought up my concerns about anti-Semitic hate speech with Human Rights Watch over the years, but the general thought seemed to be that it wasn't to be taken that seriously. Stuart Robinowitz was able to join the fray with Human Rights Watch in a way I had not—as a lawyer. He had started an e-mail dialogue with Human Rights Watch's executive director, Ken Roth (Ken had worked for Stuart early in his career when they were both at Paul, Weiss). Stuart wanted Human Rights Watch to investigate whether Iran's leadership might be inciting genocide under the standards of international law.

In international law, incitement to genocide is essentially the most extreme form of hate speech—it requires a "direct and public" call to commit genocide.

As with many human rights issues now, whether Iran might be guilty of inciting genocide is a matter lawyers can argue endlessly, but it is hardly a fringe issue. Among a long list of scholars, activists, and political leaders who signed a 2010 petition supporting the claim that Iran should be indicted for inciting genocide were David Hamburg, president emeritus of the Carnegie Corporation and appointed by UN secretary-general Ban Ki-moon to chair the Advisory Committee on Genocide Prevention; Roméo Dallaire, the former UN force commander in Rwanda; Saad Eddin Ibrahim, a prominent Egyptian democracy activist; Harvard law professor Charles Ogletree; Fouad Ajami, the head of the Middle East studies program at Johns Hopkins prior to his death in 2014; and former prime ministers and justice ministers of Canada, Australia, Spain, Sweden, the Netherlands, India, and Bangladesh.

In his correspondence with Ken, Stuart noted that President Mahmoud Ahmadinejad had said that Israel needed to be "wiped off the map." He quoted another Iranian government official who stated, "It would appear that the Israelis have understood that they are living their final days," and an Iranian military commander who said, "I recommend to the Zionists that in order to stay alive they should pack their bags quickly and return to their countries of origin."

Stuart pointed out that there is a direct link between Iran's leadership and violence against Jews—Iran supplies weapons and tens of thousands of rockets to Hamas and Hezbollah, and it has been these rockets that have been indiscriminately fired into Israel.

It would seem that Human Rights Watch agrees with this assessment. In a 2006 "Letter to President Ahmadinejad on Israel-Lebanon Conflict," the organization wrote: "The close and abiding relationship between Hezbollah and Iran, including the alleged role that Iran has played in supplying weapons to Hezbollah, gives Iran a special responsibility to raise civilian protection issues with Hezbollah leaders."

But Ken replied to Stuart that the threats made by the Iranian leadership were against the state of Israel, not Jews as a people. Stuart pointed out that the denunciations of Israel and Jews were hard to parse.

Ken's main argument, however, was that the statements of Iran's leadership did not constitute "incitement" but merely "advocacy." He told Stuart that Human Rights Watch's position was based on *Brandenburg v. Ohio*, a 1969 U.S. Supreme Court case involving a Ku Klux Klan leader who had urged violence against blacks and Jews. The Supreme Court ruled that his statements fell within the grounds of free speech and constituted only "advocacy" that could be rebutted. In the view of Human Rights Watch, Iran's leaders could not be accused of incitement to genocide unless there was imminent action after their statements. In other words, there needed to be genocidal action to prove incitement to genocide—no genocide, no incitement.

The argument baffled me. Stuart pointed out that the legal reasoning was strange, especially the reliance on a U.S. Supreme Court case, which applied the U.S. Constitution instead of the Convention on the Prevention and Punishment of the Crime of Genocide, the relevant law in this case. Human Rights Watch seemed to be comparing an Ohio Ku Klux Klan member to the governmental leaders of a state with an army, missiles, and a program to arm militant groups that have the expressed wish of wiping a country and its people off the map.

As a non-lawyer, I am still puzzled by the use of the term "advocacy" and what it means, particularly because it seems that it does not lead to any action against hate speech. I am disappointed that Human Rights Watch, which has pushed the envelope in so many other areas, has not determined this to be a problem that requires major engagement. Given the respect the organization enjoys, I'm certain that if it did take up this issue, its condemnation would be echoed in the media and from there take on a life of its own.

My recent differences with Human Rights Watch are really part of a more fundamental disagreement about the role human rights organizations should play in the world.

We started the organization in 1978 to aid the Moscow Helsinki Group, a courageous set of men and women, inspired by the example of Andrei Sakharov and led by Yuri Orlov, who had begun an effort to make the Soviet regime honor the human rights provisions of the Helsinki Accords. In New York, the aim was to use our free press to help the silenced by spreading their ideas and calling public and government attention to them when they were imprisoned. The ultimate goal was not so much to set ourselves up as critics of other countries—although we often did criticize—but to free up the citizens of those countries to speak for their own welfare.

This is certainly not to say that open societies don't go off track. They do, sometimes badly. But there are self-correcting mechanisms. A recent example would be here in the United States, where a combination of the press, concerned government officials, and civil society activists brought the issue of torture at Abu Ghraib, Guantánamo Bay, and other sites around the world to public attention.

In this case, groups such as Human Rights Watch and Amnesty were part of a much larger contingent calling for accountability and policy change.

Israel, with a population of more than 8 million, is home to at least eighty human rights organizations, a free press, a democratically elected government, a judiciary that frequently rules against the government, a politically active academia, multiple political parties and, judging by the amount of news coverage, probably more journalists per capita than any other country in the world—many of whom are there expressly to cover the Israeli-Palestinian conflict.

Israeli NGOs can hardly be accused of toeing the government line. B'Tselem, which examines human rights abuses in the West Bank and Gaza, has been acutely critical of Israel's human rights record with respect to the treatment of Palestinians, and it has dozens of reports available on its website. Other groups, such as Sikkuy, call attention to citizenship issues and lack of equality between Jewish and Arab Israelis.

I believe human rights organizations need to look at the Middle East as a whole and ask: How many NGOs in the region are able to subject their government to the scrutiny that Israeli NGOs do? Certainly, in Egypt, Lebanon, Jordan, Saudi Arabia, the West Bank or Iran, NGOs are severely curtailed and freedom of speech is limited. Moreover, as far as I know, there are no groups in these places addressing anti-Semitic attacks against Jews. Even voicing that opinion in public in many of those states would place a person at high risk of government retribution. In my view, that makes it doubly important that international human rights groups address these issues.

In 2002, a group of Arab scholars and policymakers published a very telling report on human development in Arab countries at the request of the United Nations. It included one page that denounced the Israeli occupation. The rest of the 131-page report detailed the pressing problems of the region, including joblessness and poverty in the midst of great oil wealth; a lack of educational opportunities; severe curtailment of the rights of women; corruption; and the lack of freedom of speech.

This report should have received much more attention than it did, and its message is still as important as when it was released. The approach of the authors, who recognized human rights problems in Israel but kept them in balance with the grave problems in the region, should have been an indicator for human rights groups in setting their priorities in the Middle East.

There are daily examples of the horrible human rights situation in the region, and not just with the civil war in Syria and ISIS running wild. For example in 2014, a thirty-year-old Saudi Arabian named Raif Badawi, who ran a website calling for public discussion and criticism of the country's ruling clerics, was sentenced to ten years in prison, a $266,000 fine, and a thousand lashes—to be administered in public, fifty at a time. He received the first fifty lashings, delivered with a cane in front of a mosque in Jeddah, in January 2015. International outcry and Badawi's poor health have delayed the second set of lashings at the moment but, as this book goes to press in early 2016, he remains in prison, his future uncertain.

In Gaza recently, a group of around two hundred protestors dared to publicly call for political reform. A group of Hamas security officials showed up, beat some with sticks, and dragged others off to who knows what fate.

One of the messages to the region from international human rights groups to courageous people in these countries needs to be: "We cannot solve all your problems, but we are trying to help you find ways to speak and communicate with each other. We hope that with free speech, recognizing the values of the International Declaration of Human Rights will lead to a better life for yourselves. We will do everything we can to see that you have all the possible support we can provide. We will not forget you if you are thrown in jail, and we will work tirelessly for your right to speak for yourselves."

Over the last several years I've been involved with a new organization, Advancing Human Rights (AHR), which began almost by chance. After my *New York Times* op-ed appeared, a young man named David Keyes came and told me about an organization he had started called CyberDissidents.org, which kept an online database of dissidents, democracy activists, and others who had been persecuted in the Middle East for expressing opinions that angered their governments. He wrote about them, tried to get them help, lobbied policy makers, anything he could to humanize the dissidents so that people outside the Middle East would care about their fates. It was very similar to what we had done many years earlier starting in the Soviet Union.

David and I figured we could help each other by joining forces—David had little experience with fund-raising or running an NGO, and I wanted to try to find a new way to work on human rights in the Middle East. We decided to launch a new organization called Advancing Human Rights.

Our goal is to use the Internet and new communication technologies to promote freedom of expression in the Middle East and globally. We feel that, unlike back in the 1970s when I started working with Soviet dissidents, activists now have more powerful tools, such as blogs and social media, to get their messages heard. We want to help them with that and also to rally support for them when they are repressed and threatened.

AHR quickly took shape, so much so that when the head of Google's think/do tank, Google Ideas, decided that he wished to merge a similar organization he had co-founded a few years prior with an existing organization, he came to us rather than one of the larger organizations. Movements.org became part of AHR and brought along with it hundreds of thousands of followers on Twitter. Google gave us a start-up grant of $250,000.

We expanded Movements.org to make it a place where dissidents from around the world are now able to come to make their cause known. We help them by getting their work printed, connecting them to journalists, and supplying them with legal representation.

We have been able to put together a very impressive board, including Irwin Cotler, the former attorney general and justice minister of Canada, who has also represented some of the dissidents we've been working with; Richard Kemp, a retired colonel who headed the British forces in Afghanistan, who has been effective in defining asymmetric war; and Toni Morrison, who immediately wrote a powerful piece condemning a public whipping of a woman in Sudan. (The video of the whipping had appeared on YouTube.

Toni's letter made it back into Sudan and was picked up by human rights organizations in that country.) They were joined by attorneys active in the field, from Anthony Julius in England to Gregory Wallance, Trevor Norwitz, Scott Greathead, and Rachel Davidson in the United States. Joseph Birman, a distinguished professor of physics at City College who led the New York Academy of Science's human rights committees during the Cold War years, went on the board as well. Dorothy Tananbaum, very active in philanthropy, also joined us. And David Kilgour, a prominent Canadian parliamentarian, was brought on by Irwin Cotler.

I certainly didn't expect to be so intimately involved with a new human rights organization as I entered my nineties, and I find that people are often surprised when they hear what I am doing. I was a little surprised myself, until I saw an embroidered decorative pillow in a shop window that I thought explained the situation. It said, "I'm so over the hill that I'm halfway up the next one."

EPILOGUE

ON MY SEVENTY-FIFTH BIRTHDAY, AROUND THE TIME WHEN I WAS giving up the chairmanship of Human Rights Watch, Helen and my son Tom surprised me by inaugurating the Robert L. Bernstein International Human Rights Fellowships at Yale Law School. Tom, along with many others, had been instrumental in setting up the Orville H. Schell Jr. Center for International Human Rights at the law school, in honor of Orville. Now, Tom, Helen, and others were following on the success of that effort by doing something similar in my name. Many of our friends generously contributed to make it possible.

The fellowships meant that Yale Law School graduates interested in getting started in human rights could submit proposals to work for a year on an independent project or one tied to an organization. Three would be chosen every year, and each would receive a $50,000 stipend to support him- or herself.

Having long subscribed to the principle that when you try to do good you shouldn't worry about getting the credit, I was jarred by the announcement. It is now seventeen years later. There have been more than fifty Robert L. Bernstein fellows. They have done everything from documenting abuses in the Eritrea-Ethiopia War to fighting for access to clean water in rural India. Each year a symposium is held at Yale where a different subject in human rights is discussed in depth. The fellows who are just finishing their year give presentations on their work, and many other alumni of the fellowship also return.

I have remained in touch with many of them. They have consistently opened my life to new avenues and also made me sharpen my thinking on contentious issues. That I have largely retained the admiration of many of these fellows has actually given me the strength to challenge some of the paths that major human rights groups, including the one I founded, have taken.

More recently, Richard Revesz, the former dean of the NYU Law School, started a program to bring an annual fellow from the law school to Human Rights in China. Trevor Morrison, who succeeded Revesz in 2013, picked up the idea and expanded it, working with my sons Tom, Peter, and Bill to put together the Robert L. Bernstein Institute for Human Rights at the NYU Law School, which was launched in April 2015.

The effort was tremendously boosted by a generous donation from Strive Masiyiwa, a Zimbabwean businessman who runs a telecommunications company based in South Africa. Strive and his wife, Tsitsi, run a trust in Africa—the Higher Life Foundation—which, by investing in Africa's future through education, has supported tens of thousands of young people. Tom chairs the board of the U.S. Holocaust Memorial Museum in Washington, D.C., and Strive is also a member of the museum's Committee on Conscience, which focuses on genocide prevention.

Strive helped fund the Masiyiwa-Bernstein Fellowships at NYU Law School, which, like the program at Yale, will sponsor three recent law school graduates each year. NYU is doing it a little differently, though, in that it is planning to identify organizations that need fellows and then invite applications. The first three fellows are working for the U.S. Holocaust Memorial Museum Early Warning Project, Human Rights First, and NYU's Stern School of Business, which is starting a business and human rights program headed by Mike Posner, a longtime family friend who founded the Lawyers Committee for Human Rights (now Human Rights First) in 1978 and more recently served as assistant secretary of state for democracy, human rights, and labor in President Obama's first term.

The Bernstein Institute for Human Rights will also include several programs under its umbrella. One is the U.S.-Asia Law Institute, headed by Jerry Cohen, an NYU law professor. I consider him the most courageous and effective leader in defending the Chinese legal profession, which right now is being decimated by the Chinese government.

Human Rights in China will also have a role in the institute, with a new office at the university. NYU law students will be able to get involved in research for the organization and take a class from Sharon Hom, HRIC's executive director. The affiliation with NYU should be a new source of vitality for HRIC and an opportunity for the students to get practical experience in the field.

Additionally, the institute will include NYU's Center for Human Rights and Global Justice and Stern's Center for Business and Human Rights. Finally, it will also offer a training program for judges on developments in human rights and humanitarian law. Meg Satterthwaite, a young, very sharp member of the NYU Law School faculty, is directing the institute.

As at Yale, NYU will hold a yearly symposium on a human rights issue. The first one, on human rights in China, took place in April 2015. My hope, which is now being looked into by NYU, is to have symposiums on the most controversial issues in international law and human rights, such as the call to bring Israel in front of the International Criminal Court. All sides will be open to debate. Though I realize how difficult these problems are, I'm confident that many of the positions I've expressed in this book will be strengthened by an open discussion of how law has been used in human rights arguments.

My hope is that the institute will be one of the great centers for the discussion of the issues facing human rights work—especially the areas where business, law, and government intersect—and a place where new approaches can be developed and tested.

It's an ambitious undertaking and I'm curious to see where it goes. The excitement of the launch has spurred me to take care of my health. My grandchildren have encouraged me in this effort and keep telling me that if I don't stop eating junk food, I'm not going to live long. We shall see.

While the Yale and NYU programs have had the enjoyable benefit of bringing me back into contact with twenty-five-year-olds, another recent unexpected addition to my life has been Hunter College, where I now have an office as a "writer in residence."

One of the perks is going down to eat lunch among the students. Hunter College is a special place. It's a public university, very affordable, with a prestigious academic reputation. It's hard to get into and very diverse—around 70 percent of the sixteen thousand undergraduates were born in a foreign country or have at least one parent born elsewhere. Many of the students are the first in their families to attend college.

I've been asked to speak a few times at brown-bag lunches held for students in the school's honors program who have an interest in human rights. The program is run by Lev Sviridov, a chemistry professor whom I first met in 1994, when he was twelve years old. His mom, Alexandra Sviridova, was a journalist in Russia. During the dissolution of the Soviet Union, she had exposed Russian government officials who had been KGB agents. In 1993, she came to the United States with Lev for some speaking engagements. While she was here, Boris Yeltsin attempted to dissolve the Russian parliament, an event resolved through military force. It was too dangerous for them to go back.

They went to the Lawyers Committee for Human Rights for help. My son Tom was the president, and I met Alexandra and Lev when Tom brought them to Thanksgiving dinner. They received political asylum, and we remained very much in touch over the years. When Lev was looking at colleges, he said he wouldn't need financial help as he was going to attend the City University of New York. Before his graduation in 2004, he called Helen and me, said he had a surprise for us, and asked us to come to the university a few days before the ceremony. We went, and it was announced Lev was the first City University student to become a Rhodes Scholar since 1939. Lev earned his PhD in chemistry at Oxford and took a teaching position at Hunter when he returned to New York. Given his background, he has found a way to be not only a scientist and teacher, but also to remain extremely active in human rights work, which is part of his mission with the students he mentors.

There were about sixty students at the last brown-bag lunch I spoke at. I started by asking who had heard of Andrei Sakharov—

not a single person. Next, I asked about Dr. Seuss—a forest of hands.

I was a little sad at the response but not that surprised. Looking back, Ted Geisel and Andrei Sakharov were perhaps the two biggest influences on me. I thought both were geniuses, and, though outwardly very different, I think they walked the same path—both tried to bring a little more humanity into the world. Though Ted could be dismissed as writing children's books, his real mission was to put serious thoughts into a seemingly simple form—*The Lorax* was about caring for the natural world; *The Butter Battle Book* pointed out the folly of the nuclear arms race; and *Yertle the Turtle* showed how power intoxicates and corrupts.

Sakharov gave up his position in society and his own safety to advocate for the same values that Ted held dear. But while Ted sold millions of books and lived in a glorious house in La Jolla, Sakharov, who had enjoyed a comfortable life up until he broke with the Soviet government, ended up in a tiny apartment in Moscow.

If anything shows the importance of free expression in the world, look at the millions of kids who have read and been influenced by Dr. Seuss, and then think about how Andrei Sakharov struggled to get his message out.

It strikes me that in a world where all can speak freely, the Seusses will emerge. We have to keep fighting for the Sakharovs.

ACKNOWLEDGMENTS

THIS BOOK WAS STARTED LATE IN LIFE, AFTER MY FAMILY BEGAN asking questions about how a life in publishing led me into the world of human rights.

The book could not have been written without Doug Merlino, who contributed all of the qualities of a great journalist and added patience and humor. He was indispensable. Zina AlDamlouji, my able, energetic, knowledgeable, and wise assistant, worked closely with us, and for that I am enormously grateful.

Many of those in my business life—some without their knowledge—aided in making this book possible. Leon Shimkin changed my life by firing me from Simon & Schuster; and Kay Thompson and Eloise, who disagreed with Leon Shimkin and invited me to join them at the Plaza Hotel, gave me a place to land. Shortly thereafter, Bennett Cerf, for reasons I will never know, followed up a tip from a bookseller to telephone me at the Plaza and offered me a job at Random House. During my fifteen years working for him there was never a bad word between us and even today I recognize things he taught me. Donald Klopfer, Bennett's wonderful partner, was there for me personally every step of the way and taught me most of all that when managing talented people, it's important to listen. Bob Loomis, an incomparable editor, reviewed the many incidents in this book having to do with the CIA and government, from David Wise and Thomas Ross's *The Invisible Government* to the accounts of my dealings with Victor Marchetti and Frank Snepp. I believe Random House would not have survived untarnished without Bob's extraordinary editorial abilities and his wisdom. Sandy MacGregor's memory and accuracy about many of the events during our time at Random House were a big help. When I was at Random House, he always made me feel like a great executive for hiring someone like him, who was good at everything I wasn't. I would also like to thank Sandy's wonderful wife, Marilyn, a dear friend, who worked on the book with Sandy. And how could I forget Albert Erskine, Jason Epstein, Toni Morrison, and the great editorial staff of Random House who enriched my professional life in so many ways. At Knopf, I owe an enormous debt to Robert Gottlieb, one of the greatest publishers and editors of my era, who, together with Nina Bourne and Tony Schulte, fitted my idea of publishing perfectly. They were a joy to work with and were brilliant at being independent publishers undisturbed by corporate ownership. Of course, a publishing house should always remember it is a servant of its authors, who put enormous trust in it. All of us at Random House received a tremendous amount of satisfaction from the many authors who stayed with us for long periods of time. I want to acknowledge my thanks with this partial list that came from the end of my time at Random House: William Styron (twenty-five years); James Michener (thirty-four years); John Updike (twenty-six years); Studs Terkel (nineteen years); John Hersey (forty-three years); the Berenstains (twenty-three years); Dr. Seuss (forty-eight years); Julia Child (twenty-four years); Ray Bradbury (twenty-five years); Alistair Cooke (thirty-five years); Anne Tyler (twenty-one years); Alexis Lichine (thirty-four years); Robert Penn Warren (thirty-seven years).

Many individuals contributed to my participation in human rights. Brad Wiley, who named me to succeed him as president of the American Association of Publishers, took me to the Soviet Union and changed my life. Andrei Sakharov, who gave up everything to fight for human rights in the Soviet Union, inspired me to get involved in human rights and became a close friend. His wife, Elena Bonner, was perhaps the bravest woman I have ever known, and was an amazing support to her husband. Jeri Laber put Helsinki Watch on the map with her idea to open an office at the talks in Madrid. Jeri inspired and led Helsinki Watch for many years, bravely traveling as far as Diyarbakır, Turkey, and practically becoming Václav Havel's representative to the United States. Ed Kline kept me in touch with Andrei Sakharov and reviewed the parts about the Sakharovs and the other Soviet dissidents for my book.

Sharon Hom, who gave up so much to work for the cause of bringing democracy to China, has kept me educated along the way, including reading and aiding my memory on the Chinese parts of this book. Liu Qing, a founder of Human Rights in China, suffered so much and survived to dedicate his life to trying to bring a decent government to China. I've learned a tremendous amount from the brilliant law professor Jerry Cohen, whose huge outpouring of writing and speaking has constantly challenged the Chinese government to allow a rule of law to develop. And just as importantly, his constant efforts to help endangered lawyers in China have inspired me. Xiao Qiang showed me the horrors of China's human rights abuses and introduced me to many dissidents, along the way providing me with advice I could rely on. Xu Jin, the daughter of Xu Wenli, taught me about the harsher realities of the real world and human rights abuses in her battle for her father's release from China. Her ability to adapt to a whole new life in the United States has been truly amazing to watch. I also owe thanks to Minky Worden, whom I first met in Hong Kong and who does such great work for Human Rights Watch, operating in all she does with the Vroom! last seen in *The Cat in the Hat*.

Patrick Tyler, a former *New York Times* foreign correspondent and distinguished author, read the manuscript and made many valuable suggestions for organizing it. I'm also indebted to Professor Sam Issacharoff, who gave up so much of his time to keep me straight on international law. I benefited from advice and counsel from Natan Sharansky, whose own works on human rights should be read by everybody, as well as from Trevor Norwitz and Greg Wallance, who very generously helped me with the chapters on the Middle East. David Keyes, who founded Advancing Human Rights with me, has been a source of knowledge about all issues in the Middle East. Nina Rosenwald opened a world of information to me. Edith Everett helped guide my thinking about the ways reporting on human rights can be co-opted for partisan gains. Stuart Robinowitz opened my eyes to the issue of state-sponsored hate speech.

I also want to thank Anthony Kronman, who originally put together the Robert L. Bernstein Fellowships at Yale Law School. Additional thanks are due to Harold Koh, who succeeded Tony as dean of the law school and whose advice and encouragement at many moments of my life have been so important. And thanks, too, to Robert Post, the current dean, who continues to emphasize the importance of the fellowship program at the law school.

Trevor Morrison, dean of New York University School of Law, somehow convinced himself and me to unite our efforts at NYU. I am deeply grateful for his advice and availability despite his many commitments. Richard Revesz, former dean of NYU Law, originally brought me, NYU, and Human Rights in China together. Mike Posner, a longtime advisor on so many topics related to human rights issues and now a professor at the Stern School of Business at NYU, has offered endless advice on the book and made sure I had the facts right. Strive Masiyiwa, who contributes so much of his time and financial backing to the Robert L. Bernstein Institute at NYU Law, is an inspiration to me and, along with his wife Tsitsi, has become a dear friend, for which I am very thankful.

Lev Sviridov, who came to the United States as a young boy from Russia with his brave mother, has found amazing ways to help me and is a shining example of how immigrants have contributed to the greatness of our nation. Jennifer Raab and Hunter College generously provided me with wonderful working space close to my apartment, which was a real bonus.

After I had been writing the book for a few years, Diane Wachtell of The New Press asked to read it and then asked if she could publish it. I am deeply indebted to her and The New Press, as well as to André Schiffrin, with whom I worked for years when he was at Pantheon, for starting such a fantastic not-for-profit publishing house.

Most importantly, I thank my family for both their memories and encouragement: Peter and Amy, who read and re-read the manuscript and lent their editorial skills; Tom, who helped get the book published and made many valuable changes and additions; Bill, whose enormous encouragement kept me going, along with

Andi and Lori, who wanted every story I ever told to be put in the book. And of course special thanks to my grandchildren (and their spouses): Elisabeth, who has worked diligently to put together a verbal and visual record of my life and asked some challenging questions; Nicky, who spent an entire summer interviewing me and others for the book; Lee, who is already proving that the Bernstein family interest in human rights will continue; Drew, Alexander and Lauren, Allison, Laura, Michael, Sam and Will, for always asking for more stories; and Jack, our youngest grandchild, who will one day appreciate this record of the past. I am thankful to my sister, Barbara, who has always supported me. My greatest thanks of all of course is to Helen, to whom the book is dedicated. For sixty-five years she has encouraged, endured, pushed, and advised me—and always, always expanded my horizons.

INDEX

AAP. *See* Association of American Publishers

Aaron Diamond Foundation, 200

Abrams, Floyd, 107, 114

ACLU. *See* American Civil Liberties Union

Adams, Siebert, 243

Advance Publications, 170–73

Advancing Human Rights (AHR), 318–20

Africa Watch, 272

African Americans, 84–85, 95–96; hate speech against, 311–12; Jews and, 87–92

AHR. *See* Advancing Human Rights

Alexeyeva, Lyudmila, 175–76, 206, 208

Algrant, Roland, 210

Ali, Muhammad, 95–96

Allon, Yigal, 293

Alone Together (Bonner, E.), 204–5

Amalrik, Andrei, 132–33, 142, 177–78

America Through American Eyes, 154–55

American Civil Liberties Union (ACLU), 106–7, 152

American-Arab Anti-Discrimination Committee, 302

Americas Watch, 186–87, 192–95, 199, 272

Amnesty International, 286, 299; Israel and, 304, 306, 317; letter-writing by, 151, 273

Angelou, Maya, 86

Anti-Defamation League, 89–90

anti-Semitism, 89; in Argentina, 189–90; hate speech of, 310, 312–16; interview about, 90–91; in textbooks, 313–14. *See also* Hamas

Arafat, Yasser, 294, 313

Argentina, 185–87; anti-Semitism in, 189–90; Mothers of the Plaza de Mayo in, 182, 194; Timerman and, 183–84, 188–90

Arns, Paulo Evaristo, 232

The Art of the Deal (Trump), 239

Asia Watch, 199, 257, 261, 272. *See also* China

Association of American Publishers (AAP), 97, 103–4, 118, 214; divisions within, 140; Freedom to Read Committee of, 141–42; International Freedom to Publish Committee of, xv, 142, 144–46, 158, 210

At Random (Cerf, B.), 51, 55

authors, 80; contact with, 53–54, 227–28. *See also* Chinese dissident writers; Soviet dissident writers

Bacall, Lauren, 238

Badawi, Raif, 318

Baifang, Liu, 268

Baker, James, 262

Ballantine, 228–30

Banquet Foods, 169–70

Bao Tong, 256

Barak, Ehud, 294

Barbados, 82, 210–11

Bard College, 269, 284

Barnard Medal of Distinction, 200

Beacon Press, 103–4

Begin, Menachem, 157

Beginner Books, 80

Bernstein, Alfred, 2, 4–5

Bernstein, Ann, 123

Bernstein, Barbara, 2, 5

Bernstein, Ben, 2–3

Bernstein, Bill, 38, 43, 101, 253
Bernstein, Elisabeth, 247, 288
Bernstein, Helen Walter, xiii, 99,
    137–38, 245, 321; at Beverly Hills
    Hotel, 39–40; date with, 34–35;
    honeymoon with, 37; proposal to,
    35–36; Random House and, 49, 79
Bernstein, Peter, 38, 44, 63, 97–99, 129
Bernstein, Sylvia, 2, 57
Bernstein, Tom, 38, 44, 97–99, 252,
    321; Bush, G. W., and, 286–87
Bernstein Institute for Human Rights,
    322–23
Bertelsmann, 248
Berwin, Stanley, 293
Betts, Roland W., 286
Beverly Hills Hotel, 39–40
Bitter Winds (Wu and Wakeman), 266
Black, George, 263–64
Black and White Ball, 79
Bloch, Jacob, 2; generosity of, 6–7;
    Jewish refugees and, 6–8; real estate
    of, 5–6
blockade, 303–5
The Bluest Eye (Morrison, Toni), 85
Bogoraz, Larisa, 218–20
Bonner, Alexei, 203
Bonner, Elena, xiii, 212, 224; advance
    for, 203–5; background of, 133–34;
    health of, 134–35, 202–3, 206, 223;
    internal exile of, 174, 209; Nobel
    Peace Prize and, 135–36
Botstein, Leon, 269
Bourke-White, Margaret, 33
Bourne, Nina, 27, 80–81, 83–84
Bradford, Barbara Taylor, 239
Bradshaw, Thornton, 198–99
Brezhnev, Leonid, 126, 143, 201
Brodsky, Joseph, 126
Brown University, 12–13, 288–89
Budlong, John, 63–64
Bukovsky, Vladimir, 133, 142
Bundy, McGeorge, 87, 149
Burkhalter, Holly, 189–90
Burlatsky, Fyodor, 219–23
The Burning Forest (Leys), 290
Bush, George H. W., 109–10, 262–63
Bush, George W., 286–87

Capote, Truman, 53–54, 79
Carey, John, 153
Carnegie, Dale, 23–24
Carroll, Mark, 118
Carter, Jimmy, 151, 183, 185
Casey, Bob, 114
The Cat in the Hat (Geisel), 61, 80
censorship, 123; AAP against, xv, 142,

144–46, 158, 210; by CIA, 106–7;
    Fund for Free Expression against,
    147–50; at Moscow Book Fair,
    157–58; publishers and, 101–2,
    106–7, 147
Central Intelligence Agency (CIA),
    x, 109–10; censorship by, 106–7;
    Random House and, 104–8, 114
Cerf, Bennett, xv, 47–49, 54, 70; free
    speech and, 52–53, 100; funeral
    of, 93–94; humor and, 64–65, 92;
    Klopfer and, 50–52, 55. See also
    Random House
Cerf, Christopher, 92–93
Chalidze, Valery, 129–31, 202
Chalidze, Vera, 129–30
Chanticleer Press, 58–59
Chekhov Press (Chekhov Publishing
    Corporation), 124, 130–31
Child, Julia, 59
children's books, 73; Little Golden
    Books, 25–27, 32, 39; at Random
    House, 42, 58, 60–63, 66, 80, 86–87
children's songs, 27–29, 39
China, 141, 178, 180–81; compassion
    about, 258–59, 290–91; computers in,
    284; corporations and, 263; Hundred
    Flowers Campaign in, 264–65; IOC
    and, 260–61; as MFN, 262–63,
    280–81; Neier and, 250, 253; political
    prisoners in, 255, 258; racism and,
    290; 60 Minutes on, 262–63, 265;
    Tiananmen Square in, 253–57, 276;
    UN and, 250–51; visits to, 251–53,
    267–71. See also Human Rights in
    China
Chinese dissident writers, 257–58;
    Democracy Wall and, 253–55, 277;
    Deng and, 254–56, 271–72; HRW
    and, 253, 259–60, 263–64; Liu Qing
    as, 271, 277; Wu as, 264–67; Xu as,
    255, 268, 277, 285–89. See also Wei
    Jingsheng
Chinkin, Christine, 303
Church Committee, 109
CIA. See Central Intelligence Agency
The CIA and the Cult of Intelligence
    (Marchetti and Marks), 105–6
civil rights movement, 86
civil wars, 193
Cleaver, Eldridge, 100–101
Clinton, Bill, 262–63, 294
Cohen, Jerry, 322–23
Cohn, Roy, 172
Colbert, Claudette, 81–83, 100, 210–13
Colby, William, 106
Columbia University, 93–94, 283–84

Commins, Saxe, 54
Committee to End the Chinese Gulag, 259–60
communications, 75
Condé Nast, 171–73, 247
Conrad, Andy, 164–67
Contras, 193, 195–97
control, 121–23
Convention on the Prevention and Punishment of the Crime of Genocide, 316
copyright convention, xiii, 118, 131
Cosell, Howard, 96
Cotler, Irwin, 217, 221
Cott, Ted, 19
The Courage of Strangers (Laber), 219
The Courage to Stand Alone (Wei), 282
Coward, Noël, 116
Crown Publishing Group, 234–44
Cullman, Dorothy, 200
CyberDissidents.org, 318–19

Dann, Mike, 58, 72
Dayan, Moshe, 293
de Graff, Robert Fair, 24–25
del Rey, Judy-Lynn, 229
Democracy Wall, 253–55, 277
Democratic National Convention, 98
Democratic National Headquarters, 104
Deng Xiaoping, 254–56, 271–72
Derian, Patricia, 151, 183, 185, 190
DeWind, Adrian, 153
Diamond, Irene, 200
Dicker, Richard, 259–61
Disney, Walt, 39–41
Disneyland, 39–41
Division Street (Terkel), 86
Dr. Seuss. See Geisel, Ted
Dr. Zhivago (Pasternak), 125, 237
Due to Circumstances Beyond Our Control (Friendly), 159
Duplaix, Georges, 25–26
Durant, Will, 22–23

Eban, Abba, 293–94
El Salvador, 193–95
Ellis, Charles, 263
Ellsberg, Daniel, 102–3
Eloise (fictitious character), 42–44, 46, 50
Eloise Ltd., 42–43
Ephron, Nora, 161–62
Epstein, Jason, 57, 238–39
Equal Rights Amendment, 99
Erburu, Robert, 168
Ernst, Morris, 53
Erskine, Albert, 54

Evans, Joni, 241
Explorations, 254–55

family, 1, 4–8, 63, 123, 129; Bernstein, Bill, 38, 43, 101, 253; Bernstein, E., 247, 288; as Jews, 2–3; social life of, 2–3. See also Bernstein, Helen Walter; Bernstein, Tom
Fang Lizhi, 255, 257–60, 276, 289
Fanton, Jonathan, 273–74, 295–96, 302
Faulkner, William, 54, 67
Fawcett, 229–30
FBI, 101
Fear No Evil (Sharansky, N.), 206
Federal Trade Commission (FTC), 68–69
Feltrinelli, Giangiacomo, 125
Fishlow, David, 154
Fitzpatrick, Cathy, 191, 208
Ford, Gerald, 109
Ford Foundation, 149–51, 153, 176
Forever Amber (Winsor), 64
Fox, Joe, 79
Frase, Bob, 118
Freedom to Read Committee, 141–42
Friedman, Jane, 241–42, 246
Friendly, Fred, 17–18, 149, 159
FTC. See Federal Trade Commission
Fu Xin-yuan, 276
Fuchs, George, 166
Fulghum, Robert, 245–46
Fund for Free Expression, 147–52

Gabor, Zsa Zsa, 65
Galich, Alexander, 135–36
Garbo, Greta, 222
Garland, Judy, 41
Garlasco, Marc, 306–7
Gates, Henry Louis, Jr., 92
Gaza War, 303–8, 303–9
Geisel, Ted (Dr. Seuss, Theo. LeSieg), 59, 324–25; advice from, 78–79; children's books by, 60–63, 66, 80, 86–87; humor of, 62–63, 232–36; politics of, 86–87; tribute from, 232–33
Geneva Conventions, 298
genocide: Iran and, 314–16; in Rwanda, 297, 310–11
Gershwin, George, 23
Gide, André, 69
Ginsberg, Bob, 34
Ginzburg, Alexander, 146
Glasnost Press Club, 213, 218–22
Glazer, Nathan, 91
Godunov, Alexander, 156
Goldberg, Arthur, 149–50, 176

Golden, Harry, 165–66
Golden Books, 25–27, 32, 39
Goldman Sachs, 242–43
Goldstone, Richard, 308–9
Goldstone Commission, 308–9
Goodman, Jack, 31–34, 45
Gorbachev, Mikhail, 202, 207, 209;
    publishers with, 214–16; reforms
    from, 125, 210, 223
Gottlieb, Bob, 80–85, 116, 237–38;
    New Yorker and, 240–41
Graham, Katharine, 79
Grann, Phyllis, 248
Green, Ash, 128–29
Greenberg, Jack, 153
Gregorian, Vartan, 180
Griffiths, Ed, 167–69
Grosset and Dunlap, 105
Grossman, Dick, 42
Guinzburg, Tom, 97

Haas, Robert, 53, 55
Hague Conventions, 298
Hamas, 300–301, 313; bombing by,
    303–5; charter of, 303; Goldstone
    Commission and, 308–9; against
    international law, 305–6; Iran and,
    315; against reform, 318
Harkin, Tom, 189–90
"Harlem off Our Mind?," 91
Harlem on My Mind, 87–92
Harvard, 10–12, 285
hate speech, 292; of anti-Semitism, 310,
    312–16; genocide and, 297, 310–11,
    314–16; incitement and, 315–16;
    from RTLM, 310–11
Havel, Václav, 142, 144, 224, 250
Hearst Corporation, 169
Hedrick, Helen, 84
Heller, Joseph, 83–84
Hellman, Lillian, 211–12
Helsinki Final Act, 143–44, 149, 151,
    176. *See also* Moscow Helsinki Group
Helsinki Watch, xiv–xv, 156, 217,
    224–25; Americas Watch and,
    186–87; disarmament and, 176–77;
    exiles at, 175–76; federation of,
    191–92; Madrid Helsinki Review
    Conference and, 176–78, 201; media
    and, 179–81; origins of, 151–55
Heming, Delia, 9
Hendel, David, 208
Herman, Jill, 123
Hersey, John, 17, 61, 94
Hersh, Seymour, 86, 108–9, 111–12,
    114
Herzog, Chaim, 294
Hezbollah, 300–301, 305, 313, 315

Hiroshima, 16–17
Hitler, Adolf, 310, 313
Ho, David, 200
Hoffman, Abbie, 93
Hollingsworth, Gerald, 111
Holm, Celeste, 148
Holocaust, 17, 69, 152, 310–11
Hom, Sharon, 189, 323
Hoopes, Townsend "Tim," 145–46, 157
Hoover, J. Edgar, 100–101
Hoving, Thomas, 87, 89–90
*How to Win Friends and Influence
    People* (Carnegie), 23–24
HRIC. *See* Human Rights in China
HRW. *See* Human Rights Watch
Hu Yaobang, 255–56
Huang Hua, 251
Hughes, Larry, 158
human rights, 14, 177–78, 296–97;
    International Helsinki Federation for
    Human Rights, 191–92, 213, 216–22;
    Lefever and, 187–90; staff for, 198;
    trade relations and, 142–43. *See also*
    Helsinki Final Act; Helsinki Watch
Human Rights First, 322
human rights funding, 192, 246,
    279, 319; from Aaron Diamond
    Foundation, 200; of fellowships,
    321–22; from Fund for Free
    Expression, 147–52; from MacArthur
    Foundation, 198–99
Human Rights in China (HRIC), 289,
    291, 323; funding for, 279; Li Lu and,
    258, 279–80; media with, 278–79;
    Woodman in, 277–78; Xiao at,
    276–77, 290
human rights law, 297, 299, 301–2
human rights movement, 150–51
Human Rights Watch (HRW), xv–xvi,
    200, 225, 246; Americas Watch from,
    186–87, 192–95, 199, 272; Asia
    Watch from, 199, 257, 261, 272;
    Chinese dissident writers and, 253,
    259–60, 263–64; disagreements with,
    295–96, 304–10, 314–16; divisions
    in, 272–73; hate speech and, 310,
    314–16; Israel and, 295–96, 301–2,
    304–9; resignation from, 274–75;
    structure of, 274
Human Rights Watch Middle East
    division, 272, 295–96, 301–2
Humphrey, Hubert, 98
Hunter College, 323–25

IDF. *See* Israeli Defense Forces
illiteracy, 61
In Search of Enemies (Stockwell), 112
incitement, 315–16

Index on Censorship, 149
India: education in, 17; famine in, 16;
  poverty of, 18, 86; prostitution in,
  15–16
Inside the Company (Agee), 109
Intelligence Identities Protection Act,
  109–10
International Committee of the Red
  Cross, 298–300, 306
International Covenant on Civil and
  Political Rights, 311–12
International Criminal Tribunal, 311
International Freedom to Publish
  Committee, xv, 142, 144–46, 158,
  210
International Helsinki Federation
  for Human Rights, 191–92, 213;
  Glasnost Press Club and, 219–22;
  Soviet Union and, 216–22
international humanitarian law,
  298–302
international law, 314–15; Hamas
  against, 305–6
International Olympic Committee
  (IOC), 260–61
IOC. *See* International Olympic
  Committee
Iran, 314–16
Irreparable Harm (Snepp), 113
Islam, 313
Islamists, 312–13
Israel, 137; Amnesty International and,
  304, 306, 317; blockade by, 303–5;
  disagreements over, 295–96, 304–10;
  Gaza War and, 303–8; Hezbollah
  against, 300–301, 305, 313, 315;
  HRW and, 295–96, 301–2, 304–9;
  Palestinian right of return in, 294–96;
  Second Intifada in, 296; UN and,
  308–9; visits to, 292–94; white
  phosphorous from, 306–7. *See also*
  anti-Semitism; Hamas; Jews
Israeli Defense Forces (IDF), 305–7

Jackson-Vanik Amendment, 142–43
Janeway, Carol, 205
Janouch, František, 217
Jews, 1, 6–8, 252, 294; African
  Americans and, 87–92; at Century
  Country Club, 34; family as, 2–3;
  Harvard and, 10; Holocaust, 17, 69,
  152, 310–11; in Soviet Union, 137,
  142–43, 206. *See also* anti-Semitism
John Wiley & Sons, 118; position with,
  263–64
Johnson, Anne, 204 (*See also* Anne
  Marcovecchio)
Johnson, Hugh, 66

Jones, Sidney, 257
Josephson, Marvin, 115, 206

Kaminsky, Howard, 239–40
Kampelman, Max, 176–77
Kaplan, Mordecai, 3
Kaye, Danny, 64–65
Keyes, David, 318–19
Keys, Wendy, 200
Khamenei, Ayatollah, 314
Khrushchev, Nikita, 125–26
King, Martin Luther, Jr., 101
Kirkpatrick, Jeane, 185, 188
Kissinger, Henry, 114–15, 183
Kline, Ed, 129, 153, 205; background
  of, 123–24; Chalidze, Valery, and,
  130–31; Godunov and, 156; Sakharov
  and, 133, 135
Klopfer, Donald, xv, 49; Cerf, B., and,
  50–52, 55; retirement of, 165–66. *See
  also* Random House
Kluge, John, 280
Knight, Hilary, 42
Knopf, 85, 237–38, 240; censorship
  and, 106; Mehta at, 241–42; merger
  with, 67–68; success of, 59, 68, 163
Knopf, Afred A., Jr., 67–68
Knopf, Alfred, 59; Hedrick and, 84;
  Random House and, 67–68, 83–84;
  replacement of, 80, 83–84
Knowlton, Winthrop, 146, 149
Kollek, Teddy, 293
Kopelev, Lev, 139, 175, 181
Korda, Michael, 67
Kovalev, Sergei, 218–20
Ku Klux Klan, 312; Supreme Court on,
  315–16

L. W. Singer, 69, 73, 84–85
Laber, Jeri, 176, 207, 219–21;
  background of, 148–49; Helsinki
  Watch and, 154; Moscow Book Fair
  and, 157, 210, 213; Moscow Helsinki
  Group and, 158; research by, 191–92
laogai (reform through labor), 265–67,
  277
Lash, Joe, 9–10
Latin America, 19; Argentina, 182–90;
  Brazil, 232; El Salvador, 193–95;
  Nicaragua, 193, 195–97
Lazar, Irving "Swifty," 115–17
Lefever, Ernest, 187–90
Leser, Bernard, 247
LeSieg, Theo. *See* Geisel, Ted
Leventhal, Albert, 20, 45; Goodman
  and, 31–32; Little Golden Books and,
  25–26, 32; Shimkin, L., and, 29–31
Levin, Martin, 145, 147, 168

Levy, Leon, 199
Leys, Simon, 290
Li Lu, 258, 279–80
Li Shuxian, 257–58
Lieberman, Dick, 65
Lies My Teacher Told Me: Everything Your American History Textbook Got Wrong (Loewen), 237
Lincoln School, 8–10, 86
Lindsay, John, 87, 90
Little Golden Books, 27, 32; Disney and, 39; Leventhal and, 25–26
Little Golden Records, 27–29, 39
Liu Binyan, 259
Liu Qing, 271, 277
Live with Lightning (Wilson), 120
Liveright, Horace, 21, 51–52
Loewen, James, 236–37
Loomis, Bob, 105, 111

MacArthur Foundation, 198–99
MacGregor, Sandy, 168, 229, 231, 248; Crown Publishing Group and, 243–44; five-year plans and, 163–64
Madrid Helsinki Review Conference, 176–78, 201
magazines, 109, 171–73, 179–80
Mailer, Norman, 109
Mann, Felix, 252
Mao Zedong, 251, 264–65
Marchenko, Anatoly, 158, 209
Marchetti, Victor, x, 105–8
Marcovecchio, Anne, 65–66 (*See also* Anne Johnson)
Marjorie Morningstar (Wouk), 116
Marks, John, x, 105–8
Marshall, Thurgood, 113
Masiyiwa, Strive, 322
Massler, Al, 28
Mastering the Art of French Cooking (Child), 59
McCabe, Edward, 118, 120
McCarthy, Joseph, 172
McCone, John, 105
McDowell, Edwin, 246–47
McGovern, Eleanor, 98
McGovern, George, 98–99, 103
McGraw-Hill, 242–43
McKay, Bob, 153
McNamara, Robert, 102
Medvedev, Roy, 128–29
Mehta, Sonny, 241–42
Méndez, Juan, 186–87, 196–97
Meshaal, Khaled, 303
Metropolitan Museum of Art, 87–92
Meyer, Marshall, 181–83
MFN. *See* most favored nation
Michener, James, 85, 94

Middle East, 292, 317–20; Human Rights Watch Middle East division, 272, 295–96, 301–2. *See also* Israel
Middle East Watch, 272
Miller, Arthur, 133, 152, 260
Miller, Lew, 50, 56, 65
Miller, Mitch, 28
Mirabella, Grace, 247
Mississippi, 236–37, 312
Mississippi: Conflict and Change (Loewen), 236–37
MIT, 13, 285–86
Modern Library, 51–52
Morrison, Toni, ix–xii, 148; human rights and, 319–20; meeting, 84–85
Morrison, Trevor, 322
Moscow Book Fair, 146–47, 154, 180; censorship at, 157–58; Laber and, 157, 210, 213; TASS and, 155–56; visa revocation for, 156–57
"Moscow Book Fair in Exile," 180–81
Moscow Helsinki Group, 144, 146, 158, 316
most favored nation (MFN), 262–63, 280–81
Mothers of the Plaza de Mayo, 182, 194
Movements.org, 319–20
Moynihan, Daniel Patrick, 91
Munro, Robin, 262–64, 267–70
Murrow, Edward R., 18
Muskie, Edmund, 99

Nagler, Gerald, 216–17
Nasrallah, Hassan, 313
National Broadcasting Company (NBC), 75
National Security Act (1947), 108–9
NBC. *See* National Broadcasting Company
Neier, Aryeh, 107, 311; China and, 250, 253; positions for, 152, 154, 186, 198, 273
Nevler, Leona, 230
New American Library, 63–64
The New Press, 248
New York Herald Tribune, 56–57
New York Times Co. v. United States, 102
New York University, 322–24
New Yorker, 240–41, 247
Newhouse, Donald, 170–73, 226, 248
Newhouse, Mitzi, 171–73
Newhouse, S. I. "Si," Jr., 170–73, 232, 248; celebrity books and, 239–40; management style of, 229, 240–43; meetings with, 226–27; termination from, 246–47
Newhouse, S. I. "Si," Sr., 170–71

Nixon, Richard, 99–100, 108; free speech and, 102–4; Random House and, 115–17
Nobel Peace Prize, xiii, 126, 135–36, 138
nongovernmental organizations (NGOs), 150, 178, 219
Notes of a Revolutionary (Amalrik), 177–78
Novak, Bob, 99
nuclear arms race, xiv, 210, 325; Sakharov and, 127–28

Obst, David, 105
Okrent, Dan, 106
Olson, Jane, 302
Olympics, 96, 174–75, 260–61
One Day in the Life of Ivan Denisovich (Solzhenitsyn), 125–26
Open Society Foundations, 273
Orlov, Yuri, 150, 179, 206; China and, 259; in freedom, 207–9; internal exile of, 202, 207; Moscow Helsinki Group from, 144, 146
Orlova, Raisa, 139, 158, 175, 181
Ortega, Daniel, 196
Osnos, Peter, 137–39, 206, 213
Ottaway, Jim, 287–88

Pakistan, 18, 174; anti-Semitism in, 312–13
Palestinian Authority, 294, 303, 313
Palestinian right of return, 294–96
Paley, William, 159, 229
Palmer, Helen, 59–60
Pantheon, 69, 236–37, 248
Pasternak, Boris, 125, 138, 237
Pels, Donald, 200
Pentagon Papers, 102; First Amendment and, 103–4
Petersen, Susan, 230–31, 246, 248, 272
Peterson, Peter, 169
Petrie, Donald, 170, 172
Pinochet, Augusto, 151
Portnoy's Complaint (Roth, P.), 86, 121
Posner, Mike, 322
Powell, Lewis, 113
Pressman, Joel "Jack," 82
Prisoner Without a Name, Cell Without a Number (Timerman), 188–90
Public Commission for International Cooperation on Humanitarian Problems and Human Rights, 219

Radio Corporation of America (RCA), 92; CIA and, 107; computers and, 73, 160; Conrad at, 166–67; directives from, 165–66; Griffiths at, 167–69;

NBC and, 75; profits and, 162–64; radios and, 74–75; Random House and, 73–74, 76, 159–60; reports to, 162–65; Sarnoff, D., and, 74–76, 159–60
Radio Télévision Libre des Mille Collines (RTLM), 310–11
Random House, ix, xv, 50; acquisitions by, 67–69, 228–30, 243–44; authors at, 53–54, 80, 227–28; Cerf, C., at, 92–93; children's books at, 42, 58, 60–63, 66, 80, 86–87; CIA and, 104–8, 114; compensation from, 48–49; continents from, 58–59; delegating at, 77–78; disclosure at, 67; editors at, 53, 55–56, 77, 80, 83–84; FBI at, 101; FTC and, 68–69; *Harlem on My Mind* and, 87–92; hiring by, 47–49; interview about, 76–77; Knopf, A., and, 67–68, 83–84; management style at, x–xi, xv, 55–56, 70, 77–78, 161, 231; merger for, 67–68; Modern Library of, 51–52; Morrison, Toni, at, 85; move of, 92; Nixon and, 115–17; office at, 78–79; paperback books at, 228–30; parking at, 49; partnership at, 51–52, 56, 231; promotions at, 63, 69–70; RCA and, 73–74, 76, 159–60; replacement at, 247–48; retirement from, 246–47; revenues of, 70, 161–64, 247; sale of, 167–73, 226–27, 248; salesmen at, 56; Snepp and, 110–14; social life at, 77; S&S and, 83; on stock market, 67, 72–73; Thompson at, 57; travel guides at, 58; *Ulysses* and, 52–53; valuation of, 76, 231; at Villard Mansion, 47, 49, 53, 79, 92; warehouse for, 230–31. *See also* Geisel, Ted
Randt, Clark T. "Sandy," 286–87
RCA. *See* Radio Corporation of America
Reagan, Ronald, 185–86, 193, 211, 223; Gorbachev and, 207, 214; Sharansky, N., and, 207
Red Cross, 298–300, 306
Red Star over China (Snow), 251
Reston, James, 252
Revesz, Richard, 322
Ridgway, Rozanne, 207
"Rights Watchdog, Lost in the Mideast" (Bernstein, R.), 309
Robert L. Bernstein International Human Rights Fellowships, 321–22
Robinowitz, Stuart, 310, 314–15
Rockefeller Foundation, 192
Rodgers, Richard, 23
Roland W. Betts, 286

Romero, Óscar Arnulfo, 193
Rosato, George, 243
Rosenau, Helen, 34
Ross, Thomas, 104–5
Roth, Ken, 199–200, 274, 314–15
Roth, Philip, 86, 121
Rothschild, Lord, 293
RTLM. *See* Radio Télévision Libre des Mille Collines
Rwanda genocide, 297, 310–11

Sakharov, Andrei, xiii–xv, 124, 324–25; hunger strike by, 202–3, 224; internal exile of, 174, 202, 209; Kline and, 133, 135; memoir of, 223–24; nuclear arms race and, 127–28; in Russian parliament, 223, 250. *See also* Bonner, Elena
Sandler, Herbert, 199–200
Sandler, Marion, 199–200
Sarnoff, David, 92, 107; RCA and, 74–76, 159–60
Sarnoff, Lizette, 76
Sarnoff, Robert "Bobby," 76, 160, 166
Satterthwaite, Meg, 323
Saudi Arabia, 312–13, 318
Schell, Orville, III, 268
Schell, Orville, Jr., 177, 196–97, 321; background of, 153; Godunov and, 156; Kirkpatrick and, 193–94
Schiffrin, André, 236–37, 248, 272
Schiffrin, Jacques, 69
Schoener, Allon, 87–89
Schulte, Tony, 80–81, 83–84
Schuster, Max, xiv, 21, 32, 44
Schwarzenberg, Karl "Kary" von, 216–17, 221, 224
Schwarzman, Steve, 169
Senate Foreign Relations Committee, 188, 190
The Seven Lady Godivas (Geisel), 60–61
Sharansky, Avital, 205–6
Sharansky, Natan (Shcharansky, Anatoly), 123, 137, 146, 202; Reagan and, 207; release of, 205–6
Shattuck, John, 280–81
Shawn, William, 240–41, 247
Shcharansky, Anatoly. *See* Sharansky, Natan
Sheinberg, Sid, 295
Shevardnadze , Eduard, 216–17
Shi Tao, 266–67
Shimkin, Arthur, 27
Shimkin, Leon, 23–24, 26–27; disagreements with, 30–31, 45, 57; Gottlieb and, 81; Leventhal and, 29–31; termination by, 44–45, 48
Shultz, George, 196

Silberberg, Sophie, 155
Silberman, Jim, 80, 85, 88, 110, 238
Silver Screen Partners, 286
Simmons, Ruth, 289
Simon, Bob, 243–44
Simon, Dick, xiv, 21, 32, 44, 51. *See also* Simon & Schuster
Simon, John, 100
Simon & Schuster (S&S), xiv, 21, 44, 115; advertising at, 27; art books from, 23; Carnegie and, 23–24; children's books from, 25–27, 32, 39; children's songs from, 28–29; compensation from, 20, 29–31, 45, 48; crossword puzzles from, 22; Durant and, 22–23; Eloise at, 42; Field and, 24–25; Leventhal at, 20, 25–26, 29–32, 45; music books from, 23; Pocket Books from, 24–25; Random House and, 83; storytelling contest and, 26. *See also* sales department; Shimkin, Leon
Sinatra, Frank, 76, 210
Sinyavsky, Andrei, 126
60 Minutes, 111–12; on China, 262–63, 265
Six-Day War, 293
Smith & Haas, 53
Snepp, Frank, 110–14
Snow, Edgar, 251
Solzhenitsyn, Aleksandr, 125–26, 183, 266
Soros, George, 198, 273
Soul on Ice (Cleaver), 100–101
Soulé, Henri, 59
Sovern, Michael, 283
Soviet dissident writers, xiii–xiv, 150, 156, 225, 324; Amalrik as, 132–33, 142, 177–78; Bukovsky as, 133, 142; Chalidze, Valery, as, 129–31, 202; Kopelev as, 139, 175, 181; Medvedev as, 128–29; organization of, 126–27; public protests about, 127, 180–81; Solzhenitsyn as, 125–26, 183, 266. *See also* Orlov, Yuri; Sakharov, Andrei
Soviet Union: alcohol in, 120–22; computers in, 213–14; control in, 121–23; copyright convention and, xiii, 131; customer service in, 118–19; deaths in, 125; defection from, 156; diploma tax in, 142–43; entertainment in, 120–21; Gorbachev in, 125, 202, 207, 209–10, 214–16, 223; International Helsinki Federation for Human Rights and, 216–22; Jews in, 137, 142–43, 206; paranoia in, 122–23; publishers in, 121, 123; reform in, 125, 210, 223; surveillance in, 122–23, 137–38,

218; visits to, xiii–xiv, 118–24, 131, 137–39; WWII in, 121
Soviet Union Book Fair. *See* Moscow Book Fair
S&S. *See* Simon & Schuster
Stalin, Joseph, 125, 134
Star Wars, 229
Staral, Emil, 44–45
Steiner, Paul, 58–59
Stevens, John Paul, 113
Stockwell, John, 112
The Story of Philosophy (Durant), 22–23
Streicher, Julius, 310
Stukalin, Boris, 119–21, 142, 179; censorship and, 123; visits of, 141, 145
Supreme Court, 102, 311; on Ku Klux Klan, 315–16
Sviridov, Lev, 324
Sviridova, Alexandra, 324

The Target Is Destroyed (Hersh), 114
TASS, 155–56
Temple, Shirley, 58, 72
Terkel, Studs, 86
termination, 246–47; by Shimkin, L., 44–45, 48
textbooks, 84–85, 236–37; anti-Semitism in, 313–14; sale of, 242–43
Thompson, Kay, 50; background of, 41–42; merchandise and, 42–44; phone calls from, 43–44; at Random House, 57
Tiananmen Square, 253–57, 276
Timerman, Jacobo, 183–84, 188–90
Times Mirror Company, 167–68
Timofeyev, Lev, 213–14, 218–22
Tisch, Larry, 292–93
To Defend These Rights (Chalidze, Valery), 131
Tong Yi, 270–71
Trump, Donald, 239
Turner, Stansfield, 112
Tverdokhlebov, Andrei, 129

UN. *See* United Nations
United Nations (UN), 185, 297; China and, 250–51; Israel and, 308–9; Universal Declaration of Human Rights, 150–51, 186, 273, 298
Universal Copyright Convention, xiii, 118, 131
Universal Declaration of Human Rights, 150–51, 186, 273, 298

van der Leun, Patricia, 245
Van Doren, Irita, 57

Van Ellison, Candice, 89–91
Vance, Cyrus, 259
Vienna Helsinki Review Conference, 216–17
Vietnam War: AAP against, 97; Ali against, 95–96; Bernstein, P., and, 97; Bernstein, T., and, 97–98; parents and, 97; Pentagon Papers on, 102–4
Viking Penguin, 248, 272
Villard Books, 230, 245
Villard Mansion, 47, 49, 53, 79, 92
Vitale, Alberto, 247–48
Vonnegut, Kurt, 155
Voznesensky, Andrei, 138–39

Wallace, George, 99–100, 311
Wallace, Mike, 111–12
Walter, Helen. *See* Bernstein, Helen Walter
Walter, Tony, 36–38
Wartels, Nat, 243–44
Washington Post, 102–3
Wei Jingsheng, 181, 254–55, 269; in freedom, 261, 281–84; harassment of, 281–82; letters of, 268, 270–72, 280; MFN and, 280–81; in prison, 267–68, 271–72, 281; release of, 261, 281; security for, 282–83; smoking of, 283–84
Weisgal, Meyer, 162
Weizmann Institute, 162
Welty, Eudora, 94
Werner, Robert, 229
What's My Line?, 47
white phosphorous, 306–7
Whitson, Sarah Leah, 302–3
Wiley, Brad, 118, 120, 140, 263
Wilson, Mitchell, 120
Wimpfheimer, Tony, 49
Wise, David, 104–5
Wolf, Wendy, 272
Woodman, Sophia, 277–78
Woolsey, John, 53
Words I Wish I Wrote (Fulghum), 246
Wren, Christopher, xiii
Wu, Harry, 264; on laogai, 265–67

Xiao Qiang, 281–82; at HRIC, 276–77, 290
Xu Jin, 269; positions for, 284–85; Zhu and, 285–86
Xu Wenli, 255, 277; in freedom, 287–89; in prison, 268, 285–86

Yadin, Yigael, 293
Yahoo!, 266–67
Yale Law School, 321–22

ABOUT THE AUTHOR

ROBERT L. BERNSTEIN SERVED AS THE PRESIDENT OF RANDOM House for twenty-five years. He founded Human Rights Watch, served as its chair for twenty years, and is now emeritus. In 1998, he received one of the first Eleanor Roosevelt Awards from the United States government. He is a former chair of the Association of American Publishers and has received awards from the New York Civil Liberties Union, the Lawyers Committee for Human Rights, People for the American Way, and the Association of American Publishers, as well as honorary degrees from Bard, The New School, Swarthmore, and Yale. He has been a member of the Council on Foreign Relations, chairman of the executive committee of the Aaron Diamond Foundation, and a member of the advisory board of the Robert F. Kennedy Human Rights Award. Yale Law School has established three fellowships in his name. NYU School of Law has established the Robert L. Bernstein Institute for Human Rights. He lives with his wife in New York City.

PUBLISHING IN THE PUBLIC INTEREST

Thank you for reading this book published by The New Press. The New Press is a nonprofit, public interest publisher. New Press books and authors play a crucial role in sparking conversations about the key political and social issues of our day.

We hope you enjoyed this book and that you will stay in touch with The New Press. Here are a few ways to stay up to date with our books, events, and the issues we cover:

- Sign up at www.thenewpress.com/subscribe to receive updates on New Press authors and issues and to be notified about local events
- Like us on Facebook: www.facebook.com/newpressbooks
- Follow us on Twitter: www.twitter.com/thenewpress

Please consider buying New Press books for yourself; for friends and family; or to donate to schools, libraries, community centers, prison libraries, and other organizations involved with the issues our authors write about.

The New Press is a 501(c)(3) nonprofit organization. You can also support our work with a tax-deductible gift by visiting www .thenewpress.com/donate.